# Russians, North Americans and Telugus

## The Mennonite Brethren Mission in India 1885 - 1975

*Perspectives on Mennonite Life and Thought* is a series jointly published between Kindred Productions , the Historical Commission of the General Conference of Mennonite Brethren Churches and the Center for Mennonite Brethren Studies of Winnipeg, Manitoba, Fresno, California, and Hillsboro, Kansas.*

1. Paul Toews, ed., *Pilgrims and Strangers: Essays in Mennonite Brethren History* (1977)

2. Abraham Friesen, ed., *P.M. Friesen and His History: Understanding Mennonite Brethren Beginnings* (1979)

3. David Ewert, ed., *Called to Teach* (1979)

4. Heinrich Wölk and Gerhard Wölk, *Die Mennoniten Bruedergemeinde in Russland, 1925 - 1980: Ein Beitrag zur Geschichte* (1981)

5. John B. Toews, *Perilous Journey: The Mennonite Brethren in Russia 1860 - 1910* (1988)

6. Aron A. Toews, *Mennonite Martyrs: People Who Suffered for Their Faith 1920 - 1940,* translated by John B Toews (1990)

7. Paul Toews, ed., *Mennonites and Baptists: A Continuing Conversation* (1993)

8. J. B. Toews, *A Pilgrimage of Faith: The Mennonite Brethren Church in Russia and North America 1860 - 1990* (1993)

9. Paul Toews, ed., *Bridging Troubled Waters: Mennonite Brethren at Mid-Century* (1995)

10. Peter Penner, *Russians, North Americans and Telugus: The Mennonite Brethren Mission in India 1885 - 1975* (1997)

*Volumes 1-4 were published by the Center for Mennonite Brethren Studies (Fresno)

# Russians, North Americans and Telugus

## The Mennonite Brethren Mission in India 1885 - 1975

Peter Penner

Winnipeg, MB Canada     KINDRED PRODUCTIONS     Hillsboro, KS USA

## RUSSIANS, NORTH AMERICANS AND TELUGUS
## The Mennonite Brethren Mission in India 1885 - 1975

## Canadian Cataloguing in Publication Data

Penner, Peter, 1925 -
Russians, North Americans and Telugus
(Perspectives on Mennonite life and thought; 10)
ISBN: 0-921788-40-1

1. Mennonites - Missions - India - History.
2. Missions - India - History, I. title.
II. Series.

BX8119.I52P45    1997    266'.9754    C97-920004-0

Published simultaneously by Kindred Productions, Winnipeg, MB R2L 2E5 and Kindred Productions, Hillsboro, KS 67063

Cover design by Graphic Creations, Winnipeg, MB

Book design by Graphic Creations, Winnipeg, MB

Printed in Canada by Webcom Limited, Toronto, ON

ISBN: 0-921788-40-1

# Contents

# Preface and Acknowledgements

Missionaries generally have received a bad press among historians and journalists in what sometimes is called the "post-mission era." Given their presuppositions about the inappropriateness of disturbing other cultures on one hand, and the futurism of the missiologists on the other, missionaries do not stand much chance to be recognized in modern Mennonite history-writing. This is a pity, since most of them were strong individualists and unforgettable characters, if only we can look behind the myths that surround them and reveal them, in all their relationships, as human beings.

I have no personal connection with the India Mission as explanation for such a strong interest in this story. I do however confess to an emotional tie with the Mennonite Brethren (MB) of the 1950s, in other words, with my generation born between about 1915 and 1930. I admit to a longstanding, even youthful, interest in MB history generally, and mission history particularly, at home and abroad. My interests as a Bible college student were capped by a professional interest in evangelicals, the civilizing mission of Greater Britain, and previous primary research into British India, as well as the Church Missionary Society working in North India.

Besides, this story has never been written. Others began but did not finish. To make plain such an involved and complex story stretching over three continents and three generations has been a challenge.

Though Abram H. Unruh, one of the founders of Mennonite Brethren Bible College, called for the creation of a Mennonite Brethren archives fifty years ago, those in MB studies must be grateful to J. B. Toews, who spearheaded the formation of three Centers for Mennonite Brethren Studies in the 1970s. Without such splendid resources this work would never have seen the light of day or have taken the shape of a history based on primary papers. I therefore gladly acknowledge the assistance of personnel in these three Centers: Wesley Prieb and his associates in Hillsboro, Kansas; Ken Reddig, the former archivist at the Winnipeg Centre at Mennonite Brethren Bible College/Concord College, and his associates and successor, Abe Dueck; and especially Paul Toews, director, and Kevin

i

Enns-Rempel, archivist, in Fresno, where I spent a total of eleven months spread over two stints of primary research. As well, I am grateful to the faculty and staff of Mennonite Brethren Biblical Seminary, Fresno, for treating me so graciously as adjunct faculty on these two occasions. I would be remiss if I did not draw attention to Beverly Carlson at the American Baptist Archive Center at Valley Forge, Pennsylvania. Through her generous assistance we obtained hard copy of the missionary correspondence of the Russian Mennonite Brethren working in India with the American Baptists.

I also wish to thank all those who have contributed to this unrepeatable story by sharing information in interviews and in correspondence. Their names are listed in the bibliographical note on primary sources.

I am grateful to Mount Allison University in Sackville, New Brunswick, for giving me a sabbatical year to initiate the research in Fresno. The university also allowed me to do research and writing projects during four summer months throughout my twenty-seven years on staff there. For this I always will be grateful.

I owe sincere thanks to various scholars for their editorial review and incisive criticism of the first draft of the manuscript, particularly Paul G. Hiebert, Elmer A. Martens, and Paul D. Wiebe. They have given helpful suggestions and saved me from some serious mistakes.

Bill Slusser of the California State University, Fresno Geography Department, drew the maps. I am grateful for the generous way in which Paul Toews, general editor of this work, and director of the Historical Commission, has assisted this project to its completion. Justina, bless her, has had to live with this topic as long as I have. There should be a special reward for such spouses.

Of the missionaries, if any group is to be singled out for a dedication, I choose the single women, whose remarkable story appears in these pages.

Peter Penner
Calgary, Alberta

# Introduction

This account of the Mennonite Brethren mission[1] to India represents a small part of the total Protestant effort to bring the Gospel to various language groups in all parts of the world since 1792. The dedication of these workers among the Telugu-speaking peoples of the Deccan was part of the greatest attempt to save India by spiritual means in Western terms.

Though not entirely unique, the 100 missionaries, board members, and other persons involved created so many totally absorbing and ironic situations that the story may be said to be unrepeatable. Climate and geography largely determined the rhythm of their lives between the "plains" and the "hills" within this mystical, fascinating, and puzzling Indian context. The social and economic realities among the Telugus determined the mission's pattern of becoming settlers rather than mobile evangelists.

The Mennonite Brethren were not alone as Mennonites in India. Two other Mennonite groups, the General Conference Mennonites and the Mennonite Church, ran missions concurrently in Madya Pradesh, and the Brethren in Christ worked in Bihar.[2] In addition there were dozens of other societies sponsored by mainline denominations working throughout India from the eighteenth century onwards. The great influx of "faith missions" began at the end of the nineteenth century.[3]

## The Sources

This story is based almost entirely on "primary sources." The primary, as distinct from secondary sources, are available mainly in archival centers.[4] These include materials very close to the events, such as missionary letters and reports. For many years these were printed verbatim in such conference papers as *Zionsbote*, the official North American periodical of the Mennonite Brethren Church from 1884 to 1964. Board reports, by comparison, as published in the minutes of conference proceedings, are already once removed from the primary level.

I used the standard secondary books and articles more sparingly. Two recent publications, however, have been helpful: *A Pilgrimage of Faith: The Mennonite Brethren Church, 1860-1990* by

J. B. Toews; and *Christians in Andhra Pradesh: The Mennonites of Mahbubnagar* by Paul D. Wiebe.[5] Toews has dealt theologically with the pilgrimage of the whole MB church while Wiebe has described the Church in India, the results of the MB Mission, sociologically. Findings from such field work, asking a different set of questions, prove most useful. But secondary sources have not been determinative for me at any stage. It has been necessary and possible to revise earlier accounts of people and events on the basis of a multitude of primary sources.

Items in my own research collection include notes of interviews and correspondence. This collection eventually will find its way to the Center for Mennonite Brethren Studies, Fresno. Included also are the literary results of a visit to India in 1972-73. It seems remarkable at this date to recall that I visited Mahbubnagar/Jadcherla for four days in 1973, just a short while before the "official" closing of the mission. Little did I think that two decades later I would be living with the topic of this book for eight years. What I observed and was told became the subject of letters to my family, as well as two articles for the *Mennonite Reporter*.[6]

## The Approach

I have given close attention to the least accessible sources: interviews, personal and official correspondence, letters and reports in printed form, and minutes of official missionary and board meetings. I have compared these sources and meshed them, where possible, with the most accessible: official reports given by administrators in conference yearbooks, and with more general historical accounts written by Abraham E. Janzen (1948), John H. Lohrenz (1950), George W. Peters (1952 and 1984), Anna Esau (1954), Abram H. Unruh (1955), Phyllis Martens (1971), and John A. Toews (1975).[7] These have been helpful in providing perspectives and insights different from mine.

My approach to the primary sources, in which the missionaries reveal themselves more fully, is investigative, analytic and comparative. My use of them, with respect to the mission story, may be thought of as "history-from-below." Wherever possible, I let the missionaries tell the story in their own words. These sources have helped me to know how the missionaries coped in a very difficult and sometimes hostile environment, how they justified their disturbance of

iv

another culture and, above all, how they fared as Christians in that culture. I hope I have succeeded in making this story readable and fascinating. I have chosen this story form instead of what might have become a largely faceless thematic analysis to be judged only by scholars.

I am more interested in the persons than in the institutions they developed. I begin with people and work my way to institutions as they did. But I have not been able to go all the way to tell the whole history of the India MB Church. Another person must write this story "through Telugu eyes." Having chosen this path, I freely acknowledge that others with a different predilection, even using the same sources, would have written the story differently.

I have found it impossible to give equal or full biographical treatment to every missionary or board member in this story of three generations. Because of recency, lack of historical perspective, and the greater numbers involved, I have curtailed the biographical portraits of the third generation. While it would be most desirable to have a complete survey of the missionary children's experience in education and the trauma of separation, brief sub-sections on this most important subject for each generation will have to suffice. This question of the children, whatever else may have been said to be of equal importance, was in actual fact the most serious one faced by missionary parents. The problem and its solution are discussed in family terms because each generation, despite similarities, faced this question differently.

## Openness and Honesty

The last two decades have witnessed some debate over the question of openness and honesty in historical scholarship. A consensus may be forming that we should welcome truth and openness, even controversy.[8] Given the recent emphasis on archival deposits, we can now meet these standards for openness. Whether people in the 1990s will think of a more truthful account of the past as "entering into our inheritance" remains to be seen.

Missionaries in India, perhaps more than others, were beset with dangers, diseases, deaths, and more than a fair share of tragedies. There were other unfortunate experiences that sometimes shortened careers abroad. Some of these were understandable, others–such as relationship problems, breach of promise, and loss of vocation–were less so. I have been duly cautioned by a number of missionaries not to dwell on their weaknesses, failures, and breakdowns. I appreciate the fact that missionaries lived through their conflicts one by one over the years, and that in most cases reconciliations took place in that otherwise close-knit community in a strange land.[9] My research, however, brought me to an equally inescapable conclusion that these problems and conflicts affected the total mission. While I admit that "to err is human" and to write about it irresistible, my intent is not to belittle their efforts or them. I am convinced that I would not have handled myself any better, and certain board members have acknowledged that had they been in missionary shoes they would have acted and thought much the same.

This approach occasionally brings out irony and incongruities that were glossed over in other accounts. Early in my research I became aware that the supporting constituency was told the story of India in a most selective manner. While one could say that this is always done, it seems that those stories that proved embarrassing to the board, reflected ill on the missionary, or revealed personal problems were withheld, even if, in some cases, a constituency-wide catharsis could have been wholesome. The most tragic of these stories are told in chapters seven and twelve.

What then shall be done? Most people would agree that two extremes should be avoided: the view that says "history is recorded in heaven and needs no further telling down here," or "tell everything for the telling's sake." If some readers complain that I have erred on the side of the distressful, rather than the gratifying, I offer some reasons for telling it as I have. First, there is a strong biblical precedent for acknowledging human failures and tragedies to which everyone is prone. Think of how the historian Luke dealt with such matters in his gospel and the Acts of the Apostles. One could find many other Scriptures, such as 1 Corinthians 12:21-24, which encourage this openness for the good of the whole.

Second, the results of this open approach can be wholesome for all. Some of the hagiography of the past–what J. Herbert Kane, the evangelical missiologist, calls the "myths" of the mission–should be stripped away. Mennonite missionaries in India easily adopted the use of these myths developed in the nineteenth century. In their reports, letters, and deputation visits missionaries appealed for a sense of commitment from the entire church. They elicited sympathy–in their anecdotal and illustrative style–for the plight of the "heathen," and spoke glowingly of success as seen in conversions and particularly baptisms. They frequently used the "white-unto-harvest" language, such as the "hungry heart," the "open door" or the "fast closing door" in order to keep the funds coming.[10] Perhaps board members also "massaged the truth," because there was always some degree of anxiety that unless some guilt or fear was put on their supporters, the monies would slow down.[11] This sometimes led to a degree of boastfulness. As early as 1928 Mennonite Brethren missionary John Lohrenz told delegates that "the MB conference was doing more, proportionately, than any other larger mission in America or Europe," while in 1948 he spoke of "phenomenal success."[12]

Finally, another reason for taking this approach is at last to set some people free. Through personal contacts with virtually every missionary still living, or with their children, I have found redemptive elements arising out of previous trauma. This story also shows how those who seemed to fail as missionaries–when such failure was grossly misjudged–found gratifying careers at home. From all of this I have concluded that to have "failed" in India is not a disgrace.

**What Made Them Go?**

For the early Mennonite Brethren "missionary outreach was spontaneous." Their theology of mission came later, as J. B. Toews, executive secretary of the Board of Foreign Missions from 1953 to 1963, wrote in 1993. "Their general motivation was simple: millions had never heard the gospel, and needed to hear."[13] George W. Peters, longtime secretary of the Board, thought of "missions as a way of life," for the Mennonite Brethren "a central motivation of prime importance" which "grew out of four basic factors." First was the Anabaptist-Mennonite heritage; a second was the missionary impact on Molotschna Mennonites of Pastor Wuest in the 1850s; a third was "the impact of the total Bible message" which helped to make the Mennonite Brethren church of 1860 most conscious of mission as part of their church's purpose in the world; and fourth, "the imprint of the life and words of Jesus Christ... and the example of the Apostolic Church as portrayed in the Acts and the Epistles."[14]

For most missionaries the "call" was of special significance, almost sacrosanct, while to others the question was more puzzling.[15] It will become clear that hardly anyone kept going in India without a deep conviction about being in the will of God. Sometimes this led to serious theological questions about who was really in charge: God who sent me or a Board at home? Could a missionary life be redirected because of changing times, or ministry terminated without just cause?

Among thousands of letters, articles, and reports there are intermittent references to sacrifice. Nikolai N. Hiebert, whose experiences are examined in chapter one,[16] spoke in 1927 of the [foreign] mission as an **altar**, a place of sacrifice. In the same year John H. Voth wrote of the need for a most convincing call (**Berufsgewiszheit**) and joyful willingness to sacrifice and be sacrificed (**Leidensfreudigkeit**). On the same occasion John Pankratz spoke of three who died early on, Katharina Lohrenz, Tina Mandtler Bergthold, and Anna Epp Bergthold, as having given their lives as suffering servants.[17] There is no doubt that these women, like all who went to India, were willing to take risks, exposed as they were to Indian diseases that at the very least were enervating, if not potentially deadly, for white people. Yet, in times of crisis, especially during the War of 1939-1945, concern for the family and security overrode other considerations in times of crisis. The "better country" sought (Hebrews 11) was not the heavenly, but the home country, similar to the attitude of the imperial administrator for whom India was an "exile." In times of crisis they heeded consular calls to take to the boats, borders, or the hills.[18]

### Paternalism and Colonialism

Missionaries have been severely criticized, often wrongfully, for excessive paternalism. People forget that all over the world missionaries found themselves appealing most successfully to the poorest of the poor, those who had nothing to lose by accepting Christianity and its promise of betterment. In India this was the experience of Presbyterians, Anglicans, and others, including Mennonites. They helped to fashion new creatures (I Peter 2: 9-10) of those who had no other hope of salvation from misery, poverty and a caste-ridden society that evangelicals perceived as evil and Satanic. Converts received a new dignity, though not all were given the potential to rise in the social scale. The dependency that was produced, as this story will show, seemed unavoidable.[19]

When a Madiga, an untouchable from the leather workers, left his family, he disturbed the rhythm of village life and service, and created jealousy or even enmity. Often such converts had to be detached to some extent, protected, fed, educated, and given health care. Even more would an upper-caste convert need a place of refuge from ostracism and persecution unless, of course, whole villages converted."[20]

In Wanaparty, for instance, missionary Frank A. Janzen accomplished this goal by building an imposing bungalow straight up from the main gate of the compound. Around it were placed the church, schools, dispensary and living quarters for staff. The missionary became the 'the great white father,' the person "in charge" of the station and the field of operation, the administrator of property and funds, and the only source of assistance. He and his staff provided relief, healing, and refuge for converts from Madiga *pallems* (out villages)."[21]

Somewhat more justified is the criticism of the missionaries' lifestyle. Almost invariably they adopted the colonial model of the English-built cantonments and "civil lines" for their armies and civilians, respectively. At the center was the residence of the "Collector," the official in charge of the district. He lived in style and was served by many persons, one assigned to each specific task; he preserved his distance, and was seen as a "benevolent despot." His household was geared to the preservation of health, comfort, and security.

This style was adopted first by missionaries Abraham J. and Maria Friesen, carried forward by Heinrich Unruh, and copied by John H. Voth at Deverakonda. Missionaries, it was believed, could not do justice to their work and families by conforming to the standards of Indian life. Nor could a woman be a full-time missionary without a number of servants to provide security, do the shopping in the bazaars, and the cleaning, cooking and laundry. The compound provided many jobs for a variety of tradespeople.[22]

**The Role of Women**

From the 1880s until the 1920s both married and single women were in the forefront of the world missionary effort. Many ran their own societies in Britain, the United States and Canada. After World War I an attempt, usually successful, was made to incorporate this women's work into the major societies administered by men. Some of the strongest opponents of women in leadership roles in mission were fundamentalists like John R. Rice.[23] Ironically, just as women were finally getting the vote, their role was diminished in the one movement in which they had provided remarkable leadership, both spiritually and financially.[24]

More specifically, the story of Mennonite Brethren women fits into this wider women's movement, where women outnumbered men at least two to one.[25] The married women were missionaries not only because they were married. In early years they carried many responsibilities in compound management and education. Because single women were not to be left alone on stations with their hospitals and schools, the Mission early adopted the practice of having them work in pairs (a nurse and a teacher) for company and protection.

How do Mennonite Brethren women compare with that larger movement in terms of seeking equality, or did they in fact have it? Were they intent on self-advocacy as opposed to self-denial? Unlike many single women missionaries in the nineteenth century who were paid only half of a single man's salary, Mennonite Brethren women were paid at least half the amount given to a couple. Person for person, in terms of salary, the singles were treated equally. As to self-assertion, which any woman manifested in the very act of going out, this was balanced by self-denial and acceptance of their restrictions in a maledominated world. In India all Mennonite Brethren women were equally members of the Missionary Council, comprising all the resident missionaries, and voted in plenary sessions. Some even held positions in the Missionary Council and on occasion spoke for the Mission. Mennonite Brethren women, married and single, actually were ordained until 1957.[26]

## The Organization of the Text

In order to help the reader follow this complex story of the Mennonite Brethren mission in India, I have chosen to treat the overlapping three generations, running from 1885 through nine decades, in manageable sections. To make it easier still, I have divided sections into chapters appropriate to the events and themes covered.

The first generation in this story belongs to the Russian MB Church. These first Russian missionaries came from the "mother church" and represented a well-founded, culturally advanced and fairly wealthy Mennonite community. They were the first workers in the Telugu mission field by a whole decade. In distinct ways they determined the choice of field, helped their American MB counterparts become established in their own fields, and generally provided a model for success and an operational pattern. Abraham J. Friesen at Nalgonda was their leader and father figure until 1914. He had a hand in the selection of all the other Russian candidates, who almost invariably also were trained in the Baptist Missionary school at Hamburg-Horn.

The second generation (1915-1945) is covered in two sections. This era clearly belongs to the Americans, even though some Russian Mennonite Brethren continued in neigboring areas among Telugus until about 1950 and some Canadians were added beginning in the 1920s. Commitment to overseas mission characterized the early American MB communities. This high sense of accountability and spirit of commitment culminated in the 1950s when the conference could boast one missionary to every 150 members, a remarkable statistic.[27] This occurred in spite of two world wars and the exceedingly difficult inter-war period with its worldwide depression. Unfortunately, considerable tensions surfaced within the American group, especially during the inter-war period. The period was marked by tragedy in the 1920s, and a first attempt to come to grips with the implications of biblical mission theory.

The third generation (1945-1975) is covered in two sections also. This generation belongs to the Canadians who moved into a majority position on the field as well as in the total North American constituency. This generation had to come to terms with the implications of decolonization and finally to establish an indigenous church. For reasons which are not always apparent, this period was also not without considerable stress and some tragedy, while the implementation of indigenization created considerable restlessness within the Mission, and even more in the India Church.

The following pages, chapter by chapter, tell this remarkable, unrepeatable story through three generations of men and women who focussed their activity on the Telugu-speaking people of Andhra Pradesh.

## CHAPTER 1

# Russian and American Beginnings

The first Mennonite Brethren missionaries to India, Abraham J. and Maria (Martens) Friesen, went to that country in 1889. They adopted the Telugu people as their evangelistic focus and developed the Nalgonda station in the State of Hyderabad.[1] Friesen went far toward influencing the American search for a mission field, especially during their first furlough, which included a trip to America. On the return trip they were accompanied by the first American MB missionaries to India, Nicolai N. and Susie (Wiebe) Hiebert, and Elizabeth S. Neufeld. They encouraged the sending of subsequent families from Russia to their field of concentration and were there when the first successors to the Hieberts arrived from America. These decades belong almost entirely to the Friesens.

Abraham Friesen (1859-1920) was the second son of Johann A. Friesen, a prosperous factory owner and a "carpenter and builder of windmills."[2] He belonged to the growing community of Mennonite manufacturers that spurred the later developments on the Dnieper river around Einlage.[3] According to Cornelius Unruh, Abraham was the most reliable son. The eldest and youngest were prodigal by comparison. Johann Friesen, himself an "earnest Christian and lay speaker," needed Abraham as his supporter and successor in the firm, yet it was precisely this son who believed himself called to become a missionary to India.[4] The one most likely to prosper from taking his father's business was also the one who was most needed, as it turned out, to lay the groundwork of the entire MB work among the Telugu-speaking people of India. Much less is known about Maria (1861-1917), born into the Martens family of Blumenort-Blumenau, Molotschna.

Whatever their early education,[5] they were well enough prepared to proceed to Germany for seminary training. One may assume that the training in their respective families and homes, and the teaching and discipline of the young MB church proved to be strong character-forming elements in their upbringing. These became evident in their conversion, marriage and commitment to education for missionary service. Married on 9 February 1884, the young Friesen took his wife to Germany for four years of training. They remained childless until they adopted two children in 1904 and 1905.[6]

1

Friesen attended the Baptist "Missionary School" at Hamburg-Horn in Germany. Johann G. Oncken (1800-1884) probably had much to do with its founding in 1880. Oncken, a founder of the Baptist denomination in northern Germany was also influential among Mennonites in the Ukraine.[7] This school offered four years of training, including two introductory years of preparation for theology. These were meant to accommodate those "of limited education" or those who had not completed the equivalent of secondary modern education. It is clear that Friesen and those Mennonite Brethren who followed him from Russia all took the four-year course. Grammar, style, German literature, arithmetic, world history, geography, English, and singing were offered in the first year. The second year built on these courses. Learning English was a matter of great importance to Friesen because this enabled him to read the literature of the American Baptist Missionary Union (ABMU) that heightened his interest in the Baptist work among Telugus in India. In the third year the students studied exegesis, church history, philosophy, New Testament biblical theology, Christian doctrine, homiletics, and a number of other subjects. The last year also featured ethics, pastoral theology, and New Testament Greek. Among the professors were Philip Bickel, Joseph Lehmann, and J. F. Fetzer, a son-in-law of August Rauschenbusch of the Rochester Baptist Seminary.[8]

## The Adoption of the Telugu Mission

After one year in Hamburg, the Friesens offered themselves as missionaries to the Rückenau MB Church. Following three years of studies, during which Maria took courses to help her with work among women, Friesen suggested that it was time to decide where they would work and with what association. He argued that "we are too weak to found our own mission work, but we are in a position to develop a richly blessed work . . . of an Anabaptist-minded society" [meaning the ABMU]. Above all, he urged that if they were accepted, the entire Russian MB effort should be "concentrated on one issue," on "one place," believing that such an effort would flourish, even in association with American Baptists.[9]

During 1888 and 1889 David Schellenberg of Rückenau assured the Friesens that there was much moral and financial support for this venture, and that their choice of a field among the Telugus

2

of India in connection with the ABMU was perfectly acceptable.[10] At the same time, the ABMU in Boston, the missionary arm of the American Baptist Foreign Missionary Society of the Northern Baptist Convention, acted on Friesen's application to serve in India. Its chief American seminary was located in Rochester, New York, and was later attended by numerous MB, especially from Minnesota. The headquarters of the Society, usually referred to as "The Rooms," was located in Tremont Temple Baptist Church, just off the Common in Boston.[11] Warmly supported by letters from his professors in Hamburg, Abraham and Maria Friesen were accepted in May 1889 for work in Nalgonda district of the State of Hyderabad, presided over by a Muslim prince called the Nizam.

### The Development of Nalgonda Station

Traveling from Odessa in the fall of 1889, the Friesens sailed through the Suez Canal and Red Sea, landed at Madras, and took the train to Secunderabad,[12] a twin to the capital city of Hyderabad. Here they began Telugu language study on 5 December with a *munshi* (teacher).[13] In May 1890 they made their first trip to Nalgonda, about 100 kilometers east of the city of Hyderabad. Started by William W. Campbell in 1885, Nalgonda was considered a very promising field. With the help of Robert Maplesdon, the Friesens arranged for a train of five oxcarts and, like good Russian Mennonites, laid in a generous supply of roasted *Zwieback* during the three-mile-an-hour journey.[14]

Because they were the first MB missionaries to take an overseas assignment, the Friesens took great pains to portray the world they had entered, and to interpret what their efforts meant. Whatever the hardships and opposition they encountered, and no matter how strange and "evil" the caste system appeared to them, their joy over a growing church overrode all other considerations. By adding 178 converts, they organized the first MB/Baptist congregation on 4 January 1891 and, in spite of many backslidings, could report a total of 325 baptized members by the end of that year. They attributed the harvest of converts to their dedicated preachers and Bible women who were able to go in all weather and into "Satan's stronghold" in a way they could not.[15]

It was not long before they had experienced the heat of the plains, the heavy rains of the monsoon, the ravages of "white ants,"

3

and the discomforts of life under tents, as well as the first of many bouts with illness. A first concern therefore was to rebuild a bungalow (a Bengal-style [*bangla*] house built by Europeans in India) started by Campbell earlier. When this was completed the Friesens enjoyed a spacious house that protected them from sun and monsoon and provided shelter and hospitality for many visitors. By 1894, moreover, he managed to build a complete compound (probably from *Kampung*, a Malay word meaning an enclosure, a space fenced in, a village),[16] on the model of American Baptist compounds. This large undertaking included a chapel, a two-story bungalow, a dining room for boarders, and another building for general purposes, as well as extensive tree planting. His training in Einlage as a man familiar with large undertakings and the organizational skills required now stood him in good stead.[17]

**The Fascinating World of India**

To face the prospect of a lifetime in India, broken only by intervals called furloughs, was daunting indeed. Long before Friesen's entry, many other nineteenth century evangelical Protestant and Catholic societies had forged paths into this sub-continent. Following the passage of the "pious clause" in the Parliamentary Act of 1813, they adopted an international principle of "comity," a sort of gentlemen's agreement, by which they carved up the sub-continent into fields or areas for which they would be entirely responsible to sow the gospel seed.[18] In the south, over a long period of time, Moravians, Methodists, Lutherans, and Baptists had begun their work at the coast, and then blanketed the hinterland of Madras. Those late in this drive to carve out "spheres of Christian influence" entered the so-called Deccan, even though by all accounts it was one of the biggest "wastelands" in the subcontinent. When a British official found himself in disgrace for any reason, he might find himself demoted to the Deccan. This was one of the worst "exiles" he could imagine. It consisted of a dry central plateau, subject to frequent droughts, famines, and various serious disease hazards for Europeans as well as indigenous peoples. Yet, in the 1870s the American Baptist John Everett Clough had had such tremendous success at Ongole that his work attracted Friesen to the Deccan, as well as the American Mennonite Brethren later.[19]

The Deccan could be pleasant if the rains came in profusion annually. Unfortunately, they did not.[20] In the lifetime of this story there were frequent famines brought on by extended periods of drought, the monsoon failing perhaps two to three years in a row (1919-21 and 1966-68, for example). The heat "down in the plains," where the mission work took place, became so intense (110-120⁰ F, or 45⁰ C) by April and May that a one or two-month period "in the hills" seemed imperative.

What seemed most offensive to Europeans, even in a day when patriarchy was very strong, was the caste system. The Friesens and those who followed them, especially the women, were appalled at the oppressive state in which the women generally, and widows especially, were kept. The only exception to this seemed to be among the Parsis. These were descendants of Persians and Zoroastrian in religion who had settled mainly in Bombay. The pantheon of gods, the "heathen" festivals, and the *Juggernath*, or wheel of sacrificial death, were all abhorrent. Only Christ had the answer. But the Brahman would not convert because the social and economic price was too high. Those, however, who had nothing to lose, those who had been cast out, treated as pariahs, were the ones who responded.[21]

## The A. J. Friesen Missionary Style

During this first decade, the ABMU realized that they had a Russian MB in their service of considerable ability and forthrightness. They found him frank, honest, uninhibited, and possessing considerable self-esteem. A first letter, which might have raised eyebrows in The Rooms in Boston, had to do with his perception of a shortfall in his salary. Perhaps it was only his limitations in English, or perhaps a first indication that Boston and Rückenau had differing views of shared responsibility. In any case Friesen drew comparisons between himself and a Baptist missionary named Jacob Heinrichs. Then stationed at Nellore, Heinrichs was just becoming known to the MB conference in America. He was the man named president of the ABMU seminary at Ramapatnam in 1895. In spite of this difference in standing, Friesen stated rather unequivocally that even if he did not have the same abilities as Heinrichs, he nevertheless had the same financial needs, and he would be glad for a rectification of his emoluments.[22]

A second issue involved an altercation between Friesen and Maplesdon at Secunderabad. While in the rapid building stage at Nalgonda, Friesen asked Maplesdon to loan him his assistant named

Wilson so that the gospel work would not be hindered. A misunderstanding arose between them as to funds for Wilson's support. Friesen was then experiencing a shortfall in funds from Russia. He blamed the depression on German tariffs against Russia after the fall of Bismarck in 1890. He was therefore grateful for a visit from his father, Johann Friesen, to Nalgonda. The latter solved their financial problems for some time to come.[23] Somewhat surprisingly, The Rooms deferred to Friesen in the way he had handled the case, and again in his judgment that Wilson was not qualified at that time to have charge of a station.[24] Some years would elapse before The Rooms would try to put Friesen "in his place."

Friesen also raised the question of "specifics" or "designated gifts" as opposed to general fund monies. He wrote Samuel W. Duncan:

> There are some missionaries who don't like specifics: because it is not business-like enough. Surely I would not like to be without them; yea, I could not be without them. A specific is to me not merely an amount of money [but] include many a fervent prayer especially for me and my work, many an encouragement in the work and its difficulties. . . . What has made our station [at Nalgonda] to be one of the greatest of all Protestant Missions in the Deccan? What is the cause that Nalgonda has the most preaching places, the greatest number of schools, and the largest church of our [ABMU] mission in the Deccan? The money has the smallest part in this work! . . . Where there is prayer, there is the Holy Spirit, and there the money too.[25]

While these were large claims, Friesen's subsequent treatment by The Rooms and his ability to negotiate with them suggest that he had promotional gifts, as well as statesmanlike views.

All this activity, as reflected in his reports to the *Zionsbote*, took its toll on Friesen's constitution. Supervising the building of his compound, negotiating with authorities for every step that impinged on indigenous society, and corresponding widely with officials of the ABMU in both India and America–and all of this in, for them, an enervating climate–sent them in search of cures. Maria Friesen had to be taken to the "best woman doctor" in Madras in the first part of 1895. She lamented the fact that her husband frequently had to take over her duties of supervising the Bible women, who did village work among women, and of looking after their first medical and educational work.[26] By August of that year Abraham was exhausted from the heat and the strain of the work. He went to a Christian retreat at Bangalore, Mysore, for rest and renewal.[27]

After five years in India, Friesen wrote his Hamburg professor Joseph Lehmann that he had to be a "man for all seasons." "Everything possible and impossible is demanded of us." He expressed his gratitude for all he had learned during his years in Hamburg. He wrote vigorously of defending "the rights and freedoms of our poor oppressed India Christians against unlawful actions by Muslim and heathen village officials." This letter to professor Lehman, reprinted in the *Zionsbote*, may have been quite influential. Not only had Friesen guided the construction of a model compound at Nalgonda, he had also trained preachers and Bible women, opened schools and a medical work, and found financial support from a widening circle of family and friends.[28] In retrospect, one can see that just as missionaries of the ABMU served as a model for the Friesens, the latter served as such for the MB of America.

Friesen's attention soon turned to the American scene. The first American MB support for American Baptists, and almost the first support for overseas work, was given to G. N. Thomssen working in Madras presidency. His request for $100 annually in support of an indigenous preacher was accepted by the MB conference in 1884. Within a few years about $500 was disbursed for other preachers working with Friesen and also with Jacob Heinrichs. Even though some of the growing amounts were diverted for several years to assist those interested in the German Baptist work in the Cameroon of West Africa, Friesen benefitted from this modest American support first in 1890 for one worker, and by 1894 for two.[29] The more substantial support came from Russia in addition to the general support under the initial arrangements with the ABMU. By the end of Friesen's first term in India, the work was well established at Nalgonda, and the MB Church of North America was on the threshold of a decision about that mission.

**American Independence**

This early American interest in the India mission was generated by two leading centers of the fledgling conference. One was led by Abraham Schellenberg, a brother to David Schellenberg of Rückenau who gave his blessing to the mission of Abraham and Maria Friesen. While Abraham was profoundly respected for his lead-

7

ership in the greater Molotschna MB church, he migrated to Kansas in 1879.[30] Schellenberg was the father of Katharina L. Schellenberg, the first medically-trained person to leave for India in 1907. The other center of support was among Mennonite Brethren of Minnesota, who found leadership in Heinrich Voth of Bingham Lake. His second son, John H. Voth, went to India in 1908.[31]

American willingness to support overseas mission work indirectly, as indicated, stemmed from a Mennonite Brethren General Conference decision as early as 1889 to look for a *Heidenmission* (mission to the heathen). The first committee formed for this purpose included Abraham Schellenberg and John F. Harms, the founder and first editor of the *Zionsbote*. They found this "foreign" mission in 1892 among the Comanche Indians of Oklahoma.[32] This work remained under the committee for foreign missions for many years.

Concurrently, a number of younger Mennonite Brethren studying at the German language division of the Baptist Seminary in Rochester became interested in the German Baptist mission to the Cameroon. Among these students were John Baerg, Peter H. Wedel, and Heinrich E. Enns. Baerg would have gone to Oklahoma, but illness prevented that. By 1896 Wedel and Enns were too committed to the German Baptists to accept a delayed offer of support under an independent work of the MB conference. To the great distress of the conference, the Wedels and Ennses all died in 1897-98 before they were able fully to establish their work in the Cameroon.[33] This naturally discouraged the conference leadership and other supporters of overseas enterprise. Despite this setback, the conference persisted in the search for an overseas work independent of any other denomination.

The crucial year along this path was 1896. The delegates to the conference at the Ebenfeld Church in Marion County, Kansas, were "of two minds." Abraham Schellenberg believed that the MB could work closely with Baptists because they "allow us to stand with our own confession." He represented the minority who believed that they could retain MB theological principles, even the doctrine of nonresistance, and thus could support H. E. Enns under the German Baptists just as Rückenau supported the Friesens in association with the ABMU. Enns in fact had been corresponding with A. J. Friesen at Nalgonda about joining the ABMU in India.[34] This minority view remained part of the continuing ambivalence about independence in mission.

8

John F. Harms and Heinrich Voth led the majority who favored the establishment of an independent work, though they were willing to support the work in Cameroon until they found their own missionary candidate for the field of their choice. Harms seemed most concerned to keep out all Baptist influences. Later, in a public correspondence between Harms and Friesen over this very question, the theological concern seems to have been laid aside.[35] All this time, Friesen exercised his promotional talents behind the scenes. When the decision was made in 1898 to support Nicolai and Susie Hiebert as its first missionary couple, the conference had no hesitation in also choosing India and the Telugu work as their destination.[36] Friesen had written to Harms stating that he was prepared to help the Americans either way. While he respected their decision to "go it alone," he assured Harms that there was room in India for both of them.[37]

Choosing India was made easy by the example of Friesen's successful work at Nalgonda. Many American Mennonite Brethren had heard of the "great Telugu revival" under John Everett Clough at Ongole during the previous decades. The choice was also influenced by the tragedy that had befallen the MB young people who had ventured to West Africa.[38]

**The First Friesen Furlough**

Before going to America as part of their two-year furlough in 1897-99, the Friesens spent about a year and four months in Russia. Friesen made arrangements for the eventual commissioning of Abram J. and Katharina Huebert, the second couple to commit themselves to service in Nalgonda district. They were married on 29 August 1897 at Blumenort, Sagradowka and Huebert completed his studies in Hamburg-Horn in July 1898.[39] Soon after, the newlyweds met with the Friesens at Rückenau, and then proceeded on a deputational tour. Commissioned at Rückenau, they left Odessa on 15 January 1899 and arrived at Madras on 11 March. Switching to his imperfect English, Huebert and his wife entrained for the overnight trip to Secunderabad. There they were met by Robert Maplesdon of the ABMU, who provided oxcarts to take them and their belongings to Nalgonda. Helping them get settled and taking responsibility for the medical and school work were Dr. Lorena M. Breed and Etta F. Edgerton, respectively. Friesen had requested their transfer to assist

9

with these branches of the expanding work.[40] Though Friesen expected much from the Hueberts in rather short order, Huebert explained later that he had been a man of affairs also, having been involved in sheep farming for several decades, obviously from a very early age.[41]

Once the Friesens had completed their deputation in Austria, Switzerland, and Germany, and visited their friends, they went to London, England. There they found churches in which they could report on their work in conjunction with the ABMU.[42]

Abraham and Maria arrived in Boston before the middle of November 1898, about two weeks after the North American MB Conference in Winkler, Manitoba, had chosen N. N. and Susie Hiebert from Minnesota as their missionaries for India. According to Maria they were planning to visit The Rooms of the American Baptist Foreign Mission Society only briefly and then carry on to New York to see "our dear friends, J. Heinrichs and G. N. Thomssen." From there they planned to go to Kansas to meet with MB leaders such as Harms and Schellenberg. But because Maria had been ill from the time they left Hamburg, they were detained in Boston for seven weeks.[43]

This delay meant that Friesen had sufficient time to discuss with The Rooms the continuing working relationship with the Russian MB Church, especially now that the Hueberts, and also by this time, Heinrich and Anna (Peters) Unruh, had been accepted for service in Nalgonda district. The Baptist archival records suggest that Friesen's association with the American Baptist Missionary Union had rejuvenated a Mission that had become somewhat tired and was finding it increasingly difficult to raise sufficient funds. Samuel Duncan thought of these developments as "one of the rays of sunlight amid much darkness." Hence, when the robust-looking Friesen, the author of many candid letters from Nalgonda, entered Tremont Temple Baptist church, he must have "caused no little stir."[44] From available correspondence it may be assumed that any misunderstandings generated earlier were cleared away.

### The Harms/Friesen Exchange of 1898

Achieving a similarly amicable understanding between Russian and American MB churches, especially between Friesen and Harms, took some effort. A significant exchange between them took place in the *Zionsbote* while the Friesens were detained in Boston those seven weeks. The differences suggested there, if not resolved, might have brought about a degree of tension adverse to the good relationships which had been established. John and Margaretha Harms had visited Europe, including the Molotschna, beginning in December 1897. Harms gave thirty-nine addresses in Mennonite churches, including Rückenau, where the Friesens were probably in attendance. Back in Kansas, on 30 November 1898 he published a brief article entitled: "Die schoene Missionsgabe." In it he expressed the American conference's gratitude for a gift of $919.94 from Russia "for our India mission."[45]

First, he was totally surprised by this donation. Had not "many leading brethren" in Russia recommended that both Russian and American Mennonite Brethren should work in association with the ABMU, just as the Friesens had been doing for a decade? Even though David Schellenberg had assured him that, when the Americans were prepared to send out their first missionary, support would be forthcoming, Harms had left the Mennonite colonies feeling somewhat pessimistic on that score. Hence the surprise. Second, the amount was much greater than he might have expected, and there was promise of more to come. This did not, however, minimize his perplexity in discovering that some brethren, in whom he might have had confidence in these matters, seemed somewhat casual about their confession, "which insisted on teaching all that Jesus taught." He was implying that Friesen was being hampered by the Baptists from emphasizing MB distinctives, and that Russian Mennonite Brethren were too indifferent about that. Yet, all misgivings aside, he expressed the hope that this support for the Americans was an earnest of further support and of continuing brotherly relations in mission and other projects "in accordance with our common confession."[46]

To this seemingly innocuous little article, Abraham Friesen prepared a careful response. It was published alongside Harms' as a "word of clarification." Friesen began by stating that since Brother Harms "could not possibly wish to do mischief, it is certain that he does not understand matters completely." Where Harms had detected some disunity about the mission to India and indifference about doctrinal issues between Russian Mennonite Brethren and Baptists, Friesen asserted that there was widespread support from the beginning for the path they in Rückenau had taken within the will of God led by the Holy Spirit. It would have been "sad indeed" if only a few leaders had joined the ABMU on their own.[47]

11

Friesen then stated that it was misleading to imply that Russian Mennonite Brethren were not free to teach those doctrines that were unique to them. On the contrary, the ABMU had never tried intimidation; he had never been asked to sign a Baptist confession of faith; he had been free to preach to the indigenous peoples and build up the Nalgonda work according to MB principles of faith and polity. To have been building until now on Baptist principles without making this plain to his supporters would have been irresponsible and faithless, not only to Rückenau, but also to his Indian Christians. He also made it clear that Rückenau had initiated the mission to India in 1889 in support of the ABMU, and he believed God had blessed that choice. Now, however, having just visited Boston, he was able to state that The Rooms considered Nalgonda a Mennonite Brethren work that the ABMU was supporting. Nalgonda was in effect a "daughter church" of Rückenau. Their preachers, Bible women, and Christians were "their missionaries" serving more than 700 members. Friesen obviously did not wish that Harms' misleading interpretation of the association with Boston should gain currency. For nine years now they had served in India under the signal blessing of God in a mission "in which they were free to teach all that Jesus commanded." While he was thankful for gifts and prayers from America, Friesen concluded on a note of regret that his American brethren (whom he was about to visit) had not long since taken action to satisfy the mission interest that was very evident. On behalf of Rückenau, Friesen wished the readers of the *Zionsbote* God's blessing in the pursuit of an independent mission.[48]

To this brotherly rebuke and explanation, Harms gave "a word of clarification." He now regretted that he had misjudged the doctrinal integrity in the relationship with the ABMU. He now understood more fully the nature of the relationship between Rückenau and Boston. Meanwhile, the Rückenau mission committee had confirmed all the points Friesen had made in his statement. In light of this exchange, Harms "took back" what he had previously written.[49]

In the same issue it was announced that the Friesens would be making a tour of the churches and be present at the meeting of the American committee at Ebenfeld, Kansas. There, on 11 April, the delegates, led by Heinrich Voth, confirmed the decision that the Hieberts would proceed to Nalgonda. In due course they adopted a field within a large area between Nalgonda district and other ABMU stations to the south of Hyderabad. Friesen assured them that The Rooms were inclined to leave this region for an independently-working American Mennonite Brethren Mission. All told, this meeting with Friesen created an opportunity to obviate any possible misunderstandings, to minimize any damage that may have been done by the Harms-Friesen exchange, and to assure the Hieberts that all was well in the relationship between Ebenfeld and Rückenau.[50]

## The Historic Voyage to India

After the Friesens had completed their tour among the MB churches and their obligations to the ABMU, they were joined in New York toward the end of June 1899 by the Hieberts and Elizabeth S. Neufeld of Kansas for the trip to India.[51] This included a stopover in the Molotschna and at Sevastopol in the Crimea where Heinrich H. and Anna (Peters) Unruh from Spat-Schoental, the Crimea, were to join them. At Sevastopol on 1 September 1899 14 persons bid farewell to the whole party of Friesens, Hieberts, Unruhs, and Elizabeth Neufeld. Among these were various persons related to Friesens, as well as *Reiseprediger* [itinerant preacher] Hermann Neufeld.[52]

## The International Scene

While this party was en route in their historic trip, momentous events gripped the world's attention. The years 1899 to 1901 were fraught with danger and great trials, not least for the missionary cause. The Treaty Powers, including Russia, were carving China into spheres of influence at the same time as America was taking over the Philippines. While Rudyard Kipling was enlisting the Americans to join his British Empire in shouldering "The White Man's Burden, "[53] some groups of Chinese known in history as "The Boxers" took their revenge on the Treaty Powers (including the United States since 1844), and particularly on the Christian mission. Among those killed in 1900 were 243 missionaries. The China Inland Mission, a faith mission founded a generation earlier by J. Hudson Taylor, suffered more casualties than any other mission."[54]

In retrospect, this period may be seen as the "high noon" of empire, and colonialism as an attitude and policy showed few signs of wasting away. Yet the British Empire was deeply troubled on several fronts, not only in China. Queen Victoria's Empire had taken on the Boers, the white South Africans, in the infamous Boer War (1899-1902). Britain almost lost the battle, and found world opinion against her. The readers of the *Zionsbote* heard about the tragic elements of that war from their missionary friend G. N. Thomssen. Hardly could he know the vast consequences that would flow from the English treatment of the Boers.[55] It has been shown that much of the determination and theological rationalization of the policy of apartheid in a white South African republic was born among the survivors of the Boer War. [56]

More importantly, when the MB missionary party arrived they saw the aftermath of the devastating famine in British India, particularly severe in Bengal, but reaching serious proportions in the Deccan also. In Calcutta Viceroy Curzon was faced with sharp criticism for British India's land settlement and other oppressive policies. These had reduced the vast majority of India's people into a subsistence existence on the land." At such times the Deccan was most vulnerable. Any dislocation in the pattern of the rains in any part of India could swiftly impinge on the people. Shortages of food led to rising prices. Rising prices brought food to those who could pay and starvation among those existing on an inadequate diet even according to Indian standards. MB missionaries frequently experienced such calamities in the Deccan. Disease and death followed unless timely relief could be given.

The famine of 1900 came in the midst of a number of calamities, not the least of which was a severe economic depression, whose costs British India's government passed on to the Indian people between 1895 and 1905 by a devaluation of silver. One American critic quoted a leading British civil servant who admitted that India's people earned an average of 27 rupees per year. He knew what many missionaries never seemed to realize that the cause of India's poverty lay in "the simple fact that India is a subject land, ruled by a foreign power, which keeps her tributary to itself, not only politically, but commercially, financially and industrially, and drains away her wealth in a steady stream that is all the while enriching the English people, and of course correspondingly impoverishing the helpless people of India."[58] Most people believed that it was not the British, but the Indians themselves and their money lenders who were to blame for India's poverty.[59]

## The Hieberts and Elizabeth Neufeld

Once in India, and having completed the initial language study at Nalgonda, the Hieberts and Neufeld, advised by the masterful Friesen, chose urban Hughestown as the preferred site for a first American MB station. Hughestown was a suburb of Secunderabad, and therefore lay within an area worked by the ABMU. Here a combination of illnesses and an intervention by Jacob Heinrichs seemed to force the early retirement of the Hieberts.

Some pains must be taken to explain why the Hieberts left so abruptly before the hot season of 1901. They were long since back in Minnesota before Harms printed material in an apparent attempt to clear up questions about that early return. It involved publication of an intervention by Jacob Heinrichs in January 1901, but Harms delayed the clarification until 1903.

To begin, Hiebert became seriously ill and was advised to return home in the midst of language study. Susie was also not immune to illness in India, perhaps because of complications during pregnancy. Her infant daughter Susanne, a twin, died in August 1900. Abram J. Huebert, getting settled at Suryapet, was intending to tour south of the Krishna river. While there, he expected to buy a strong pair of oxen for the Hieberts.[60] They never needed them.

Many persons must have asked at the time: was it really necessary for Nicolai and Susie Hiebert to return home before completing their language study at Nalgonda, and then to remain at home? Was the decision to leave based only on the fever that brought N. N. Hiebert near death's door, or was it because he also suffered a nervous breakdown early in 1901? Elizabeth Neufeld, who travelled to India with the Hieberts, and who was on the scene, wrote in 1945 that Hiebert's nerves had broken at this time.[61] If fever had been the only cause, then Hiebert could have stayed in India, or could have returned after convalescence in America, as others did. Clearly, he recovered sufficiently to travel home. More than that, he had recovered from fever once before. After all, his very supportive friend, Abraham J. Friesen, suffered from both fever and nerves throughout his time in India. For these reasons it seems legitimate to ask whether the medical advice to return to America might have been based on his tendency toward nervous exhaustion. Furthermore, how well was Hiebert when he was sent out in 1899? At least one

15

respected leader has suggested that Nicolai Hiebert was not medically fit for such an assignment.[62]

Compensating for this loss was the knowledge that the Hieberts at least had been able to lay the foundations of the work. Everyone in India came to "believe," as he stated, "that the Lord Jesus has commanded us to return home."[63] This was most unfortunate in that they had been recommended to the conference by Heinrich Voth and the board as an answer to prayer. Voth had written to the churches in the *Zionsbote*, "Now as Brother N. N. Hiebert travels through the churches the beloved brethren and sisters raise the question, 'Is this the brother?' Who offers the clear answer?"[64]

## CHAPTER 2

# The American Baptist Plan of Cooperation: 1902 to 1905

The period from 1902 to 1905 produced complex negotiations between Abraham J. Friesen and The Rooms about the place of the Russian Mennonite Brethren in the ABMU India mission program. Mixed in was an attempt to bring the American Mennonite Brethren into a three-way association. Friesen's model of Russian MB-Baptist cooperation was in jeopardy only when Friesen used the possibility of closer Russian-American MB cooperation as leverage in his negotiations. Working out the relationship between Russian Mennonite Brethren, the American Mennonite Brethren and the American Baptists of the Northern Baptist Convention was, if not unprecedented, certainly quite unique. In this Jacob Heinrichs, located at Ramapatnam, the India headquarters of the ABMU, was a key player.

## The Heinrichs Intervention

Even though it was clear that the Baptists welcomed Americans to the open space between Secunderabad in the north, Palmur (later called Mahbubnagar) to the south and west, and Nalgonda to the east, it became apparent that any allocations were to be made in the "correct" way. When Nicolai Hiebert chose Hughestown without Friesen's referral to the India-based Reference Committee of the ABMU, this was interpreted in Ramapatnam as a breach of comity. This intervention in December 1900/January 1901 might have led to a break in the relationship between American Mennonite Brethren and American Baptists, except for a timely explanation in the *Zionsbote* in August 1903.

On that occasion, John F. Harms printed in full a brief article from the *Baptist Missionary Review (BMR)*, dated January 1901, as well as a subsequent explanatory letter from Jacob Heinrichs. Leaving Heinrichs' explanation aside for the moment, the article made five points: 1) until now there has been full harmony between the ABMU and the Russian Mennonite Brethren; 2) but because Hughestown is encompassed by Secunderabad station, the common courtesies expected between two mission societies would dictate that Hiebert should offer to go to an area left vacant until now;

3) there are vacancies elsewhere and we need to retain our interest in Secunderabad; 4) last year (1900) in Minnesota, we discovered that one segment of opinion in America did not support this independent effort, and we made our point (of working together, like the Russian Mennonite Brethren) with them at that time; and 5) most surprising of all (even after discussing the whole issue with Hiebert personally at a conference), the *BMR* pointedly remarked that the last reason for opposing this plan is that Hiebert "is too good a missionary to be used for this experiment (at an independent station in the midst of a Baptist field)!"[1]

This raised questions in Harms' mind, but he did not publish them until August 1903, not until Heinrichs had written him in July. Even Harms asked at this late date whether a drastic mistake had been made in the choice of Hughestown. Furthermore, was the *BMR* statement the cause of Hiebert's doubts about Hughestown? According to Harms, "[Hiebert's] illness seemed like an answer from God that Hughestown had to be given up."[2]

Heinrichs defended their statement. He had first consulted with William B. Boggs of the Reference Committee, as well as with Friesen and Hiebert at Bapatla, an ABMU station to the east, before letting it go to press. This suggests more reasons for detecting some incongruities here. If the ABMU Missionary Hopkins of Secunderabad and Friesen of Nalgonda had approved of the Hughestown location, and presumably of the MB strategy of working out from an urban center, why did Boggs as editor-in-chief of the *BMR* and Heinrichs print this article? Was it to teach Friesen, the Russian "general," a lesson on how to work through the India Reference Committee?[3] Would this not be necessary if a firm plan of cooperation was to be worked out?

### Heinrichs' and Friesen's "Unorthodox Manner"

The answer seems to be, yes, they wanted to see mission comity and common courtesy observed. Heinrichs explained that the article of January 1901 had not been directed at Harms and colleagues who preferred to remain independent, nor against the Russian and American Mennonite Brethren who already had been warmly welcomed into their midst. What he and Boggs wanted was to avoid any unpleasantness and embarrassments between Ramapatnam and Nalgonda. Correct protocol should have dictated a reference to the committee at Ramapatnam. Whatever Friesen,

Hopkins and Hiebert agreed was desirable and possible did not make it official! Heinrichs stated that to have gone to a vacant area within the larger ABMU sphere would have been better, "but now that we have become used to the unorthodox manner in which [this decision] was made, all of us in the ABMU in India want you to stay among us."

Heinrichs then showed his hand. He did not shy away from stating they still hoped that American Mennonite Brethren would join with the ABMU as the Russian missionaries had. To paraphrase Heinrichs: let us unite in a work among Telugus that is so vast that the ABMU will never be able to do justice to its needs. Let us unite because you will never be completely independent of us, no, not in fifteen years or so. Even if Hiebert's successor locates [in Malakpet, as he did, as an alternative to Hughestown], he will still unavoidably rub shoulders with us. Let us unite because he will have to send his promising preachers to Ramapatnam for training in ministry. And they are most welcome. Moreover, you will adopt the "station plan" [compound system] that we use. Heinrichs concluded: "Gladly would the stronger ABMU take the fledgling American mission by the hand until it is strong enough to run alone. That is how the Canadian Baptists did it for many years until they were able to go off independently." Heinrichs ended on a note of good will, suggesting that, if Harms wished, he would be willing to send some articles for the *Zionsbote*. Obviously, he wanted to mend fences.[4]

### Rückenau: with American Mennonite Brethren or ABMU?

If Friesen's tactics with the ABMU seemed somewhat strange, it must be remembered that during these years he was playing his chosen mission off against the fledgling "American Mennonite Brethren Mission Union," as it was called then.[5] From the evidence one cannot help but conclude that Friesen (like Jacob Heinrichs) was really trying to influence the Americans to work with the Baptists as he was. Yet Friesen pressured Boston by stating that if the ABMU did not make arrangements satisfactory to the Russians, his people might be tempted to come out under the American board. One opportunity to do this had come in 1900 when the Americans approached the Rückenau committee about a working relationship. David Schellenberg replied decisively that they preferred to continue their association with the ABMU "under [the direction] of Missionary A. Friesen," and would therefore "not go along with them." The report on this correspondence and two letters written by N. N. Hiebert from Nalgonda were brought into discussion at the American conference held in Kansas in October 1900. Before the Heinrichs intervention of January 1901, Hiebert was inclined to work closely with Friesen, even if he understood his board's desire to remain independent. After all, Friesen had assisted him in locating a site in a suburb of Secunderabad, and the local Baptist missionary Hopkins had supported this choice. Furthermore, the urban setting for a first station seemed practical and strategic. But Hiebert's request that a second couple be sent out soon, and other matters of principle, led the Conference of 1900 to reaffirm the decision to remain independent of the ABMU.[6]

Friesen kept pressure on The Rooms for several years, especially once it was clear that the Hieberts would be returning home for health reasons. This turn of events only encouraged Friesen to use every possible argument. Harms, having heard Hiebert's report of their good experiences at Nalgonda, had written to say that they were now "favourably impressed" with the work of the ABMU. Friesen knew that some American brethren had wanted to know whether they could work with the Baptist mission, but "not without giving up their missionary organization."[7] Heinrichs, in Minnesota in 1900, had discussed these points, and had found some supportive voices. In light of this Friesen now asked The Rooms: "Will the constitution of the ABMU permit a union with the [American Mennonite Brethren]?" Though such a union did not materialize, the answer from Boston was in the affirmative and Friesen and his associates continued to hope for such an arrangement, at least until John H. and Maria Pankratz arrived in 1902 to replace the Hieberts.[8]

### The Successors to the Hieberts

In the midst of these events, N. N. and Susie Hiebert returned home, thus jeopardizing the independent American MB mission program. Who would ensure continuity? Found in 1902 were two missionaries, John H. Pankratz from Minnesota, who was married to Maria Harms, and Daniel F. Bergthold from Oklahoma, who was single. Whereas Pankratz had studied at the Rochester Baptist school, Bergthold attended first the German-language division of McPherson College of the Church of the Brethren in Kansas and then the interdenominational Moody Bible Institute in Chicago. The MB conference at Bingham Lake in 1901 examined both men and accepted them for India. Whereas the Pankratzes were sent out in 1902, Bergthold, by then married to Tina Mandtler of Dalmeny, Saskatchewan,[9] was kept back. Chairman Schellenberg, who exercised great power at the time, asked Bergthold to serve at home as an evangelist of the conference for three years. Openly, on the conference floor, he implied an element of mistrust. A year later Bergthold was humbled further by having to confess that he had expressed attitudes unfavorable to the conference while at McPherson College. The chairman asked for an expression of confidence in his suitability as a candidate for the Mission.[10] It is hard to avoid the conclusion that the difference in education and background between the two candidates and this treatment were felt in the Mission for the next two decades.

Soon after they arrived in India, John Pankratz was invited to attend an ABMU convention at Nellore, where he became acquainted with the Russian Mennonite Brethren as well as many American Baptists. Just as with the Hieberts earlier, Friesen took them to a convention at Palmur to meet Edward Chute, and to Coonoor, one of the favorite hill stations, for the beginning of language study. Language training, as was usual, delayed the initiation of their evangelistic work for almost two years.

When Pankratz was ready for touring, having advanced in his language study, Friesen spent ten days with him in November 1903, going over the field of Malakpet. Elizabeth Neufeld and Anna Suderman, a missionary who shifted from the Alliance Mission in Gujarat to the AMBM in 1899, had discovered this as a suitable field of evangelism. This was the beginning of the occupation of a field that ran south of Hyderabad/Secunderabad to the river Krishna, about 160 kilometers in length and 50 kilometers wide. This was bordered to the east and south by the American Baptist fields, and to the north and west by Methodists.[11] At Malakpet, between November 1903 and March 1904, John and Maria Pankratz, assisted by Neufeld, a teacher, and Suderman, a nurse, inaugurated the first church of the American Mennonite Brethren Mission in India.[12]

**Preparation for the Missionary Task**

Almost without exception this first generation of MB men who went to India were trained in Baptist seminaries at Hamburg-Horn or Rochester. Only Franz J. Wiens from Siberia was trained at St. Chrischona in Basel, and Daniel Bergthold at McPherson College and Moody Bible Institute. All had met fairly high standards, but not because they found them **prescribed** in a MB policy handbook. Friesen, who had set the pace and the standards for Rückenau, believed that academic training could be a positive good, but spiritual strength, language ability, and practical skills were more important. These first missionaries were highly valued for their practical capabilities, their common sense, as well as their spiritual stability. Their work was duly noted in Hamburg and Boston. When Friesen's illness in 1904 drove him to Russia for a second furlough, Carl Schneider took the opportunity in his first history of the seminary in Hamburg-Horn to extol the work of their five graduates in India (all Mennonite Brethren) among the Telugu people. "These brethren have earned for themselves an enviable and enduring place in the esteem and admiration of their colleagues and continue to work with energy and acumen based on sound principles."[13] About the same time, the seminary teacher, Fetzer, strongly urged The Rooms to consider accepting more Hamburg graduates, in this case Johann G. Wiens and Cornelius H. Unruh. Barbour expressed Fetzer's sentiments this way: "Their recognition of the quality of manhood which your people in Russia send to missionary service makes their wish very strong that it might be possible for these additional workers to come into their fellowship."[14]

In every case, the Russian Mennonite Brethren who indicated an interest in going out as missionaries were examined before they were sent to Hamburg and then to India.[15] Normally, the candidates were presented at the annual conference or mission festivals at Rückenau, where leading brethren would examine them. Among these was David Schellenberg, who served as chair of the Rückenau committee, at least until he withdrew in 1909.[16] Another may have been Heinrich Jacob Braun (1873-1946), who became a key figure, but who lived in Neu-Halbstadt. Most strings in the mission story involving the Molotschna lead to Braun. He was also trained at Hamburg-Horn. Not only was he trained for the ministry as few were, he acquired two estates, making him one of the wealthy Mennonites. He became a director of the Raduga publishing firm in 1903, served as secretary/treasurer of the overseas mission, and was appointed as the MB member of the faith commission in about 1910.[17]

Among the American Mennonite Brethren missionaries, the earliest candidates (those who elected to go to West Africa and those who were prepared to establish a field in India) were all trained in Rochester, except Bergthold.[18] This was all the more remarkable in light of John F. Harms' objections in 1896 and 1898 to having anything to do with Baptists.[19] Gradually, however, his objections were minimized, if not completely withdrawn. The other committee members on the American MB side do not seem to have been educated up to seminary standards, except Henry W. Lohrenz, who had degrees from four institutions, among them Princeton Theological Seminary and Southern Baptist Theological Seminary.[20] Lohrenz later led the MB Board of Foreign Missions and also served as president of Tabor College and as chairman of the General Conference of MB Churches in North America.

### The Launching of *Das Erntefeld*

In 1900 Abraham Friesen began *Das Erntefeld* (The Harvest Field), a quarterly publication of the Russian MB missionaries in India. One might suspect that Friesen's desire to have his own publication arose out of the failure to bring the two streams of Mennonite Brethren together organizationally. Another reason might be found in the debate which surfaced between Friesen and Harms over apparent differing theological perceptions, as indicated earlier. It is more likely, however, that he was urged by Rückenau on his first furlough to give his constituents a newsletter of their own. A more concrete reason lay in the need to report quarterly to the ABMU anyway. These reports were written at first by Friesen and then translated into German for *Das Erntefeld* by Heinrich Unruh. Friesen's position in the founding of the Russian mission and his intermediary role in the establishment of the American one demanded a paper. His paper was not a rival to the *Zionsbote*. Both were widely read in both countries until the *Das Erntefeld* was discontinued in 1914. In all probability it reached many who did not subscribe to the *Zionsbote*, realized greater financial support, and ensured coverage of what was considered important from the vantage point of Nalgonda district.[21]

Given the education of the Russian Mennonite Brethren in a European context where world awareness was sharpened by imperial rivalries, the contributors to *Das Erntefeld*, both men and women, including the American Mennonite Brethren, provided

23

material of a sociological and anthropological nature, perhaps more so than the *Zionsbote* did at the time. For example, Katharina Huebert very perceptively wrote on the differences between Christianity and Hinduism.[22] Abram Friesen was favorably impressed with the Parsi community in the Bombay area, where European learning was highly valued and their women had a high status in society. By contrast, he used the work of Pandit Ramabai, a Christian advocate on behalf of women,[23] to assess the oppressive nature, as he and other evangelicals saw it, of the doctrines of both Hinduism and Buddhism, and how some, like Max Mueller of Oxford University, had misguided Europeans into overlooking these negative aspects. It is evident that the Hamburg professors provided some lectures on Buddhism.[24]

### Abram and Katharina Huebert at Suryapet

Abram J. and Katharina Huebert arrived in Nalgonda in 1898. Once the Friesens had returned from their second furlough in 1905, an earnest effort was made to establish a second station for the Hueberts with the same relationship to the ABMU and to Rückenau as that of Nalgonda. The site chosen was Suryapet (Sooriapet), north of Nalgonda. Friesen had targeted this village before leaving on furlough and had presumably discussed the site and its potential with Huebert at Rückenau. While in Boston Friesen had deposited $2,200 with The Rooms and, while in Chicago, he received another $800 from Rückenau "towards the expense of opening up Sooriapet (Suryapet) in the Nalgonda field."[25]

Early attempts with Friesen's help to obtain land for a second station were frustrated by Muslim hostility to Christianity generally. Hopeful, however, that the British presence at Secunderabad would help them, the Hueberts rented a "little house" in order to keep pressure on Muslim officials. While there they were visited by Thomas S. Barbour from Boston. By June they had been able to buy land, had purchased some building materials, but had no building permit.[26] In May 1903 Huebert was still living in a traveler's bungalow at Suryapet and struggling to get permission to build. Huebert wrote Barbour from the heat of May 1903: "We have to wait a long time .., but we believe it is our duty to stay here. If we give up this time, no one will get land for Mission purposes in the Deccan, but it will be easier after this has been fought out." Just how long they waited was indicated on 13 July: "We have been now three hot seasons here in the plains in this little house and we feel that our health is giving in, and if we do not get a suitable house soon to live in, we may break down." Barbour saw the struggle as a "[contest] for the radical principle of religious liberty. I am glad you have the strength to refuse a concession . . . and to stand for a final victory that shall secure freedom in Christian work to all Christian workers."[27]

Around October 1903 Huebert finally secured permission from the Nizam's administration to build, but then seemed stymied by lack of funds from Boston. Whereas Barbour sounded very discouraging in October 1903, he was able to write in February 1904 that the bungalow as such had been "authorized." Funds would be forthcoming from somewhere. The committee decided that "your need must be met." He added a sentence that may have caused some problems later, assuming that "the Property Committee will have general oversight of plans for building." In fact, Huebert was reprimanded for overspending on the bungalow.[28] It was reported finished in August 1904, when Huebert wrote that "we praise the Lord that he has been with us, and through him we got the victory, although it was a very long fight."[29]

### Heinrich and Anna (Peters) Unruh at Jangaon

Heinrich and Anna Unruh who went to India in 1899, as noted, also had a long struggle to establish a third station at Jangaon. This was on the railway line north of Nalgonda and Suryapet. First they lived in Secunderabad for two years, waiting for permission to build. Then Unruh was asked to assume charge of Nalgonda during the Friesens' second furlough (1904-05). When he was finally given permission to build in 1904, Unruh worked the Jangaon field from his base in Nalgonda and built only a small house and kitchen until he and Anna could actually move there.[30] Following the Friesens' return, Heinrich Unruh spent the year 1906 building up the station. He wrote the *Baptist Missionary Magazine*: "I never had any idea what it meant to build up a new mission station."[31] He was being all too modest. Jangaon's compound became the model for John Voth at Deverakonda. Both Unruh and Voth later justified the lifestyle.

### The Ongoing Discussion between Rückenau and Boston

In spite of the strong fellow-feeling between The Rooms and the Russian MB workers in India, and the pressure being exerted from Hamburg-Horn to accept more of their graduates,[32] a skirmish about salaries became a prelude to more difficult negotiations in the future.

By the fall of 1902, Friesen had asked Thomas Barbour to guarantee the salary of the Hueberts, as well as that of two additional couples, Johann and Helene Wiens and Cornelius and Martha Unruh, who were soon to be available for service. He reminded The Rooms that when the ABMU failed to persuade the Rückenau committee to guarantee the Hueberts' salary, the latter, together with Heinrich and Anna Unruh, had been accepted "unconditional[ly]."[33] Obviously, Barbour had mistakenly concluded that Rückenau could easily afford to build and keep up three stations, given the practice of designating Russian funds. In response to his request that Friesen confer with Huebert and Heinrich Unruh about this, Friesen wrote they were unanimous in thinking that "the Mennonite Brethren Church in Russia" (which he thought had a total membership of about 4,000) was not able to support their three stations wholly. Some sharing between Rückenau and Boston would be necessary. Whether he exaggerated a view to make his point or not, Friesen explained why "specifics" (designated gifts) were forthcoming even if guarantees were not: "our Churches have had no missionary training, have no missionary literature, and no missionary tradition and experience." His Nalgonda committee had agreed that if Boston did not insist that Rückenau guarantee "our personal salary," they were sure that sufficient funds would come from Heinrich J. Braun "to carry out the **evangelistic** mission work of our three stations without any financial aid" from the ABMU. If they did insist on this point, the ABMU might lose the entire operation to the American Mennonite Brethren.[34]

In April 1903 while at Ootacumund, Friesen again spelled out the reasons why his committee at home still felt they could not guarantee the salaries. That should be done by Boston. The Russian people were giving more than enough toward the building of Nalgonda and Suryapet. He was supremely confident that his friends would continue to give ample amounts as long as they saw their work placed on a solid footing, where salaries were guaranteed from general funds.[35]

Once Friesen had consulted with Rückenau, the discussions reached a stage of more concrete recommendations. From that perspective much more had already been donated than the "cost of the support of the missionaries," and therefore David Schellenberg's committee would rather see their missionaries in Nalgonda district work independently than be forced to meet "conditions." Taking this implied threat as an assurance of support, Friesen and his colleagues recommended to Rückenau that they "guarantee the outfit, passage money to India, and cost of a personal teacher (munshi) of all their missionaries"; also "all the expenses of the evangelistic mission work" emanating from the three stations, and any others that might be opened by "our brethren in Hyderabad, Deccan, under the auspices of the Missionary Union"; and to give "as much as possible so that their total contribution shall not be less than the cost of supporting all their missionaries" for the items listed.[36]

Obviously, some definitive arrangements had to be struck soon. As a third stage Barbour asked Friesen to have a "frank conference" with the India Reference Committee, so that "all questions concerning our relations now and in the future may be wisely determined and fully understood." This was precisely the time of Heinrichs' letter to Harms of July 1903. After more behind-the-scenes correspondence about salary guarantees Barbour replied: "Our committee are desirous of a solution that shall be seen to be entirely just to you and that... shall [also] be just to all the interests for which the [ABMU] must care."[37]

### Friesens' Second Furlough

These negotiations were delayed when the Friesens returned home on account of ill health. Maria, whose "chronic condition" was probably aggravated in India, wrote about being set aside "in order to learn a lesson" and of having the sympathetic support of those at Nalgonda in 1900 and until they left for Russia in July 1904. After the furlough in the Molotschna, Peter A. Penner, an American Mennonite missionary at Champa, Madya Pradesh, found her "quite sickly" when he visited Nalgonda.[38] Besides, Abraham had not found a cure for his heart trouble in the hills. He explained: "In March [1902] I had a severe attack of heart trouble due to weakness of nerves. Since then my health has been poor." In 1904, sent to Madras by Dr. Lorena Breed for a further consultation, he was ordered home to Russia for one year. Heinrich Unruh wrote that as long as

Friesen was touring, even vigorously, he felt better, but "as soon as he has worries or does mental work, he feels much worse."[39]

Friesen's heart and nervous condition likely was related to stress over the need to reach an agreement with Thomas Barbour of the ABMU, or perhaps because of his conflict with Jacob Heinrichs. The discussions of these complex issues had remained too inconclusive. From 1902 to 1904 these negotiations overlapped with Heinrich Unruh's need for a compound with its requisite buildings at Jangaon, the coming out of Johann G. Wiens and Cornelius Unruh, and the attempt to persuade the Russians to make "specific gifts' available to the general treasury. Friesen had also suggested that if Cornelius Unruh was not accepted he might well come out independently, taking some hitherto supporters of the ABMU with him. Meanwhile, Barbour had written to say that the ABMU needed to be assured of regular support from Rückenau as much as the Russian committee.[40]

Besides the question of health, the Friesens had another good reason for the second furlough. Since they went back with two children in 1905, one can hardly expect the adoptions to have been made without prior consideration or correspondence. Maria's brother, Jacob Martens, and his wife Anna had nine children. After allowing Aron, the fifth child, to live with the Friesens while on furlough, they permitted a formal adoption which was necessary for taking him to India. Young Aron therefore took the name Friesen in 1905. The second adopted child, a Mariechen (Mary), was an orphan of Prussian Mennonite parentage.[41] One of the reasons for the adoption might have been to provide a family role model for their Christian as well as non-Christian Indian families.[42] One might conjecture that not having a family was seen in India as being unblessed by the gods. How frequently they must have been asked: "Don't you have any children? How sorry we are for you."[43]

Once Friesen had arrived home, he found that Johann Wiens, who had weak lungs, was at the moment not under consideration. Hence Rückenau had focused its entire attention, rather persistently, on getting Cornelius and Martha Unruh to India, especially since there was more than enough money available for their passage.[44] By a fortunate coincidence Barbour had to go to Europe. He offered to pay Friesen's expenses for a meeting in Paris or Hamburg. When the illness of his father persisted, Friesen tried to make arrangements for the Unruhs to go to Hamburg, near Martha's home town, in order to meet Barbour. Another complication arose when Rückenau declared that Wiens was now healthy enough to go. Would the ABMU also accept Johann and Helene Wiens on the condition that if his health broke down, the return journey would not be charged to the Boston treasury ?[45]

What delayed any advancement of the discussion was the illness of Friesen's father back in Chortitza. Friesen could not, however, avoid pressure from two sides: from the ABMU's committee in India, and from Braun at Neu-Halbstadt who was "asking again and again: what is the Committee in Boston going to do with regard to our young men [Johann G. Wiens and Cornelius Unruh] who are ready to go to India?" Friesen tried his best to restrain the impatience of Rückenau and asked them "to wait until final settlement" could be reached.[46] Meanwhile Barbour received recommendations from India that emphasized how crucial it was to have some assurances of the amounts of money that could be expected from Russia, especially since the ABMU work extended to "so many mission fields and so many countries."[47]

**The Stockholm Plan of Cooperation**

Though some correspondence is missing, Friesen must have made a hurried trip to Stockholm, Sweden, sometime in September 1904, to meet with Barbour. There they agreed on a "Plan of Cooperation Between the Mennonite Brethren of South Russia and the Executive Committee of the Missionary Union," and this plan was ratified in Boston on 26 September 1904. In Rückenau, however, Friesen did not distribute the complete document until the end of the year. Only the "points" of the Plan were "unanimously accepted" there.[48]

The Plan promised to accept any missionaries recommended by the Rückenau committee if indeed the "needs of the work and the resources available" justified such appointments. Such missionaries would be recognized by the ABMU as "representing themselves and the full constituency of the Union, as well as their brethren in Russia." It was clearly stated that the Boston committee had the last word, and that the India committee "of the [Baptist] Telugu mission" would referee placement, total appropriations to be spent on all missionaries so appointed, and monitor the amounts coming to the Nalgonda district. The sharing principle as finally approved stated that the Rückenau committee would be financially responsible for everything except half the salary; the missionary residence (other building needs would have to be covered by special appeals or by appropriations as necessary from Boston); half the cost of outfitting; half the costs of "return passages" for furloughs; and half the costs in retirement or widowhood caused by death.[49]

Though acceptance of this plan should have created some delays in the matter of appointments, and Friesen was clearly told that in the matter of Johann Wiens he had to wait for "medical endorsement," Barbour found himself faced with an accomplished fact. On 25 October 1904 Friesen stated that since Wiens and Cornelius Unruh had waited so long, he had made arrangements for their passage. "I am very sorry [they] had to be sent to India **before** receiving the decision of the committee in Boston, but it could not be helped." He promised, however, to persuade Treasurer Braun to send Boston the appropriate amount "directly during the winter of each year." Meanwhile, he expected to have a positive ratification from Boston of his action regarding Wiens and Unruh.[50] This procedure of paying up after the fact was not understood, or well liked, and caused controversy later.

### Successful Renegotiation

As it was, Friesen did not hear from Barbour until the spring of 1905. Meanwhile, the Rückenau board had met and taken exception to the second clause in the Plan, which opened the way for Russian Mennonite appointees to be sent outside the Nalgonda district, or even outside the Deccan. Led by David Schellenberg, they decided that if and when the work in the Nalgonda stations were fully supported, and there were acceptable and qualified recruits who agreed to be appointed outside the area in which Friesen had initiated the MB work, they would give them their blessing, but could not promise to furnish their support.[51] To this Barbour and the India committee had strong objections. In principle every missionary accepted by the ABMU should be "available where the need is most urgent." It would be "inequitable," on such grounds, to see certain stations understaffed, and the Russian MB stations overstaffed. Barbour promised, however, that "no assignment to another station will be made without full correspondence and mutual understanding," but he would not alter the clause in the Plan nor make this "agreement" look as though a "temporary" assignment elsewhere should require "exceptional action."[52]

While still in Russia completing his health cure, mainly in St. Petersburg, Friesen reminded Barbour that the Plan, as written down, had entirely omitted a further item of responsibility: the medical work. The Russian treasury could only cover the expenses "required for the [evangelistic] work of these missionaries." In August 1905 Friesen wrote that "our committee will not sign any agreement, in which it is not clearly stated that the Executive Committee of the Union is responsible for all expenditures required for the Educational and Medical Mission work in the care of the missionaries working under the agreement." For a church that was far from using legal counsel in that day, they were relatively shrewd bargainers. As a result of this demand, the relevant clause added the words: "direct evangelistic." The Rooms understandably claimed the right to final authorization for any expansion in other areas of service. Almost immediately Friesen found himself over budget for evangelistic work, but he attributed this to the open doors created by the revival of 1906.[53]

On these points Rückenau was seen to have registered a successful protest. Though there were some exceptions, as a general rule, and as it worked out, given illnesses, deaths, and furloughs, all of the Russian MB missionaries, including the single women who came as teachers or nurses, managed to stay or rotate in three locations. This concentration of Mennonite personnel aroused the fear among Baptist missionaries in India that the Russians with their large stations and many converts would in fact declare their independence or perhaps even join the AMBM. Friesen actually had occasion to reassure Barbour on that point: "I'm glad to think that you know better."[54]

## CHAPTER 3

# Missionary Fellowship and Revival

The two Mennonite Brethren working groups in India before 1914, Russian and American,[1] had a very close relationship, though they were separated organizationally. Their association in India has never been fully investigated.

One can lay aside the myth that Mennonite Brethren in India had many relational difficulties because of their isolation from each other. During the period 1904 to 1915 their "exile," to borrow a term from the British in India, was made tolerable and enjoyable by their frequent contacts for spiritual, social, and practical purposes. In this the Russian Mennonite Brethren took the leadership, by virtue of their prior position. They formed part of a larger unit for fellowship and policy discussions.

The Russians assisted the pioneer Americans in staking out territories within the larger Baptist field so that their respective areas came to be from fifty to one hundred fifty kilometers apart. Until 1914 the Americans closely identified with the Russians in terms of help, fellowship, and perhaps even with some feeling of dependence. They did not initiate a separate decision-making structure until then. The Americans welcomed Russian hospitality, accepted arrangements for language training, as well as indigenous preachers. This pattern had been established with the arrival in 1899 of N. N. and Susie Hiebert, Elizabeth Neufeld, and John and Maria Pankratz. All were soon subjected to trying times, yet all were blessed by the revival of 1906. All shared their methods, results, and concerns about the mission with supporting constituencies through their respective papers.[2]

## The Political Background

Many anxieties disturbed the Russians around 1905. That year marked the disastrous defeat of the Tsar's forces at the hands of Japan. The resulting Russian revolution of 1905 led to disturbances that were felt in Odessa while the Friesens awaited departure for Nalgonda. Katharina Reimer, a teacher who was going to India with them, observed a variety of demonstrations.[3] European diplomacy between 1908 and 1914 barely kept Russia out of the Balkan Wars. In the midst of this, the Mennonite world continued to prosper, and normality seemed to return after the scare of 1905. Most

Mennonites, not least the MB missionaries to India, were favorably disposed toward the Tsarist regime, especially if their way of life in the Mennonite colonies and their outreach beyond was not curtailed. According to historian Peter M. Friesen, most Mennonites identified so closely with the Tsar's regime that they criticized even the Liberals (the *Kadets*) for their demands for democratic reform. Most were quite content that in the October Manifesto of 1905 the Tsar had gone far enough, and were probably secure in the knowledge that the Duma under Count Peter Stolypin was overpowering the revolutionary voices.[4] Perhaps Friesen was more liberal than some, for in the midst of his furlough (1904-05), he enjoyed seven weeks in St. Petersburg, where he found not only a cure for his heart ailment, but also some "spiritual refreshing," which coincided with expectations for "an era of liberty of conscience."[5]

**The New Recruits from Russia and America**

Cornelius H. and Martha (Woltmann) Unruh were well prepared for their work in India. Cornelius (1873-1941) served in the Mennonite forestry service in Siberia and elsewhere for four years before leaving to attend the Hamburg-Horn seminary (1899-1903). While there he met a young woman from a Baptist family, Martha Woltmann, who was a nurse in training. They married in 1902 and were commissioned for service a year later.[6] They left for India in 1904 and served at Palmur (Mahbubnagar) for some time, before taking over the work at Nalgonda when the Friesens retired in 1908. The stint at Palmur, as a replacement for Edward Chute, preceded the arrangements between Barbour and Friesen, and the understanding about concentration.

Already at this early stage Cornelius evinced a vigorous independence comparable to Friesen's. When he believed he was being cut back in appropriations promised to Chute, Unruh gave vent to a sharpness that occasionally got him into trouble. The issue at this time was money for Palmur's indigenous preachers. If the agreement was not kept his preachers would surely starve. With some sarcasm, he wrote: "They can't board in heaven and work in Palmur field." Still in a very junior position, he stated his conviction that surely God was above even the ABMU and he was responsible to God![7]

Though Abram J. Huebert had preceded him by six years, it was soon clear that Cornelius Unruh would succeed Friesen as the dominant figure, the leader and executive of the Russian Mennonite Brethren. He drew closer than Friesen to the ABMU and this for a good reason. After Friesen resigned, the funds that came as "designated gifts" tended to dry up. Coming as he did from the Crimea, Unruh simply did not have the circle of well-to-do friends to whom Friesen had appealed. By 1909 Unruh had decided he did not like the "specifics busyness" at all, preferring to see all designated funds accounted for in the Boston office.[8] At the same time, he did not want to hear about cutbacks, least of all for Nalgonda, which had been like a "firstborn" to Friesen, the builder of that station.[9]

**Johann and Helene Wiens**

Johann G. and Helene Hildebrandt Wiens went to India in the midst of Friesen's negotiations with Thomas Barbour. Wiens, from South Russia, was a member of the Mennonite Church in Lichtenau. He attended Hamburg-Horn school during the years 1899-1903, along with Cornelius Unruh. He joined the MB Church in 1900, was ordained in 1903, and served at home until 1904.[10] While much less is known about Helene she had some nurse's training in preparation for India.[11]

Between language study and their enforced departure in 1910 because of Elizabeth's illness, the Wienses served temporarily at Hanamakonda (1906-08), the site of Dr. J. S. Timpany's hospital. They covered Suryapet in 1908 when the Hueberts left on furlough, and stayed at Jangaon in 1909 when Heinrich and Anna Unruh went home for a rest. Though he disliked having to serve as a relieving missionary, Wiens learned much from these experiences, especially in the matter of appropriations. At Hanamakonda he had taken money intended for medical work, so that he could undertake touring in the villages. This was because the system of funneling money from Russia to the ABMU as arranged by Friesen and Braun was not working smoothly. Wiens criticized the system in September 1909. He suggested that Heinrich Unruh, and not Friesen, should now serve as the link for funds from Russia. Despite his views on funding arrangements, Wiens was a strong advocate of the principle of concentration on behalf of Rückenau.[12]

Wiens had the distinction of being called to teach at the Baptist Seminary at Ramapatnam, in response to an emergency staffing situation. The appointment as acting vice-principal was to be for two years. Though the family actually moved to Ramapatnam, north of Madras, in late 1910, the desperate illness of their daughter forced them to heed medical advice and take her to Germany. As Cornelius Unruh explained, the Wienses were standing between two mountains: their "precious work" and the call to Ramapatnam (after having moved four times in five years) on the one side, and the life and future of their daughter on the other. As expected, they chose to leave for Europe in mid-term, 1911.[13] They might have chosen to take her to Vellore for treatment. Had they done so, Wiens could have remained at Ramapatnam, and the family would have avoided the war and revolution that prevented their return.

Wiens reported to the Mission on his daughter's progress until his formal resignation in 1913. Even then he hoped one day to return to India. Elizabeth, born in November 1905, died in 1917. In 1912 they moved to Tschongraw in the Crimea. Immediately after the War (and during the Revolution), Johann G. Wiens was instrumental in launching a Bible school there.[14] When Wiens in 1922 applied to return to India instead of leaving for Canada in the intended migration, the troubled American Baptists found it "absolutely impossible" to entertain his application, whether as missionary or at Ramapatnam.[15]

**The Single Women from Russia and America**

Though the work of the four single women who came to India from Russia is not insignificant, much less is known about their background, and the course of their work, than is the case with the married couples. This disparity of information is not exceptional for that day. Furthermore, their time in India was in each case short lived. Katharina Reimer came out with the Friesens in 1905. She was a teacher, and obviously quite gifted as a writer. Her mastery of German was exceptional.[16] She may have been related to the Friesens, probably from the Martens side. She retired from the field in 1908 because of illness. She then took up teaching, though it has been difficult to isolate her from others of the same name and also involved in education. That she taught the four children of Heinrich and Anna Unruh, left at home in 1911, is clear.[17]

Anna Epp arrived with Cornelius and Martha Unruh in 1904, and then married the young American widower Daniel Bergthold in the very next year. Anna Peters came to India as a nurse in 1909 in the company of Franz and Marie Wiens and served as a nurse at Suryapet with the Hueberts. She contracted tuberculosis of the spine and had to return to Russia in 1912. For the short time she was in India, she distinguished herself in language study. She adopted an Indian orphan, and made frequent and interesting contributions to *Das Erntefeld*, one of them a study of India's women.[18] Aganetha Neufeld accompanied A. J. Friesen in 1913 on his last visit to India. As a nurse, she probably replaced Peters at Suryapet. She seems to have carried on until 1923, when she left for North America with those seeking a new citizenship.[19]

**The Two Katharinas: Lohrenz and Schellenberg**

Katharina Lohrenz (1882-1913), also had a short career in India.[20] She studied in the German language division at McPherson College. Eventually she qualified as a teacher, but felt called to go abroad, even though, as the eldest and unmarried daughter, she might have been expected to stay at home in view of her mother's prior death. She was accepted as a missionary at the MB General Conference in 1907. She traveled to India in the company of John H. and Maria Voth. At Malakpet, while in language study, she made her home with Anna Suderman. Since Elizabeth Neufeld had left the field because of ill health, Katharina took her place as head of the school at Malakpet. As her brother John suggested, hers was a heavy burden. She became director of the school, taught, served as role model to indigenous teachers, and mothered seventy-five children. When Muslim opposition closed Malakpet station, she had to make do in more crowded conditions. She and Anna Suderman moved their work to the Ismiah Bazaar, where the local population was decimated, perhaps as much as 30 percent, by the 1911 scourge of typhus, cholera, and a plague of boils.[21]

Lohrenz took a trip to Agra in 1911 and to Darjeeling a year later, particularly enjoying the Taj Mahal and Mount Everest. These recreational tours, however, were not sufficient to keep her alive. Her promising career was cut short by death from the dreaded typhoid fever on 5 September 1913. This and the death of Heinrich Unruh at Jangaon in November 1912 and of Anna Epp Bergthold in

1915 had a profound impact on both the American and Russian missionaries and their supporting constituencies.[22]

Katharina L. Schellenberg's career in India proved more fortunate for the Mission. It fell into the period when North American women had built up a vast network of missionary support and endeavor. Her preparation for medical work was not unusual, given the broader spectrum of women's missionary societies.[23] For example, the ABMU had Dr. Lorena Breed at Nalgonda for some years before Schellenberg went to India.[24] In the AMBM, however, Katharina's career choice was unusual and unique. There was no other MB doctor–male or female–until Jake Friesen went there in 1951, six years after her death.[25]

As the daughter of Abraham Schellenberg, Katharina volunteered for service in India as early as 1900 but was encouraged to become medically qualified. This she did by taking a four-year course at "a homeopathic school of medicine" in Kansas City.[26] She left for India in 1907 and started her mission at Malakpet, where her work was interrupted by persecution from the Muslim population. She then went to Nagarkurnool, where she laid the foundations for a hospital. She subsequently worked at Shamshabad in conjunction with John and Maria K. Lohrenz.

Because of these earliest experiences, one of her fundamental interests became the Muslim women who lived in a village purdah world, insulated from the outer community. As a female doctor she had access to the *zenana* (a place of seclusion) where even a male Indian doctor would be excluded.[27]

### The American Pioneer Couples

John and Maria (Harms) Pankratz, who arrived in 1902, were followed in 1904 by Daniel and Tina (Mandtler) Bergthold [and as his second wife, 1905, the Russian Anna Epp], John and Maria (Epp) Voth (1907), and eventually Frank and Elizabeth (Dickman) Janzen (1910). These four couples became the "pioneering four" whose work stretched to the Second World War. They came to join Elizabeth Neufeld (who actually left India in 1906 because of illness)[28] and Anna Suderman, who became the third wife of Daniel Bergthold in 1915.[29]

Daniel Bergthold and his first wife, Tina, found a suitable building site at Nagarkurnool, near a reservoir for the rice fields in the area. This was at the southern reaches of the large field of 50,000 square kilometers, which the AMBM had assumed from the Baptists during Hiebert's short stay. Fortunately, getting permission for land and for building was not as difficult here as for the other pioneers. They were more or less settled into a compound by 1907. This meant that the Bergtholds were isolated for some years from both the Pankratzes as well as from the Russian Mennonite Brethren in Nalgonda district. Once Deverakonda to the north-east and Wanaparty to the southwest were settled, the distance from each other did not seem so great.[30]

While looking for a second AMBM field, the Bergtholds were soon introduced to the Madigas, the leather worker caste. Daniel Bergthold wrote that "though they live in the dirt of India, we have our greatest success with them." Observing them in their suppressed condition, and comparing the caste system with an earlier civilization as he conceived of it, he became quite convinced that Darwin's theory did not apply here. His view was that the caste system had "reversed progress" from that earlier civilization.[31] Pankratz, touring with them in their first years, nevertheless thought that the people of this area were more ready to hear the Gospel than those in Malakpet, and thought the prospects for a successful work were very good.[32]

### John and Maria Voth

The third couple, John H. and Maria (Epp) Voth, came from Bingham Lake, Minnesota. This second son of Heinrich Voth was seen in his youth as a model of a wholly dedicated person. Nicolai N. Hiebert, who remembered him as a close associate in a young men's group, saw in him the value of an "early conversion," though some church leaders had questioned the advisability of baptizing such a "small boy." His long-time associate, John Pankratz, wrote about him as the "unforgettable" one, a person "who proposed to serve his Lord and Savior to the utmost of his ability."[33] Following his education at McPherson College and the German division of Rochester Baptist Seminary (1903-06), he married Maria Epp, who was educated in a Bible school at Mountain Lake, Minnesota, and at Moody Bible Institute in Chicago.[34]

Voth received the field of Deverakonda in 1910 through the auspices of Cornelius Unruh at Nalgonda. As Unruh explained, Deverakonda was simply too far from Nalgonda district for the kind of supervision it deserved. These circumstances, and the search for a field by Bergthold, Pankratz, and Voth between Nagarkurnool and Nalgonda led to the choice of Deverakonda, one of the "most poverty-stricken" areas of the Deccan.[35] Voth worked intensely, giving almost his whole attention to evangelization. Not only was he the most prolific propagandist for the Mission,[36] he also raised more money through designated gifts than all the others. This factor was undoubtedly one of the reasons for bad feelings between the Voths and others, yet, over the years, benefitting from the impact of the revival of 1906, they garnered a large number of baptized believers in over one hundred villages.[37]

Voth later compared the beginnings at Deverakonda with John E. Clough's experience at Ongole fifty years earlier. He told how A. J. Friesen, before 1908, had been approached by an indigenous Christian named Wankayalpetty Jacob. This evangelist came from south of the Krishna River, but felt called to preach to the lower caste people of Angadipett, near Deverakonda, where he had some relations who were "without the Gospel." When Jacob died of a heart attack while at a Nalgonda district meeting, Friesen felt constrained to organize the group of Christians left behind at Angadipett. This church formed an early core in a Christian community that Cornelius Unruh handed over to the Voths in early 1910. Voth was careful to declare his indebtedness to the Russian Mennonite Brethren for this location.[38]

### Frank and Elizabeth Janzen

Frank A. and Elizabeth (Dickman) Janzen were the last American couple to settle in India before the Great War. Born in 1880, Frank was not converted until age twenty one when he heard John Pankratz preach. Immediately feeling the call to witness for his Lord, he attended Hiebert's Mountain Lake Bible Academy. Here he made some converts, perhaps even Elizabeth Dickman whom he married in 1907. Impressed by the needs of India, and hearing of the early death of Tina Mandtler Bergthold, he decided to train for ministry in India. In 1904 he joined John H. Voth at Rochester and graduated in 1907. Here he worked in the Rochester city mission.[39] Meanwhile, Elizabeth Dickman took her Bible training at Moody Bible Institute. Following their marriage, they engaged in conference evangelistic work for several years before being ordained for missionary service by Heinrich Voth and N. N. Hiebert in 1910. In that year they left for India and, following language study at Malakpet, took up residence at Nagarkurnool during the Bergthold's first furlough.[40]

### The Russian/American MB Fellowship in India

Occasions for fellowship between the Russian and American Mennonite Brethren missionaries were largely determined by the rhythm of life between the "hills" and the "plains." Fortunately for those who followed them, the Friesens had already taken the precedent of "going to the hills." This meant that the children from the schools came to the plains to be with their parents at Christmas, and the parents met somewhere in the Blue Hills during the hot season. At this time the choice was either Ootacumund, more than two thousand meters up in the Nilgiri Hills, the site of Breeks Memorial school for missionary children, or Coonoor station, the location of the Hebron girls' school. Both had vacation homes for missionaries during the hot season.[41] In 1900 Nicolai and Susie Hiebert probably benefitted greatly from their only visit to Coonoor station in the company of the Friesens, Heinrich and Anna Unruh, and the single women Neufeld and Suderman. Every new family arriving or departing by train in Secunderabad was an occasion for getting together. In February 1901 they all met in Secunderabad to say farewell to the Hieberts and their surviving twin.[42] Once the Pankratzes built their station at Malakpet, their bungalow served as a central place of contact.[43]

Pankratz responded to Russian assistance by visiting their stations in February 1904. This coincided with the farewell for the Friesens who were going on their second furlough. While others traveled by oxcart, Pankratz rode his bicycle all the way to Nalgonda (one hundred kilometers). There he enjoyed the "very best hospitality." On the way to Suryapet, Friesen insisted that Pankratz take the Nalgonda ox team half way. Back on his bicycle, he forded a river at low tide, and arrived at the Hueberts during their intensive building program. Quite coincidentally, or because of the opportunity of company, Huebert planned a buying trip to Secunderabad. They sent their oxcarts ahead, led of course by trustworthy servants, and then each cycled westward on the main road running to Secunderabad. They probably spoke Low German, and enjoyed *Zwiebach* made by their spouses. What Pankratz remembered from this jaunt was how "rejuvenating" the fellowship had been. Particu-

41

larly observant also of how the Friesens and the Hueberts had laid out their compounds, this fellowship "enlarged his experience and enriched his understanding."[44]

One of the next occasions for anticipated fellowship turned out to be a sad one, ending in a funeral. During November 1904 the

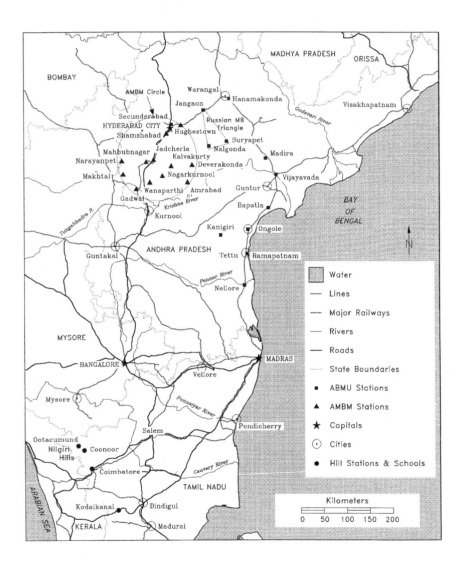

Bergtholds, accompanied by the Pankratzes and Elizabeth Neufeld, left for Nalgonda in order to attend their first Baptist Telugu Convention.[45] They had also accepted an invitation from the Hueberts to visit them before returning home. After five days of conference in Nalgonda, the party left for Suryapet. On the way Tina Bergthold became ill. Conjecture had it that she contracted the dreaded smallpox virus while staying in a traveler's bungalow on the way. Even though the missionary doctor, J. S. Timpany from Hanamakonda, an ABMU station to the east, arrived a few days later, he was not able to save her life. She died at Suryapet of smallpox on 26 November 1904.[46] Because it was not possible to wait with burial for more than one day, Abram Huebert worked during the night to prepare a coffin and a grave. Pankratz expressed the gratitude of the American families when he praised Katharina Huebert particularly for her generous hospitality, given the sad circumstances. This fellowship in bereavement had drawn them all closer to God and to each other.[47] Tina Mandtler Bergthold's only child, Viola, who later came to India as a missionary, recalled that "none of us had been vaccinated against any disease." Her parents were told by the MB mission board to put their "complete faith in God alone."[48]

Happier occasions followed. In 1904 Cornelius and Martha Unruh and Johann and Helena Wiens arrived, while Anna Epp married Daniel Bergthold the following year. Epp, from Tiege in the Molotschna, had trained as a nurse in the Bethel Deaconess Home in Berlin.[49] While Abraham J. Friesen, on furlough, was negotiating about their support and the financial arrangements of the continuing relationship with the ABMU, this party traveled via Hamburg and Southampton to Madras. They were met by Jacob Heinrichs and Heinrich Unruh. They were glad to have the latter aboard the train, to help with the strangeness of the land they had entered. On their way to Nalgonda, a station not located on the railway, the locomotion was by oxcart. The whole party stopped at the Pankratz bungalow at Malakpet. Cornelius wrote: "We were pleased to learn to know and love these fellow believers."[50] Anna Epp remained at Malakpet until she married Daniel Bergthold in 1905.

For Christmas 1905 Daniel and Anna Bergthold traveled to Suryapet for the annual Deccan Association meeting of the ABMU. They went first to the Pankratzes at Malakpet, where they were joined by Jacob Heinrichs from Ramapatnam. Together they traveled to

Suryapet, where they met not only the Russian MB missionaries of the Nalgonda district, but also the Baptist missionaries from Palmur and Secunderabad. Revival was the main theme of this convention, and for the Bergtholds it was a time of orientation to the larger Mennonite/Baptist community.[51] Cornelius Unruh commented on how fully the American Mennonite Brethren had come to be identified with the Russian members of the ABMU: they were "thought of as belonging to us."[52] One of the reasons why the Americans did not organize themselves into a field council of their own until 1914 lay in the gratification received through the frequent social contacts which provided fellowship, inspiration, and cultural insights.

All of this was surely indicative of a most cordial fellowship between the two MB groups. These contacts increased as missionaries moved from oxcarts to automobiles in the inter-War period.

**The Testing of Character**

Wholesome fellowship helped as the missionaries' faith, commitment, patience, and character were much tested by delays, official hostility, illnesses, accidents, and hazards. Hardly anyone was wholly prepared for the price to be paid for trying to impact on India's civilization. Nor did it ever take long to feel the enervating climate of the Deccan. All who came in conquest of India's wealth or of India's soul paid a high price, not least of which was severe illness, if not broken health.[53] One such warning could have come from even a cursory survey of the fate of the Bengal Civil Service of the East India Company. This revealed that about one-third of all males, who thought of their stay in India, quite realistically, as an "exile," never achieved the desired goal of retirement in England. Even though they soon developed hill stations in the south and north where they could stay during the hot season, the mortality rate of their wives and children in the nineteeth century was much higher.[54] For the Mission the compelling command of the Great Commission of Jesus Christ overrode common sense and history, which warned white people to stay away from India or West Africa.

Only a few examples of illness must suffice. Anna (Peters) Unruh broke down in 1905 and badly needed a furlough. Her precarious health probably was the main reason for leaving four children in Russia in 1911, if it was not caused by the toleration of an annual pregnancy.[55] Though herself a nurse, trained in Germany,

Martha (Woltmann) Unruh lost five children at infancy or in still-birth from having to travel one hundred kilometers by oxcart to Secunderabad to have an English doctor deliver her baby. Only two boys survived.[56] Family life and missionary work were made most trying because of travel by oxcart. On Friesen's visit to Nagarkurnool in 1908, just when the birth of Martha Bergthold was announced, he noticed that the Indian climate was taking its toll on the family, even though Dr. Katharina L. Schellenberg was stationed at Nagarkurnool.[57]

## The Revival of 1906

This revival, seemingly the only one of its kind to overwhelm the MB in India during the entire period of ninety years under consideration, greatly enhanced fraternal relations. As a result both MB groups realized quite substantial results in both conversions and baptisms.

The person most affected by the experience, and who interpreted it as a baptism with the Holy Ghost as promised in Acts 2, was Johann Wiens. During the hot season of 1906 three of the Russian families–Friesen, Huebert, and Wiens–went to the hill station of Ootacumund for a rest. In their search for spiritual renewal, the men left their wives and children behind at Ootacumund to attend a weekend conference arranged by Plymouth Brethren at nearby Coimbatore.[58]

The meaning and significant results of this weekend experience can only be noted briefly. The wives, informed of what was happening at Coimbatore by daily cards sent in the mail by Huebert, also received a new sense of the holiness of God. What Wiens and company learned at Coimbatore was that the Spirit's blessing was invariably withheld until there was full confession of sin and reconciliation with fellow believers.[59] Wiens led the way in sharing his wonderful experience with articles in *Das Erntefeld*, beginning in August 1906. Friesen and Huebert followed, explaining what the renewal meant to them personally. When they returned to their stations, they found the revival sweeping over their Christian congregations in the Nalgonda district,[60] even though the two Unruh families had not been present at Coimbatore. Yet when the Unruh families visited the Pankratz family at Malakpet on 30 September 1906, the renewal movement came to Hyderabad also. Nor were the

Bergtholds at Nagarkurnool uninfluenced by the revival. In fact, they followed the Wiens' invitation to Hanamakonda, where in October they found the Friesens, and Katharina Reimer, the Hueberts, and the Pankratzes. Bergthold wrote home: "the news of the revival spread to the four corners, and we too wanted to be renewed 'with power from on high.'"[61] The Deverakonda area also benefitted from the revival that continued to spread over southern India.[62]

**Family Considerations**

Two intimately related concerns were the matters of income and education for missionary children. The salaries established for American couples in 1912 were $1,000 annually, or $83 monthly. Each child had an annual allowance of $100. Single women were paid 50 percent of the allowance for couples without children.[63] This meant that missionary couples were paid almost three times as much as *Reiseprediger* at home, and far more than N. N. Hiebert or subsequently even Henry W. Lohrenz, who were paid an honorarium for their work as facilitators of the mission.[64]

Though there were periods of financial hardship for the missionaries, nearly all seemed to have enough for the necessities of life, including provision for their children's education. The depression of the 1930s made matters very difficult for some, but even then travel, housing, and expenses on the field in conjunction with their work were covered by annual appropriations. By some standards missionary salaries were very low. Yet, because their work was interspersed by furlough travel, some missionary families did manage to circle the globe during their lifetime and see many things denied to those supporting them.[65]

**Molotschna, Ootacumund, and Coonoor**

Another more than ordinary concern of the missionaries was the education of their children, who had to be sent to a distant school in India, or to the homeland in the care of relatives or friends.

The practice of sending children off to distant schools was adopted from the British administrators by Baptist and other missions. As mentioned, for the Mennonite Brethren in India the choice was either Breeks Memorial school for missionary children, or Coonoor station, the location of the Hebron Girls' School.[66] Both schools were founded by the Plymouth Brethren and were run on regimented but evangelical lines, designed to prepare children of tea planters, business men, and missionaries for entrance to Cambridge University colleges. In conjunction with her discussion of these schools, Viola Bergthold Wiebe took the occasion to quote Rudyard Kipling, who wrote: "A man should, whatever happens, keep to his own caste, race and breed." Breeks and Hebron schools seemed to have done that until about 1930.[67]

Though they knew about the virtues of these English schools, the pioneer Russian Mennonite Brethren preferred arrangements in their home country. The Friesens personally escaped the worst of this ordeal because the children they adopted and took to India in 1905 returned to Russia three years later when the Friesens had to retire because of ill health. Meanwhile, Aron [Martens] Friesen attended Breeks for one term. The Hueberts were the first to leave children in Russia. In 1909 they left their Abram and Katie with Heinrich J. Braun, a "fellow student" at Hamburg-Horn, and later the treasurer in Neu-Halbstadt. Following stints at Ootacamund and Hebron, Heinrich and Anna Unruh left their four children–Henry, Marie, Martha and Arthur–in Russia with members of the family at the end of their one furlough (1910-11). These children were only reunited with their two youngest siblings, John C. and Elizabeth, when their mother returned to Russia after Heinrich's death in November 1912.[68]

In 1911, given the fact there were now eight of them in the Molotschna–two Hueberts, four Unruhs, and two of their own–Abraham J. Friesen raised the question of the need for a school in Russia for missionary children.[69] The Unruh children, particularly, ran into trouble over an attempt to integrate them into a Mennonite school in the Molotschna. Family lore has it that they were regarded rather strangely because their experience at Breeks had been much more rigorous, disciplined and advanced.[70]

## The Ordeal of Separation

American MB missionary families mostly followed the example set by Cornelius and Martha Unruh, who sent their two sons Cornelius and Henry to Ootacumund or, as in the case of the Voths and the Bergtholds, to Coonoor. Even though some of the children suffered from the separation, most came to appreciate, with the help of sensitive parents, that a sharing of the sacrifice for mission was necessary. Nearly all made a successful transition to North American secondary institutions and found their preparation for the professions, in many cases, second to none.[71] Most found gratifying places in a variety of government services, as well as nursing, teaching, and medicine.

Some trauma did come with the separation. Viola and Martha Bergthold, twelve and six in 1915, were about twelve hundred kilometers from home. Their father Daniel appeared in September to convey to them the sad news that their mother had died in childbirth two weeks earlier. They received a new mother, Anna Suderman, in 1916. She was someone they knew and had already learned to love.[72]

Martha's life at Hebron and Breeks illustrates to what degree such a child could become totally anglicized by this experience. Having been introduced to tennis by her father at Nagarkurnool, she benefited from the athletic opportunities at "Ooty." She remembers defeating her tennis rival and closest friend, Pamela Walker, and receiving the top award from Sir Robert Staines, a Coimbatore tea planter, at Ootacumund's "Wimbledon."[73]

Arnold Janzen, the youngest son of Frank Janzen, described how the structures at Breeks affected even sibling relationships. His oldest brother Leander, a prefect (a senior student monitor) was quite unapproachable on the school grounds while his brother Edwin, the middle one, "could be talked to at a distance." When his parents were present at Ootacumund for weeks at a time, they could attend as "day scholars." He remembers Teddy Voth and Henry Bergthold as friends with whom he would "shoot at bee-hives high in the eucalyptus trees with our catty-y's." After his father's death in 1927 he was grateful that he could stay with his mother Elizabeth until he went off to medical school in Kansas. All in all, he found his Minnesota school "far inferior" to Breeks, whose disciplined study habits served him well .[74]

48

A. J. Friesen's
Nalgonda Station, 1901
Credits: C.C. Unruh,
Pittsford, NY

Preparing Food at
Nalgonda, c. 1900:
Susie W. Hiebert (with
child), Katharina P.
Huebert (with child),
Anna P. Unruh,and Maria
M. Friesen with their
servants.
CMBS/F

The First Missionary
Families from Russia, c.
1905
Standing: Aron Mar-
tens Friesen, A.J. Friesen,
A.J. Huebert;
Seated: Maria M.
Friesen, Katharina
Reimer, Katharina P.
Huebert.
On the carpet: Abram
Huebert, Jr., Katie
Friesen, Katie Huebert
Credits: Susan Reimer,
Vineland, ON

Russians and Americans together, at Nalgonda [December] 1899: Standing: Anna P. and Heinrich H. Unruh, Elizabeth S. Neufeld (later Wichert, Wall), Maria M. and A.J. Friesen;
Seated on chairs: Etta F. Edgerton (ABMU), A.J. and Katarina P. Huebert (with children Abram and Katie), and Dr. Lorena Breed (ABMU);
Seated on floor: Nicolai N. and Susie W. Hiebert, and Anna Suderman (later Bergthold)
Credits: P.M. Friesen [1911], CMBS/F

Russian Mennonite Brethren in India, c. 1905 Standing: Johann G. Wiens, Anna Epp (later Bergthold), Martha W. and Cornelius H. Unruh;
Seated: Helena H. Wiens, Heinrich and Anna P. Unruh;
Children: John Wiens Jr., Marie and Henry Unruh, and Martha (on lap of her mother)
CMBS/W

The American Missionary Family, 1920:
Back row: Lydia Bergthold, Elizabeth Voth, Viola Bergthold, Leander Janzen, Helen L. Warkentin (Canada), Bertha Bergthold, Anna Hanneman;
Back row, seated: K.L. Schellenberg, Elizabeth D. and Frank A. Janzen, John H. and Maria K. Lohrenz, Maria C. Wall;
Front row, seated: Daniel F. and Anna S. Bergthold, Maria E. and John H. Voth;
Children seated, back row: Menno Voth, Sarah Voth, Martha Bergthold, Henry Bergthold, Arnold and Edwin Janzen;
Children in front, Mathilda Voth, Samuel Bergthold, Theodore Voth,
Credits: Sarah Voth Ferris

John H. and Maria H. Pankratz, with Rubina, Ernest, Linda, and John, c. 1910:
Credits: Sarah Voth Ferris, Tulsa, OK

Russian Mennonite Brethren about 1914:
Standing: John A. and Anna N. Penner, Katharina P. Huebert, Aganetha Neufeld (later Hamm);
Seated: Franz J. and Marie W. Wiens, A.J. Huebert, and A.J. Friesen
The three Wiens boys: Henry, Frank (on lap) and Jacob
CMBS/F

Anna Hanneman Katharina and L. Schellenberg, c. 1920
CMBS/F

Frank and Elizabeth D. Janzen, at Wanaparty, with Arnold and servant, in their Ford Convertible, about 1920.
Credits: Arnold Janzen, FL

The Wanaparty Residence of the helpful Rajah
Credits: Peter Penner, 1973

The Wanaparty Bungalow built by Janzen
Credits: Peter Penner, 1973

The C.H. Unruh Family, 1933, at Acadia University, Wolfville, Nova Scotia;
Standing: C.H. Unruh, Henry C. and Cornelius C. Unruh
Seated: Elizabeth (youngest daughter of Heinrich Unruh), and Martha W. Unruh.
CMBS/W

Henry W. Lohrenz, Chair, BFM
CMBS/F

Jacob W. Wiens, Treasurer, BFM
CMBS/F

The Missionary Group of 1934
Standing: Catharine Reimer, Annie B. Dick, Margaret Suderman, Anna J. Hiebert, Elizabeth K. Balzer, Peter V. Balzer, Daniel F. Bergthold, Jacob J. Dick; Seated: John N.C. Hiebert, Viola B. Wiebe, Maria C. Wall, Katharina L.Schellenberg, Anna S. Bergthold, Helena L. Warkentin, John A. Wiebe, John H. Lohrenz (Maria K. Lohrenz is missing); Children: from Hiebert, Wiebe, and Dick families
Credits: Sarah Voth Ferris

Dr. Schellenberg's Hospital, Shamshabad, durning the 1930's
CMBS/F

## CHAPTER 4

# Territorial and
# "Ownership" Considerations

Circumstances changed drastically for both the Russian and American Mennonites around 1914. For the former the causes lay in the administrative differences between Boston and Rückenau/Nalgonda, in the brief missionary career of Franz J. Wiens, and the totally changed position of the Russian situation by the outbreak of the Great War. The Americans were shaken by the extreme difficulties that John H. Pankratz had in establishing his work in the Nizam's Hyderabad. Getting established in this Muslim state was much more difficult than in the state of Madya Pradesh where the General Conference Mennonites and the Mennonite Church had missions. This was pointed out by Peter A. Penner, a Mennonite missionary working at Champa, Madya Pradesh. From his visits to John and Maria Voth at Deverakonda, Penner concluded perceptively that, being part of British India, as his state was, made the GC Mennonite Mission's relations with government easier than for the Mennonite Brethren in Hyderabad.[1]

### The Early Vicissitudes of John and Maria Pankratz

The Pankratz's first years at Malakpet seemed promising. Abraham J. Friesen was present at the formation of the first India MB congregation under American leadership on 27 March 1904.[2] During the winter months of 1904-05, while skilled tradesmen were building at Malakpet, Elizabeth S. Neufeld initiated a boarding school (like other missions had done), and Pankratz went on extensive tours into the villages, only interrupted for the Christmas celebration. They welcomed the three Russian MB families: Heinrich and Anna Unruh, Cornelius and Martha Unruh, and Johann and Helena Wiens. Maria Pankratz wrote: "Because we had so many Germans together, we wanted to hear the Christmas story [and sing] in our mother tongue." Such joys were diminished when John Pankratz, touring in the villages, fell from his bicycle and broke his arm in early April. In August it had to be broken again "in order to fix it right."[3] Cornelius Unruh told how Pankratz was present at a missionary conference at Ramapatnam during the Christmas vacation of 1905-6, and spoke there on the theme of "revival." During the next year Pankratz participated in the Deccan Association meeting held at Hanamakonda, where they were hosted by Johann and Helene Wiens. He experienced renewal here and built up his expectations for the future of the mission in India.[4]

Peter A. Penner's observations about government relations were soon borne out by the difficulties Pankratz encountered at Malakpet in 1910. In April of that year, the general Muslim opposition to Christian missions was considerably intensified when Pankratz baptized his first converts from Islam.[5] One of the reasons given for the opposition was that the Pankratz's station was too close to an existing mosque. This concerted opposition forced the Pankratzes to delay a planned departure on their first furlough. According to Cornelius Unruh, Pankratz was "nearly broken down over this turn of events."[6] Upon their return, he had to give up Malakpet at the order of the government. Its officials did, however, cooperate in acquiring property for the AMBM in Hughestown, just across from the location chosen originally by the Hieberts in 1900. This property was dedicated at the end of December 1914. Unfortunately, this area was found to be malaria-infested, and the first mission was moved further south to Shamshabad in 1920.[7]

## The Frank Janzen/Hiebert Altercation

At about the same time, Frank and Elizabeth Janzen began to search for a fourth field of evangelism. Though the story is not entirely clear, the MB General Conference at Hillsboro, Kansas in 1912 was told that the Rajah of Wanaparty had offered a site for a mission station in his large domain, southwest of Nagarkurnool.[8] Even then permission had to be secured from the Nizam's Government in Hyderabad, about 150 kilometers away. Janzen rode his bicycle that distance during the hot season in order to seek permission. Having secured it, he was dumbfounded in 1914 to discover that N. N. Hiebert (who was now serving as executive secretary for the MB Board of Foreign Missions) was not treating Wanaparty seriously as a fourth station. Edward Chute had assured Janzen that he had no further designs on the area, even though Chute at Palmur was justified until then of thinking of Wanaparty as part of the old American Baptist field. The elderly Chute explained that he had not been able to devote any effort to Wanaparty and, with the wholehearted support of his Palmur congregation, was willing to hand it over to the American MB represented by the Janzens. Strangely, the Conference of 1912 had accepted Wanaparty as a new station, and yet Janzen had to argue the case for adequate appropriations with Hiebert two years later.[9]

Janzen's letter of 14 June 1914 must be seen as symptomatic of the difficulties the early American missionaries experienced in their correspondence with N. N. Hiebert as secretary of the Board, a position he held from 1906 until 1936.[10] This letter shows the beginnings of irritation with Hiebert because of his slowness to act, and his increasing pessimism. This exchange resembles those between Friesen and The Rooms about Rückenau/Boston relations. One may conjecture that the American "pioneering four" began to organize as a Missionary Council in 1914 for this reason.

Janzen was surprised to find it so hard to convince the Board at home that Wanaparty really constituted a field separate from that of Nagarkurnool, and that it required a new missionary jurisdiction, supported by adequate funds. Even if it were possible to evangelize Wanaparty from Nagarkurnool, the Bergtholds could hardly be expected to provide accommodation for them.[11] The conference decision of 1912 notwithstanding, Janzen took great pains to explain, once again, that he, supported by his peers on the field, wanted to settle at Wanaparty. This should be considered a separate field, and **not** as part of Nagarkurnool, as Hiebert seemed convinced that it was. Frank Janzen's complaints were based on statements of reservation and evasion, which he copied back to Hiebert, and were pointed enough for Hiebert to become defensive of his actions.

In light of his failure to obtain funds for Wanaparty, Janzen was well aware of the promptness with which John Voth had received funds while living at Malakpet, yet developing far-away Deverakonda. Thinking that his situation at Nagarkurnool, filling in for the Bergtholds, was similar, Janzen was mystified to think that Deverakonda was given generous support because there were already many Christians there, while Wanaparty was still virtually unevangelized. He was more than irritated by Hiebert's rationale: we cannot send support according to the number and location of missionaries. What determines financing is the number of converts, size of field, and institutions already established.[12] Janzen found this reply astonishing, because it certainly did not coincide with the view of missionaries in India.

### Rückenau versus Boston

Beginning about 1909 Friesen had a somewhat similar altercation with George B. Huntingdon, assistant secretary in Boston. This was shortly after Friesen had retired the first time. From all accounts Friesen would have carried on for some time, and perhaps opened a new station, except for illness in his family. While on a rest cure at Ootacamund, Friesen learned that his adopted son Aron, at Nalgonda, had typhoid fever. The youth of 11 years had barely recovered with medical help when Maria Friesen "broke down with nervous prostration." Consultation with others confirmed that she should retire from the work altogether. With the unhappy prospect of having to leave the work (Katharina Reimer being ill as well), Friesen worked to consolidate the Russian MB forces. Since the Hueberts were planning a furlough in the spring of 1908, as were Heinrich and Anna Unruh in 1909, there would be a vacancy or two that should be filled with "representatives of our churches." Friesen returned to his theme: since Russian Mennonites had been involved in foreign mission work for only eighteen years, Barbour should not think his request strange. They needed to have a "specific place" for their donations and the concentration of their people.[13]

The new station he had in mind was Mirialagoodam. Early in 1907, while touring with his entire family, Friesen stopped at this district town twenty-eight miles from Nalgonda. He was encouraged greatly because the revival was still spreading. This area had about 600 church members, 117 having been baptized in the previous year. He counted three organized churches and nine preaching places. He baptized twenty-eight from among the school children who had been converted in the previous August. What was required was the opening of a new station. Friesen already knew of acreage he could buy from a Christian for about 500 rupees. Moreover, he had access to "75,000 bricks and heaps of stones" which had been gathered as a make-work project during a recent famine. What was most important, Friesen emphasized, was obtaining a "bright, godly, young Mennonite."[14]

Once home, the Friesens resigned as working missionaries, stating that they did not expect financial assistance from the ABMU.

Friesen requested however that they might maintain "a connection with our Union," perhaps being listed as "honorary" members. Barbour assured Friesen he would always be thought of "as related to the Union," and that he would always be remembered in India as well as America, by both Baptists and Mennonites.[15] In practical terms, it is evident that Friesen continued to function as the leader of the Mission, at least until 1915.

Friesen was barely home a year when Huntingdon, standing in for Barbour, found an occasion to fuel the continuing tension between Rückenau and Boston. In 1909 Huntingdon instructed the Union's treasurer in India to send only half the salary for Johann Wiens and Cornelius Unruh. He had not understood that since the Stockholm meeting (1904) Friesen had expected the total salary to be sent from Boston, and treasurer Braun would replenish the treasury during succeeding winter months. This came on the heels of Friesen's urgent request to accept Franz and Maria (Warkentin) Wiens as the new missionaries to maintain staffing of the three stations. They were prepared to go to India with the returning Hueberts who had arranged to leave their children Abram Jr. and Katie in Russia with the Heinrich Braun family. Friesen, still in charge at Rückenau, responded in language resembling that of about nine years earlier. "I have done some hard thinking to find out what was the reason for such an order [to send half salaries], quite against our agreement. On account of this unhappy order our missionaries think the time has come to begin an independent work." Friesen found Huntingdon's letters most unsatisfactory, and directed his replies to Barbour. In his view the Union had shown "lack of justice and confidence" toward the Mennonite Brethren missionaries. He insisted that since 1889 Rückenau had always contributed more than they had promised, even without the guarantees Barbour would have preferred. According to Friesen's calculations Rückenau was close to 6000 rubles ahead of the Union in terms of the monies postulated in the agreement of 1904-05.[16]

Huntingdon now pressed the point that it would help a great deal "if the contributions can be sent directly to our treasury." His perception was based on the circumstance that Braun, whose English was weak, preferred to send money to the ABMU's India treasury. Once his contributions reached Nalgonda, they were sent on to Ramapatnam. Friesen, of course, assumed these were being fully credited there and in Boston. When Friesen realized that Huntingdon was interpreting all this as a shortfall in contributions, he resorted to an accusatory tone: "Has the ABMU not had the whole benefit of the money sent to the treasurer in Boston through the local treasury of India?" He was particularly irate about a negative vote registered in The Rooms and conveyed to him in this conditional sentence: "so long as contributions sufficient to meet these payments are sent to the Treasurer in Boston." He feared that the whole matter had been misrepresented to Boston or, worse still, The Rooms as such had "no knowledge of the relation that has existed more than **eighteen** years." If he was wrong, he stated on 20 July 1909, he would apologize; if not, that note should be stricken from the record.[17]

Meanwhile Friesen asked for $250 annually for his deputation work in Russia on behalf of the "Telugu mission." Though he had refused any salary when he resigned in 1908, now he explained that he was editing *Das Erntefeld* and spending virtually all of his time on behalf of the Russian relationship to the ABMU. More importantly, though he did not ask for funds for this purpose, he and two members of the Russian committee, mission treasurer Braun and conference treasurer Wilhelm Dyck of Millerowo, wished to attend the international missionary conference planned for Edinburgh in June 1910. He therefore asked for letters of reference from The Rooms.[18]

Huntingdon tried to placate Friesen, but not until March 1910. He confirmed that the accounts in the two treasuries were considered to be in "substantial agreement." Friesen also learned from this letter that Barbour had visited India, was traveling through Europe on his way to Edinburgh, and was expected to confer with him "regarding several points . . . raised in correspondence with you and other representatives of the Russian brethren in India."[19] Friesen apparently waited in vain for communications about such a conference and, instead of going to Edinburgh in June, as he had hoped, he "visited [MB] churches in Turkestan." As Barbour seemed to disappear from the correspondence, one may conclude that he was not well enough to meet with Friesen in 1910, or that he was making one final trip to American Baptist fields before his retirement.[20] What is known is that Barbour visited India and Cornelius and Martha

Unruh at Nalgonda in January 1911 and had only high praise for Friesen.[21]

## The Illness and Death of Heinrich Unruh

For the missionaries in India, certain events and issues overrode all other anxieties. Heinrich Unruh's severe illness and death was one of these. It was a terrible letdown for everyone. Their return from Russia in 1911 had been eagerly awaited for many reasons, not least a shortage of personnel to supervise the three stations.

In April, before his illness set in, Heinrich Unruh sent a report to Rückenau in anticipation of the annual meeting of the Russian MB conference. In this report he shared the burdens of the India work. The separation from their children and the death of little Anna caused them more sadness than they thought possible. Fortunately, during their absence and under the care of Franz J. and Marie Wiens, new missionaries from Siberia, the number of converts had increased, for they had begun to wonder whether they had made a mistake to build at Jangaon, a railway town. The persecution, especially by Muslim elements, never seemed to cease, going so far as trying to ban Christians from access to water supplies and jobs. He was not unaware of the difficulties the Pankratzes were experiencing in Malakpet at the same time.[22] Another problem was the all too frequent return of indigenous preachers to their former life style, causing great embarrassment and disappointment. Yet for all that, Heinrich hoped that the conference at home would consider expanding the work in Nalgonda district. The fields allotted to each missionary couple were simply much too large to do justice to the Great Commission. When he recommended that three more stations be opened in the Nalgonda district, he pointed to the American MB mission as a model of aggressively going forward: Malakpet, Nagarkurnool, Deverakonda, and Wanaparty, all taken up since 1903. He was grateful for the sacrificial way in which many in far away places in Russia like Samara and Siberia, who were otherwise in less prosperous situations than in the Molotschna, had contributed to the Mission during his deputation.[23]

Unruh attended his last district missionary conference in mid-September, and became very ill at Jangaon soon after. All converged on Jangaon as quickly as possible: from Nalgonda, Franz and Marie

Wiens, who had their own family illnesses to worry about; Dr. J. S. Timpany at Hanamakonda, who sent to Nellore for additional medical help; and Anna Suderman from Malakpet. Nothing, however, could be done to save him from the deadly typhus.[24] Unruh died on 23 October 1912 and was buried almost immediately. Wiens and Huebert dug a grave overnight, lined it with concrete to protect the remains from jackals and white ants, and conducted the funeral service the next day. Tirmalajah, one of Unruh's preachers, spoke broken heartedly, while Huebert gave a tribute in German and Franz Wiens in Telugu. Especially poignant was the sorrow of little Cornelius, who had been separated from his siblings in Russia, from his sister Anna who died, and now from his father. In later life he came to believe that "missionaries should never leave children behind for any reason. [The separation] made my brothers and sisters bitter."[25]

Marie Wiens, who stayed in Jangaon for some time, followed up this account of the illness, death, and funeral of Unruh with a firsthand account of the fortitude with which the bereaved Anna Unruh, who was pregnant again, carried on, managing the entire station of Jangaon. She always had guests to feed, and without Marie's help and the usual number of servants, her situation would have been quite desperate.[26] Anna left Jangaon on 29 January 1913 and was accompanied to Bombay by Franz Wiens. She and her children were met at Trieste, Italy, by Cornelius and Martha Unruh, who were still on furlough. She traveled to the Molotschna in order to stay with a Reimer family. Provision was made for her support and that of her six children.[27]

Franz Wiens at Nalgonda recalled the "last words" that he and the innermost circle of missionaries had heard from Heinrich Unruh on his deathbed. He had appealed to the Russian MB supporters to heed the message of one who had given his life in service, one whom they had commissioned to serve on their behalf. Unruh called for young people to leave all to come to India. Others must give up their accumulated rubles for the work. There were not enough prayers and encouraging letters. Unruh's other major concern was this: on furlough he had noted how MB's were disputing over dogmatic questions rather than focusing on the mission beyond them. Unruh died in peace, having put his house in order.[28]

## Cornelius Unruh's Admonition to Rückenau

Coinciding with Heinrich Unruh's furlough and Johann Wiens' forced return to Russia was a felt unease about loss of commitment in the Rückenau church. Johann Wiens had become increasingly disquieted, since his spiritual awakening in 1906, by the prevailing attitude of indifference towards mission work in the relatively wealthy Molotschna.[29] By 1914 this concern surfaced in a lamentation by Heinrich's brother Cornelius Unruh. He recalled that the Friesens and Katharina Reimer went home ill in 1908, Johann and Helena Wiens with their daughter Elizabeth in 1911, then followed the death of his brother in 1912. The early departure for America of the Franz Wiens family was so great a blow to him that he wondered what would become of their Mission. This was before the Great War closed off Russian funds. The only prospects as substitutes were a young couple, John and Anna Penner from Rückenau, and a single woman, Aganetha Neufeld. Hence he was moved to make this appeal.

While on furlough, Cornelius Unruh delivered a message to the readers of *Das Erntefeld*, which was based in part on a reconsideration of the meaning of God's call in the light of his brother's death. Unruh reminded his readers that the Mission to India was everyone's, not only the missionary's; that God had given the Nalgonda field to the whole constituency. Workers and prayerful supporters were needed, not negative criticisms, he wrote. He placed the mission in the context of an older, more heroic view of the missionary as witness, ready to be sacrificed. He quoted Gustav Warneck at length,[30] emphasizing the element of the cross and its suffering for Christ's sake. "Whereas every disciple of Christ needs to carry his cross, those in foreign mission work have more than their fair share of distressful and thornfilled situations: deadly climates, persecution, ridicule and slander at the hands of their neighbors, travel hazards, a sacrificial existence, separation from children, disappointments and trials of all kinds." If only all could be totally convinced of the motto: "He [Christ] is worthy," then "our mission could triumph."[31]

## The Question of "Ownership" of Nalgonda

The dispute about the ownership of Nalgonda district stations flowed essentially from two things: the coming of the Great War, and the Russian MB wish to consolidate their work – to claim "ownership." Not surprisingly, the many misunderstandings, especially with George Huntingdon, brought the Russian committee and Friesen to think of segregating the Nalgonda field for their own. Whatever the reasoning behind this attempt this time, Friesen seemed to give the "union" of Rückenau and Boston a new twist. "You know of course of the mutual understanding which exists between [the two] concerning the Nalgonda mission field with its 3 stations... : that as long as the Mennonite Brethren are able to supply men and money to carry out their share of the mission work... , **they shall be considered as belonging to our churches.**" He then reviewed his role in shaping this relationship since 1888 and added: "This mission policy of concentration to one field has helped our churches to have also love for a world wide mission; but the Nalgonda mission field is the uppermost in their heart." For this reason he wanted Heinrich Unruh's place filled, and suggested John A. Penner for the role. Penner had been "heartily endorsed" and sent to Hamburg in preparation for work among the Telugu people.[32]

Friesen returned to India in 1913-14 in hopes of having Mirialagoodam accepted by the India committee as another station. He came back without Maria, but brought Aganetha Neufeld, as well as John A. and Anna (Nikkel) Penner, in order to help the staffing situation during the unexpected delay in the return of the Cornelius Unruh family. The new foreign secretary in Boston, Arthur Charles Baldwin, deplored the fact that Friesen had felt compelled to return for such a reason.[33] But was there another compelling motive? Although Friesen was not implicated directly, it was soon apparent that Franz Wiens, of little experience and perhaps influenced in Rückenau by the desire for greater independence, carried that wish too far when he published some sentiments in *Das Erntefeld* which may have led to his dismissal in 1913.

Franz Wiens, son of Jacob G. Wiens, an elder in the MB church, came from Siberia. He had prepared for missionary service at St. Chrischona and Bielefeld. Marie, the daughter of Henry and Agatha (Loewen) Warkentin of Sagradowka, trained as a nurse in Berlin. They were married near Omsk in Siberia. Once commissioned at Rückenau in 1909 in the presence of the Friesens and the Hueberts, they proceeded to Nalgonda for language study. Once they were ready to take charge of Nalgonda, they found themselves very quickly overburdened by having also to supervise Jangaon, left vacant when Anna Unruh and the children returned to Russia. What became so crushing for Wiens was the terrible poverty of his people from famine conditions precisely in these apprenticeship years. By the end of 1912 his language suggests fairly extreme personal prostration because of the desperation of his "brown brethren," the ravages of cholera, and the death in November of Heinrich Unruh. Yet he was uplifted and grateful for the outpouring of money from Rückenau in response to a telegraphic appeal in this critical time. He was at great pains to explain to his readers just how he and the others had distributed the five thousand rubles sent for the poor.[34]

Wiens' statement to the readers of *Das Erntefeld* may have been triggered by a letter from Huntingdon in about June 1913. In it he wrote concerning the difficulties occasioned in Boston and Ramapatnam when funds from Russia were not sent directly to The Rooms. Huntingdon took the occasion to inform Wiens of the financial agreement made with Friesen nearly a decade earlier. Perhaps because of this missive, and in view of the overwhelming response he had received, Wiens seems to have expressed a desire for independence, regardless of the consequences. Wiens wrote, "we who are overseas are grieved to think that all that potential for giving and growth in Russia can be restricted by a committee comprising people different from us, determined by considerations strange to us." Going even further, he stated that if the Russian MB were to grow to their potential, they must be prepared to work "**against the rules**" of the Union "to which we are subservient. Only then will we be able to show the world to what extent the Molotschna could carry this magnificent work.[35]

Though some letters are missing in the papers of Franz Wiens, one must conclude that he knew that such opinions would be perceived in Boston as very wrong indeed. Given the friendly relations established between Heinrichs at Ramapatnam and Friesen over the years, his action seems very strange. But Wiens probably had not learned to know Heinrichs. It is likely that Wiens almost immediately regretted having sent these strongly-worded statements to *Das Erntefeld*. They might not be read in Boston, but they would be by Jacob Heinrichs at Ramapatnam. Wiens therefore sent his letter to Heinrichs, who had no choice but to alert The Rooms. They chose to accept Wiens' letter of 14 October 1913 as a form of resignation.

Huntingdon wrote him on 26 December 1913: "We believe that you have deeply and truly repented of the wrong and for that reason measures have been taken [toward] helping you to a new start." Wiens was told that the "main facts" of his indiscretion would be kept confidential to a very small number of people, but that he could not return as a missionary once his furlough had ended. When it became clear during 1914 that it would be inadvisable to return to Russia, they decided to make their home in California.[36]

Only five days after writing the letter, of which copy is missing, Wiens wrote the *Friedensstimme* (a Mennonite newspaper published in Russia) in words that suggest a complete nervous breakdown. He told his readers not to be too surprised if they had to give up their position in India never to return. If he feared reprisals for anything he had sent off to *Das Erntefeld,* he gave no indication. Yet, if this was published in November 1913, he must have written those expressions of unilateral action about the time he wrote Heinrichs and the *Friedensstimme.* Wiens only wrote on 4 February 1914 that they were leaving for California within two weeks. In a article full of pathos, Wiens stated that his heart was failing him. This may have been so, but his written utterances suggested a nervous breakdown over some issue other than their great workload in trying times. And there was no indication, then, that Marie was ill.[37]

**The ABMU Takeover in 1914**

At this juncture one must balance several considerations. Certainly one factor was Franz Wiens' indiscretion with respect to "going it alone," whether or not encouraged by Friesen's principle of concentration, and his oft-repeated threats to take an independent line. Another was the fact that the Russian Mennonite Brethren missionaries were cut off from funds by World War I. They therefore had no alternative but to beg the ABMU to take them over until they could recover their position. Since this proved impossible, given the revolution, famine and Mennonite emigration from Russia, the takeover became permanent.

In the background was a simmering dispute about money for education at Suryapet, which unfolded between 1911 and 1914. Abram and Katharina Huebert wanted to extend the educational work at Suryapet and Friesen had brought the teacher Anna Peters to India with them for this purpose. They had appealed for assistance through the required channels, but now the India committee of the American Baptist Women's Missionary Society had turned them down, stating that the Hueberts would have to make their appeals to the Molotschna churches. Friesen wrote that "considering the present agreement . . . this is not in order." He made it clear to Barbour that if the Suryapet work suffered because the educational work did not find support as agreed, Huebert would seek "specifics" for this purpose. The consequence would be an acceleration of a growing feeling of "prejudice against the board in Boston." Friesen concluded this letter, dated 24 September 1911, with the ominous suggestion that "the only thing that will help is to ask the ABFMS [in Boston] to hand over the entire care of the Nalgonda, Sooriapett, and Jangaon fields to the Mennonite Brethren of Russia." Fortunately, he added the sentence: "I wish we could talk this matter over with you."[38]

Almost on the heels of what must have been a disturbing missive in Boston, Friesen returned with thankfulness for gifts in the amount of 1,500 rupees from the ABWMS in support of Anna Peters' work. Friesen acknowledged that "the Lord is answering **before we cry**," that his board at home had "expressed great gratification" with the linkage with Boston that had existed for the last twenty-two years, and that "has brought so many blessings to our churches." He now asked for the kind of conference Huntingdon had suggested in 1910.[39]

Yet by 1914 Abram J. Huebert complained that monies were not forthcoming for Anna Peters' educational work, as expected and promised. The real reason for this became evident in the fall of 1914. Three or four letters came to Huebert from Baldwin. Quite apart from the war alarms in America, donations were in decline, and The Rooms found themselves "seriously in debt." Moreover, The Rooms had received word from treasurer H.J. Braun of the "failure of the Russian funds" owing to the war. Baldwin wrote, "I wish you could have heard the words of sympathy that were expressed." There evidently was a "deep desire" to see the MB work continue. But if Braun in the Molotschna could not send the $1,500 he had in hand, Huebert was told that support beyond January 1915 was seriously in doubt. If a special appeal to the Northern Baptist Convention did not bring in funds, the three stations could find themselves without support. Five days later Baldwin wrote that the "entire question" would have to come before their board in order to "decide whether or not they can advance funds on the basis of Mr. Braun's assurances" that he would repay the funds as soon as possible. Having heard from Braun that he had tried to send drafts to India, but that they could not be cashed, he was deeply grateful that even "under war conditions the Mennonites hope to keep their work going." Baldwin even suggested to Braun that he try sending money to India through the office of Standard Oil. In the hopes that this would work, he cabled the India committee to continue the work after January 1915.[40] The irony between Franz Wiens' view of the great potential for support from Russia and the sudden collapse of the Russian funds is great.

### Friesen's Last Plea

Abraham Friesen, having left India in September 1914 for the Crimea, heard this bad news from Baldwin, but not before early January 1915. He was grateful for the expressions of "sympathy" in that letter. Based on his previous experience with Huntingdon, however, Friesen was not completely trusting of the new situation. He felt he had, once again, to review the history of the relationship since 1889, and particularly 1905. While freely acknowledging that the three stations "legally belong to the [ABFM] Society," he returned to his former style of reprimand: "we are greatly astonished and deeply pained" at the thought that this temporary halting of funds should become the subject of an embarrassing appeal to the Baptist denomination to prevent stoppage of the work after 1st January. Yet this was quite a reversal. Now the three stations were clearly theirs. "We are asking no favour from you, we are only asking you to help carry over **your** work" until these difficult times are ended. "My dear Brother Baldwin, we are under no obligations whatever to the ABFMS but, humanly speaking, you are under great obligation to our churches for caring so lovingly and freely for **your** work for **twenty-five years**." He assured Baldwin there was "no risk" involved in sending what he estimated to be 1,400 rupees a month until the end of the War. **"If this is refused by the board and the work at Nalgonda... stopped, our churches will be alienated [from] the ABFMS forever."** Friesen claimed, on the basis of discussions with the ABMU before he left Nalgonda in September, that there were two funds in India "from which to draw." To be given such short notice of a possible work stoppage when there were, apparently, other paths to take was most shocking to Friesen.[41]

## The American Baptist View of the Mennonite Brethren

In "A Statement Concerning Needs of the Mennonite Work in South India," Baldwin made a special appeal to the ABFMS not to allow the three stations to decline for lack of support. It was obviously based on Friesen's anxiety and arguments, and may therefore be dated early 1915. Because it is revealing of what the Russians actually contributed over the years, and of how the American Baptists viewed their Mennonite associates, this "statement" must be considered equally as significant as the Plan of 1904-05.

Baldwin explained to his board and denomination the nature of the political strictures hampering treasurer Braun. The Mennonites expected to repay this "loan" when conditions were set right in Russia. He emphasized how meaningful the twenty-five year relationship had been. He made it clear that in 1914 alone, before the War stopped the flow of money, the Mennonites had contributed $4,146. This was more than the combined contribution of the ABMU and the women's branch ($1,830 each) to Nalgonda district. Besides, the Russians had contributed an average of $6,176 toward the work annually. Given their three large magnificent stations, having a total Christian church body numbering about 4,000, the Society should support this great work until the end of the war as an "extraordinary expenditure." He thought this could be "justified" for the sake of maintaining those institutions as well as "for the sake of the Mennonites."[42]

In the midst of these arguments he expressed what must have been the prevailing opinion in The Rooms of the Russian Mennonite Brethren. The contrast with Friesen's portrait in the *Das Erntefeld* was somewhat startling. The Mennonites were certainly highly respected, but their contribution was more diminutive when seen within the larger Baptist body. While Baldwin defined the role of each based on the 1905 Plan of Cooperation, he was concerned to impress on his board that "if this Board should refuse the request [for assistance], it could not help having a most unfortunate effect on the Mennonites." As though echoing Friesen's last protests, he wrote: "They would feel that they were not trusted, that their fidelity through these years has amounted to nothing and the influence which American Baptists . . . have been able to have upon them would be lost." Baldwin thought of these Mennonites as "Baptist in all but name and, like the Quakers, are a peace loving, peculiar people who are exempt from military service. Their missionary interest has been slowly developing [something right out of Friesen's arguments!], indicating a larger appreciation both of the gospel itself and their responsibilities beyond themselves."[43] While this portrait was probably not as flattering as Friesen would have liked, he felt better about every succeeding missive that reached him in the Crimea.[44]

As is known from the Huebert and Cornelius Unruh papers in the Baptist archives, correspondence between the Molotschna and Nalgonda district virtually ceased by the year 1916. Eventually the Huebert children were cut off from their parents in India.[45] Apparently Braun had received India letters from Cornelius Unruh and Huebert in 1918. When, however, mail from Russia to the outside world more or less ceased, The Rooms would not necessarily know that in Russia the accumulation of funds for the mission continued. By 1918 a sum of 60,000 rubles had been set aside to repay Boston for their support of the continuing work in the Nalgonda district by the Cornelius Unruh, Huebert, and Penner families. It was believed that an additional 20,000 rubles could be anticipated. In addition, in September 1918 the MB Conference in Russia voted to increase the support money from 500 to 1,400 rubles on behalf of Anna Unruh and her six children.[46] It is, of course, unlikely that this was ever paid, given the Bolshevik Revolution and the end of the Tsarist regime.

### The ABMU and the AMBM in 1915

Over the years some have asked why the American Mennonite Brethren did not take over the three stations built up by their Russian counterparts. This has been interpreted to mean that severe tensions existed between the two missions.[47] Actually, it would probably be quite accurate to say the AMBM never even dreamed of taking over Nalgonda district. At this time, Pankratz was not settled at Hughestown, nor did Voth have a compound at Deverakonda, and Janzen was worried about his status. Neither did the Russian Mennonite Brethren ask the AMBM to incorporate them. The good relations between them were maintained and recemented as

Cornelius and Martha Unruh returned to Nalgonda. When war broke out in August 1914, they were still on furlough, visiting Martha's family near Hamburg. As Russian citizens, they were fortunate not to have been held for the duration, given the hostility between the two nations. Whereas German nationals working as missionaries in India were either interned or sent home, the ABMU, with the assistance of the U.S. State Department, was able to free the Unruhs for a return to India.[48]

Nothing evidently was said about integrating the two missions until Pankratz mooted the possibility with Henry W. Lohrenz in June 1922. This corresponded with the attempt by the Russian Mennonite Brethren to gain Canadian citizenship during a furlough year. Pankratz thought that if the Russian Mennonite Brethren, including earlier supporters of the Russian MB/American Baptist tandem, migrated to North America anyway, they might agree that such an integration could take place.[49]

The Nalgonda district with its three stations in 1914 represented a Christian church comprising over 4,000 members.[50] Their missionaries, perhaps in line with their more longlived ABMU, seemed to think of their work as very nearly complete. In his 1909 report, written at Jangaon, Johann G. Wiens stated that once Hindus and Muslims had heard the preaching of the Gospel, and acknowledged that what they had heard was true, then "if they [were] not saved it is their own fault."[51] He did not, however, say that giving the Gospel once to every area absolved the missionary of further responsibility for the people in that area. Each compound was rated highly for their model institutions: schools, medical clinics, churches and bungalows, all of which attracted a following and reshaped the social and economic environment.[52]

The four stations–Malakpet/Hughestown, Deverakonda, Nagarkurnool, and Wanaparty–being developed by the American Mennonite Brethren missionaries, must have appeared relatively primitive at that stage. Statistical numbers for the AMBM work for this early date are scarce. John H. Voth claimed 825 baptized members on the Deverakonda field in May 1915. His father told the MB Northern District Conference in 1917 there were about 2,000 Christians on the field of the AMBM.[53] The American conference report for the year 1914-1915 showed that $15,031 was paid out for *"Heidenmission,"* including the work among the Comanche Indians in Oklahoma.[54] The Russian Mennonite Brethren, by comparison, had been giving $6,176 a year as their share of the ABMU expenses.[55]

## CHAPTER 5

# The Pioneering Missionary Conference

World War I and the subsequent revolution in Russia drastically changed the outlook of everyone, not least that of the Russians who remained in India. All stood more directly under the leadership and funding of Ramapatnam and the ABMU committee. This left the American Mennonite Brethren to fashion their own structures, cut off from home as they were by the War. Until then these pioneering brethren seemed to have little need for keeping minutes of formal consultations. Only Daniel Bergthold was settled in a compound at that time. Most social, spiritual, consultative, and recreational needs had been met by attending the annual Deccan Telugu Association and other meetings of the ABMU.

While it is not clear whether the Board of Foreign Missions asked John Pankratz as the senior missionary to call the first Missionary Conference meeting, there are minutes extant of such a consultation on 13 December 1914 in conjunction with the dedication of the Hughestown station. Their first formal discussion, recorded by John Voth, focused on the needs of their four stations, and raised, above all, the issue of designated gifts. Reservations about them were swept away on the grounds that their friends at home might be deflected from giving if they could not designate the project and the missionary.[1]

Quite apart from any urging from America, the issue that spurred the four couples to meet in consultation likely was Frank Janzen's experience with N. N. Hiebert in 1914 regarding recognition of Wanaparty as a fourth station. They now needed a united and strengthened voice from India to make certain that the secretary in Minnesota and the treasurer in Kansas followed through on their questions to him. They needed to consolidate their positions, just as Friesen and company had done in Nalgonda district. They, like the district collectors, the "men-on-the-spot" who knew what was required, took advantage of the weak constitution at home to acquire considerable authority as to how the Mission would be run, and by whom.[2]

## The Missionary Council and N. N. Hiebert

Whatever feelings lay dormant as long as the Americans were in the orbit of the Russian Mennonite Brethren, they surfaced not long after the initiation of the Missionary Council in India. In the midst of their severe settlement trials, the American pioneers patterned less-than-tranquil relationships with the home board. All being strong individuals, no one missionary emerged as the leader, although John H. Voth became the dominant figure in several significant ways. He was the secretary of the Missionary Council for many years, and certainly helped to consolidate much of the determining power in India within the Missionary Council.

When Voth's father, Heinrich Voth, died at Vanderhoof, British Columbia, on 26 November 1918, Henry W. Lohrenz became chair of the Board of Foreign Missions. His close associate in Hillsboro was treasurer Jacob W. Wiens. Secretary N. N. Hiebert, living at Mountain Lake, Minnesota and burdened with many responsibilities, became vulnerable to the criticisms of the missionaries. He, like the others, was only a part-time facilitator, and lived miles apart from the other two, without long distance telephone service.[3] He was somewhat slow of action, pessimistic, and of weak nerves. Some of this came out in a letter to John Voth in India, dated March 1919. Hiebert seemed incapable of measuring up to all the demands on his time. He deplored the scarcity of funds in the treasury, the poor state of his health, and confessed that "sometimes I can hardly meet the obligations." Along with Voth, Hiebert mourned over the loss of Heinrich Voth.[4] More publicly he suggested that he would now like to be released from these many demands on his strength. He seemed so discouraged and pessimistic that he wrote: "If this were not the Lord's work, one would hardly want to take on any more obligations."[5] Such sentiments surfaced in a 1921 conference sermon on the "scolding Jesus" (Matthew 11:23ff). Perhaps they deserved it, but to borrow a phrase from India, there never could be "an auspicious moment" for such a sermon.[6]

One of the early demands on Hiebert was H. W. Lohrenz' request for materials in order to prepare a well-rounded historical report on MB missions. Much preoccupied with the development of Tabor College, a Mennonite Brethren college founded at Hillsboro, Kansas in 1908, Lohrenz sent Hiebert a list of twenty-seven questions in late 1914. He thought that Hiebert, with the help of Heinrich

Voth in Minnesota, could bring together resources and answers. Resources must have been scarce at the time, as he, at Tabor College, could not even lay hands on all the issues of the *Zionsbote*. It does not appear that Hiebert met this request, for Lohrenz did not publish any full-length report on the Mission until 1939.[7]

One of the ironies of this period was Hiebert's view on gearing appropriations to results, while at the same time anxiously trying to have some control of the treasury. Already in 1914 Frank Janzen was completely taken aback when Hiebert wrote that he could not have money to build up Wanaparty even if he had authorization to start a new station. The measuring stick for grants was results: the number of Christians. The implication was that since Voth at Deverakonda already had many converts, he should get more money. All Janzen wanted at that stage was to engage two preachers in the villages.[8]

Not long after this, Hiebert may have become aware that John Voth was getting unauthorized money for construction purposes through treasurer Wiens.[9] Voth had complained to Wiens in 1919 that Hiebert was slow in sending money already allocated by the Board. Was Wiens really playing favorites and had he accepted the argument that payment should follow results? Was that one reason why Voth received so much more than the others? Did the temporary withdrawal of Bergthold from the Missionary Council allow Wiens to think he could permit the aggressive Voth to take advantage of the fact that he was in charge of three fields for some time? Wiens wrote a number of letters to Voth in 1919-1920: "Your work shall not suffer for lack of funds, and you need a car." Hiebert seems to have come around to this view by March 1920. Writing to Wiens, Hiebert stated that if Voth became very demanding during this term in India, it was understandable because the "results in the Mission are very gratifying."[10] Voth was still playing this game in 1930. He wrote that he now had more Christians than all the others together, and therefore he should get more funds.[11]

**The Ambivalence Between Hiebert and Voth**

Though Hiebert had good fellowship with Voth when he was on furlough 1916-18, this feeling continued only until 1920. By the first half of the 1920s, Hiebert hardly knew what to do with Voth. The latter had become so abrupt, so harsh in his correspondence, so demanding, that Hiebert almost despaired. Moreover, Hiebert criticized Voth's general sloppiness and almost illegible handwriting. He suggested that the Board send a letter of admonition to India so that the Missionary Council would appoint a different secretary.[12] These anxieties began in 1920 when Voth "struck out into the blue" with his request for an Overland automobile. This was an expensive vehicle, when others were satisfied with Fords. Hiebert complained to Lohrenz: "Here at home things are so bad that [not even] Ford cars are being purchased, and he wants an Overland, retailing at $1,600 before transport costs, and have it sent into a land of hunger and death!"[13] Ironically, at about the same time Voth wrote Wiens in Hillsboro that he tried to live and work in peace with other missionaries. "We may occasionally disagree but Christian manliness makes it possible to overlook problems and work together."[14]

A long succession of irritations served to make Hiebert very weary, even if Voth's attitude to him apparently had changed by 1924. As Voth's second furlough drew near, Hiebert took a less pessimistic tone when he wrote that he hoped that Voth's return might be a blessing to many. He knew that the Hueberts and Unruhs, on furlough in Canada around this time, had expressed fears as to what harsh demands Voth might make once he arrived home. Unruh had told some brethren in Canada that Voth was a little "pope," and Hiebert sensed that a degree of coolness had developed among the missionaries in India. His confidence in the Missionary Council had been severely shaken.[15]

### The Role of Henry W. Lohrenz

This view of Voth was sharply reinforced by the critical period Henry W. Lohrenz was experiencing in the 1920s. Lohrenz feared Voth's possible machinations during that furlough (1925-27). Following one term as a missionary teacher, Anna Hanneman wrote Lohrenz that John Voth wanted to have his father's position on the Board. He would then wield power in the Conference and Mission from his Minnesota base.[16] In response to such warnings, Henry Lohrenz wrote his brother John H. Lohrenz, who was very new in India, that he had been aware of Voth's "propaganda" and his camp following for some time, in fact since the time of his election to a nine-year term at the Minnesota conference in 1919. He knew Voth had friends among Lohrenz' critics at Tabor College and firmly believed some of his "co-workers" would use Voth, if they could, to remove Lohrenz from the presidency.[17]

Added to the alleged conspiracy was Lohrenz's fear that John H. Pankratz had been turned against him by some "slanderous tongue." Another cause for stress were the warnings from Lohrenz's brother and Anna Hanneman in India that neither Pankratz or Voth wanted him to visit India in 1925. Hanneman wrote that such attitudes were "certainly unworthy of [the missionary] calling." There was another source of discouragement in this matter. Such a trip was not to be undertaken without conference approval, and this was not forthcoming.[18]

By the end of this period there was no clear view of how to deal with the Missionary Council in India. This fact was reflected in the problem in getting Katharina L. Schellenberg and Anna Hanneman back to India. Lohrenz posed the question with Hiebert in March 1925: should they write once more to ask whether the Board needed to wait for Missionary Council minutes before acting on the return of missionaries? Why did he have to write Hiebert at all? This was necessary because they could not get together quickly to make decisions.[19]

### Appropriations, Salaries, and Gifts

Donations for the mission by constituents and churches were registered and distributed by treasurer J. W. Wiens in three categories: 1) general; 2) designated for special projects or missionaries; and 3) endowment, or trust (emergency) fund. Salaries remained the same as before the War: $1,000 for a married couple for the first term, $1,200 for the second. Allowances for children were minimal and clearly spelled out. Single women received half the salary of a married couple. Pension contributions were not a consideration until 1936 and nothing substantial in that regard was done until much later. In addition to travel allowances, as required, the general appropriations in 1919 were $2,400 for one year, though the Janzens at Wanaparty got $1,000 less, at least for that year. Appropriations per station were cut to $2,000 at the conference of 1921. The schools in the compound got from $1,250 to 2,000, as required, while medical work received rather small amounts initially.[20]

These sums represented larger salaries than any other conference workers, except perhaps those engaged as teachers at Tabor
College. In India their salaries were about 30 percent of what an
experienced British collector of a district was paid. Even then some
missionaries, especially the Pankratzes, found it difficult to make
ends meet on these allowances.

In terms of basic compensation, all missionaries were relatively equal. But they were quite unequal when it came to designated gifts, and such felt inequities caused much vexation. Not only
had John Voth invested $3,000 of his own money, presumably at
Deverakonda, in addition to his general appropriations; during the
decade 1915 to 1925 he had also received over $22,000 in gifts listed
in the *Zionsbote*. In terms of such assistance for his empire building–and it was perceived as that–he stood in a ratio of five to three
for John Pankratz, five to two for Daniel Bergthold, and five to one
for Frank Janzen.[21] These figures reveal that John Voth came to dominate the field, not only in the number of conversions, but also in
the income he generated. His superhuman promotional efforts had
much to do with this success. During his entire career in India (and
he never stopped writing even during furloughs), he published approximately as many letters in the *Zionsbote* as the other three couples together. Though he did not want to boast of their achievements at Deverakonda, he once used the device of denying boast-
ing to draw attention to his work.[22]

### The Continuing Frustrations of John and Maria Pankratz

The matter of getting settled in a suitable, permissible location in order to do the work of the Gospel was not a simple matter
for any of the four founders. It seemed unusually difficult and trying for John and Maria Pankratz. They were pushed out of Malakpet,
where they had developed a station plan, just as they were ready to
leave on their first furlough. Following their return in 1912, they
had barely dedicated their new settlement at Hughestown[23] across
the street from the first location chosen by N. N. Hiebert and A. J.
Friesen in 1900, when they were advised to leave because the area
was plagued by fever. Furthermore, a plague of rats had driven
their school out of the Ismiah Bazaar. They chose as their third site
Shamshabad, southwest of Hyderabad.[24] Some of Pankratz' preachers had already reached out to this area, and in 1915 Katharina L.

Schellenberg and Anna Hanneman began to provide medical and school services there.[25]

Before attempting to settle in Shamshabad, John and Maria Pankratz, in India without their older boys since the previous furlough, returned home once more.[26] At that point they were uncertain whether to bring them to India with them, or stay at home in America because of them. They had received medical advice suggesting a rest as early as January 1918. They were even more exhausted a year later when influenza swept through their field, causing 400 deaths a day. Pankratz also underwent a hernia operation, yet they waited until the Voths returned from furlough. Having a car in 1919 allowed them to make a farewell visit to the Unruhs and Hueberts to the East, and the Voths to the south, 500 kilometers in 6 days. Ironically, tired as they were, they made a side trip of four weeks to the China field at the request of the Board. They left from Bombay mid-April 1919.[27]

When they returned in 1921 with two sons, Ernest and John, they found that life in Shamshabad was not necessarily easier, even though it was considered a healthier place. John and Maria began conducting monthly meetings at Shamshabad while the famine of 1919-1921 was still raging. Ernest was appalled to see so many emaciated people at their doorstep every day. Maria wrote in 1922 that their area had experienced only two good crops during the past decade. According to some, conditions had not been so desperate in forty years.[28] Nevertheless, they managed to build a first small house in that year, and even moved the Bible School to Shamshabad while Daniel F. Bergthold at Nagarkurnool was on furlough. While Pankratz regretted that the twelve acres or so at Shamshabad did not yet look like a compound, there was "beauty here and promise."[29]

### The Period of Heavy Construction

Building a large compound as a headquarters and a haven was still an unquestioned assumption during the inter-war years. Bungalows and other station buildings came from appropriations and special gifts. The Bergtholds had completed their compound at Nagarkurnool in the previous decade. The children remember it as a happy retreat, surrounded by gardens and trees, an atmosphere created by Bergthold and his eye for appointments.[30] Even if they and others did not try to duplicate Friesen's Nalgonda or Unruh's Jangaon as to size and comforts, the approximation was significant. The Voths and the Janzens, on the other hand, found themselves building their bungalows and compounds during the worst of the famine years 1919-21, when construction and relief monies were used to create employment.

John H. and Maria Voth's construction period in very difficult times was bookended by furloughs in 1916-18 and 1925-27. Because of the overlapping of furloughs in the case of the other three couples, Voth virtually had the care of their stations also during some of that period. After twelve years of unsettled living conditions, between Hughestown and Nalgonda, the Voths finally had a good bungalow as their home. It was a commodious, two-story structure at the center of the compound, measuring 3,720 square feet on the ground floor, including the usual verandas around the house. All other buildings on their compound represented much less square footage.[31] He had already justified this European life-style as early as 1916. In response to a much publicized contemporary charge that missionaries lived too well and achieved little of value for all the money raised in America, Voth did a survey and concluded that it was unwise to live close to the more primitive conditions in which they found most of their converts. Just look at the long British experience in trying to prevent breakdowns in health, he was told. They and most missionary societies had found it imperative to build comfortable bungalows.[32]

His construction period corresponded to years when poverty around them was so heart-rending that Voth ceased going to the villages. He simply could not take it emotionally. The poverty-stricken were constantly at their gates. At the same time he appealed very aggressively to wealthy Mennonite Brethren at home to give generously. At one point he warned that God would hold them personally responsible for lost souls. He acknowledged that their 4 stations with 3,000 members, over 100 preachers in the villages and over 600 children in school, cost much more than 10 years go, but they were also starting a publication, *Suvarthamani,* for their believers. There was also the Bible school, and so he felt justified in asking for ever more funds.[33]

If Voth received designated gifts during this decade in a ratio of five to one compared to Frank Janzen at Wanaparty, this means the latter relied on other kinds of assistance to build his enormous bungalow. Actually, Janzen received $3,000 from general funds for construction in 1921, when Voth and Bergthold received only $500 and Pankratz $1,000 for Shamshabad.[34] There was assistance from the Rajah of Wanaparty between 1912 and 1921, but the interpretations differ considerably. Because he had attended a mission school in Madras, the Rajah was not opposed to having a missionary in his domain, but he was somewhat reluctant to see his subjects become Christians.[35] In any case, Janzen's relationship with this petty prince was unique in the MB India story. Before their furlough in 1919-21, the Janzens constructed only a small house, which would serve as a schoolhouse later. For this and other construction, the Rajah provided "wood, lime, and stone." Following their return from America, they began to construct the main house, which was two-storied, having eighteen foot ceilings at each level. According to Viola Bergthold Wiebe, the Rajah insisted that the interior must match the interior of his country residence. Hence, during a time of extreme famine in the Deccan, the walls were coated with plaster "mixed with thousands of egg whites to make a smooth shiny finish," a treatment reserved for palatial houses.[36] Strangely, not much was said about the proportions, larger than Deverakonda, and the quality of the workmanship, in publications or in correspondence. Missionary lore has it that the Rajah wanted to have a suitable house in which to stay whenever he came to Janzen's compound.

Where Pankratz was unfortunate in most of his settlement endeavors, John H. Lohrenz, who went to India in 1920 and took up residence at Shamshabad in 1926, was able to make up for lost time. By the fall of 1927 the main bungalow was completed and the hospital, a building almost as large, was underway. Katharina L. Schellenberg remarked after her return to India in 1926 that she had been in India nearly two decades and "still [had] no hospital."[37] It finally was dedicated 4 April 1928. Eventually a ladies' bungalow, only slightly smaller than the main bungalow, was also constructed. Lohrenz was quite boastful of his constructions in Shamshabad, both in letters to his brother, Henry, as well as at a 1928 conference. They were, he remarked, simply "the best" on the field anywhere.[38]

The AMBM thus had four prestigious stations by the year 1930. If the statements made by these showpieces were ambiguous to the critics, it was obvious they were there to stay, just as in the case of those in Nalgonda district.

## Other Tensions

As difficult as construction work was, these problems were nothing compared with the tensions in the years 1917 to about 1921 over other issues. Clearly, the question of the Bible school, and who would have it, became one of the most significant questions. Strong individualism, wounded feelings, and aggressive behavior by all toward the sensitive N. N. Hiebert characterized this period. Apparently Abraham Schellenberg had told his daughter Katharina to expect such problems. She reminded him of this when she wrote privately in December 1917 that "the relationship among the missionaries is not what it should be. There are in fact two sides: one where self-will rules; the other grieving over this. . . . The problems are so severe[39] that one can hardly stand it, and one does not know where it will end. But God sees and knows all, and He can change things!" Surprisingly, this letter was printed verbatim in the *Zionsbote* by her brother, Abraham L. Schellenberg, who was then the editor of that paper.[40]

Since the Voths were on furlough when Schellenberg wrote about this strife, John Pankratz, probably supported by Frank Janzen, formed one side, and Bergthold the other. An official letter from Pankratz to the Board, dated 2 May 1918, suggests that he saw Bergthold as the problem, though the latter blamed the others. Pankratz stated that they delayed sending this letter, hoping to become reconciled with the Bergtholds, but had been totally unsuccessful. They, Pankratz said, had withdrawn and working with them in the Mission seemed impossible. The fact is, Bergthold absented himself from at least three Missionary Council meetings (August 1917, December 1917, and January 1919), even though as chairman he had called for the August meeting. One of the problems, apparently, was that he sometimes discussed Missionary Council agenda items with indigenous preachers, or simply wrote that he and his preachers were not going to attend scheduled meetings. Mystified, Pankratz wrote that they were trying desperately to avoid an open breach in the Mission. They, Pankratz wrote to the board, "are being blamed for excluding the Bergtholds from our Christian love, whereas the opposite seems to be the case. What shall or can we do? The work in India is suffering."[41]

Bergthold, on the other hand, in several letters to Heinrich Voth during this period, gave vent to his feelings about the Mission. He wanted Voth, the pioneer evangelist and mission spokesman, who had helped to persuade him to enter missionary work, to know that he now had serious doubts about the quality of his co-workers. He characterized them as spiritually impoverished, selfish and aggressively self-willed. "I fear that God will not be able to use such as ourselves here. If you can find others who will bring greater glory to God, we are willing to step aside." He thanked Voth for the kind way in which he had been treated, yet asked forgiveness if he had offended anyone in the Board. He repeated much the same view in a letter that must have reached Voth's widow after his death in December 1918. Bergthold added that hardly anyone seemed to care whether reconciliation took place on the field or not. They felt deeply wounded.[42]

One wonders whether this harked back to Bergthold's early troubles, about 1901-03, especially with Abraham Schellenberg as the chair of the Board of Foreign Missions. To the embarrassment of Bergthold, Schellenberg had implied in 1903 that Bergthold was not ready for overseas work. Was he prepared to go, "in all humility, according to our Mennonite Brethren understanding, and remain in close contact with the Board?" Bergthold at that time was practically forced into begging forgiveness for some attitudes he had manifested while at McPherson College.[43]

In 1919 another issue arose, involving a division between Wanaparty and Nagarkurnool over a church member named Isaac. Excommunicated by Janzen at Wanaparty, Bergthold had accepted Isaac at Nagarkurnool. The case involved misuse of money. Whereas Bergthold said he would abide by the decision of a committee of indigenous brothers who should arbitrate the matter, Janzen would not concede. He felt that Wanaparty alone could rehabilitate Isaac if he were truly repentant. Bergthold, on the other hand, wrote to J. H. Voth and the others that if the question could not be resolved in the manner suggested, then "he failed to see how they could work alongside each other [in the Missionary Council]."[44] Of course, N. N. Hiebert was very discouraged by these developments, and particularly by Bergthold's stance.

One of the recurring questions that often triggered problems was the "stationing" of new missionaries, or of filling vacancies and taking "charge" when senior missionaries went on furlough. Such a case arose in January 1917. Katharina L. Schellenberg, the senior medical person, preferred to stay in Hughestown, to which she had been assigned. Maria C. Wall, just out of language study, wanted to stay with her. All agreed to this except the Bergtholds, who wanted Wall to go to Nagarkurnool.[45] Daniel Bergthold, in his isolated location, required help there. Wall was eventually assigned to Nagarkurnool temporarily, but served most of her time in India at Deverakonda.[46]

### The Beginnings of Bethany Bible School

Many other questions rippled the waters. One concerned automobiles to facilitate the work. Another recurring aggravation was the seeming inability to deal profitably with the rate of exchange between the rupee and the dollar,[47] especially in times of war, or famine. The most contentious question, however, without considering the placement of new workers, was that of the Bible school, an institution essential for training preachers and Bible women. This work and the principalship that went with it seemed to receive the highest status on the field.

The initiation of a school project came from India; the proposal was probably brought home by Pankratz on furlough in 1919. The conference in Mountain Lake reacted favorably to the suggestion of independence in this matter.[48] While there may have been other considerations at Deverakonda and Nagarkurnool, such as lower literacy levels and problems of financing,[49] a deciding factor in 1920 was a controversy between J. H. Voth and W. E. Boggs of Ramapatnam's seminary staff. What brought on the separation was Boggs' reaction to an anti-war tract circulated among Indian Christians by Voth during the last years of the War. While Boggs might have agreed with the stress on the "unrighteousness of war" in that tract, he interpreted it as a "thoroughly anti-British pamphlet." Voth, who took nonresistance seriously, protested that he too was loyal to Britain, as were members of his family who lived in Canada (but still were American citizens) and supported the Mission.[50] He did not like to be characterized as "disloyal," nor was he thought of as such by English officials to whom he had explained his position. They professed to understand the tract as pacifist rather than anti-British. If anything, it was directed against Prussian militarism.[51]

This problem might not have arisen if Heinrichs had still been at Ramapatnam, or Friesen still in India. Voth demanded an apology from Boggs for not having discussed the matter with him before drawing it to the attention of British officials. In retaliation, he characterized Ramapatnam as an institution that "upholds war and militarism," and stated that the AMBM would no longer send students to Ramapatnam. Boggs was surprised by this attack. In response he tried to sort out the justifiable and traditional theological differences between Baptists and Mennonites in the matter of war. He felt that Voth had misinterpreted his true position on war and hoped that he and Bergthold (Pankratz was on furlough) would reconsider their decision regarding Ramapatnam.[52]

Shortly after this exchange, Bergthold, as the second most senior missionary, suggested that Voth should start a school in a small way at Deverakonda. If not, would Voth support him if he started an appropriate school at Nagarkurnool? In July he considered it advisable first to discuss the matter with the junior missionary John H. Lohrenz, who had hoped to teach in such an institution, and with Schellenberg at Shamshabad. Bergthold's August letter informed Voth that he planned to begin in September of that year. He asked Voth to make available J. Y. Abraham as a teacher. If that were not possible, Bergthold asked if he should find someone else. With regard to course work, he asked Voth to teach biblical synthesis and exegesis, theology, homiletics, and church history.[53]

Regrettably, this discussion did not proceed without Voth feeling hurt. When Bergthold wrote from Nagarkurnool next, on 22 September 1920, he expressed regret that Voth felt aggrieved. He reminded Voth that he had been given every opportunity to start the school, but he had declined ostensibly in favor of Nagarkurnool. The whole issue, he wrote, was complicated because the Board at home was intervening in the two new ventures of that time: the publication of a Telugu paper called *Suvarthamani*, which Voth had started, and the Bible school. This only served to disturb the division of labor between Bergthold and Voth. Hiebert, according to Bergthold, "had not read the protocol" regarding the initiation of *Suvarthamani*, and had mistakenly urged Bergthold to start it, even though the latter had indicated to Hiebert that he would not take on any new work. Bergthold expressed thanks for Voth's cooperaton in sending teachers and students from Deverakonda.[54]

## N. N. Hiebert's Intervention in the Bible School Question

The years 1920 to 1923 were complicated by problems involving communication and lines of authority between the Missionary Council and the Board of Foreign Missions. Nicolai N. Hiebert was increasingly burdened by all the requests from India. Utterly exhausted, on 12 March 1923 Hiebert responded to the fourth missive blaming him for interfering in the affairs of the Bible school.[55] The troubles intensified once the Pankratzes returned to India in 1921 and the Bergtholds had gone home. The former, as senior missionary, took the Bible school to the still imperfectly developed Shamshabad station. Hiebert had misgivings about Pankratz' health, as well as his wish to develop the school at Shamshabad. Because of such considerations, he had recommended to his Board at home that the considerably younger John and Maria Lohrenz should take charge of the Shamshabad station.[56]

John Lohrenz soon discovered that this disturbed Pankratz a great deal. The latter believed he had a mandate from the conference in 1919 to take over the school, if not to launch it.[57] Hence, in response to this suggestion, Pankratz protested vigorously to H. W. Lohrenz as chairperson. He was "in charge" in Shamshabad, was he not? If not, "where shall we go?" he asked (implying a belief that there was room for only one male missionary at any one station.) He complained that the Missionary Council had not been consulted, hence the decision at home was unconstitutional, ill-considered, and impractical. Thus, he would ignore the directive. It was for a discussion of this issue that the Missionary Council members had come together during the summer. For some the journey to this meeting had involved four days by oxcart. All they received from Hiebert was a postcard acknowledgement about which they were most unhappy. "If there is not more interest shown for our work among the heathen, and greater zeal for lost souls," they remarked, "then we also become discouraged."[58]

In connection with this drawn-out controversy, Hiebert, who must have felt he was walking on eggs, suggested to H. W. Lohrenz and J. W. Wiens that not everything they considered at home needed to be revealed to the Missionary Council in India, and they should avoid as many criticisms and alternative suggestions as possible. He referred to instances of criticism by the Missionary Council for neglecting the minutes they sent home, for not reacting to them, as though the stronger case was being made in India.[59]

Patiently, Hiebert explained again why they had written as they did previously. In consideration of the work load carried by the Pankratzes it would be well if the Lohrenzes were also at Shamshabad to assist with the new Bible school. He had not intended to dictate to them, but to consult with them. It was, however, "our advice and wish" that they should consider this sharing of the work. John Lohrenz, having been there long enough to observe the situation, wrote his brother that it would be better if one couple (meaning themselves) were clearly assigned to the Bible school. The work was significant enough for specialization.[60]

By November 1923 Pankratz wrote home that he was prepared to adjust to the advice of the Board. This change of attitude seems to have taken place upon return from furlough of the Bergtholds and their visit to the Pankratzes at Shamshabad on 16 September 1923. The Bergtholds were now reconciled to the Missionary Council once again. Pankratz was able to write: "we were blessed together."[61] He now wrote that he had given the Bible school back to Nagarkurnool. Their own family needs, he admitted, had reached an embarrassing stage. The schools in the Hills were really not proving "to be suitable" for their boys. They must return home and for that they would need financial assistance.[62] Once the Bible school had returned to Nagarkurnool in 1923, where it stayed for the next six years, and where the Lohrenzes assisted for three of those years, the turmoil over who would have the school ceased for awhile.

## CHAPTER 6

# New Missionaries
# and a New Citizenship

While the American newcomers, John H. and Maria Lohrenz, and Peter V. and Elizabeth Balzer, were getting settled in India, the missionaries from Tsarist Russia, specifically Abram and Katharina Huebert, Cornelius and Martha Unruh, and John and Anna Penner, became desperate to find a new country. This search for a new citizenship overlapped with the early part of the migration of Russian Mennonites to Canada in the years 1923 to 1927.

## New Missionary Couples from America

For their apprenticeship years, John and Maria Klaassen Lohrenz resided at Nagarkurnool while the Bergtholds were on furlough, and began their language study there. For the next few years, they helped at Shamshabad while the Pankratzes were away, and with the Bible school once Bergthold had taken it over again at Nagarkurnool. Not surprisingly, one of the first letters John Lohrenz wrote from India to his brother had to do with finding "a permanent work." He wanted to establish something comparable to Deverakonda for the Voths and Nagarkurnool for the Bergtholds.[1]

The area targeted, between Shamshabad and Nagarkurnool, was ill-defined for a number of years. In 1921 Lohrenz named it Janumpet, but by 1922-23 it had been renamed Kalvakurty and included a portion of what had been assigned to Nagarkurnool earlier. Yet Lohrenz thought of Kalvakurty as strategically located on the railway where major roads crossed. Acquiring the land was not easy. The political restlessness of the country caused by the fallout from the agitation for "Home Rule," the failure of the Lucknow Pact (between Hindu and Muslim) of 1916, and especially from the massacre at Amritsar (1919),[2] seemed to slow down the granting of permission for the opening of more Christian compounds. Cornelius Unruh told Lohrenz that the ABMU had tried for years to get sanction for a station in that area and had failed. If the AMBM was more successful, he would be glad; the Baptists were cutting back.[3]

John Lohrenz, because his brother chaired the Board of Foreign Missions in Hillsboro, played a larger role than other junior missionaries in shaping policy on the field. Appointed as treasurer,

Lohrenz soon questioned the wisdom of permitting designated gifts, especially after J. W. Wiens had explained the three kinds of funds to him and added, "designated gifts are not the best for the India Mission!" As Kalvakurty was slow to develop, Lohrenz wrote that any special gifts assigned to them should be placed in the general fund.[4] He did not think large appropriations for education should be sent unless there was proof that station boarding schools (elementary and middle) were being overseen as they should be. He suggested that these contributions could be reduced by 33 percent, if only there was more unity on the field.[5]

But how could there be more unity on the field if they had difficulty as junior missionaries working with the Bergtholds in the Bible school? In 1925 the Lohrenzes had such a difficult year with the Bergtholds that they decided not to assist in the Bible school again.[6] They felt slighted by an error about monies for their projected furlough. The Missionary Council had decided that the Lohrenzes were to have their first furlough before the Janzens had their second, but J. W. Wiens, apparently urged by Hiebert, sent travel money to the Janzens first. Henry Lohrenz intervened on behalf of his brother, saying that John had had "a particularly difficult period for a number of reasons which he did not want to document."[7] As it was, John and Maria Lohrenz postponed their furlough until the spring of 1928, and thus were able to complete the main bungalow and hospital at Shamshabad.[8] It is clear that John Lohrenz could manage building projects where Pankratz had faltered and demonstrated strategic insights. More than others he hammered away at the need for clear policy statements. He, too, was never quite satisfied with Hiebert's way of conducting business.

During their furlough the Lohrenzes both engaged in studies at Central Baptist Seminary in Kansas City, and earned B.D. degrees.[9] Furthering their education was a matter of great concern for them, especially since Henry W. Lohrenz had taken a leave of absence from Tabor to pursue further studies at Princeton. John Lohrenz started a trend among Americans in the interwar years. Whereas the missionaries, both Russian and American, who studied at Hamburg or Rochester felt confident with their educational preparation (none of them ever took further studies), their successors seemed always to be upgrading their educational attainments, as though what they received at Tabor College was not sufficient.

## Peter V. and Elizabeth Kornelson Balzer

The Balzers, from Oklahoma and Nebraska respectively, went to India in 1923. They found language study difficult. At first they were assigned to Bhongir, a station east of Secunderabad, on the railway to Jangaon. Here they encountered strong resistance to their first venture into the villages, finding themselves interrogated by police and village officials.[10]

They did not stay at Bhongir long enough to establish a new work. Like the Lohrenzes, they were looking for a pioneering place of their own and had some hand in starting the new station at Kalvakurty. Their lot as apprentices, however, was to fill in while their predecessors enjoyed furloughs. When the Voths went home in 1926, they took over the Deverakonda station. Here they began work on a hospital building for Marie C. Wall, and experienced a severe drought and rising grain prices.[11] When the Voths returned, the Balzers invited them back to Deverakonda, as was expected. A junior missionary placed in charge gave way to a senior missionary returning to his station. Earlier, the Lohrenzes had to do this even though they were sent to teach in the Bible school.[12] Thus developed the pattern of playing mission "musical chairs." After several years at Deverakonda, the Balzers took over Wanaparty, left vacant by the death of Frank A. Janzen. As the Lohrenzes were leaving on furlough in 1928, the Balzers took over the Shamshabad station where Balzer continued some of the building projects started by Lohrenz. There Elizabeth showed signs of an illness that would plague her during much of her time in India. Balzer thought they might have to return for health reasons as early as the spring of 1928. Two English doctors at Secunderabad found severe spinal damage and placed Elizabeth in a plaster of paris straitjacket. She was able to remain in India, either convalescing in station or in the hills during the hot season.[13]

The other two couples from America before 1930 were John A. and Viola (Bergthold) Wiebe (1927), and John N. C. and Anna (Jungas) Hiebert (1929). Their story will be left to the next chapter. The only other new couple of this period, from Russia, were John A. and Anna (Nikkel) Penner, whose story will be told in connection with the ABMU. Coming to the aid of Katharina Schellenberg was the nurse Maria C. Wall and the teachers Anna Hanneman and Helen L. Warkentin. Over time Schellenberg and Hanneman formed a team, working together longest at Shamshabad, while Wall and Warkentin served most of their long careers with the Voths at Deverakonda. Death ended the work of the first team in the 1940s, while the second continued until 1957.

### The Medical Doctor Katharina L. Schellenberg

Schellenberg (1870-1945), the only woman medical doctor sent out by the Mennonite Brethren, began her medical ministry in 1907 in connection with the Pankratzes at Malakpet. (This was forty-five years before another medical doctor came to India.) When Malakpet closed because of Muslim persecution, she moved to Nagarkurnool. There she began a dispensary in conjunction with Anna Epp Bergthold, who was trained as a nurse in Russia. Following four years of work there, Schellenberg moved to Hughestown, a most feverish place, where she first teamed up with Hanneman. Until she settled at Shamshabad in 1922, Schellenberg said that her work was a bit "scattered," running between the two. This was presumably possible because she was one of the first to have a car, by 1918.[14] Also, she followed Anna Suderman's pattern of going to assist whoever in the Mission was in dire need of help. For example, the two of them tried to save Katharina Lohrenz in 1913, and helped with the birth of a child to Anna Epp Bergthold.[15] In October 1927 she and Hanneman went to Wanaparty to assist Elizabeth Janzen and her three boys.[16]

Schellenberg took only two furloughs between 1907 and her death in 1945. Often she was "alone in the plains, of the whites," probably urging her colleagues to take to the Hills during the hot season, but not persuadable herself.[17] Even though she did not manage to dedicate a full hospital facility until 1928, she had an enormous patient load. Even without that facility, she and her staff saw over 52,000 patients between September 1916 and August 1918.[18] The conditions under which she worked were difficult. The average life expectancy in India was about twenty-four years as late as 1930. Millions died in infancy. Among the many serious diseases were small pox, cholera, leprosy, fevers, and diarrhea. Other hazards to life and limb, for missionaries also, are too many to mention here.[19]

Katharina Schellenberg's furlough of 1922 lengthened to four years because of John Pankratz's resistance to her return. Prior to her return in 1926, Henry W. Lohrenz wrote her, "I think you might go back and work on a station where you are welcome! Perhaps the Lord will change the circumstances so that all can be set right again."[20] But many of the anxieties followed her return. In light of the difficulties she experienced with the Pankratzes, she wondered who would build the necessary facilities. The answer came with the return of John and Maria Lohrenz.

Schellenberg got her hospital at Shamshabad in April 1928. Her workload increased so dramatically that by May, 1929, she went to Coonoor for a rest. According to Anna Hanneman, Schellenberg was suffering from "nervous exhaustion."[21] As in most evangelical missions of the day, Schellenberg emphasized that medical work was not an end in itself, but a means to bring about salvation of the soul.[22]

## Anna Hanneman

Sharing the heat and burden of the work in the plains during this decade, as well as the frustrations of being kept at home because of an recalcitrant John Pankratz, was Anna Hanneman. Born in Kansas in 1890, she attended Tabor College at the same time as Maria Klaassen (Lohrenz). President Lohrenz thought of her as a worthy successor to his own sister, Katharina, who had died in Hyderabad in 1913. He wrote: "Her quiet ways, her diligent application to her duties, her excellent physical condition, and her firm faith in God spoke for her as an ideal missionary." She committed herself to service in India in January 1914, interrupted her training as a teacher, and arrived in India in August 1915.[23] After working closely with Katharina Schellenberg for one term, she returned to Tabor College and graduated in 1925 with the A.B. degree. Lohrenz had been quite impressed with her oration at Tabor's commencement exercises in that year.[24]

Once in India, she was immediately immersed in the work, setting up her first mission school in the Shamshabad area. She also continued to supervise the school in Hughestown, an area that proved pestilential and feverish. Her first teaching, while learning Telugu, was conducted in English. By the fall of 1918 her school was recognized as an Anglo-Vernacular Middle School, grades five to seven, by the Nizam's education department.[25] In a 1929 report, she showed a keen perception not only of their ultimate objective in education, but also of the potential for failure. She noticed among her children, basically all from outcaste families and now disoriented from their former circumstances, the strong motive to acquire enough education to qualify for an occupation providing independence. Though she understood this, Hanneman was idealistic enough to say: "Among truly born again persons, this striving for earthly gain should not have such high priority, and so we ask ourselves whether we have done our best or been earnest enough in prayer."[26] She hoped that some would grow up to serve the Mission and Church.

Hanneman also illustrated the promotional role that the women missionaries undertook, both single and married. In 1925 at a Mennonite Brethren Conference in Brotherfield, Saskatchewan, she and Maria Wall were the only mission representatives present. She spoke on behalf of H. W. Lohrenz, who insisted that she give greetings and report on India.[27] She was not the first woman to report to the Conference from the platform. Maria Pankratz may have been the first to do so as early as 1920, and she wrote many of the Pankratz articles for the *Zionsbote*. They limited themselves, whether by request or not, to speaking of their children's well being, or about work among women in India, or about the "boardings." At the MB Canadian Conference in 1923, Katharina L. Schellenberg appealed for support for a hospital at the new station Shamshabad, "and for similar things."[28]

### Maria Wall and Helen Warkentin

Mention has been made of Maria C. Wall and Helen L. Warkentin, who were paired at Deverakonda for many years. Their strength was not in promotion of their work nor of themselves. Their impact on India was cumulative, better appreciated as they neared retirement. Wall, from Munich, North Dakota, was trained as both a teacher and a nurse. Like others of this period, she was "ordained" for missionary service, arriving in India in the early fall of 1915. One of her first experiences was a shock to all: the "totally unexpected" death of Anna Epp Bergthold, and the frustration of not getting there with a rented car in time to help because of the torrential rains.[29]

As mentioned, in 1917 Wall found herself at the center of a controversy over stationing. During her first years in medical service, she discovered how crushing the burden of the "heathen world" could be. Whether she was at Nagarkurnool in time to help during the rat plague of 1918, or at Deverakonda, she was overwhelmed with patient demands, with the needs of orphans and battered wives and was glad to get to the hills in 1920.[30] She kept at her post faithfully, except for excursions to Coonoor, and hardly wrote anything until her partner at Deverakonda, Warkentin, became ill in 1930 and had to go to Bangalore for a rest.

Helen Warkentin was the daughter of Johann and Sarah (Krahn) Warkentin, from Winkler, Manitoba. Johann was a leading convert from the evangelistic outreach of the MB General Conference by Heinrich Voth and was a longtime leader of the first MB church in Canada.[31] In 1920 his daughter became the first Canadian to join the AMBM in India. Of all the missionaries, she was one of the most infrequent correspondents, always apologizing for being tardy. Warkentin admitted she could not keep accounts very well.[32] In 1930 Warkentin had such a strong premonition of her mother's death in Winkler, Manitoba, that she became depressed. A year later, according to Maria Lohrenz, Warkentin was "sick unto death" with typhus.[33]

### John A. and Anna Penner

John A. and Anna Nikkel Penner, one of the last couples to arrive from Russia to work with the ABMU, were contemporaries of Anna Hanneman and her generation. John A. Penner came from the Molotschna colony. At the age of sixteen, he went to Lichtfelde for training in carpentry under a Johann Dick. Here he was converted, baptized by Peter Regehr and joined the Rückenau MB Church. He developed his carpentry skills and trade to the point of engaging others to work for him. He was influenced spiritually by Jacob Reimer and others in Rückenau, and was trained in German for his further studies by Cornelius Unruh at Sagradowka. Penner felt called to prepare for foreign mission work to India, so he, like others, attended Hamburg-Horn from 1909 to 1913.[34]

Penner's planned trip to England to study English for six months was cut back to six weeks by the staffing needs of the Nalgonda district, where Heinrich Unruh had died in November 1912,[35] and where A. J. Friesen was preparing to return because of severe shortstaffing. Friesen wanted to take Penner with him, but the latter was still unmarried. This he found quite disconcerting. He wrote: "I was forced to go in search of a wife by letter [from England]." In this way he contacted, and on 10 October 1913, married Anna Nikkel from Münsterberg, Molotschna. Jacob W. Reimer of Rückenau officiated. Anna had prepared for mission work and nursing at Steglitz, near Berlin, and at Riga.[36]

Their departure for India was so hurried that they could not do any visiting in the churches. They were accompanied to India by A. J. Friesen and Aganetha Neufeld from Orenburg. In the Crimea they visited Johann G. and Helena Wiens, who had to retire from the India work because of their daughter's illness.[37] They were welcomed at Jangaon by Franz and Marie Wiens, as well as by the local Christians. They immediately saw the stress that had overwhelmed the Wienses by having charge of Nalgonda as well as Jangaon in a time of famine. Of the young Penners an Indian leader said: "We note the self-denying way in which they have come into our midst, having left parents, friends and country behind." The Penners began their language study at Nalgonda.[38]

At first the Penners took the Jangaon field, vacated by the Wiens family. From his annual reports, one gleans a sense of the responsibility placed on the young couple. With the help of fifteen indigenous workers they were trying to reach 300,000 people living scattered over 1,500 square miles. Among the troubles that nearly overwhelmed these poverty-stricken people, if not themselves, were plague, cholera, influenza, and famine. Malaria struck Anna in 1918 and she was once "at death's door."[39]

Though it is clear that Penner felt he had a "distinct call" to serve in India, and "there was never any doubt about his priorities," he became very frustrated with administrative details. When he was reprimanded for not sending the receipt for the annual car license, he showed some sarcasm. Penner wrote "In Indian logic that receipt had to be attached to the car for which it was issued...Do I send [Ramapatnam] the whole car–so [the treasurer] can see I spent the money?"[40]

This report and another concerning the worsening famine, when "whole pallems" (out villages) were devastated, evoked interesting responses from ABMU secretary Joseph C. Robbins in New York. He was impressed with Penner's ability to teach Indian boys industrial craftsmanship. Penner had established a workshop in which his proteges produced industrial items of amazing ingenuity, such as school desks and chairs, and machinery for farming and transport.[41]

### International Changes

Soon after the Penners left Russia the Great War began. Few people dreamt how this would bring to an end the glory days of the Russian Mennonite community.[42] This had vast implications for the Russian Mennonite Brethren in India. Not only were they dependent financially since 1914 on the American Baptists, they were now cut off from their homeland, and had to find a new citizenship. Quite apart from any other consideration, the Great War had an enormous impact on the financing of the American MB work. Nothing curtailed the pioneering four like the relief effort to save the starving Mennonites in Russia. Mennonites everywhere took literally the injunction to reach out "to those of the household of faith." Treasurer J. W. Wiens and secretary N. N. Hiebert repeatedly expressed the hope that less money would be required for Russia,[43] but this hope was not fulfilled for many years, as the lists of givings in the *Zionsbote* show.

### The Role of Joseph C. Robbins and the ABMU

The foreign secretary of the ABMU during much of this period was Joseph C. Robbins, a native of Nova Scotia, Canada. Robbins proved helpful in many complex situations during the inter-war period. Because the Unruhs, Hueberts and Penners were enjoying such fruitful years, despite frequent famines in the Nalgonda district, he took them into his confidence. Beginning just after the Great War, Robbins annually informed them of the theological tensions within the Northern Baptist Convention. He explained the reasons for the removal in 1920 of the Society's headquarters from Boston to Manhattan. More importantly for the ABMU, the 1919 Denver Convention of the Northern Baptist Convention had managed to bring greater theological unity to the denomination. Modernism, one of the big issues, had seemingly been laid to rest. Robbins also shared his vision of what the Northern Baptist Convention could do with a large amount of money anticipated from oil baron John D. Rockefeller.[44] For one thing, more money would be forthcoming for famine relief. Rockefeller had promised $1,000,000 for foreign missions, if the entire denomination raised $6,000,000 for its work at home and abroad. Actually, the Northern Baptist Convention was committed to raising $100,000,000 toward the Interchurch World Movement's goal of $336,775,572.[45]

As though the three missionary families did not quite trust the situation, and in spite of the seeming assurances of grandiose funding projects, Cornelius Unruh, Abraham Huebert and John A. Penner approached Robbins with a number of requests on 14 June 1920. First they thanked the ABFMS for "carrying the whole burden of these [Russian MB] stations during the [six] long years of war and struggles." On the basis of reports about the revolutionary situation in Russia, especially as it affected the Mennonites, they were now convinced there was no hope that Rückenau would ever be able to take up the support again. They had heard falsely that Friesen had been among thirty-five Mennonite men recently hung by the Bolsheviks. They were also disturbed by rumors that some ABMU stations were to be given up. They assumed that the Nalgonda district would be targeted. Since the time for furloughs was approaching for all of them, and since they were virtually stateless, they wished to have their status with the ABMU clarified and confirmed. It was clear, however, they wished to maintain the relationship with the ABMU established a full generation ago.[46]

Though Robbins was genuinely sympathetic to the plight of the Russian Mennonites, he was just then in the midst of helping to move the entire ABFMS headquarters from Boston to New York City. In January 1921 he replied to their joint letter, assuring them of continuity. They need have no fear of becoming unemployed even though the Society was experiencing a financial crunch. The campaign of the post-war years had reached only about 50 percent of its goal. This would therefore require some radical adjustments.[47]

### Becoming Canadians

John A. Penner, eligible for furlough in 1922, was the first to initiate the question of seeking a new citizenship in North America. Now that they were completely cut off from Russia, each Russian Mennonite family longed to attain citizenship elsewhere, preferably in the United States. Penner spelled out the poignancy of the situation. For the sake of their children they needed a country they could call their own.[48]

When furloughs for the Hueberts at Suryapet, and the Unruhs at Nalgonda overlapped, in large part, with that of the Penners, they found themselves together in California. To their dismay, however, they could not bypass the five-year residence rule in the USA. When it was discovered, alternatively, that they could gain their citizenship in Canada within a twelve-month period, Unruh helped make possible a change in residence to Canada and the realization of Canadian citizenship for all three families. Another crucial factor in all this was the spiritual nourishment and practical assistance that the three families found at First Baptist Church in Vancouver, led by J. J. Robb. Unruh wrote they particularly enjoyed Robb's fine sermons. "After having been so long alone in India in the jungle, and having struggled with Satan, darkness, ignorance and superstition, where we were the only authority [in] religious matters... where we have to give out every day and very little chance to take in... We rejoice in having this time and help."[49] At this time there were no MB congregations anywhere in British Columbia.

During the years 1922 to 1925, Robbins' assistance was crucial in immigration matters. As a former Canadian, he facilitated the process toward Canadian citizenship by persuading Canadian and then British immigration officials to allow former Russian citizens, working under American sponsorship in India, to fulfill residence requirements in Canada during the usual furlough time and then return to a British colony in a state of unrest. By any standards that was quite a feat. Unruh even wondered whether the State of Hyderabad was sufficiently part of British India to allow them to return as missionaries if everything else could be worked out.[50]

At no time did Cornelius Unruh show his genius for getting things done as he did during this furlough. These years, 1923-25, coincided with the beginnings of the migration of about 21,000 Mennonites to Canada from the Soviet Union. While Unruh was visiting in Waldheim, Saskatchewan, he took up the cause of his brother Heinrich's family. He earlier had ensured that Anna Peters Unruh with her six children would be cared for in Russia. As Anna had died in 1922, Cornelius, with the help of his brother Benjamin in Karlsruhe, Germany, and the Canadian Colonization Board in Rosthern, contrived to bring all of his nieces and nephews to Canada. They arrived in 1924 while the Unruhs were waiting for their Canadian citizenship papers. Having adopted John C. and Elizabeth, Cornelius and Martha made suitable arrangements for housing and schooling in Manitoba for Henry, Marie, Martha, and Arthur. They took Elizabeth back to Nalgonda with them, where she attended Breeks School at Ootacumund.[51] He also managed to send money to the Crimea so that his brother Abram H. Unruh and family could migrate. Not knowing how to send the money in those uncertain times, he took $1,100 of borrowed money, sealed the cash in an envelope, "prayed over it and dropped it in the mail box." Amazingly, the Unruh family received the bundle intact in the Crimea.[52]

**An Overview of the Two Missions in the 1920s**

If the three stations in the Nalgonda district had about four thousand Christians in 1914, one may assume there was some growth, based on such mass movements as Cornelius Unruh, once back in India, experienced in the cool season of 1929-1930 when about one thousand were baptized. He reported Christians in 225 villages out of 700. He was optimistic that their five thousand Christians would double within ten years, and that "there will not be many Malas and Madigas in Nalgonda field, but Christians." Of his thirteen congregations, eleven were self-supporting and preachers' support levels ranged from forty rupees per month in the compound church to sixteen rupees in the villages.[53] Abram Huebert reported eight congregations in the Suryapet field in 1930 but did not give any figures, while John Penner at Mahbubnagar stated that the Jadcherla congregation was quite self-supporting.[54]

By comparison, in summary, the AMBM had over four thousand converts on five fields in 1929. Assisting the missionaries were about two hundred village preachers and Bible women. The latter taught about four hundred children in village schools, while the missionary women, assisted by thirty-five trained teachers, conducted four station boarding schools with about four hundred children enrolled.[55]

In 1929 Anna Hanneman reported that the Bible School had enrolled 190 men and women since 1920. Of these 150 had finished the course and 119 of these were active in the Mission. Four were serving under other missions, twenty-one had entered other occupations, and five had died.[56]

Total giving by the organized churches was well under one thousand dollars. Ten years later many of the figures were the same, though there was a good increase in the number of organized churches (56) on ten fields, and baptized believers (nearly 12,000).[57]

## CHAPTER 7

# Tragedy and
# Trauma in the 1920s

The story of Mennonite Brethren mission work in India is dotted with heart-wrenching tragedies and stories involving serious trauma, especially the Pankratz family. No generation was immune. The first generation experienced the trauma of deaths from India's diseases, and the deaths of mothers and infants from the difficulties of giving birth in the age of the oxcart. This pathos was intensified by unusual deaths in two periods of anguish: the first between 1922 and 1927; the second between 1950 and 1956.

## The Tragedy of 1922 at Reedley

Franz and Marie Wiens were introduced earlier in connection with the death of Heinrich Unruh in 1912, and the takeover of the three Russian MB stations two years later. As noted in Chapter 4, they proceeded to Nalgonda in 1909 and, when Heinrich Unruh died, they served at Jangaon until the cool season of 1913-14. Even though they had land in Siberia, they chose not to return to Russia. It is not clear whether they already saw political problems developing in Russia, or were swayed by embarrassment over the disappointing conclusion to their service with the ABMU. In any case, they relocated to southern California. A venture there in orange growing failed, after which they moved to Reedley, California. There Franz found work in a bank, while he and Marie served in various capacities in the Reedley MB Church.[1]

It was in Reedley, on 31 July 1922, in the company of two of his boys and visiting missionary John A. Penner, that Franz J. Wiens lost his life in a most abnormal episode. Late at night, coming home from a trip to their new farm at Livingston, California, Franz was at the wheel of his 1920 Ford when he approached the Kings River bridge at Reedley. He found himself confronted by a civilian posse, in this case firemen without badges, who had set up a road block to catch a murder suspect and escapee from a Fresno prison. Not trusting the situation, Wiens tried to run the roadblock. He only slowed down enough to ask what the men wanted, but then sped away when he saw them reaching for their guns. At least five other cars, out of about seventy-five, were fired at that night. While the fire-men, hastily recruited, had orders to shoot only at tires, only Wiens was struck by a bullet at the base of his neck and killed. When Penner, in the front seat, saw blood discharging from Wiens' mouth, he pulled him over, and young Jacob climbed into the front seat. To-gether they managed to keep the Ford under control and brought it into the yard of their house not far away from the scene of the shooting.[2]

When Marie Wiens was called from the house to face the death of her husband, she wrote: "There under the open sky the children and I knelt beside our dear Papa and called upon God for cour-age... because human strength was insufficient. O, that unforgetta-ble, sad, midnight hour!"[3]

The uniqueness and pathos of the situation was not lost on the people of Reedley. While the Wienses had already become Ameri-can citizens, having been in the States since 1914, the chief witness in the case was his friend, John A. Penner, a missionary to India under the aegis of the ABFMS, New York, but hailing from Russia, a country he could no longer call his own. The Penners had arrived from Jangaon with three children in May 1922. A *Fresno Morning Republican* staff correspondent wrote: "Coming half way around the world to rejoin his comrade of missionary days . . . only to have him gasp out his last breath in his arms after being shot,... Penner [asked for] a thorough probe of the slaying of Frank J. Wiens." He was not calling the shooting a crime, but wanted the truth of the matter established through the proper channels.[4]

The inquest by jury called for manslaughter charges against two firemen: C. W. Fridley, who fired the fatal shot, and W. A. Seger. They also charged gross negligence against J. T. Kennedy, a county detective, for using a posse that was not duly sworn in nor properly instructed in the use of firearms. When Fridley and Seger were charged, it was Penner who signed the "complaint" against them, saying that his friend had been killed in a shooting that was "un-called for and unprovoked." The two firemen were held over on 22 August for trial by a higher court.[5]

Both the inquest and funeral attracted large crowds. To show respect for Wiens and a family bereft of husband and father, the bank where Wiens had been employed as head bookkeeper was closed for the day, and all businesses in Reedley for two hours in the afternoon. John Penner gave the funeral sermon, assisted by the Reedley MB church leader John H. Richert.[6] The editor of the *Reedley Exponent* expressed the opinion that "the verdict of the jury and the evidence in the case show that a crime was committed." But what could be done for the family? He assumed from the stance of the *Fresno Morning Republican* that no assistance would be offered by the City of Fresno. He stated that the *Exponent* had been advised that unless something was done, the three boys would likely be deprived of an adequate education "to fit themselves for life's burdens. They will have to become bread winners when they should be in school... and counted among the less fortunate." The editorial asked "the people of Reedley" to make an effort "to see that Fresno makes such provision."[7] When a committee of citizens called on the Fresno city officials to consider remuneration for the loss of a bread winner, the city attorney turned back the plea, stating that there was "no legal liability on the city." Nor could the city make a gift of money. Such funds would have to be raised by a volunteer citizenry.[8]

It is not known whether such funds were raised, nor to what extent the Reedley MB church helped the Wiens family. In the long run, the Wiens boys did not suffer the lack of education that was predicted. They worked hard in the fruit harvest of the San Joaquin valley and at a variety of jobs during school years. Jacob became a teacher and school administrator and retired after thirty-nine years to Hemet, California. Henry (1910-1968), a Berkeley graduate, ended his career as a diplomat for the federal Department of Labor and as a consultant to the World Bank. Frank, the youngest worked in overseas assignments with Mennonite Central Committee for many years and later entered the field of social work in Kansas.[9]

### John and Maria Pankratz, 1923-1926

In earlier sections, notice was taken of the exceptionally troublesome times experienced by the Pankratz family. Despite these disappointments, they seem to have tried to consolidate their family position at Shamshabad. Whether or not they were seeking recognition for the building up of a station, similar to the builders of Deverakonda, their proceedings brought the Board at home and their colleagues in India considerable anxiety.

After their furlough in 1921-22, they had three sons at Ootacumund, and a daughter at Coonoor. Much criticized for taking the two older boys back to India, the year 1924 found them in dire straits. They were embarrassed because their land holdings in America had not produced enough to help their financial situation. By July Pankratz explained to treasurer Wiens that they had tried to be most careful to evade criticism of their lifestyle and had tried to get by on their mission income and the travel funds made available. He was most thankful to the Board at home for timely assistance in that year.[10]

Whatever serenity or gratification they had found in moving to Shamshabad was broken by a number of traumatic incidents. Among the trying situations was the plague in the fall of 1924, when over half the inhabitants of Shamshabad temporarily ran away. Thereupon they inoculated all Christians and their school children. In spite of all the problems of getting settled since coming to India in 1902, the Pankratzes celebrated the twenty-fifth anniversary of the AMBM at Malakpet/Hughestown/Shamshabad with some joy, emphasizing particularly what they had accomplished in training faithful indigenous workers. They pointed to the contributions made by their missionary colleagues: Elizabeth S. Neufeld, Anna Suderman, Katharina Lohrenz, and Anna Hanneman and their changing staff of thirty-one, who had instructed 662 children. They could point to sixty-six workers who had left their schools for service in their field alone.[11] Not all was lost.

The most discouraging and traumatic event, however, was the fatal shooting of Preacher J. P. Samuel at the hands of Ernest Pankratz on 5 January 1924, a story never made public. The Pankratz family was on tour in the oft-visited area of Ibrahimpatnam. After they and their company of preachers had lunch under a tree and were readying the tents for overnight camping, Ernest suggested he would try to bag some doves or quail for their supper. Taking his .22 caliber rifle in hand, he reloaded the gun, only to accidentally touch the trigger. Unknown to Ernest, J.P. Samuel had left the group and found himself in the path of that bullet. Though every attempt was made to save him, Samuel died from a gunshot wound to his lower body. Ernest was most heartbroken, as was the entire family, and all the Christian workers on the Hughestown/Shamshabad field. As Pankratz explained to the Board at home, Samuel of all the preachers was closest to their two sons, who had been welcomed back very warmly as helpers in the work.[12]

This naturally brought up the question: why did missionaries have guns on the field? Pankratz explained that he had resisted the idea of possessing and carrying a weapon. In reality, he argued, a gun was needed for self-protection against such wild animals as panthers, boars, jackals, and especially stray dogs. When the missionaries discussed this question, they decided they needed them "in station."[13]

This unfortunate accident and the fact that Ernest and John had not adjusted well to Breeks school at Ootacumund led to a decision to return them to America. Ernest wanted to go to Wheaton College and John to an engineering school. They left India in March 1924 following an affectionate farewell at Shamshabad. Their father took them to Karachi on the Lower Sind River for embarkation. "The separation was very hard." This period of intense trauma drove John and Maria to the Hills for a rest. They were totally exhausted and needed some relief from the toil, sweat, and tears in the plains.[14]

Though overburdened with work, the Pankratzes resisted the return to Shamshabad from furlough of Katharina L. Schellenberg as doctor and Anna Hanneman as teacher. Henry W. Lohrenz believed that it was because Pankratz had requested that their children, Peter H. and Rubina Ewert, should be sent out to take over Shamshabad during their absence. Lohrenz did not think that Ewert's health was up to the task, nor should stations be transferred in a nepotistic manner. John H. Voth, himself a problem to N. N. Hiebert, wrote to the Board privately saying that if and when the two women returned from furlough, they should be prepared to be gentle with John and Maria Pankratz, to "carry them," as though they had become burdensome to all.[15] At the end of the ordeal, John and Maria returned to America and stayed home from 1926 to 1938.

### Criticism from Cornelius Unruh

Meanwhile, Maria Pankratz may have innocently drawn Cornelius Unruh into a critical appraisal of their current relationship to the ABMU. In light of all their troubles, in 1923 Maria acknowledged that it might have been easier for them in 1902 if they had become an auxiliary of the ABMU, as Jacob Heinrichs had advised in the pages of the *Zionsbote* two decades earlier.[16] She noted the departure of the Russian MB families (also Aganetha Neufeld) for North America in search of a new citizenship. It was obvious that "old Russia was no more!" When beggars came to the door, she related how they used news of the terrible famine in Russia to put them off. Life is bad for Mennonites too, she told them.[17]

At about the same time, John Pankratz suggested in 1922 that it might now be possible for the Russian MB work in India to be integrated into the AMBM. Pankratz had suggested privately that if many of the former Russian MB supporters of the mission to Nalgonda District, now moving to Canada, would agree to such an integration, this would be worth pursuing.[18] A different influence arose from Unruh's visit to the Northern Baptist Theological seminary, Chicago, where J. P. Klahsen, Abram Huebert's son-in-law, was studying and Jacob Heinrichs was now teaching. Unruh called Heinrichs the "most influential missionary ever to have worked in India." From there the Unruhs went to see J. C. Robbins in New York, the secretary who had been immeasurably helpful to them during their search for a new citizenship.[19]

Back in Nalgonda, Unruh noted that when the stations of the Nalgonda district were attended by American Baptists rather than Mennonite Brethren, that some support from American Mennonite Brethren for the Russian work had been diverted to the AMBM.[20] Reflecting on all of this, Unruh put his thoughts on paper to Hermann Neufeld in Winnipeg. While he recognized the changed situation, Unruh insisted that they "could not have fallen into better hands" in Friesen's day than those of the ABMU. That Society had treated them "more nobly and generously than any other." Except for the ABMU the Russian Mennonite Brethren could very well have faced closure of their stations and personal unemployment. Unruh asserted that if tomorrow the clock could be turned back in Russia, the ABMU would gladly revert to the former partnership.[21]

Unruh drew out what the Pankratzes would see as an invidious comparison. Indirectly he suggested that they might not have fared as well had they been taken over by the American Mennonite Brethren in 1914. Perhaps he should have stopped there, but Unruh chose to take the inference one step further. Referring to the downturn in support from America, Unruh wrote that "it was not a good policy to take bricks from your neighbor's broken-down house in order to build your own." John Pankratz took offense at this, while John Lohrenz thought the remarks were in bad taste. Unruh was casting the AMBM in an "unfavorable light." When Unruh apologized, the problem was cleared up quickly and the good relations between them, built up since 1904, continued.[22]

## The Death of Frank Aaron Janzen, 1927

The Mission soon faced another tragedy for which there was no easy explanation. On Friday, 7 October 1927, around midnight, Frank A. Janzen awoke in his Wanaparty bungalow with severe intestinal and abdominal pain. He did not call his wife Elizabeth, but she was awakened a few hours later by his moaning. According to Katharina L. Schellenberg, Elizabeth tried such remedies as she possessed, but by morning his heart began to weaken and his limbs grew colder. At first he resisted the suggestion to leave immediately for Secunderabad's civil hospital, about 160 kilometers away. But as he grew weaker, Elizabeth engaged a driver for their vehicle, and asked her compounder Philip to help get her deathly-ill husband to town. They had a terrible time. First there was heavy rain, then a punctured tire. Only half way to Secunderabad, Frank Janzen died in the car. The death-dealing blow to this otherwise healthy person had taken only 17 hours.[23]

Instead of proceeding directly to the city, they stopped at Shamshabad to inform John and Maria Lohrenz, Schellenberg, and Hanneman of the calamitous event. As quickly as possible the Lohrenzes and the two single women took their car and accompanied the Janzen car, first to Secunderabad, where they reported the death, and then to Hughestown station, where they packed the remains in ice. Sunday morning they sent messages to Cornelius Unruh at Nalgonda, to Wanaparty station, to the Bergtholds at Nagarkurnool, and to Hillsboro. The message N. N. Hiebert received was that Janzen had died unexpectedly from a "bowel obstruction."[24]

Janzen's son Leander, who had just been home, was on his way back to school when his father died. He was asked to return to Secunderabad immediately. Sons Edwin and Arnold at Breeks Memorial School in Ootacumund did not know until their mother Elizabeth Janzen went to Ootacumund to convey the sad news. Meanwhile, the Lohrenzes ordered a grave to be prepared in St. George's Cemetery, where Katharina Lohrenz was buried in 1913, and planned to have the funeral service in late afternoon, with Unruh as one of the speakers.[25]

**Suspicions of Foul Play**

Surely some questions about the cause of death must have crossed the minds of the missionaries, yet no one expressed any suspicions of foul play. Perhaps they were too numbed by the sudden catastrophe to have thought of such a possibility. Schellenberg wrote: "We all would not have thought about it, but here come along some police officers, and tell us of this suspicion ... that [Janzen] might have been poisoned."[26]

The funeral was conducted as planned, but the police intervention delayed the burial. When they heard the news that Janzen, who would have been known to the authorities, had died in rather mysterious circumstances, they requested that a 'post-mortem examination' be done. Bergthold wrote: "Because we had no certain knowledge of the cause of death, we had not until then thought of an enemy hand in the matter...." It had been quite impossible to have any medical doctor examine Janzen before he died. "We were completely in the dark about the cause of death." Bergthold discovered later that if permission had not been given, the police would have insisted on an autopsy.[27] This was carried out the next day, Monday, the 10th, by a government doctor, in the presence of Katharina Schellenberg, as well as Dr. J. S. Timpany of the ABMU, who had been notified about the sudden death. Schellenberg wrote that the autopsy "only revealed to us that nowhere in the body could there be found the cause of death." Given this result, it was decided to permit further "chemical and bacteriological analysis." When this seemed to take an inordinate amount of time, the Mission decided to ask the American consul to expedite the matter. The results were not known until the end of February 1928. At that time Bergthold published the conclusion of the matter: "The chemical analysis made by the Public Examiner in Hyderabad and in Madras fails to disclose the presence of any poison in the specimens submitted for examination." This denial of poisoning was confirmed in a statement by Consul Ed B. Montgomery.[28]

The pathos of it all came home to Maria C. Wall. Along with others she attended a convention at Wanaparty for which Missionary Janzen had made elaborate preparations. "Somehow I almost dreaded to go there, because of the sad feeling... Mrs. Janzen stood alone on the [Wanaparty bungalow] veranda to meet us. No words were spoken, only tears were flowing." Wall retold the story for Helen Warkentin who was away in Winkler, Manitoba. Between midnight and 3:00 a.m. on that Saturday Frank Janzen had "wrestled with God." She interpreted this and other of Elizabeth's memories to mean that somehow God had prepared her husband for this hour. His last will and testament was "in good order"; he had kept boards for a casket when required, and he had asked Elizabeth to look for a picture of himself. But Wall could not get away from the question: "What did Bro. Janzen die of?" Even though she did not have the February 1928 report and denial of poisoning, by 12 November she could write: "Everyone believes it has been poison."[29]

One of the British doctors in Secunderabad, named Hunt, was quite convinced that Janzen was poisoned. If so, who could have been responsible? Had Frank Janzen, by all accounts a man of great integrity, commanding wide respect,[30] made enemies who would dare to murder him in his own bungalow? According to Wall, Hunt believed that three persons would be chargeable, if the chemical analysis proved positive. These were Samuel, the previous compounder, who had been dismissed because of adulterous activity,[31] the Janzens' cook named Paul, and "a preacher Joseph." This may have been the preacher whose case of adultery had been discussed at a previous meeting of the Missionary Council. Wall wrote: "It seems that Samuel, as soon as he had known that Mr. Janzen was taken to town, he followed right after on the train with some Reddies [a caste designation]–that he had been hanging around [with] to find out how things would develop. This whole affair has made a stir among the Europeans, Missionaries, as well as officials."[32]

To this day missionaries believe that Janzen was poisoned, the denials in the press notwithstanding. Neither the missionaries nor the sympathetic doctor had any control over the subsequent analysis. Schellenberg called it "Moglai work,"[33] meaning a government agency run by Muslim officials who generally resisted the preaching of the Gospel. She believed that the specimens sent for analysis were switched; in other words, someone bribed someone to falsify the evidence.[34]

**Fatalism or Faith?**

Even if that were so, the missionary community left it in the hands of God. As Hiebert wrote to the churches, and told the aged parents of Frank Janzen: "the dear Lord in His wisdom had taken this brother... so unexpectedly out of the work." John Lohrenz stated that "we cannot doubt that it was an Almighty God who allowed this to happen." Given hindsight, it may be hard to believe they could be so resigned, but that was the only way to find comfort and carry on. (And it was in this spirit that Elizabeth Janzen returned to India in the year 1938, the only widow on the field.) At the Hillsboro conference in 1933, Hiebert referred to Wanaparty as the station built by Janzen "in his time," and "where he was permitted to complete his ministry." The German sounds much more fatalistic: "*und wo [er] auch seinen Lauf vollenden durfte*," as though while his death was meant to be, that is where it was meant to happen.[35]

The two calamities of 1924 and 1927 are touching but contrasting. The official silence of the mission regarding the accidental death of Samuel at the hands of Ernest Pankratz, and the almost fatalistic attitude at the mysterious death of Frank Janzen set a pattern for news management. Whatever tragic event could be used to glorify God and appeal for prayer and new recruits was told in some detail. If, however, something happened that reflected on a missionary's judgment, perhaps an element of incaution or carelessness, or if it was the death of someone outside the Mission family, this was withheld from the constituency. Comparable situations would arise later where this practice was followed in the 1950s.

**Trauma of Separation**

All parents suffered trauma in the separation from their children at age six onwards. The greatest "agony," however, came when children were sent to North America or left there, as young people, usually with substitute parents so that the parents could return to their life's calling. For example, John and Maria Pankratz left three children in America in 1912: Rubina, who had been to Breeks for several years, and John and Ernest. This was, as N. N. Hiebert explained in 1914, a "painful separation, felt by all supporters of the Mission." In 1920 they took John and Ernest back to India, as noted, and then suffered again in a different way following the death of Samuel.[36]

The Voths particularly made some hard choices which involved separation from children by returning to India. They left the eldest, Elizabeth, Sarah, and Menno, at home in 1928. The girls had teaching positions and Menno was at Tabor College. They found family separations more painful than some.[37] Viola Bergthold (Wiebe) came to understand why this question of the children loomed so large in missionary families: even though most children adapted very easily, they were not in India of their own choosing; they were exposed to many strange diseases; they needed special schooling and she, once she had her own children, thanked God for those who had the vision to establish schools in the Hills. She suggested that Ootacumund helped them develop a special sense of the sacrifices made by their parents as well as an understanding for the separations that appeared necessary for the well-being of all.[38] Generally, there was always a strong orientation toward service vocations such as teaching, medical and dental studies, nursing, and government service.

Of the Russian MB families, John and Anna Penner as well as Cornelius and Martha Unruh had no regrets about sending their children to Ootacumund. Waldo Penner and the Unruh brothers, Cornelius and Henry, all had good experiences there. All went to Baptist-related Canadian universities, Penner to McMaster in Hamilton, Ontario, and the Unruhs to Acadia University, Wolfville, Nova Scotia. As Penner wrote: Breeks had good traditions and "set us up for future study." In Penner's case it was his father who most influenced him by his zeal and commitment, as well as by making such times as they had together into positive experiences. Neither he nor his sister Hulda, or other siblings, were left with any lasting resentment for the separation.[39] The most trying period for the Unruhs was the separation from parents at the end of high school, and the social adjustment required for the university scene. During the depression they experienced the university of hard knocks. As Henry Unruh wrote, they had "Ivy League master's degrees," but had to take summer jobs in the years 1934-37 that paid twelve and one-half cents an hour and deducted four dollars a week for room and board. "You talk about a depression!"[40]

In one of her articles Viola Wiebe wrote of these young people as "Little Missionaries." But did any of them ever follow the footsteps of their missionary parents? The answer is mostly in the negative. In fact, many children of MB missionaries left that church. Only she, Waldo Penner, and Katie Huebert of this period, returned as missionaries, she as the wife of John A. Wiebe, Waldo as a missionary under the Canadian Baptists, and Katie with Jacob P. Klahsen with the American Baptists. Somewhat later Esther and Ruth Wiebe, and Paul Hiebert entered missionary service.

## CHAPTER 8

# The Board of Foreign Missions in Depressed Times

The difficulties that befell both Henry W. Lohrenz and Nicolai N. Hiebert during the 1930s were not entirely caused by the world-wide depression and the corresponding Dust Bowl experiences of the prairie states and provinces. But funding, precarious in any year, declined sharply during this period. Missionary salaries and appropriations were cut back, particularly impacting the indigenous workers in India. North American support was still generated mainly from agriculture, and all missionaries understood that income for their families and for retirement was dependent on a farming economy. Many missionaries owned acreage in North America worked by someone in order to supplement their support or for investment purposes.[1]

In many ways this was the last period characterized by an "agricultural way of life" when many mission supporters were "tied to the sod by economic toil and obligations." Even then, by the 1930s, as Abram E. Janzen wrote, "the missionary potential of the brotherhood was larger than the conference . . . and the yield of workers and means outstripped the cautious faith of the conference board."[2] Annual district and triennial general conference sessions stressed "the faith of our fathers." Tabor College was seen as a bulwark against satanic influences of various kinds. In the most difficult years Tabor could be cast in the light of a "faith work" as legitimate as any so-called faith Mission.[3]

In the midst of this faith community not all was as serene as the trouble-free portrait in most AMBM publications. There were severe tensions between missionaries on the field, between missionaries and N. N. Hiebert in Minnesota, and many hurt feelings that sometimes lasted for years.[4] Abram E. Janzen, former president of Tabor College and executive secretary of the Board since 1945, as was his style in public, in 1948 treated these as "minor problems" that "quickly faded from existence in the light of a united ministry in world evangelism."[5] The problems, however, did not go away and probably diminished the effectiveness of those involved.

### Henry W. Lohrenz and Tabor College

The career of Henry W. Lohrenz was much entwined with the early years of Tabor College in Hillsboro, Kansas. The school was founded as a societal college in 1908 as a successor to the German-language division of McPherson College, which many Mennonite Brethren had attended. Henry Lohrenz was president of Tabor from the beginning until 1931. In addition to his election to the chair of the Board of Foreign Missions in 1919, he also had four three-year terms as moderator of the General Conference of MB Churches. This triple role was stressed considerably by the difficulties in gaining conference support for Tabor with the addition of a new Bible and missionary training department.

In spite of the depression H. W. Lohrenz and N. N. Hiebert were able to establish a "Bible and Missionary School" at Tabor, supported by the Conference. This would assure solid MB-oriented Bible training for all potential conference workers. Though Tabor had emphasized Bible training since its inception, this was the first attempt to establish a conference training school sponsored by the Board of Foreign Missions. The planners originally expected that Lohrenz would remain president of the College as well, that Peter R. Lange at Buhler would teach, as well as N. N. Hiebert and J. H. Pankratz (in India, 1902-1926) who was still in America.[6] For the year 1931-32 Lohrenz and Hiebert were assisted by A. H. Unruh of the Winkler (Manitoba) Bible School, who traveled from Manitoba to Hillsboro for some weeks in the fall term, and ended the spring term with lectures.[7] For two years, 1932-34, Lohrenz taught Bible and biology, an interesting combination, at Bethel College, a General Conference Mennonite school in North Newton, Kansas. Meanwhile, Tabor ground to a halt during the 1934-35 school year as the Conference was repeatedly being asked to render full support.[8]

Since the issue of full support for Tabor with its new Bible department was intrinsically tied to the Mission in India, Henry Lohrenz was at pains to explain to his brother John and others in India why he was being unseated as president. In the spring of 1930 when he was urged to keep Tabor afloat, he already had cause to think that certain persons on the Board were working against him. When Lohrenz, however, stayed as professor of the new Bible department and thought all was well, there was a second assault, this time led by former students, indicating a vote of no confidence in his leadership. Lohrenz confided to John N. C. Hiebert in India that "the revolution that was inaugurated the week of the Bible Conference [1931] has set a limit on my personal energy." He went on to say that an attack of the flu on top of the "grief that all this caused me" had left his heart "in a disturbed condition."[9] To his brother he wrote: "Not only did they accept the motion of non-confidence, but they tyrannized me and spread half truths at best. What they did differed only in degree from Brutus' betrayal of Caesar!" he wrote. "To be cast aside by your own 'offspring' does hurt a great deal." Now it was clear that if he stayed at all, he was welcome only as professor of Bible, but even a "professional etiquette would not permit that."[10]

He was also disappointed that the Hillsboro church was less than supportive of the Bible school. He thought the congregation should return something for the benefits it received from the presence of the educational institutions in Hillsboro.[11]

**The Question of Leadership and Authority**

One of the most crucial missiological questions arose in the midst of this crisis: "Who's in charge?" Generally speaking, it was always assumed that a sort of hierarchy existed in Mission structures: board members in the sending country had ultimate authority, whatever seniority might dictate on the field. This assumption applied to the AMBM also, but Daniel Bergthold's relations with N. N. Hiebert in 1933 once again showed up the weakness in America.[12] Bergthold was convinced that Hiebert was a drag on the coach, in spite of the depression circumstances. What brought them close to a break was Bergthold's need for family travel money. They had to come home before furlough time in 1932 because of illness. They wished to return in the summer of 1933 rather than wait for the October conference, as requested by Hiebert. Bergthold thought he had made a very reasonable case, practical and missiological, for leaving in August, and ultimately went without any charge to the Conference when his travel expenses were paid by a widow.[13]

Bergthold was deeply offended at Hiebert's statements in the *Zionsbote* of April 1933. Bergthold felt that his reports to the constituency, including his insistence that no important decisions should be made before the October conference, could only make supporters ask: Are the Bergtholds going out independently? Bergthold stated openly that he would like to have seen a word of explanation in Hiebert's public statement about the Bergthold's continuing attachment to the Conference. But it was not there. Statements such as granting support in difficult times only because he "wanted to bring joy to the workers on the field" irked Bergthold. He had gone to India at the command of Christ, not for an adventure which the secretary at home could turn on or off. How could they keep on working if the secretary was constantly saying that we are "constrained to move ahead with hesitation?" This was no way to act under God. God knew the difficulties of these days, Bergthold suggested, without being reminded of them constantly.[14] What was needed was a shakeup of the organization. Bergthold went so far as to state that the larger Board should have chosen a different secretary when they had an opportunity in September 1933. They needed one who could command the confidence of all the missionaries and who was "spiritually and physically well."[15]

Throughout the spring of 1933 Bergthold assured H. W. Lohrenz that he wished to remain in working fellowship with the Board, but he wondered whether all the brethren understood the reasons for their choice in leaving early. Despite these "desperate times," and the rationale for holding back, Bergthold seriously questioned whether such statements should be printed in the conference paper when missionaries' criticism of Board decisions, according to a ruling of 1915, was not to be published.[16] The whole experience soured Bergthold toward the Board. He appeared ready to break with the Mission altogether. In 1933 Bergthold returned to the basic missiological question: who is the highest authority here: the Board or the Lord? Bergthold demonstrated that he was only being obedient to his call; he chose to see Hiebert as inflexibly authoritarian, interpreting God's will narrowly.[17]

In September 1933 Hiebert was still preoccupied with the Bergthold's going out "at their own risk." Perhaps to strengthen his position with the delegates at the coming conference in Hillsboro, Hiebert wrote that "experience will speak out and that is what leads to these lines." Taking Acts 13 as his guide he argued that when financial shortages occur, missionary candidates were expected to have patience and show their commitment by working at home. This the Bergtholds had refused to do.[18]

By the middle of 1935 Hiebert had backed away from his hard line and suggested that the Board stood as facilitators between the constituency and the missionaries.[19]

## N. N. Hiebert and the Depression Blues

According to Bergthold, Hiebert showed very little basic missiological trust in the Great Provider, but rather a general penny-pinching attitude toward disbursement, perhaps based on the farmer's concept of an uncertain income. Even if that was too severe a judgment, this spiritual but somewhat hapless man seemed cast in the wrong role. He saw the world too pessimistically to be effective.

Finding sufficient funds proved difficult in the best of times, and the world-wide depression of the 1930s brought the worst of times. This period, called the "dirty thirties," brought horrendous Dust Bowl experiences to the prairie states and provinces.[20] The fundamental concern during the depression was not to incur any debts. **Hilfeleistung** (relief for Mennonite brothers and sisters in need) took large amounts of money during this time, and often gained a more sympathetic hearing than foreign missions. This helped to shrink the budget for Mission work. In 1929-30 a third of the monies raised flowed into the general fund, slightly more than a third from "designated gifts," and a third went into the Mission Fund for a total of about $115,000.[21]

During the period from 1915 to 1930, the Conference raised $1,217,412 for overseas Mission; during the years 1930 to 1945 only $1,061,213, even though the membership was greater. The downturn in missions giving in the first half of the 1930s was sharp and lasted until about 1941-42. Only a sharp upturn in the 1942-45 period brought the fifteen year total to a respectable amount.[22]

In the exchange of letters between H. W. Lohrenz, who had felt the financial crash at Tabor College, and N. N. Hiebert, concerned about paying for India cars, the depression reality indicated that severe adjustments would have to be made.[23] Hiebert acknowledged that there was a serious shortfall by the summer of 1931, but he did not yet want to cut back missionary salaries. He saw both sides: the reasoned requests and the necessary denials, and "was reduced to weeping." In June 1932 things were even more desperate, as wheat prices went down, and giving was reduced considerably. If the next three months were as bad as the last, he would have to consider cutting back missionary salaries, and payments to indigenous workers. This situation led to serious discussion about dwindling finances at the Canadian Conference in Herbert, Saskatchewan later that year. The debate reinforced the view that they were governed "by the principles of our fathers" not to incur debts. The upshot was a recommendation to carry on, but missionaries should not undertake any new building projects, nor privately solicit for designated gifts, lest this create offense.[24]

In 1933 Hiebert described the treasury as "empty." In October the general fund had a balance of $103 and the designated fund, $3,226. Meanwhile, the Mission Fund showed a deficit of $2,854. Giving for foreign missions in 1932-33 declined to half of that three or four years earlier. Cutbacks in salary and field programs were accepted as necessary.[25]

Regardless of these conference guidelines and circumstances so distressing to Hiebert, John Voth in 1934 intervened in the business of fund-raising. He received "designated gifts" while on furlough, and took the occasion to write: "That's the way it should be! Just send money for my preachers, evangelists, Bible women, orphans and the poor of Deverakonda directly to me. I will contact our treasurer Brother Wiens, and we will see that these monies are sent to John Wiebe who is in charge of Deverakonda in my absence." He gave out his mailing address and then itemized the degree to which depression cutbacks were affecting those dependent on him in India. Hardly anyone could beg like Voth, and no one else would have dared to try this money-raising tactic.[26]

As to pensions for "worn-out" workers, John Voth responded before the depression by saying that the question was premature and hoped he would never have to use pension funds. Hiebert raised the question in 1933, not because of the depression, but in connection with another intimation that he might resign. At that point he argued theologically that pensions were not in God's plan. "Life was a struggle and labor is the lot of the Christian until life's end. God may have 'prepared a rest for His people,' but never here below. Entrance to the work of Mission is a sacrifice and must remain so, so also during its progress, as well as after the eventual withdrawal from the work, if we understand the work of the kingdom correctly."[27] Hiebert's position must have seemed out of touch with opinion elsewhere, for by 1936 a pension fund had been set up "for those who had given their best years" to missionary service.[28]

Yet for all that, when Hiebert retired[29] from the Board of Foreign Missions executive in 1936, he could point to a total income for the Mission in the amount of $1.5 million within a period of thirty-eight years. This represented close to $40,000 annually. On the field there were approximately 7,000 souls that had been won for Christ. These had been won by "about thirty-five workers" under the guidance and support of the Conference. What seemed much more important to him was that "none of these workers has become objectionable because of doctrinal error or sin." He thanked God that for these thirty-eight years he had been privileged to work as a facilitator in the "*Heidenmission*," in a number of ways. It had not always been easy, and many "tears have been shed privately." His services had in the last analysis been modest, he stated. He and Susie retired to the West Coast.[30]

**Henry Lohrenz and Promotion of the Mission**

In 1936 Henry W. Lohrenz replaced N. N. Hiebert as Mission secretary and in 1937, with the death of J. W. Wiens, also became the treasurer. One of his first tasks was to strengthen the authority of the Mission board and administration, particularly in shaping Mission publicity. While he was able to exercise more influence at home, even with these positions he and the board were not able to direct affairs in India any more than had been the case during the previous decade.

Lohrenz knew that a trip to India to see the work first hand, as various missionaries had requested, would be helpful. Earlier, during one of his periods of deepest gloom over the situation at Tabor College, he had considered making such a trip, as other Mennonite Mission executives already had done. Even though there were risks involved, he would rather "die at sea," he wrote, than stay in his present situation. Even here he struck out. His brother John replied that, yes, he should come, but not now, since some senior missionaries would not welcome such a visit, least of all, presumably, J. H. Voth.[31]

To say that there was a tug-of-war in the matter of promotion and news management would be to exaggerate. Nevertheless, there seemed to be some competition for leadership in promotion between India and home. The first two booklets about the India Mission program, published in 1929 and 1931, were edited by J. H. Voth/Anna Hanneman and D. F. Bergthold, respectively, and printed in India.[32] Whereas John Voth had launched *Suvarthamani* in about 1919, a paper for their literate Christians, J. N. C. Hiebert early in his first term was concerned with establishing a paper called *The Harvest Field*. Hiebert began this missionary periodical in 1931. It was written in popular style, but was spiritual in tone, and comparable to Friesen's *Das Erntefeld*, for readers in America.[33] At first it was published and circulated very infrequently, but seems to have achieved sufficient support in the Missionary Council and at home by 1936 to consider that as the starting date. In 1937 when Elizabeth Balzer was editor, the masthead read as follows: "*Harvest Field* is the recognized organ of the AMBM in India. It comes to you [six times a year] laden with the exceedingly interesting and still warm experiences, of your fellow labourers, direct from our now much enlarged [with the acquisition of Mahbubnagar/Gadwal] Mission field."[34] Hiebert managed to build up a circulation of over 1,000 by early 1942. Even Henry Lohrenz' suggestion in 1939 of an alternative paper to be edited by a full-time person in Hillsboro, and which would serve India, China and Africa Mission interests, did not deter the Missionary Council.[35]

Meanwhile, in 1936 Lohrenz brought out another booklet, the last one to be written in German. Like Bergthold's *Licht und Schatten* (1931) this included numerous contributions from the missionaries on various subjects. Lohrenz included Bergthold's penetrating statement on the mistaken policy of dependency-building among their India workers.[36] The next publication produced by Lohrenz, entitled *Our Mission Among the Telugus* and published in 1939, drew some ire in India. It was prepared in India by J. N. C. Hiebert, J. A. Wiebe, and J. H. Lohrenz, and was designed to promote and explain the work of the Mission to the constituency. When the published copy arrived back in India, J. H. Lohrenz pointed out some "grave errors" of fact, while "the Mission is pictured [as] far too promising and glorious."[37] John N. C. Hiebert was openly critical of "the one who rewrote the material" and who had "found it of interest to insert some of his own ideas." For example, Henry Lohrenz apparently had wanted to Americanize the images of India by making American cereal crops grow in India. This disappointment aside,

Hiebert wrote an enquirer from Buhler, Kansas, that he was willing to cooperate with any effort to "stimulate missionary interest."[38] Even then the publication committee reiterated these criticisms at the Missionary Council meeting of 3-5 January 1940, and passed a resolution that Hiebert and Wiebe should prepare a list of desired revisions for a second printing. They softened the criticism by adding that they believed "the report will be a blessing in general."[39]

When the *Harvest Field* was discontinued in 1942 because of the war, Henry Lohrenz initiated a series of booklets entitled *Greetings*, as a way to bring Advent greetings and present Mission information. These pamphlets, for example, featured articles about Anna Hanneman (who died in 1941), and J. H. Voth (who died in 1943). The last in this series was a "Memorial Number" to Henry W. Lohrenz who died on 17 March 1945.[40]

The principal vehicle of information, inspiration, and promotion of Mission before and after World War I for all MB conferences was the *Zionsbote*, initiated in 1884. Before 1945 the *Zionsbote* and the *Mennonitische Rundschau* provided the primary forum for letters, reports and appeals. Missionary J. H. Voth wrote about 400 letters to the *Zionsbote* between 1908 and 1943. It is doubtful whether any were ever refused, though he suspected that some were.

As the Lohrenzes and others knew only too well, those who write history make history. John Lohrenz, before going to India in 1920, prepared a master's thesis on MB Church history. It was published in 1950 by the Board of Foreign Missions under the title, *The Mennonite Brethren Church*.[41] Since that time MB Mission history has been written almost exclusively by missionaries or board members, who tended to protect their interests. As A. E. Janzen put it in 1964, it was necessary to prepare material "that will present an image by means of which [hopefully] our young people can be challenged."[42]

Throughout these years the missionaries on furlough undertook deputation tours through the constituencies. They elicited sympathy–in their anecdotal and illustrative style–for the plight of the "heathen," and spoke glowingly of success as seen in conversions and particularly baptisms. A recurring promise was that the upper caste people were just about to turn to the Gospel.

## Russländer and Kanadier

Mission work in India seems to have suffered during this era as a result of discrimination against the **Russländer**, immigrants to Canada of the 1920s. Some members of the Board of Foreign Missions, notably Heinrich S. Voth (the brother of Missionary John Voth) wanted to limit access to missionary service to those who stemmed from the Russian immigrants of the 1870s. In Canada they were called **Kanadier**, though in many cases, as with the Voths, they were really **Amerikaner** living in Manitoba or Saskatchewan. In the case of H. S. Voth, for many years the leading minister at Winkler, Manitoba, this feeling probably began with the coming to Winkler of a famous trio of Bible school teachers from the Crimea, Johann G. Wiens, (the former missionary to India), Gerhard Reimer, and Abram H. Unruh. These three launched Winkler Bible School in 1925. Evidently Voth felt overshadowed by these better educated **Russländer**. Whereas Voth served on the Board of Foreign Missions for many years, it was A. H. Unruh who was known as the educator and Bible expositor. Unruh later became associated with the Bible department at Tabor College and chaired the Conference Education Committee for many years.[43]

One of the things that ruffled the feathers of the **Amerikaner/ Kanadier** in the 1930s was the rise of the **Afrika Missions-Verein**. It had its origin among supporters of African missionary Heinrich Bartsch, all of whom were graduates or strong supporters of the Winkler school. This Society tried to persuade the Conference to support its venture. Even if A. H. Unruh and his son Abram A. Unruh were not involved in the promotion of this second independent Mission to the Belgian Congo, it appears that the son's acceptance as a missionary to India was delayed because of feelings over this and other differences between the two culturally diverse groups within the MB conference. In the end the younger Unruh was accepted for service in 1936 largely because he had married Anna Elias, the daughter of a **Kanadier**, J. M. Elias, who served as Canadian treasurer of the Board of Foreign Missions.[44]

## The Unruhs and Gadwal

Such difficulties aside, Abram A. and Anna Unruh left for India late in 1936 with four daughters, ranging in age from eight to two.[45] Following language study they were assigned to Gadwal, an area in the extreme south of the Mission's field of operation, and newly-acquired in connection with the Mahbubnagar purchase from the ABMU. Though the area had been neglected by the Baptists because of its distance from their epicenter on the east coast of India, Gadwal proved to be the most successful field in terms of numbers and self-support. The Unruhs also reincorporated the so-called Adoni field which lay on the British (south) side of the Tungabhadra River, thus giving them a large field of service. There were Christians in 160 of the more than 400 villages, an immense responsibility. Their daughter Kathryn, who had already had the experience of being bitten by a mad dog, and survived, wrote from Ootacumund: "Daddy, do you preach much? Are you busy?"[46]

**The Last Missionaries from Russia**

In 1933, most unexpectedly, the family of Jacob J. and Anna Berg Dick appeared in India, having trekked across the mountains through China from Stalinist Russia. Upon their arrival in India, they were accepted as missionaries by the mission.

Both Jacob and Anna Dick were converted at Alexanderkrone, Molotschna, in 1923, and they married two years later. Though they might have emigrated to Canada with many others during those years, they felt called to serve in mission at home. During winter months Jacob took classes in what he called a "wandering Bible school." Once Stalin introduced the first Five-year Plan, preachers like Dick were disenfranchised. They were directed to labor on the great hydroelectric dam on the Dneiper river, near Chortitza, named Dneiprostroy. Encouraged by the Lord, as he claimed, the Dicks, with their seven-year-old daughter Helga, fled the Soviet Union via Moscow, across Asiatic Russia and into northwestern China. From there they crossed the Tian Shan mountains and then the Hindukush mountains into northern India. From Kashmir they journeyed south to Delhi, to Agra, and "with the protecting hand of God on their lives," arrived in 1933 at the General Conference Mennonite Mission at Champa. Here they were given refuge and Helga, supported by the Mennonite Mission at Dhamtari, was sent to Woodstock school in Mussoorie, North India.[47]

Dick later explained how they became convinced to stay in India as missionaries:

During this time in the Orient [having already observed and learned so much about the needs of India at Champa and Dhamtari], we have come to face the question of missionary service here as a life's work. Of course we did not want our peculiar circumstances to be the only determining factor. We wanted to be certain God was leading us. Now, after prayers on the part of many, we have committed ourselves and provision has been made for service [at Kalvakurty].[48]

Henry W. Lohrenz considered their acceptance somewhat unorthodox, but once it was clear to N. N. Hiebert that the Dicks were strongly recommended by the Voths and others, he notified the constituency that Jacob Dick, despite the difficult situation from which he had come, was an ordained MB minister, and had been accepted as a new missionary. Given the financial exigencies of the time, however, it would be necessary for the Dicks' relations to help with their support.[49] By the hot season of 1936 they felt quite at home. They had spent considerable time at Ootacumund with Abraham and Katharina Huebert, who had a cottage there. Present also were Jacob and Katie Huebert Klahsen, as well as Cornelius and Martha Unruh. Dick explained to his relations in Canada: "All those mentioned here come from Russia and are working with the American Baptists."[50]

As with these Russian Mennonite Brethren, who were stateless after the Russian Revolution until they went to Canada in 1923, the Dicks (who were doubtless considered traitors to the Soviet Union) tried to obtain British citizenship from British India, but this would have meant residence in a state other than Hyderabad for one year. When this plan fell through, Dick received assurances through Benjamin B. Janz, the seasoned Mennonite "diplomat" at Coaldale, that the Coaldale MB Church would provide all the assistance required for them to land in Canada and to become Canadian citizens.[51] During their furlough the Dicks had a very busy schedule, including conferences from Coaldale to Toronto, some schooling, and some deputation. The Dicks occupied the Wanaparty station during their second term, and stayed in India throughout the war. They were accustomed to danger, Dick wrote in 1942.[52] After the war they sent Helga, age 19 to live with relatives in Leamington, Ontario, while on her way to Tabor College.[53]

### Jacob P. and Katie Huebert Klahsen

The Klahsens, also recently from Russia, came to the ABMU field as full-time missionaries in 1930. Katie and her brother Abram were left in Russia by their parents during their first furlough in 1908. While Abram was lost during the Revolution, Katie went to Canada in 1923, assisted by Cornelius Unruh and his brother Benjamin Unruh in Germany. She came in time to be reunited with her parents, the Hueberts, who were seeking citizenship in Canada. There, in Vancouver, she met Jacob P. Klahsen who had attended school in Halbstadt, Molotschna, with her brother. Klahsen survived severe wounds received during the war, as well as typhus, and spent several years in Germany where he attended university classes in Berlin and Munich. His trip to Canada via Halifax and Rosthern eventually ended in Vancouver where he went to the Baptist church attended by the Unruhs, Penners, and Hueberts. Pastor J. J. Robb baptized him and also officiated at his wedding to Katie Huebert in June 1924.[54]

As a result of an invitation from Jacob Heinrichs, who was then teaching at Northern Baptist Seminary, the young Klahsens spent three years there in preparation for mission work with the American Baptists. While back in Canada in order to obtain their own citizenship papers, they farmed at Coaldale. From there they went to India, to a station named Madira. When Katie's parents retired in 1936, the Klahsens took over their work in Suryapet, at least until John and Anna Penner moved there from Mahbubnagar. During their furlough in 1937 Katie and their children stayed at Ootacamund with the Hueberts. Jacob returned to Chicago via the Middle East to continue his studies, acquiring both a Bachelor of Divinity and a Master's degree.[55]

### The Second World War

The Second World War changed everything for the MB missionaries in India. The early war at sea brought German battleships into the Indian Ocean. Hitler launched a campaign against the Soviet Union in June 1941; Japan struck Pearl Harbor in December of that year and overran South East Asia in short order. Just when Japan was threatening the British position in India in 1942, Mahatma Gandhi's Congress Party staged its "Quit India" movement, designed to paralyze the Government into granting independence immediately. At this point, given the choice of leaving or staying, those missionaries with large families such as the Unruhs and the Hieberts preferred to risk their lives en route home. In March 1945 the Unruhs were asked to consider a return to India. Their only concern was whether the conditions that induced them to leave India, the "safety of their children," had changed sufficiently. They returned in February 1946, departing from Seattle, Washington, travelling with four other Canadians, part of the post-War wave of missionaries: Julius and Eva (Block) Kasper, Emma Lepp, and Helen Harder.[56]

The Mission also experienced the war when young Indian men from their stations arrived back from "government service" around the world. Having earned far more money than was earlier imaginable, and having been exposed to the wider world, John Wiebe suggested that the Mission would have to adjust to these new realities.[57] This, and the deaths during the war of five missionary stalwarts (Maria Harms Pankratz in 1941, John Voth and Anna Hanneman in 1943, Katharina L. Schellenberg and H. W. Lohrenz in 1945) changed the Mission's complexion sharply.

## CHAPTER 9

# The India
# Missionaries "in Station"

By mid-century, the "pioneering four" couples and several singles of the pre-Great War years had become seniors. These master builders in the hierarchy were the Pankratzes, Bergtholds, Voths, and Janzens, in the order of their seniority, and the two women Schellenberg and Hanneman. Securely in succession were others who might be termed intermediate or "journeymen" missionaries. In chronological order between 1915 and 1945, the following fit into this category: John and Maria Lohrenz, Peter and Elizabeth Balzer, John and Viola Wiebe, John N. C. and Anna Hiebert, Jacob J. and Anna Dick, Abram A. and Annie Unruh. Whereas John A. and Anna Penner and Jacob P. and Katie Klahsen carried on under the ABMU, Cornelius and Martha Unruh and the Hueberts retired during this period.

Within this context of overlapping, succeeding generations, unwritten rules were formulated to cover seniority privileges, deferences, stationing, and furloughs. Certain positions and compounds, or a combination of these, were considered more prestigious than others.[1] It also came to be assumed that seniors returned to their places following a furlough. First-time missionaries devoted themselves to language study and evangelism and said very little at Missionary Council meetings, while women were not expected to say anything. In effect, the seniors decided where those ranked below them would be stationed, who would conduct the Bible school, and who would form the executive of the Missionary Council.[2]

While the stated goal of the Mission remained evangelism in the villages and towns, station work seemed to consume more and more time. Education for children became fully developed through "boardings" at each headquarter station. In order to train converts from these schools to become village church planters and evangelists, the stabilization of the Bible school was crucial. In spite of strong suggestions from many quarters that medical work should be undertaken for its own sake, Katharina L. Schellenberg and the nurses insisted on an evangelistic purpose as their goal. Besides Shamshabad, hospitals were developed at Deverakonda under Maria C. Wall and at Wanaparty under Margaret Suderman.

## The Last Term of the Pankratzes

John and Maria Pankratz worked in America from 1926 to 1938. Their prolonged stay at home was based on health and family considerations.[3] In the fall of 1930, their furlough privileges having run out, they took up duties in a German Baptist church in Beatrice, Nebraska. During those years John Pankratz had many invitations to preach in MB churches, and even served on the Board of Foreign Missions during 1937-38. On 9 April 1938, while Pankratz was keeping the minutes, the Board decided, with some reservations, to recommend another term in India for them. Though advanced in age, it was like old times. They took up duties at Hughestown, where they had built up a station years earlier. They wished to buy the buildings back again in 1940, but had not succeeded by January 1943. By that time they were in danger of losing the whole Hughestown congregation to the Methodists or Baptists. In fact, the congregation split soon after John and Maria Pankratz moved there.[4] Regrettably, Maria Pankratz died within three years from a severe case of jaundice. Maria Wall wrote in November 1940: "If only [Maria Pankratz] would take better care of herself... but she will try to work in spite of it all." This loss induced John to retire at age 74 in 1941. He lived until 1952, cared for by his daughter Linda in the city of San Diego.[5]

## Elizabeth Janzen

Elizabeth Janzen, the widow of Frank Janzen, also returned to India in 1938 and performed useful service teaching children and helping Indian women, first at Nagarkurnool, and then at Hughestown, for some years. In many ways, her courageous return was as heroic as any. For many of these years, her son Edwin worked in India, while Arnold, a radiologist with the United States Army, was stationed in Algeria. Though all American women and children were advised to return home as the war developed, Elizabeth chose to stay, even at the height of Gandhi's "Quit India" resolution against the British.[6]

Elizabeth recovered from a "slight stroke" during the cool season of 1942-43. She had "high blood pressure" during the hot season of 1944, but wanted to see Kashmir before she left India. She planned to take that trip with missionaries Wall and Warkentin from Deverakonda during the cool season of 1944-45, and she also hoped to return home in the spring of 1946 by way of the Belgian Congo to see the work of her brother-in-law Aaron A. Janzen. It seems that these plans did not materialize, but she spent some time in Bangalore with her son Edwin and his wife in the fall of 1945. She arrived home in August of that year, and retired to Buhler, Kansas.[7] Elizabeth died unheralded in 1960. The *Zionsbote* correspondent said only that Elizabeth Janzen was one of "two weary pilgrims" who had died at Buhler. Her three sons "came from far" to be at the funeral. Abram E. Janzen, representing the Board of Foreign Missions, gave the eulogy.[8]

### John H. and Maria Voth

While the cumulative benefits of the Pankratz and Janzen years was curtailed by the unusual interruptions in their careers, the field of greatest influence was left to the Voths and the Bergtholds. Daniel Bergthold is reputed to have been the more profound theologian, but matched neither Voth's ability to communicate effectively in the *Zionsbote* nor his promotional zeal. Between 1926 and August 1943 (including two furloughs 1926-28 and 1934-37) Voth contributed more than one hundred articles in German, and welcomed the new *Christian Leader* as another channel of communication.[9] Bergthold, in this same period of eighteen years, published only nineteen such articles, concentrating on a few themes.

While Voth became an irritant to both Henry Lohrenz and N. N. Hiebert during the 1920s, most of the missiological positions he took were quite balanced and judicious. He was, however, critical of some aspects of both the Mission and the MB Conference. He thought that the trust fund was ill-managed, and that the Conference was losing the struggle in church extension at home. He also was quite jealous of Cornelius Unruh's ability to arouse interest in America, and opposed his plans to raise money for the ABMU during his furlough in North America in 1933-34.[10] Yet at the same time, he devoted several admiring articles to Abram and Katharina Huebert of the ABMU, who were planning to retire in India.[11] When he expressed criticism of his own country, based on bi-cultural perceptions after a generation in India, he cited Mabel Lossing (Mrs. E. Stanley) Jones, whose husband's writings were unacceptable to MB fundamentalists at home.[12]

In 1930, overwhelmed by the work, he asked how he, his wife, and two single women could be expected to cope with 3,500 Christians scattered in 120 villages among a population of 350,000. In a survey of 1,000 families he discovered 105 Christians who were not yet baptized. "Our work here is really very superficial," he exclaimed. He wanted more full-time workers for village church consolidation. He was critical of his "brown brothers" who did not seem to share his sense of responsibility for the lostness of souls.[13] Though Voth never dwelt on his many contacts with Hindus until 1943, he obviously enjoyed the prestige attached to a visit to Deverakonda by the Nizam's government leader.[14]

At the same time, Voth revealed several other sides to his character. At the preparation of the manuscript *Our Mission Among the Telugus* in 1939, John Wiebe noted that Voth wanted to stand out as an "individual," having clearly topped all the others in terms of converts and Christian membership at Deverakonda.[15] At that time the number of "baptized believers" claimed was 11,943, but these figures by then encompassed ten stations. Voth's colleagues had serious difficulties with these 1939 figures, since it was Voth who had already claimed three thousand converts for Deverakonda ten years earlier when there were only four thousand in total on five stations. The "official" statistics of 1970 indicated that Deverakonda had only 1,877 church members.[16]

He also never let up on the issue of designated gifts. Almost to his last days Voth protested any attempts to channel all giving into the general treasury. Already at home, and probably ill, he voiced his complaint that Wiebe's revision of the India budget in 1943 was creating hardships at Deverakonda. Henry Lohrenz always remained sensitive to Voth's supporters "in certain quarters." Once Voth's influence had abated and majority opinion favored an equalization of appropriations according to need, designated gifts were not discouraged, but appropriations were downsized accordingly.[17]

Voth's last term was shortened by ill health. After returning home in 1942, he died of heart failure in Tulsa, Oklahoma, the following year. John Wiebe, who observed Voth in his last months on the field, found him with an ailing heart, quite deaf, and very fatigued from all the requests that came to him. His widow Maria lived until 1968.[18]

## Daniel and Anna Bergthold

During the term when Bergthold had openly criticized the Board at home (1933-1939), he set up the Mission's own press, and began to print *Suvarthamani* and other papers like *The Harvest Field*. Once the Wiebes were established at Mahbubnagar, the press was moved there. Later, a Bergthold memorial press building was created.[19] In 1937 Bergthold undertook to complete a well project at Nagarkurnool and, with the help of J. A. Penner, erected a windmill. One catches a glimpse of family solidarity in spite of separation from children in his letter to daughter Martha, age 26, in 1935. While pursuing her own career in America she helped with Lydia's and Henry's education expenses. The youngest, Samuel, was then at Kodaikanal. Father wrote: "We would not have known how to support them if it had not been for your generosity all these years."[20]

Daniel and Anna Bergthold went back for one more term, their sixth, in February 1941, before America became directly involved in World War II. They returned in the spring of 1946 and settled in Alhambra, California. While he was prepared to concede that India should be politically free he still believed that "unlimited independence, plus the greatest measure of civilization, will never break the shackles of idolatry and sin; this can only be made possible through faith in the Gospel, which is the power of God."[21] Daniel Bergthold died of heart failure towards the end of 1948. Anna Bergthold lived until 1957.[22]

## The Last Years of Katharina L. Schellenberg and Anna Hanneman

These two unmarried pioneers, while working with John and Maria Lohrenz at Shamshabad, had very productive years between 1926 and the war years. While Hanneman took one furlough during these years, for health reasons, Schellenberg took none. She vacillated about this for years. Though she suffered from "nervous exhaustion" in 1930, having come through a long building period in which her hospital (1928) and bungalow (1929) were completed, she wondered what she would do in America. If she went home in 1936, would she be allowed to return? She chose to stay, unafraid of the upheavals caused by Gandhi's agitation, and taking her rest by trips to Bangalore and Kashmir, or to visit her friends Wall and Warkentin at Deverakonda. Having reached the point where she was "too tired to do what she liked," she died at her work on 1 January 1945 in her 74th year.[23]

Nearing her 70th year, Schellenberg ruminated on the virtues of her single state. She did not openly ask "why marry at all?" but inferred that remaining single, as she and Hanneman had done, could be a viable option for young women schooled at Shamshabad, if only India's cultural demands in matters of marriage could be broken down. She told the story of Mara (the grieved one), whom she had met in Kashmir. Mara was denied marriage twice because the man she liked was perceived to be above her socially. When she was pushed into a marriage with someone from her caste, but who did not meet her educational level, she remained unhappy.[24]

In connection with her long medical service to India's poor, Schellenberg raised the question whether these people were worth serving and saving. "At a time like this when life seems to be counted so cheaply, and where so many have to lay down their life [sic] in this great world struggle [the War], it sometimes seems almost ridiculous to fight for and work with some poor life and spend time, energy and means to save it. Yet that is our work, to go on undauntedly and do what we can, even if it does not seem to be worth very much." She realized that God would do the "weighing and balancing" as to what was worthwhile, and his view would be just. She did not want to be "found wanting."[25]

Anna Hanneman, though 20 years younger than her colleague Schellenberg, may be considered among the seniors of this period, especially since she died at the early age of 52 in 1943. She built up a reputable middle school at Shamshabad and became involved in the debate about the number and location of the middle schools. Eventually this was resolved by having one central high school, first at Shamshabad, and four middle schools instead of one as she recommended. She kept requesting that a full-time couple be sent to take responsibility for such a central school, and she preferred to see a man in the principal's position. In the matter of meeting government educational standards and curriculum, she was reminded by H. W. Lohrenz in 1939 that the policy of the AMBM was clearly to train for Christian growth and eventual evangelism of their own people. This did not lighten the pressures on her, and she felt the strain physically.[26]

Except for her declining health, Hanneman might have made quite a mark in India. She served as treasurer of the Missionary Council during John Lohrenz' furlough and Voth liked her editorial work.[27] Though Katharina Schellenberg was critical of the haste with which people left the work in the plains for the hills,[28] she understood Hanneman's need to seek periods of rest in Bangalore. The latter admitted defeat in the attempt to "win the victory over my physical and spiritual weaknesses." Henry Lohrenz wrote of the difficulty "of distinguishing between bodily ailments and the conflicts with the spiritual powers of darkness." In May 1933, while on furlough, with the help of Reedley pastor George B. Huebert, who was holding meetings in Bakersfield, she sought spiritual healing to overcome her despondency, even if she could not always enjoy full physical strength for her work. On that occasion, following prayer over her by members of the church, Hanneman experienced "the power of God" coming over her, and felt "anointed with the oil of gladness." She wrote: "God did not see fit to remove every weakness at that moment, but from that day, He has continued His work. God has done nothing less than a miracle." She more readily found "God's grace sufficient for her."[29] Hanneman returned to America in September 1940 and died of a stroke in February 1943 in her fifty-third year.[30]

### The Apprentices Become the Journeymen

Those missionary couples of intermediate rank who remained in India until the period of great change from 1957 to 1960 were John H. and Maria (Klaassen) Lohrenz and Peter V. and Elizabeth (Kornelsen) Balzer. Among the women were Maria C. Wall, who arrived in 1915 and Helena L. Warkentin in 1920.

Much has been written about John Lohrenz. He was a source of strength to his brother Henry at home in this critical period for Tabor College and the Board of Foreign Missions. John matured into a shaper of the Mission, partly through his extensive writings. Though his was a pedantic and plodding style compared to Voth, Lohrenz made his influence felt through repeated emphasis of certain themes. As Missionary Council treasurer, a position he held for about three decades, Lohrenz was irritated that J. W. Wiens could not seem to separate his official duties as Board treasurer from his personal interest in, and perhaps even favoritism toward, missionaries such as John Voth. As treasurer in India, Lohrenz hammered away at Hillsboro's failure to take into account the adverse currency exchange costs. He was also much more decisive than Henry in the matter of designated gifts. John must have been quite upset when in 1939 the Missionary Council restored the subsidies for preachers to a former level. This only increased the requests for assistance and slowed indigenization.[31] Cornelius Unruh would have agreed.

Faced with the prospect of another famine in the middle of the decade, Lohrenz evinced a simplistic view of India's poverty. He wrote that "it is a small thing for God to give daily bread to the millions of India!" Perhaps he was not aware of the basic causes of the many terrible famines in the political economy that the British had fashioned since the 18th century.[32] Nor could one expect him to have asked why the Nizam was not making rice available at moderate prices in times of drought when he was one of the richest men in the world. At about the same time Peter Balzer rationalized the withholding of God's blessing on India by reinforcing the myth that the Indian people were themselves to blame: "When we note the excesses of the heathen, is it any wonder that God withholds his blessing in order to in some way draw these people to Him."[33]

More significantly, Lohrenz was quite disturbed that there was no clear set of principles and policies for many facets of the work. Often during the 1930s and 1940s he asked for such a statement. He could hardly have been satisfied with the new constitution of 1936, especially if it really meant greater "centralization" in Hillsboro. He was not afraid to tell his brother that learning how to run the Mission was a reciprocal thing, not one-way from Hillsboro.

At Shamshabad Lohrenz became known as the chief builder of that station, having completed the hospital in 1928, the ladies' bungalow in 1929, the well in 1931, and the church in 1933.[34] Also at Shamshabad Maria Lohrenz helped Anna Hanneman with the boardings, and took charge when the latter was on furlough or seeking to recoup her health in excursions to Bangalore.[35]

### Peter and Elizabeth Balzer

The Lohrenzes and the Balzers, like Abraham and Maria Friesen before them, were childless couples. While the Lohrenzes wrestled with the question of adoption and thought of taking in a Russian Mennonite child, the Balzers never seem to have done so. Both Maria

Lohrenz and Elizabeth Balzer were frequently sidelined by illness. Maria, despite her depression at such times, was vigorous. She underwent a serious operation in Secunderabad and survived, whereas Elizabeth's illnesses associated with her spinal damage limited the work she could undertake in India or at home.[36]

Despite this weakness, Elizabeth Balzer carried a significant share of the work, as her reports and her editorial role in the *Harvest Field* attest. Her story does, however, suggest that insufficient attention was given to careful screening of candidates as to their health. If ordained missionary spouses were indeed expected to be missionaries, to carry responsibility for a school or dispensary, then the qualifications for married women should have been as rigorous as for single women who were employed full-time. But even after 1947 they were not expected to meet the requirements for being "in charge," namely "a college education" and a "theological course."[37] In any case, the Mission could ill afford to carry the infirm, and perhaps should not have sent childless couples to India if providing a Christian family model was important.

It was unfortunate that the Balzers' very first furlough had to be an extended one, from 1930 to 1934. Nicolai N. Hiebert explained at the 1933 conference that they could not go back in that year for two reasons: financial stringencies and Elizabeth's health. Balzer was unhappy with this, for if the Bergtholds could leave in August 1933, as explained in Chapter 8, when they were asked to stay until after the conference in October, why could they not go back and, by inference, be employed and salaried as missionaries? Lohrenz had to reassure the Balzers they were not being pushed aside. It was Elizabeth's probable need for further convalescence that influenced the board's decision. They stayed home until 1934. Fortunately Balzer found employment in a Bible school at Hooker, Oklahoma during 1933-34.[38]

Peter Balzer's deployment or "stationing" brought him into responsible positions not given to most first term workers. During the first Lohrenz furlough (1928-29), he took charge of Shamshabad, conducted the Bible school, and supervised the construction in progress. In 1936 the Balzers were living at Shamshabad again while the Lohrenzes were in America for further education. At the same time Balzer also had charge of Nagarkurnool while the Bergtholds were on furlough. In between they lived at Wanaparty, where they dedicated a church in September 1936.[39] While earlier misgivings about the Balzers were largely erased, they took furlough in 1942 when the Unruhs and Hieberts left because of wartime fears for their children, even though this created severe shortstaffing. The Balzers returned to India in the spring of 1945.

## Maria Wall and Helen Warkentin: an Inseparable Team

The American nurse Maria Wall became closely tied to Deverakonda, along with Helen Warkentin, the Canadian teacher. Wall's earliest experiences were with Katharina L. Schellenberg. Now at an intermediate stage in their span of service, Wall and Warkentin labored together at Deverakonda from 1920 to 1957. Infrequent correspondents, they nevertheless carried the burden of the hospital and educational work for those years. They were among the unsung heroes of the Mission. Helen gave one of the best descriptions of station schools, called "boardings." Not only did the children from the villages do the state curriculum; they also received training for a life of service.[40] When the Voths went on furlough in 1936-37, Wall and Warkentin were left with the responsibilities of the station but without the corresponding additional salary. In fact, one of the married men stationed elsewhere would have been "in charge."

While she was on furlough Warkentin had charges brought against her at Deverakonda. These came from discontented teachers and a few other disgruntled persons who had been disciplined spiritually. Nevertheless, she had widespread support in the Deverakonda field. Both the Missionary Council, which investigated them, and the Board at home, dismissed the charges.[41]

During the war, these women faced Deverakonda, "the Hill of the Gods," again. They experienced the death of Maria Pankratz in 1941, the departures of Hanneman and the Voths because of illness, and saw the Hieberts and Unruhs depart in favor of protecting their families. Shorthanded on the field, they lived through the "Quit India" movement of 1942 and the terrible drought of the next year when they stayed down in the plains. Wall had inadequate medicine and Warkentin little food to feed her children and orphans.[42]

When Warkentin was involuntarily retired in 1957, having worked at Deverakonda for thirty-seven years, she was widely honored as "Mother Helen Leena Warkentin of Deverakonda." She was very effective as a missionary teacher in bringing forward leaders for the Mennonite Brethren Church of India. The well-known M. B. John, one of the early India MB leaders, wrote of her: "I had the unique privilege of being one of her favourite students from 1920 to 1926." She was very devoted to the most unfortunate of her pupils, the orphans.[43]

### The Juniors or Apprentices

The first-term missionaries during the depression years were John and Viola (Bergthold) Wiebe (1927) and John N. C. and Anna (Jungas) Hiebert (1929). Both couples were from Mountain Lake, Minnesota. In addition, Jacob J. and Annie Dick, with daughter Helga, arrived in 1933, having come across the Chinese mountains from Stalin's Russia. Eventually, since they had family in Coaldale, Alberta, and received Canadian citizenship during their first furlough (1939-41), they came to be thought of as **Russländer** Canadians, just like the immigrants of the 1920s. The first of these to be accepted, as noted in the previous chapter, were Abram A. and Annie Unruh of Winkler, Manitoba. As a son of Abram H. Unruh, A. A. Unruh was nephew to Cornelius and Heinrich Unruh of the ABMU. Three single women, whose work will be discussed below, completed the wartime roster of the AMBM until 1946.

### Enlarging the Sphere and Changing the Focus

The careers of these first-term missionaries could not flourish by pioneering building programs. Enlargement of the field of activity came slowly. Kalvakurty was added in the 1920s, but the acquisition of the former Palmur field eluded them in 1927. This area, which encompassed the Mahbubnagar, Jadcherla, and Gadwal fields, was not acquired from the ABMU until 1936-37, and then only after lengthy negotiations between Henry Lohrenz and J. C. Robbins in New York.[44] An opportunity presented itself in 1926, but N. N. Hiebert turned back the offer without consulting the Missionary Council in India. John Lohrenz was very upset by this, because he saw this as the "greatest opportunity [perhaps for themselves] for the development of our Mission here in India."[45] But his brother thought such an opportunity was likely to recur, and he recommended acquisition when this was possible. As it was, John and Maria Lohrenz were not in India when these developed stations were purchased from the American Baptists.

With such a possibility in mind, however, John Lohrenz formulated a strategic plan whereby the addition of this area, including Jadcherla on the railroad, southwest of Shamshabad, and west
of Wanaparty, would give the AMBM a new focus, a strategic center
far from Deverakonda, which was actually extracted from the
Nalgonda district. Though Mahbubnagar was a larger center it could
not compete with the twin cities of Hyderabad and Secunderabad
as the chief urban center providing goods and services. Yet the railroad junction at Jadcherla would provide a new hub for the AMBM,
and the outlying stations from Deverakonda and round to Wanaparty
were connected by adequate roads.[46]

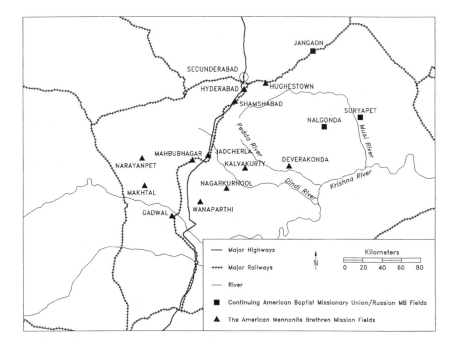

In time, the epicenter of the AMBM, in line with Lohrenz' vision, was moved to Mahbubnagar from Shamshabad by the development of the central high school there, and after 1950, the creation of the central hospital at Jadcherla.

## The Wiebes and the Matter of "Stationing"

The acquisition of Mahbubnagar had vast implications for John and Viola Wiebe. Their experience illustrates the perennial problem of stationing. During their first term they had to satisfy themselves with serving at the undeveloped stations at Kalvakurty and Janumpet. It is clear that Wiebe was one of those missionaries who would have liked to have pioneered in a new location. Hence he chafed at the fact that the treasury was too empty for him to build where he was, while others, obviously John Lohrenz, were completing the compound at Shamshabad.[47] By 1933, when the Bergtholds returned, they had to vacate Nagarkurnool. All seniors, no matter how self-effacing at other times, expected after a furlough to return to the stations they had built. There was in effect an unwritten rule that rarely went unobserved: first-term missionaries had to move into and out of undeveloped stations or, like the Balzers, move ahead by taking short-term responsibility for a large developed station.

Even if a missionary thought it should be otherwise, Wiebe found that any request for higher appropriations could not be decided without recriminations, emotions, and disunity.[48] For this reason John Wiebe wrote Henry Lohrenz that "we need a definite assignment." Lohrenz had received a similar plea from his brother John a decade earlier. Wiebe said, in effect, that those who did not "have charge" of a field were considered junior, inferior, and were to be patronized. He wrote: "If we have five fields, but one is downgraded, it is natural to become rebellious about it. I struggle long and hard against such feelings. Those who consider others are thought of as weaklings."[49]

Whatever the criteria for "rating" a field, whether the number of unevangelized people, or results, or whatever people were told at home as justification for carving out another field requiring a station compound setup, the junior missionaries had to have patience.

Once back from their furlough (1935-36), and having learned much, it was not surprising to note that the Wiebes, who might have been given Nagarkurnool or Wanaparty, jumped at the chance to take Mahbubnagar, the station acquired from the ABMU in 1937. Once assigned there, they were indeed grateful for this "definite assignment." John A. and Anna Penner were glad to turn that station and the charge of Jadcherla over to them. But staying there was not guaranteed, and confirmation did not come without further tensions about stationing. For example, in 1939, when the Bergtholds went on furlough, the question of stationing someone there was placed on the agenda. Would it be the Hieberts or the Wiebes who had seniority? Once the confirmation came that they would stay at Mahbubnagar, Wiebe admitted: "we had inward struggles about this, but we are glad in the conviction that the Lord is with us."[50]

The Hieberts' experience with stationing was somewhat different in that their path went from places of some rank to lowly Kalvakurty. As confusing as this may be to the observer, in their first term they vacated Shamshabad, moving to Hughestown to make way for the Balzers who, as senior people, took Shamshabad and the Bible school during the Lohrenz' furlough. In their second term Hughestown had become available when Maria Pankratz died in 1941 and her husband went home. In 1942, as the Voths returned home permanently, the Hieberts found the Balzers claiming Deverakonda and had sufficient influence to move the Bible school there from Shamshabad. When the Lohrenzes were induced to take Hughestown because the Dicks apparently refused to leave Shamshabad, the Hieberts were sent to Kalvakurty, lowest on the prestige ladder, and still used as a "moving-up" place. All of this took two full sessions of the Missionary Council. At these meetings Hiebert argued for more equitable appropriations for the newest stations so that they could be built up to standard, for the sake of the missionaries, the prospective graduates of the Bible school, and others who looked to the compound for employment.[51] After all this, the Hieberts were probably glad to leave for America in that year, even risking wartime travel.

Involved in the seniority ladder was the question of furloughs, always a sensitive issue. These were pursued as rigorously as in any modern-day association concerned about vacation privileges. The feelings aroused may be illustrated from a summer Missionary Council meeting, where the matter of Voth's furlough was on everyone's mind, if not on the agenda. Wiebe observed how sensitive some were if others did not offer encouragement to anticipate the furlough coming, and how hurt they were if someone pushed their rightful claim to furlough too much.[52]

Whereas the Hieberts and the Unruhs, among missionaries with children, returned home in 1942 because of the war, the Wiebes and Dicks stayed in India throughout that year. Wiebe advocated a novel idea to help with understaffing: young single men "in close touch with the Master" should "now come and help till the very serious crisis has been bridged."[53] Actually, the Wiebes stayed in India undisturbed for ten years without a furlough from 1936 to 1946. Without them understaffing would have been most severe.

## Should Mahbubnagar Have Been Acquired?

While Voth and Bergthold diverged widely on missiological questions, as the next chapter will show, Voth supported Bergthold in his argument against the acquisition of Mahbubnagar in favor of reaching into more unevangelized areas.[54] Bergthold believed that the whole settled compound approach was not consistent with the Apostle Paul's way of doing missions, and that by acquiring Mahbubnagar they were saying that Paul was wrong, the Mission right, and that there was more money in America. Faced with this criticism, Wiebe wrote an elaborate rationale, invoking the Apostle Paul's method of keeping Antioch as a center from which to move out. Centering on certain areas was justified, even as Voth had justified building up Deverakonda.[55] Bergthold disagreed with his son-in-law on this point, resorting also to the model of the great Apostle. He argued for a new, totally "unevangelized," field, knowing that the Baptists had worked the Mahbubnagar area since 1898. What he had in mind was certainly remarkable. He suggested turning to the Chensulus, who lived on a plateau to the south. Who could be challenged to come out for such a task? "It will require a heart full of compassion, patience and self-sacrifice to live among the poorest of India's teeming population." This was also, interestingly, the home of "panthers, jaguars, tigers, several species of deer, and bear and, of course, various kinds of monkeys."[56] The Chensulus never were fully evangelized.

If Wiebe could not build, he wanted at least to utilize the large buildings by centralizing some institutions there. In 1938 he proposed planting a strong, complete middle school in Mahbubnagar, rather than continuing with the present two such schools at Deverakonda (Helen Warkentin) and Shamshabad (Anna Hanneman). Interesting too was his argument that the indigenous Christians should have more of a democratic say in the location of such schools and that, of course, they should pay accordingly.[57]

## The Hieberts: Handling Illnesses

As in earlier decades there were frequent illnesses, involving particularly mothers and children. The first and second terms of the Hieberts especially were marked by many such anxieties. John Hiebert and Anna Jungas were married in the summer of 1927, and the first six of nine children were born within ten years, four of them in India during their first term. Concern for the health and well-being of their family rose sharply in 1932 when Helen Luetta died very young, and other family illnesses seemingly followed at regular intervals in the next few years. For them and for Anna it seemed imperative to spend as much time in the hills as possible. John wrote in July 1935: "Bringing up children in this heathen land is attended by many problems. It is not easy to leave children at a tender age so far away [at Ootacumund], but we are happy to report that God is giving grace for this too."[58]

Hiebert wrote about the nervous strain on all missionaries in 1939, and all held their breath when Viola Wiebe became "distressingly ill" during the Christmas recess in 1939-40, while her son Paul was very ill with a throat infection.[59] As always, the missionary family rallied round during illnesses. For example, when Helen Luetta died and was buried in St. George's Cemetery, all families were there except the Bergtholds. Maria Wall, Katharina L. Schellenberg, and Margaret Suderman all converged on Wanaparty when John and Anna were both ill in 1934.[60] Even without such experiences there was much more visiting, in this age of the car, especially on the Shamshabad compound, which was on the way to shopping in Hyderabad.

### Single Women of the 1930s

The three single women added to the missionary force during this period were Margaret Suderman, a Canadian nurse from Morden, Manitoba (1929), Catharine A. Reimer, an American nurse from Buhler, Kansas (1931), and Anna Suderman, an American teacher from Michigan (1938). Anna Suderman travelled to India with Margaret Suderman and Helen Warkentin, who were returning from furlough. The two Sudermans formed a formidable team at Wanaparty for two decades, while Reimer served only one term. While Margaret Suderman and Catharine Reimer did not leave behind many letters or reports, Anna Suderman made up for them by her prolific writings, sometimes in a controversial manner. While Anna too was fairly typical of first termers in that she did not correspond much with the Board of Foreign Missions directly, she was not reticent about writing for the press. In fact, she became the most outspoken correspondent for the press, sometimes embarrassing the Board, but not until well into her second term, and in her "Memoir" of 1983.

Having nursed for some time in Detroit, Michigan, Catharine Reimer was welcomed at Hughestown, Hyderabad, in January 1931 by the Lohrenzes and Voths. Though she worked mainly with the Bergtholds at Nagarkurnool, she filled in at Deverakonda while Maria Wall was on furlough.[61]

Reimer had definite views about what needed to be done and what she would like to do in India. Perhaps even before the Jadcherla station came into the possession of the AMBM in 1937, she wanted to see a hospital built there. This question caused her considerable spiritual struggles. In a 1937 letter to Henry Lohrenz, she confessed she was not as "surrendered and yielded" as she would like. For her furlough in 1939 she went to Bakersfield, California, where she claimed to have "absolutely surrendered" her life to God. There she was still wrestling with the question: is the project of a "Maternity Hospital and an Industrial Home for Women" in Jadcherla something God wants me to do, or is this just my own will? "If God has now given the MB this station," she wrote directly to the Missionary Council in India, "am I to see in this the hand of God?" At the same time as she was succumbing to what the Lohrenzes considered an unhealthy "*Geistesbewegung*" (a form of Pentecostalism), she was finding quite a bit of support for her Jadcherla project. She claimed that "the Lord had put it into her heart to pray for $15,000 for this project." While she was using the George Mueller "faith mission" approach through prayer alone, those in Hillsboro and Shamshabad wondered whether they would be able to use her in the Mission. Though she was made welcome to return to India, she never did. John Lohrenz wrote that "if she cannot have her way she may leave us and join the Pentecostals."[62]

As for Margaret Suderman from Winkler, Manitoba, she trained as a nurse and then supported herself while taking Bible classes at Moody Bible Institute in 1927-1928. Throughout her time in India, especially after Anna Suderman from Michigan joined her at Wanaparty, Margaret left communication to Anna. Interesting, however, was her comment upon arriving on the field: "How did our people ever find a mission field here?"[63] It was not clear whether she found it hard to adjust to the environmental extremities of the Deccan, and therefore questioned the wisdom of the choice, or whether, as her first writing assignment shows, she was overwhelmed by the plight of the widows and the orphans. She found the treatment of widows abusive in the extreme. Because of a plague of unusually deadly diseases, she found herself providing healing for these ostracized persons and for children bereft of their parents. Clearly, she felt the strain of the work and was glad to leave on her first furlough in 1936.[64] Her second term extended from 1938 to 1946.

Like almost every other missionary Anna Suderman seemed anxious to convey her first impressions of India. Whereas Margaret was taken up with orphans and widows, Anna focused on the caste system. She was thoroughly convinced that the outcastes' "only chance of advancement is in Christianity."[65] After she completed her language training she was assigned to work at Wanaparty with Margaret Suderman, where the Balzers were in charge. But as in the case of Maria Wall in 1915, this was achieved only after "a tug of war" in the Missionary Council.[66]

Anna Suderman's report of the 1943 Missionary Council at Deverakonda showed her style. Voth had retired and died in Oklahoma, leaving Warkentin and Wall with the boardings and hospital work, a model for the Suderman women. Conscious of the continuing war and the restrictions caused by it, Anna wrote: "the Lord's work must go on in spite of war and rumors of war. Satan's hosts must be conquered." Then, in the third person, she stated that "the Wanaparty sisters are thankful for the addition of a few necessary rooms [a second bedroom and a small office] to their dwelling." Clearly, this was not the bungalow they wanted, but they were grateful for such improvements.[67] After five years as the boardings supervisor at Wanaparty, she wrote Henry Lohrenz of the discouragements she encountered. Given the difficulties in getting food supplies, she wondered if it would not be better to close the schools and simply take to the villages to evangelize. It was obvious that most of the graduates of their schools were mainly concerned about upward socioeconomic mobility, not about reaching out with the Gospel to their own kind. She then compared this lack of passion for souls with the same lack at home. "The spirit of the times is to make money, but that is not only true in India, is it?"[68]

John N.C. Hiebert loading the van at Kodaikanal (June 1950): Credits: Dilwyn Studebaker. Modesto, CA

Ernest and Evelyn Schmidt, and John and Anna J. Hiebert, Mahbubnagar, c. 1950 Credits: Ernest E. Schmidt, Fresno, CA

The Women at Coonoor, 1950, in Sunday Dress
From the left: Mary Doerksen, Helen Harder, Maria Wall, Emma Lepp, Rosella Toews, Eva B. Kasper, Margaret Willems, Helena Warkentin, Edna Gerdes.
Credits: Dilwyn Studebaker

The Ladies' bungalow, Wanaparty, built by Anna Suderman and Margaret Suderman.
Credits: Dilwyn Studebaker

The Missionary Family in 1951
Back Row: Rose Krause, Helen Harder, Mildred Enns, Mary Doerksen, Rosella Toews, Margaret Willems, Edna Gerdes, Emma Lepp;
Next Row Standing: Julius Kasper, Ernest and Evelyn S. Schmidt, Beatrice K. and Herman Warkentin, Anna J. and John Hiebert, Mildred H. and Dilwyn Studebaker, Abram and Anna E. Unruh;
Seated: Margaret Suderman, Maria Wall, John and Maria K. Lohrenz, the H.K. Warkentins (parents of Herman), Peter and Elizabeth K. Balzer, Helena Warkentin, and Anna Suderman;
Children Kneeling: Gwen Hiebert, Margaret Unruh, Elizabeth Hiebert, Joanne Hiebert, and Louise Unruh.
Others: Schmidt, Warkentin, Kasper, and Studebaker children
Credits: Beatrice K. Warkentin, Fresno, CA

Missionary Children at Kodaikanal, about 1954:
Back Row: Paul and Herold Dick, David and Paul Wiebe, Donald Unruh; Front Row: Garth and Garry Schmidt, Jackie Kasper, Willie Dick, Marilyn Wiebe, Elizabeth Dick.
Credits: Ernest E. Schmidt, Fresno, CA

The Board of Foreign
Missions, c. 1950:
From the left: J.B.
Toews, H.S. Voth, Waldo
Hiebert, P.R. Lange,
John Baerg, J.A. Harder,
H.H. Janzen, G.W. Pe-
ters, and A.E. Janzen,
secretary.
CMBS/F

The Missionary Family in 1958:
Back Row: Emma Lepp, Helen Dueck, Helen Harder, Margaret Suderman, Margaret Willems, Anne Ediger;
Next Row: Henry Poetker, George Froese, Henry Krahn, Katie Siemens, Rosella Toews, Marie Riediger, Regina Sudennan;
Next Row: Anne B. Froese, Alice B. Krahn, Edna Gerdes, Anna Suderman, Jake and Ruth B. Friesen, young couple unknown, Ted Fast;
Seated: Julius and Mary D. Kasper, Viola B. and John A. Wiebe, Peter V. and Elizabeth K. Balzer, Annie E. and A.A. Unruh, unknown, Esther H. Fast;
(Also Froese, Krahn, Friesen, Kasper, and Fast children).
CMBS/F

India MB students at Yeotmal Seminary, 1960s:
Back row: K. Nathaniel, J. Paranjyothy, R.S. Lemuel, Kenneth Bowman, principal, N.P. James, B.S. Joseph, M.A. Solomon; Front row: Spouses of Paranjyothy, Lemuel, Joseph, and James.
CMBS/F

Bethany Bible Institute Teachers, Shamshabad, 1969:
Standing: Peter M. Hamm, V.K. Rufus, N.P. James, S. Joseph; Seated: Betty H. Hamm, Mrs. N.P. James, Hannah Kompelly Joseph, Mrs. Paranjyothy, Mrs. D.J. Arthur, Katie Siemens.
CMBS/F

Education Committee, 1958
Seated: A.S. John, Gadwal; J.A. Wiebe, Mahbubnagar; R. David, Shamshabad; P.V. Balzer, Shamshabad; B. Abraham, Hughestown; Anna Suderman, Deverakonda; Anne Ediger, Gadwal; Edna Gerdes, Wanaparty; Katie Siemens, Nagarkurnool;
Standing: Benjamin, Wanaparty; D.J. Franz, Hughestown; A.A. Unruh, Wanaparty; Premayya, Shamshabad; Henry Poetker, Hughestown; M.B. John, Mahbubnagar; Julius Kasper, Gadwal; N. S. Abram, Kalvakurty; Henry Krahn, Narayanpet; Gerhard; K.E. Paul, Shamshabad; Caleb Bella, Narayanpet; Emma Lepp, Shamshabad.
CMBS/F

The young P.B. Arnold, Sharada and child, Wanaparty: J.Friesen, Reedley, CA

R.R.K. Murthy and his family, c. 1960 CMBS/F

The Missionary Family of 1964:
From the left: Regina Suderman, Emma Lepp, Frances and Paul Hiebert, Rosella Toews, Peter and Arlene Block, Esther and Ted Fast, Frieda Neufeld, Helen Dueck, Anne Ediger, F.C. Peters, Ruth Friesen, Katie Siemens, Jake Friesen, Anne Froese, Marie Riediger, George Froese, *(Unknown)*, Anna Frantz, Henry Poetker, Annie Unruh, Peter Funk, A.A. Unruh, Helen Harder, *(Unknown)*.
CMBS/F

The Ordination of P.B. Benjamin Gollipelli Village, 1966
A.A. Unruh, Preacher Gerhardt, and H.P. Poetker officiating.
CMBS/F

Some Members of the Governing Council, Mahbubnagar, 1970s:
Henry Poetker standing, J. Paranjyothy, M.B. John, D.J. Arthur, B.A. George .
CMBS/F

Staff of M.B. Medical Centre, Jadcherla, A.P, 1972
In the row seated on chairs: M.C. Emmanuel, Malakpet, is on extreme
left, Jake and Ruth B. Friesen in the center, and Regina Suderman on the
extreme right.
Credits: Regina Suderman, Reedley, CA


The Secretariat at India Church Gathering, 1972:
In the foreground: Jake H. Epp, M.B. John, and Vernon R. Wiebe (kneeling); to Wiebe's left
are M.C. Emmanuel, B.A. George, and P.B. Richard.
CMBS/F

Dan Nickel on a visit with the author to Nagarkurnool, 1973, the station built by D.F.Bergthold.
Credits: Peter Penner, 1973


The India Delegation to Mennonite World Conference, Winnipeg, July1990, at the home of George and Anne Froese:
Standing, left to right: S. Solomon, Bethany Bible School, Peter and Betty Hamm (2, 4), Joseph and Hannah Kompelly (8, 9), Karuna and C. S. Joel, (11,12), Agnes and M.C. Emmanuel (13,15), Prabakar, Zephaniah, P.B. and Sharada Arnold, Jadcherla (18,21), R. S. Lemuel and his wife (22,23), Divakar Rao and his wife Pramilla, Winnipeg (seated 3rd from right), Prasangi, David Wiebe, Nebraska, his wife Lorma (seated second from right);
  Kneeling: Anne and George Froese (2,4); Seated on grass: D. Puroshotam, G. Daniel, P.S. Zechariah, friends of the Rao family (5,6), and children, and Cathy (Froese) Baerg at the end.
  Credits: Peter Penner

## CHAPTER 10

# Mennonite Brethren Missions: Theory and Strategy

In the 1930s Mennonite Brethren Bible schools frequently taught a course called **Missionslehre** (teaching about mission). It was a course based on the Book of Acts and on books borrowed from evangelicals. J. B. Toews has suggested that during the first half of the twentieth century "our theology of mission, strategy, and methods of church planting, were largely an adaptation from the Baptists without an independent study of the Scriptures to determine the New Testament patterns."[1] This observation, as well as the experience of the India mission, does raise the question about the extent to which early MB schools prepared young people for mission thinking and cross-cultural experience. Might the Conference have developed a biblical missiology (the science of missions) for its schools on the basis of the India experience?

What follows is a brief overview of Mennonite Brethren education for mission and the Indian context in which its leading missionaries experimented with theory and strategy in the pre-War decade.

### Missiology, the Mennonite Brethren, and the Bible School Movement

At the turn of the century leading Mennonite Brethren in Kansas, Minnesota, and Manitoba possessed some general knowledge of the significant missiological contribution made by the Anabaptist/ European experience of suffering and witness. They also knew something of the significance of William Carey's going to the Danish colony of Serampur in 1792. They all seemed to know about the principles of indigenization: self-support, self-government, and self-extension, as developed by Henry Venn, secretary of the Church Missionary Society between 1851 and 1866.[2] One may assume that all those missionaries who studied at Hamburg-Horn, and at Rochester between 1885 and 1914, were taught about such issues in their mission courses. If they had not also heard of the work of Rufus Anderson, they surely had heard of J. Hudson Taylor's "faith mission" concept in connection with China and how he adapted to

Chinese culture.[3] They probably knew about the developments in mission thinking and strategy as exemplified in the famed Edinburgh Conference of 1910, organized by John R. Mott.[4] As noted, Abraham J. Friesen had wanted to attend that conference but was prevented.

More broadly speaking, what developed out of the well-known modernist/fundamentalist controversy of the 1920s, as it impinged on foreign missions, was a vast network of Bible schools all over North America. For example, at Prairie Bible Institute in Three Hills, Alberta, a school launched in 1922, the entire curriculum, residential life style, worship services, and its press promoted prayer, missions, and dedication to a Christian vocation. Long before that Chicago's Moody Bible Institute became one of the leading schools in this movement toward serious Bible study and missions. Large numbers from agricultural communities, small towns, and lower income families attended these many fundamentalist schools, and thousands were propelled overseas. Those who have studied this phenomenon, however, discovered that the missionaries who came from these schools, and joined such missions as the China Inland Mission (70 percent of them women) tended to play down a well-rounded educational preparation and contributed little to the development of missiology, such as cross-cultural studies, when there was already much they could have built on.[5]

Even if many Mennonite Brethren attended these schools, and their administrators borrowed from them, there still was potential for developing a missiology which might have captivated young minds for the mission cause. Even a cursory survey of the early MB Bible schools shows up some degree of home-grown **Missionslehre**. As founding editor of the *Zionsbote*, John F. Harms must have taken his knowledge of the early MB missionary enterprise with him when he founded Herbert (Saskatchewan) Bible School in 1911. Reports from Russia and America were available also in the Winkler (Manitoba) Bible School and Bethany Bible Institute at Hepburn, Saskatchewan, both founded in the 1920s. At Bethany, the Three Hills influence toward outreach was very strong because G. W. Peters and Jacob H. Epp, who both attended Prairie, taught at Bethany in its early years. The many MB students who attended Prairie Bible Institute and then taught in MB Bible schools undoubtedly strengthened the mission emphasis.[6]

A. H. Unruh, one of the founders of the Winkler Bible School, had two brothers, Heinrich and Cornelius, in India as missionaries at that time; Johann G. Wiens, another of the school's founders, had actually served as a missionary on the same Telugu field in the first decade of the century. It is clear that Winkler emphasized MB history and missions well before others precisely because of this reason. The son of Abram Unruh and the nephew of Heinrich and Cornelius Unruh, Abram A. Unruh, a graduate of 1928, wrote that "encouraging enthusiasm for missions is not enough. The school must have a program which prepares its students for their responsibilities in the mission field."[7] Since most of the later Bible schools in Canada were staffed by graduates of Winkler Bible Institute, it may be assumed that their courses of study also included these subjects. Even then some graduates who compared the mission emphasis at Winkler with that of interdenominational schools, such as Winnipeg Bible Institute, found Winkler relatively weak in this regard.[8]

In the United States the foremost training center, as noted, was the Bible Institute organized by H. W. Lohrenz and N. N. Hiebert in 1930 at Tabor College. The MB congregations in America were not far behind Canada in the number of locally-supported Bible schools that attracted young people during winter months.[9]

It is admittedly difficult to determine just how much MB church and mission history was taught at MB schools. A survey of persons who had experience in MB Bible schools in the 1930s and 1940s only confirmed the view of David Ewert that "the history of missions got short shrift in most of our schools."[10] The Canadian Conference as such did not specifically encourage the teaching of Mennonite and MB history until 1945. This recommendation grew out of an elaborate report on the Bible schools by George Pries, another teacher at Winkler.[11]

**The Challenge from Gandhi**

If it is true that Mennonite Brethren schools were much more oriented toward **Glaubenslehre** (matters of faith) than **Missionslehre**, how much less of Indian history must have been known by Mennonite Brethren unless they were reading the national press? Yet there were interesting developments in India, and J. H. Voth and John Lohrenz occasionally shared their views of

Mahatma K. Gandhi, who emerged as a challenger to all Christian mission.[12]

The absence of training in missiology meant that many missionaries and members of the Board at home were prepared to accept British India's pronouncements that the British were good for India and that India was far from ready for independence.[13] For thinking Indians, however, who knew their history under the British, it was much like having "Christianity without Christ" in their country. In 1930 John Voth was not aware to what extent Gandhi had come to believe in the "four-fold ruin," economic and political, cultural and spiritual, that British India had brought to the subcontinent in the past 150 years.[14]

Under Gandhi's leadership India produced a home-grown method for its own redemption. Gandhi had returned home to India from South Africa in 1915. There he had developed **Satyagraha**, a strategy of nonviolent civil disobedience against white racism and discrimination. Gandhi was not wholly against Britain if India was compensated fairly in terms of political freedoms. In fact, he favored aiding Britain against Germany if that were the result. When Britain failed to deliver on the promises of 1917 for considerable advances along the path to self-government and added unprovoked repressive measures to the India Bill of 1919, the Indian National Congress was disenchanted, to say the least. When demonstrations led to the Amritsar Massacre (April 1919), and Conservatives in England applauded the perpetrator, General Dyer, Gandhi turned against the Empire, declaring a **hartal** (complete work stoppage) against this "infamous" government that had proven itself unworthy of support.[15]

Taking the long view, the missionaries and Gandhi were working toward similar goals, **harijan** (outcaste) uplift, by vastly different means. Though mystified by him, the missionaries could not help but take notice of Gandhi, this "heathen" and "socialist," as the missionaries thought of him. John Voth claimed in 1926 that Gandhi could not help the Indian people, because the problems of India were spiritual. They required not political and economic, but spiritual solutions, even though Voth was quite aware that the Gospel had social and political implications.[16] When in 1929 Gandhi led in the declaration of independence from England, Voth told Canadian delegates he could see deeper into the mind of the Hindu and

Muslim. He believed that the Telugus were more concerned about salvation of their souls than about political independence from England. Perhaps the untouchables, yes, but he was wrong about the Hindu and Congress leaders. As a convinced pacifist, however, Voth was aware, "to the shame of militant Christian nations," that it took "Gandhi, a heathen" to teach them "the non-resistance which our forefathers for 400 years had tried to bring to the attention of the nations."[17]

Voth most certainly could not accept Charles F. Andrews' view of Gandhi as India's Mahatma (Great Soul).[18] Voth was equally skeptical of Jawaharlal Nehru, the Allahabad lawyer who had been to Harrow and Oxford for his education. In 1937 Voth saw him as pacifist, anti-English, and socialist.[19] John H. Lohrenz noted every act of civil disobedience against the British by action of the Working Committee of Congress, meeting in Allahabad, Uttar Pradesh. The *hartal*, the declaration of independence of 1929, and the Salt March to Dandi at the sea in the next year, always seemed to cause the missionaries some anxiety. Lohrenz gave some recognition to Hindu reform movements, such as the Arya Samaj. He saw it as a "reformed liberal" Hinduism, puritan, but not willing to recognize Christianity as such.[20]

This was the Indian context in which the AMBM found itself in the 1930s. Gandhi dominated the political and social scene and, to the astonishment of many, successfully applied civil disobedience and other methods to India on a large scale in his goal of achieving political autonomy.

### The Missionary Goals of John Voth

John Voth and Daniel Bergthold wrestled with the question of biblical church planting most seriously. Theoretically close, they diverged widely in practice. Both knew that the mission should not become church, and the church should not become dependent on the mission.[21] In 1925 Voth translated the four most important words of mission: "Go, preach, baptize, teach," into two broad program aims: evangelization and indigenization.[22] Evangelization meant taking the gospel to all the people for whom a missionary like Voth had taken responsibility. It was assumed that no other mission would enter the area covered by Deverakonda. Indigenization meant forming converts into believers' churches and training its members to take responsibility for self-support as well as for outreach as quickly as possible. How to achieve these goals with a united strategy, given the reality of poverty, was a problem that all involved in the India program wrestled with for many years.

John Voth was conscious at Deverakonda of the need for indigenization. He had been warned by Cornelius Unruh at Nalgonda as early as January 1917 that he should not make his preachers dependent on the Mission. Distributing money to the poor because of the shocking poverty, as had been done by Franz Wiens, was a mistake. Unruh pointed out that Christian families who received support tended to have more children. "Our whole task is to make our Christians independent," Unruh expostulated, "else we will lose everything."[23]

With this in mind, Voth began teaching self-support in 1924 for the day when his disciples must be independent. Three years later he argued for a "golden mean" between the extremes of pushing self-support prematurely, and fostering a child-like dependence. For the most part he felt he had no choice but to look on his converts, impoverished and crushed socially and economically as "children" who would need tutoring for a long time. In 1932, having worked the villages, in some cases "door to door," he discovered that the India church was not ready for the administration of their own funds, even though it already had its own "home mission." Voth knew that his program was too compound-centered, but he was also the one who most emphasized building enduring and solid institutions, to show all classes they were there to stay.[24]

Voth also had a vision of reaching the caste people. Hence he was very disappointed to have to admit only two years before retirement that among four thousand Christians at Deverakonda he had only forty-four converts from higher castes.[25] He was likely aware that some of the first mission societies in India tried to win the "upper ten thousand" of the Hindu caste system, including Brahmans. Some argued that if this could be achieved, surely the blessings of the Gospel would more than filter down to the lower castes, and to the outcastes. The famous Scot, Alexander Duff, tried this approach with limited success. Neither the American Presbyterians in the Punjab[26] nor the Church Missionary Society working in the Ganges River Valley were successful with the upper castes. Nor did Voth himself have confidence that the Brahmans would have tried to convert their untouchable servants.[27] The Brahman, Warrior, and Merchant castes who accepted the benefits of English education proved impervious to the Gospel, except in isolated cases.[28] Like Gandhi, some individuals among them were prepared to adopt certain elements of the Gospel into their value system and programs, but never wholly from Christian and biblical premises based on radical conversion. Certain Indian merchant families became partners of the British Indian commercial community, but most of the latter were at best nominal Christians. British and Indian merchants worshipped money and power in the same way.[29]

It must have been some consolation to Voth to know that most missions found themselves working almost exclusively in behalf of the poorest elements in Indian society. They naturally began to build educational institutions from the bottom of the pyramid, using the vernacular languages.[30] The best known example of how unavoidable this approach was comes from the life and work of the ABMU's John Everett Clough at Ongole. The story of his mass baptism of untouchables in the 1870s was heralded everywhere. When in 1927 Clough's widow seemed to criticize the strong social motive for upward mobility in the conversion of outcastes, Voth countered this by pointing to the fact that, of the thousands who were baptized under Clough's ministry, only a small percentage had fallen back into idolatry. Besides, as no one else, Voth had confronted the reality of trying to bring spiritual uplift to the depressed classes and knew that it was successful, at least to a degree.[31]

Increasingly Voth found the aim of indigenization frustrated by poverty as well as by the physical lack of endurance of the missionary. Abram E. Janzen faced this question in 1949: how could missionaries expect their poverty-stricken church leaders in India to do well when so many missionaries were on furlough, or in the hills during the hot season? When Voth gave his talk on "the foundation and consolidation of churches in our Mission" at the Missionary Council meeting at Shamshabad in early January 1939, he had concluded that the poverty of their converts would make this almost impossible to attain and they would be dependent on Hillsboro for some time, except for a small number of converts from among the farmer caste. And that number was discouragingly small.[32]

145

### John Lohrenz and Daniel Bergthold

Others too were finding that the twin aims of evangelism and indigenization were not easily achieved. The young John Lohrenz wrestled with this question in a paper for the Missionary Council in 1930: in view of the widespread faithlessness and breakdowns among indigenous believers in training, how does one inculcate spiritual motives and aims without taking on a fatherly role? This could only be done by avoiding the extremes of forced independence or slavish dependence. "Leading without lording" was the way Jesus had used. Lohrenz concluded that the Missionary Council should look to Pauline methods of converting, founding churches, and making them dependent on their own support.[33]

Though they diverged considerably, John Voth and Daniel Bergthold both believed that self-support rather than dependency among converts was the ideal. In this debate about withdrawing life supports both used Pauline texts, but Voth, as noted, seemed to bend more to field realities.[34] He became convinced that self-support would be long in coming. Bergthold decried the dependency syndrome, believing that he also had the Apostle Paul on his side. He wrote Henry Lohrenz twice that "we are sending the wrong signal with our money."[35] In his missiological position, published in *Unsere Mission in Indien*, Bergthold stated that "by writing this I am going strongly against the grain of those who assert that, for a successful mission, we need money and more money." He realized he could not work in India without any support, yet his call implied a radical alteration in missionary tactics.[36] His views crystallized in the midst of serious scarcity of funds in the 1930s, though he too thought the problem was more spiritual than purely financial. A lack of funds came from the absence of prayer, he said. While this economic factor and the depression may hurt the Mission, he argued that it created an opportunity to place the work on a new footing of independence from foreign funding. Where earlier courage to say no to increased funding had failed them, the new reality would make it imperative.[37]

Bergthold pointed to this mistaken policy of the last forty years. He explained that from the very moment that the AMBM had taken the first promising youngster into their boardings until he was prepared for preaching in the villages, he had been made dependent on money from the Mission. Confirming what Cornelius Unruh had found, Bergthold wrote: "No man, woman, or child, was appointed to any job without first coming to an agreement about a wage." No Madiga or Mala convert initiated anything on their own. "We pushed them into evangelism among their own people and paid them to do so." Having made them entirely dependent on North American largess, they never learned to give out the Gospel or themselves free of charge. Bergthold wanted a radical alteration in thought patterns and methodology. In his words, "it is my deepest conviction that, even if monies should again be available in rich measure, as say fifteen years ago, we should not return to the policy of driving this work with American money. . . . We are giving entirely the wrong impression with our money, both among the heathen as well as among the Christians, and the healthy beginning and end of the work will be made difficult." They simply had not been using the Pauline method of evangelizing and then moving on after several years. While it may be "100 times easier to do our work with much money," it was nevertheless a short-sighted policy, he argued. He predicted that each generation of junior missionaries would have to repeat the disappointments of the past if this policy was continued.[38]

Even before this N. N. Hiebert, informed of the depleted state of the treasury, had given a rationale for using indigenous persons wherever possible. Twenty workers, he calculated, more familiar with the language and culture, could be supported with the money for one missionary.[39]

Cornelius Unruh reinforced these views when he told the readers of the *Mennonitische Rundschau* what he had done when, during his furlough of 1933-35, his appropriations had been cut by fifty percent. In the midst of India's political unrest he feared that his Nalgonda Christians would need all the courage they could muster. He now had to put in place a new way of teaching self-support. According to Unruh, as long as they paid them, Indian workers were spoiled into thinking support from abroad would continue indefinitely. Unruh advised praying for a hard heart, or else they would not be able to stand the constant expressions of disbelief at the idea that the funds have dried up. "For the workers the adjustment is inexpressibly difficult" as "our old methods . . . lie broken at our feet." What he proposed was an earlier principle of Mennonite self-support for preachers. They would have to find employment or return to the land to support their families, except in the case of the appointed itinerant evangelists. He provided an illustration of one of his preachers who had laid aside his dress clothes for native working clothes in order to work the land. Unruh knew how difficult this was for an educated Indian.[40]

Bergthold returned to the subject two years later. He feared that as long as Indian Christians were paid to evangelize their own, they would likely never do it solely in obedience to the Holy Spirit, and would consider it the duty of the Mission. He predicted that it would require a radical political upheaval in India or a world-wide war to see a change in methods. "For me it has become a matter of the heart and conscience to adopt a more biblical method, though I may not even then be able to do more than announce that I do not agree with the current practices." Nothing disturbed him more than the fact that they as missionaries were not united in making such an adjustment.[41] Peter V. Balzer echoed the same regret in 1939: there had "never been unity . . . as to how we should proceed [on indigenization]."[42] For all that, Voth could not bring himself to cut off any of those who had become dependent on him for livelihood. Such principles of self-support were put into practice in the AMBM, as Bergthold predicted, only when indigenization could no longer be circumvented.

**The Lack of Recognition**

Even if there were differing views on indigenization, this alone need not have prevented Voth from preparing an adequate book on **Missionslehre**. His many published statements indicate that he had the ability to absorb and evaluate the writings of others and to organize his material. Peter C. Hiebert came closest to recognizing Voth's potential in this regard. He knew that Voth had been urged to remain at home in order to devote his talents to the Conference in other ways. John H. Pankratz wrote of Voth as "the unforgettable one" who had "made many contributions to our directing policies of mission work."[43] From what was said of Daniel Bergthold in retrospect, it might appear that he would have been the person to write on the science of missions. He was a devoted student of the Bible, a good teacher, had built up a fairly large library, and had very clear principles about indigenization. He did not, however, cover as many bases, nor could he place mission theory into the historical and social context like Voth. Bergthold was asked to give a mission course at Tabor College in 1946, but the notes he left behind indicate that he taught essentially the Books of Acts without much application or evidence of wide reading.[44]

There was, however, no indication that the idea of bringing such teachings together, even if it occurred to Henry W. Lohrenz, was ever pursued. In this respect the American Mennonite Mission at Dhamtari seems to have surpassed the AMBM. George J. Lapp of the Mennonite Mission published *The Christian Church and Rural India*, a well-researched missiological document, in 1938.[45]

### Reflections on the 1936 Constitution

A new constitution adopted in 1936 by the Mennonite Brethren Conference of North America offered an opportunity to strengthen the requirements for missionary education. The pre-1936 constitutions left a leadership vacuum that was filled by the strongly individualistic missionaries who pioneered the AMBM in India and who were now the seniors. While Henry Lohrenz was a good choice to succeed Heinrich Voth as leader of the Board of Foreign Missions in 1919, he had been far too busy with educational matters during this decade to do justice to the position. Nicolai N. Hiebert, as secretary for three decades, was preoccupied with the material maintenance of his family. The other reality for him always was the "weak treasury." The hard times of the 1930s pressed heavily on his spirit. Hiebert at least had been in India long enough (1899-1901) to appreciate what the American pioneers and builders of the first four compounds were going through. He and Susie had been there "to turn the key, if not to open the door," as he said.[46] Though the pioneers Pankratz, Bergthold, and particularly Voth provided him with MB **Missionslehre**, he never developed it fully. Bringing order to these ideas and making them usable in the schools was not his strong point.

Nevertheless, the preparation of a new MB General Conference constitution over a period of six years, 1930 to 1936, created an opportunity. But Voth's writings from the 1920s and early 1930s were not incorporated in the mission segment of that constitution. One does not like to think that Voth's many "practical suggestions" were pushed aside because of the coolness between him and Hiebert. As shown in a previous Chapter, Hiebert did bring together some missiological questions, but primarily under pressure to answer issues raised by Bergthold.

The constitution of 1936, while making fundamental changes in conference structures, did not strengthen the educational requirements for missionaries in the article on foreign missions. It stated only that missionaries should have the "necessary education and training" without specifying what that was.[47] Spiritual qualifications were uppermost, just as in Abraham J. Friesen's day. Other considerations, spiritual, psychological, and church-related, were considered more important than actual educational preparation. While their call, character, and loyalty to the MB Church were very important, nevertheless, more emphasis, especially before 1960, might have been placed on special preparation for overseas and cross cultural ministry. It became clear in some cases later that spirituality alone could not make up for such deficiencies. The Board of Foreign Missions did not provide the requisite policy handbook until 1947.

### Translating Missiology into Adequate Funding

If there had been a better home-grown **Missionslehre**, actively taught in Bible and Sunday schools, would this have reduced the gap between rhetoric and funding? If Voth and Bergthold agreed that the problem with their outcaste converts was spiritual, could not the same criterion be applied at home? Should the hard times under this guideline have permitted the general penury of the Conference in the 1920s, or even in the depression of confidence in the 1930s? More than once it was stated: "We have always governed ourselves by the treasury." And yet, just at the divide between the relatively prosperous 1920s and the "dirty 'thirties," H. W. Lohrenz echoed a plan, the vision of one of the missionaries. In a well-formed 1930 speech in Hepburn, Saskatchewan, he stated the potential of full staffing: if all the India fields could be fully staffed for the next fifteen years, the conference could realize the planting of one hundred "independent churches" in India.[48] This vision could not materialize at a time when understaffing prevailed.

Understaffing hurt American work much more than the Russian Mennonite Brethren on their three stations a decade or so earlier. This situation resulted from overlapping of furloughs, rather than staggering them so as to keep all stations with their preachers and Bible women adequately supervised. In his 1936 report, for example, H. W. Lohrenz stated that only eleven of thirty-two missionaries were on the seven stations. Very few prospective candidates, if there were any from all those Bible schools, could be sent. Yet money was found to bring entire families home. And money was found in 1936-37 to purchase two more fields, Mahbubnagar and Gadwal.[49] The problem of understaffing was further exacerbated when the Unruhs, Hieberts and Balzers chose to leave the field during wartime and risk the dangerous trip home. This meant that each missionary patriarch had charge of two stations.[50]

### The Neglect of Cross-cultural Education

As indicated in this Chapter, training MB missionaries for cross-cultural exposure and contextualizing the message into local cultural forms was largely neglected during this era, not only by the MB, but by Protestant missionaries generally.[51] John Voth may have been interested in pursuing such questions, but perhaps he deliberately played down such ideas which might have been misunderstood at home, especially during the modernist-fundamentalist conflict which affected some Mennonite colleges from the 1920s to the 1940s. It seems that MB missionaries in India were probably much more ecumenical and irenic in their attitudes toward missions more liberal in their theology than they ever admitted in their published statements. In 1943 John Voth recalled some of the notable liberal Christians and prominent Hindu thinkers he had met since 1909.[52] Had he lived longer he might have shared more about the cosmopolitan world in which he and his colleagues circulated.

That such education was possible and desirable may be seen from one who did explore this dimension in the mid-1930s. J. P. Klahsen became unusually well-versed in the area of cross-cultural studies when he took courses at the University of Chicago in Hinduism and ancient religious history and literature. He subsequently requested permission to continue such studies in Madras during his remaining furlough months. The ABMU secretaries in New York considered this so intriguing that they asked Klahsen's advice on the value of such studies for others. Klahsen wrote,

> It is very interesting and helpful to find the historical points of contact of ethnic religions with Christianity . . . because it helps us to understand better the minds and background of those

people, whom to lead to Christ is our first concern. We missionaries are in danger to lose the point of contact with our educated Indian Christians because we fail to appreciate that part in them which is essentially Indian.[53]

Klahsen was convinced that a person "of an independent mind and [who] comes to India with a well defined objective can succeed here as well as in any other country." He also thought it desirable for North Americans to study mission history in a South India setting. Had Mennonite Brethren from Russia and North America taken such courses, Klahsen claimed, the promise of upper-caste conversions might have been more fully realized.[54]

Neglect of this cross-cultural interest may have resulted from lack of acumen at the conference level, or lack of inter-mission contacts to spur such a project. Or they awaited someone like Gerhard Wilhelm Peters, who grew in cross-cultural understanding from a variety of educational and mission experiences. He was a 1930 graduate of Winkler Bible Institute, and then attended Prairie Bible Institute in Three Hills, Alberta, for one year. He was influential in the founding of the Hepburn Bible School and the Western Children's Mission in Saskatchewan. Peters criticized the North Saskatchewan conference leadership as being "unenlightened and uninformed" with regard to the international nature of that Mission, and challenged the Board of Foreign Missions to begin work in South America in the early 1940s. He later pursued graduate studies at Hartford Seminary in missiology, theology and philosophy of religion. Peters completed a doctoral dissertation at Hartford in 1947 entitled "The Growth of Foreign Missions in the Mennonite Brethren Church." Not only did he deal with personnel and methodology on the India, China, and Africa fields, he also included sections on geography, some anthropology, and the prevailing religions on these mission fields. This dissertation, published under that title by the MB Board of Foreign Missions in 1952, was the first documented history of MB mission work overseas, and proved very useful to all subsequent writers, especially Abram E. Janzen who became secretary-treasurer of the Board of Foreign Missions in 1945.[55]

Some cross-cultural awareness also was fostered by Mennonite Brethren Bible College in Winnipeg, which offered a special "missionary course." In 1948-49, for example, about twenty students participated in this course, which included the study of tropical diseases and other religions.[56] Those not in a position to take this course did, however, have the ability, as Vernon R. Wiebe argued, "through experience and common sense to become quietly cross-cultural."[57] All too often, missionaries arrived in India, like the young English civilian of the nineteenth century, thinking that all that was needed for cross-cultural understanding could be learned in language study or during an apprenticeship term. This approach had its limitations, as Helen Harder learned. She was unprepared for India and had the misfortune to arrive in Calcutta amidst violent Muslim agitation against the English plan of 1946 for a united India. She commented later that there should at least have been a reading course to prepare new missionaries for the cultural context into which they were entering.[58]

The missionary who most appreciated the cross-cultural value of two years of mandatory language study was Henry G. Krahn. He noted in 1957 that "we learned the radical difference between our way of thinking, our standard, our entire outlook, to those of people of the East."[59] The educational requirements in the 1961 and 1963 statements of mission principles and polities were never as onerous as they might have been, even with orientation sessions, in consideration of the cross-cultural task before them in India. Not until 1977 did the Board touch on this dimension specifically.[60]

## CHAPTER 11

# The Missionary Council in Post-War Andhra Pradesh

The Missionary Council was not oblivious to the new post-War realities, but it seemed to carry on as though there was no time-table for handing over church governance to the India MB nationals. In the same way, some seniors wanted to hold power over juniors in the established way, causing considerable grief. The missionary relationships at Gadwal, Wanaparty, and Mahbubnagar reveal how senior/junior equations worked themselves out over a period of years. In fact, it seemed like a replay of the period from 1917 to 1926.

Meanwhile, the constitutional change in the State of Hyderabad and in India generally provided an opportunity for Canadians to come to the fore in this last generation in India. The American influence remained strong, however, in resolving the post-war question of the education of their children, by electing Kodaikanal over Ootacumund.

### Bringing the Nizam Into the Union

While India became independent, the Muslim-led State of Hyderabad, landlocked in a Hindu-majority Union, could not remain so, and was aligned in 1948 by "police action." The Nizam would not accede voluntarily, and only capitulated after a tight economic blockade. This action by the forces of Jawaharlal Nehru so close to home served as the "handwriting on the wall" for the Mission. Whereas missionaries in wartime tended to take to the boats, if advised to do so, in this case they took to the borders or the hills.

One of the most complete accounts of Nehru's action against the Nizam came from the pen of Gadwal's Abram A. Unruh, whose family had removed to the hills. In the midst of the rising crisis, Peter V. Balzer suffered "heart failure and nearly died." Since he had the Bible school at Deverakonda, the Balzers requested that Unruh should come to take charge of the school. In doing so, Unruh was caught by the threat of military intervention against the Nizam. While moving about, he discovered that nearly everyone in the Mission had left by 10-11 September 1948, at the strong recommendation of the consular services. Only the Balzers remained at Deverakonda.[1]

One of those who left was Emma Lepp, only two years in India. Advised to evacuate by the United Kingdom's High Commissioner, she made her way to Ootacumund. It might have been safer in Shamshabad. Near Madras her train struck a truck loaded with potatoes. She was held up all night. On the way to Ootacumund, the locomotive of that train gave out causing another delay.[2]

Unruh sent messages to his family at Ootacumund with the departing Suderman women. He got back to Gadwal as best he could. Though all was quiet there and his Christians advised him to leave also, he stayed throughout the short period of invading action by Union troops. The Nizam's "Razakars" (Muslim reserves at best) could not have resisted for long had they tried. They were about 1,500 strong at Alampur, and the "police action" there lasted about four hours. There was, however, great fear in the compound because the Gadwal bridge across the Krishna river suffered severe damage, and invasion of Gadwal was possible. Once the Muslims of Gadwal had evacuated and the Maharani of Gadwal assured the Union forces that Gadwal was essentially defenseless, the conflict was over in two days. Some Muslim records and property were destroyed in Gadwal in the "victory celebrations." For about a week, Unruh's family was without news of him. His reward on the 23rd was the gratitude of the compound people for having stayed with them. He was able to leave for the hills a few days later.[3]

The Mennonite Brethren most threatened by Nehru's incorporation of the Nizam's Dominion were two couples working in the Baptist field: John and Anna Penner at Suryapet, whose compound east of Hyderabad city was actually bombed from the air, and Jacob P. and Katie Klahsen, at Madira east of Suryapet. The Penners actually evacuated their compound, taking about one hundred boarding children with them. Many of the Klahsens' possessions were taken, and the Christians there fled. Klahsen was able to return to his field in October. Even then, Jacob Dick, who had left Wanaparty for the border city of Kurnool, was confident that under Nehru's Union government full opportunities would be given to continue mission work.[4]

## The Canadian Generation

The Dicks, Penners, and Klahsens, all new Canadians, helped to boost the number of Canadians on the field so that by the middle of the 1950s they outnumbered the Americans as long-term missionaries two to one.

John A. Wiebe, taking note of this new phenomenon, had to accept the fact that this new national imbalance was caused, at least in part, by the international power politics of the day. Indian nationalism, hastened by Gandhi's influence after 1919, brought independence to India.[5] Independence demanded decolonization: the dismantling of all foreign controls and the end of political dependence. While Nehru's India became a Republic in 1947, it remained within the Commonwealth headed by the United Kingdom. Nehru's attempt to form a bloc of nations who would remain non-aligned diplomatically upset the American State Department. The Bagdad Pact, part of the Eisenhower/Dulles plan to encircle the Communist countries, was formed on the eve of the Nehru-led Bandung conference of April 1955 and included Pakistan, a sworn enemy of India. This circumstance of American military installations so close to India made Americans less welcome than Canadians. The Commonwealth connection, however, eased Canadian entry.[6]

That was a primary reason why it may be said that this third and last generation (1945-1975) belonged to the Canadians. They were there to close the Mission in 1973. Many of those working on the Board of Missions/Services and its Secretariat were of Canadian origin also: John Wall, Bill Wiebe, and Jake H. Epp before the office was moved from Hillsboro to Winnipeg, and Fred Epp, Victor Adrian and Peter Hamm afterwards. This seemed fitting since the Canadian MB membership overtook the American before 1950, as also did their financial support in due course.[7]

John Wiebe hinted at other implications of this imbalance that are fascinating in themselves:

> Since a majority... now come from Canada, the Canada way of procedure comes to the front more and more. This and some other related situations make me think at times that this field... will be left to our Canadian friends.... It would not be well to burden our Board of Foreign Missions with certain conflicts

157

which arise. Such conflicts exist and it is our duty ... to overcome [them].

Six months later he added to the ambiguity by stating that policies were now being shaped "more in keeping with Canadian Church policy," and that meant significant adjustments on the field. "I wish we could [therefore] turn missionary responsibilities to leading Indians sooner." Either he was implying that the indigenization process was being slowed down by Canadians, or that Americans should be the ones to process it.[8]

**The Education of Missionary Children**

Until World War II all children attended either Breeks Memorial or Hebron School. Ootacumund and Coonoor remained the favorite sites for recreation away from the heat in the plains. In 1939, however, the first steps were taken to shift recreation and schooling from Ootacumund to a more American atmosphere and curriculum at Kodaikanal. While Canadian families like the Unruhs and Dicks, given the continuing British curriculum influences in Canada at that time, might have continued at Breeks, the John Hieberts viewed the American school as a better choice for their children than the English ones with their rigid curriculum and regimen. Hiebert wrote, "The question of the training of our children is indeed one of our greatest problems. After prayerful consideration we felt that this school would better fit our children for the life in America." He acknowledged that Breeks was theologically conservative, and worried that Kodaikanal revealed "a more liberal element." Several years later he admitted that "our children do not receive the kind of spiritual guidance they might expect at home." They tried to remedy this by having special events for the children at the semi-annual Missionary Council meetings.[9] While the Hiebert children were taken to America in 1942, the Wiebe children were moved to Kodaikanal and stayed throughout the War years.[10]

After the War and their return to India, Hiebert tried to persuade Mission Board Secretary A. E. Janzen that American Mennonite Brethren now required a home at Kodaikanal and a matron for the missionary children.[11] Rose Krause came to fill that position in 1950. She and her husband Herbert had worked under John Hiebert at the Reedley Academy. Herbert taught at Kodaikanal while Rose became matron in the home called Bruton, purchased in 1949. During her three years she established a comfortable and comforting co-ed home for up to twenty-five MB children. Rose also coped with the parents who came sometime between April and June of each year. While the Krauses stayed on and Herbert became the principal of Kodaikanal School, they were succeeded at Bruton in 1953 by Linda and Jacob Ewert.[12]

Before independence Bruton was occupied by English government officials. When it was first put up for sale it was prohibitively expensive, but by 1949 its price had been cut by half, making purchase possible. Missionaries promptly moved from Ootacumund and occupied this spacious house on thirteen acres on the first of June. Though the missionaries disliked the name "Bruton," Hiebert wrote, it was never renamed.[13]

The experiences of Phyllis Hiebert, Katie and Hilda Klahsen, Donald Unruh and Ruth Wiebe, all born in the inter-war years, are illustrative of the Ootacumund style. None of those who attended both schools spoke of Ootacumund in the same appreciative tone as the generation of missionary children before them. All more or less detested the drill-like marching from the boarding house to school, the unfairness of teachers eating roast dinner within sight of the students who had to do with lesser fare, and the demeaning punishments for minor infractions. Ruth Wiebe (Friesen) stated that moving from Ootacumund to Kodaikanal was like "going from a cold shower to a warm bath."[14] The Klahsen sisters, born in 1927 and 1929 respectively, attended Ootacumund only. They were there when their grandparents, the Hueberts, retired at Ootacumund in 1936. When furlough considerations during the war were waived because of the dangers involved in travel, Katie (who finished at Breeks at age 16) went to Nellore and then to Women's Christian College in Madras. There she prepared for medical studies in Canada. Hilda remained at Ootacumund. After the war both registered in science courses at the University of Western Ontario.[15]

Donald Unruh, the youngest member of this family, spent five years at Ootacumund before transferring to the more congenial atmosphere of Kodaikanal in about 1950. He did well professionally in Canada even though he had to change high schools many times–Kodaikanal, Winkler (Manitoba) High School, Mennonite Brethren

Collegiate Institute in Winnipeg–and had his schooling shortened by one-and-a-half years.[16]

More difficult for many missionary children than attending these boarding schools was the culture shock that came from the re-entry to North American society. One missionary child wrote that they knew there was "some big authoritative institution behind all this, which we did not want to know about or meet." Once back in North America the differences between the missionary children and a richer lifestyle was all too evident.

> "But nothing prepared me for the change to a powerful life-commanding institution like *that* MB Church. . . . I can't describe the damage done. I'm still trying to recover. It was this religious angle that affected adversely all other aspects . . . including my social life, which now became unnatural and emotionally unsatisfying." When missionary children were taken on deputation visits to the churches, there was pressure to "present a good image of mission fields," to put on a good face.

They usually found themselves faced with a woeful ignorance of India, if not of the world generally. Some missionary children came to feel sorry for church members in North America who had never traveled, whose educational standards fell short of Kodaikanal's, and whose social graces and sense of fun were under-developed compared with life in the hills of India. Fortunately, the social atmosphere at Tabor College was a little more cosmopolitan than most small Mennonite towns, and many graduates of Kodaikanal enjoyed the Tabor experience.[17]

### Missionary Relationships in the 1950s

After World War II there were six senior couples and four single women on the MB India missionary field: John and Maria Lohrenz, Peter and Elizabeth Balzer, John and Viola Wiebe, John and Anna Hiebert, Jacob and Anna Dick, Abram and Annie Unruh, Maria Wall, Helen Warkentin, Margaret Suderman, and Anna Suderman. Their ranks were thinned by the recall of the Hieberts in 1951 and the departure, for family reasons, of the Dicks in 1957.

Among those missionaries who arrived in the late 1940s intending long-term service were Julius and Eva Kasper (Nagarkurnool), Ernest and Evelyn Schmidt (Mahbubnagar Central

High School), Dilwyn and Mildred Studebaker (Wanaparty), Herman and Beatrice Warkentin (Kalvakurty), teachers Mildred Enns, Edna Gerdes, and Emma Lepp, and nurses Helen Harder, Mary Doerksen, Rosella Toews, and Margaret Willems. The teams of single women formed here were Gerdes and Willems at Gadwal; Lepp and Harder at Shamshabad; Enns and Toews at Nagarkurnool.

Those who arrived between 1950 and the early 1960s also still intended long-term service: Peter and Arlene Block (Deverakonda hospital), Ted and Esther Fast (Deverakonda), Jake and Ruth Friesen (Jadcherla Central Hospital), George and Anne Froese (Jadcherla hospital), Peter and Betty Hamm (Kodaikanal and Shamshabad), Paul and Frances Hiebert (Shamshabad), Daniel and Helen Nickel (Mahbubnagar), Henry and Alice Krahn (Narayanpet, Mahbubnagar), Henry and Amanda Poetker (Hughestown, Kalvakurty), teachers Anne Ediger and Katie Siemens, and nurses Frieda Neufeld, Marie Riediger, and Regina Suderman. With the construction of the central hospital at Jadcherla the new nurses were focused there, while the teachers moved about.

Coming to relieve the medical doctors during furloughs were David and Lorma Wiebe and dentist Ronald and Marianne (Peters) Wall. The house parents at Bruton were Herb and Rose Krause, Jacob and Linda Ewert, Peter and Betty Hamm, Jerry and Nancy Neufeld, and David and Martha Friesen. After serving at Bruton for one term (1958-1962), the Hamms joined the missionary staff at Bethany Bible Institute, Shamshabad. Other Mennonite Brethren who came to Kodaikanal to teach during the last years of the AMBM were: Kathryn Unruh, Anna Frantz, and John, Carol and Donna Wiebe. Margaret Enns taught at Hebron School beginning in 1959.

These new missionaries came to India after a period (1936-1946) when no new missionaries had arrived and understaffing had been acute. As a result, the new missionaries associated with seniors in assignments previously not accorded to juniors until their second or third terms. Potentially, they faced greater relational problems without an intermediate group to shield them. Some felt the full force of the seniors' desire to protect privilege and place.[18] This kind of behavior, however, became more and more unacceptable to younger missionaries and not everyone coped equally well. Staying only one term when a life-time commitment was intended placed the onus of explaining a "casualty" on the missionary and the Board.

When faced with such problems, the Board was prone to accept the seniors' view of unhappy situations. Since the seniors dominated a powerful Missionary Council until 1960, they supported each other. Both the Missionary Council and Board tended to discount those who became one-term missionaries.[19]

### The Story at Gadwal

Margaret Willems and Edna Gerdes formed a team at Gadwal where the Unruhs had worked since 1936 except for a wartime furlough. Gerdes was sent home in 1960 while Willems withdrew in 1961 because of illness and her own disillusionment. The problems Willems and Gerdes faced in India were duplicated among other nurses and teachers, to some extent.

Willems was from a well-known family in Saskatchewan. Following Bible school and nurse's training in Manitoba she went to India in 1946. Assigned to Gadwal, she found a ready response to her combination of evangelism and healing ministry. But her station supervisor, A. A. Unruh, did not want her to be too independent. Whatever she wished to do would have to be cleared by him. Though she was aware that juniors, especially singles, were expected to be quiet during their first term, she let Unruh know he would have to adjust to her way of doing things. More than that, she wanted to expand her nursing facilities. Encouraged by John Hiebert, she used earnings from her grain farm in Saskatchewan to build her own hospital with a water system and access roads. Even if Unruh was not happy with her independent spirit, the home office was pleased to have pictures of her enlarged facilities.[20]

During her furlough (1953-55) Willems gave up to 240 talks about her work in India, almost more than any other missionary of the AMBM. Soon after her return, she and Gerdes were transferred to Wanaparty to work alongside the Unruhs. There Willems extended the work left by Margaret Suderman. She added an operating room, a ward for upper caste patients, and a tuberculosis ward. More mobile with the new Chevrolet she took with her to India, she organized and led a large girls' camp for three years and also adopted two orphans, Lois and Eunice.[21]

Gerdes was Willems' associate at Gadwal and then Wanaparty, working alongside the Unruhs since their first appointment. Gerdes always felt, given her German Lutheran background, that she was not wholly acceptable to those born into Mennonite families. After her first year of language study, the Unruhs and the Dicks wanted her to look after their children in the hills. She had not come to India for that. Besides, she and others found that, whatever the grounds, some had very little patience with the idea that single women should be on the field, and even less with their teaching Bible in the schools.[22]

### The Situation at Wanaparty

When Dilwyn and Mildred (Heinrichs) Studebaker, of Church of the Brethren and MB background respectively, went to India in 1949, they were hardly prepared for the difficulties attending their initiation into that country. Originally planning on an assignment in Colombia, the Studebakers were reassigned by the Board to India.[23]

Following language study the Studebakers, though expecting a teaching assignment, were assigned to Wanaparty as station missionaries. This station had been vacated by the Dicks, who were on furlough. The assignment brought the Studebakers into close contact with the "Sisters" Margaret and Anna Suderman. This team of seasoned missionaries, working well in tandem, alone for a year and virtually in charge, did not take easily to the young California family. Studebaker recalled that the "relationship was strained at best" and fellowship restricted.[24] Suderman wrote in April 1953 that relations "have been strained, but are improving. Difference in background, age, experience, and other factors enter in." It was clear to the Studebakers that the sisters and others stumbled over the non-Mennonite name.[25]

When the Studebakers arrived at Wanaparty, the Sudermans had gone through a very tiring period of work and some trying situations. Anna Suderman, the writer and spokesperson, had managed to complete a new women's bungalow in the spring of 1950. In October she suffered a severe back injury in a bus accident and was in a cast from hip to neck for six months. Even then she exhibited a sense of humor by referring to "this restricted cast system." In addition to her responsibility for a middle school, which was establishing accreditation and about to receive government "grants-in-aid," she was developing a passion to distribute Christian literature in Telugu.[26]

The sisters were upset by some of the Studebakers early actions. About one month after their arrival at Wanaparty, Dilwyn took a pregnant Mildred to the Vellore hospital. From there he took Mildred and their newborn son Keith to Kodaikanal, where they remained during the hot season. Back at Wanaparty the sisters interpreted this delay as an abnegation of responsibility, since Dilwyn was gone for several months.[27] This response was ironic in view of A. E. Janzen's hopefulness that they would all work well together. He wrote Dilwyn: "No doubt your being stationed at Wanaparty... pushed you into the water so that in many respects you had to swim without much assistance, although, of course, the Sisters Suderman were available in an emergency."[28]

Given the myriad activities of this large station, there were many opportunities for the clash of two mindsets. In this situation, three factors exacerbated what was essentially a struggle for control: 1) Chendriah, the head custodian; 2) the chain of command and the method of giving directions; 3) the matter of cars.

Chendriah was a very important factor at Wanaparty. This Madiga Christian, who had been taking orders from the sisters for some time when the Studebakers arrived, was very glad when a male missionary arrived to be "in charge." Conflicts arose when the sisters on occasion countermanded directions given by Dilwyn. Mildred's role as interpreter for her husband, using her grasp of the local Telugu, was grossly misunderstood.[29] To the Suderman sisters, who were used to having younger women and men defer to them, this was most unusual and unacceptable.

Another recurring and complicated question had to do with motor vehicles: whether to buy them in India or ship them from America, where the money would come from, and who would get the cast-off vehicles. The emotions that arose over this question were part of the difficulties between the Sudermans and Studebakers. Until each had new cars brought to them in 1952, Studebaker used Kasper's Chevy. The Sudermans were trying to make do with the twenty-one year-old Chevy left on the station by the Dicks. To an earlier suggestion from the Missionary Council that they could buy this old car, Anna responded: "We still do not have complete joy to do that." She explained they had already had one accident with it when one of the wheels fell off.[30] Because of this they became dependent on a missionary whose view of the transportation problem was different from theirs. Studebaker wrote Janzen in Hillsboro: "Since their work is limited to the compound they have use for a car only to go to the city for supplies."[31]

During 1949 the women had hoped that Margaret Suderman's home church in Manitoba would raise money for the Willys utility van that they wanted. As it turned out, Janzen told them they would have to "comfort themselves" with Romans 8:28. Hardly satisfied with such an attitude, in March 1951 Anna Suderman spelled out the specific ways in which they needed a vehicle. Her lucid article, "Ox-Carts or Motor Cars," caused some irritation in Hillsboro. In it she effectively made the case for cars as a necessity and left the question hanging in the air: why do we still have to resort to the travel methods of the 1920s? "Only nine motor cars, such as they are, and a million and a half people to be reached in thousands of villages, in an area of about 5,000 square miles." She made a special case for the women in ways the Board may not have expected: "Out of five mission hospitals and dispensaries only two have old cars, the others have none at all." Margaret was not far behind Anne in the lucidity of her arguments. Having a vehicle over which they could claim some "ownership... would make things run more smoothly for us on the mission station." They finally got their Willys utility van in the fall of 1952, but not without being reprimanded by the Board through a third party. Anna later apologized for their action.[32]

As the question of cars occurred repeatedly for administrators, it is helpful to reflect on the relationship between the oxcart and the very poor of India. The bullock-drawn cart as burden-bearer was the lifeline of the poor. The oxen drew water, ploughed, trampled the grain and when worn-out, provided meat and leather for the Madigas. For missionaries, since 1920, to rush past an oxcart caravan in their cars was to separate them, symbolically, from almost everyone in the emerging India church. Even for Pankratz forty years earlier to ride his bicycle while he sent his preachers ahead overnight by oxcart could be seen as a separation. On the other hand, the missionary's wife and young children, riding along overnight in one of the carts with their unyielding axles, remained closer to the attending Bible women and servants. Had they been successful in making converts from the upper castes and had therefore settled in cities and large towns, the difference in class distinctions would not have been so great. It was only exacerbated by the white-walled tail-finned new cars of the mid-1950s.[33]

## The Matter of the Well

Back at Wanaparty, an even more exasperating issue arose in 1953 over the need for a "hospital well." The labor costs of supplying the hospital with precious water from the "big station well" were very high. To prevent contamination of the well, proper masonry work, septic tanks and latrine drainage were required. At about the same time Studebaker was giving the compound a face-lift. This included whitewashing the huge two-story bungalow, some extensive renovations, and the installation of a 500-gallon tank on the roof so that flush toilets could be used on both floors. Studebaker also built a trailer suitable for touring in the villages. Someone in California had provided money for these things. Needed for the trailer was a team of white oxen, in addition to two other teams, one for ploughing, and another to pull up the water. These additions and more elaborate and expensive equipment for the kitchen and the laundry led to much criticism.[34] When difficulties arose during this time, Anna complained to the Board, bypassing Studebaker. In her April letter she admitted her mistake in having shared a former letter with other missionaries but "not with the station missionary." This "mistake" led to "an unhappy situation... which we regret."[35] About that time the Studebakers went to the Hills leaving the supervision of the well construction to the Sisters and a reluctant Chendriah. Though she said that the matter had been resolved by open discussion, Anna returned to the problem in June, saying: "Satan is behind the mis-understandings, trying to hinder Christ's work.... Unguarded remarks made to the fellow workers at the beginning of their work... created false impressions and prejudices which seem impossible to erase no matter how hard one tries."[36]

Anna managed to salvage the well project and even had a meal for all the well diggers, many of whom were not Christians. Ironically, when this was all over and the Studebakers had left, Anna confessed that it was "lonesome here without the Studebakers." Besides, the sisters were asked to move to Deverakonda field (there displacing Wall and Warkentin), to make way for a younger team, "the two capable sisters" Willems and Gerdes.[37]

## Under a Cloud

The Studebakers felt themselves the target of unnecessary behind-the-scenes abuse, especially since they were sent home in 1954 on a medical certificate. Mildred's problems with jaundice began before the well construction, and Keith developed allergies affecting his breathing. Their daughter Judith at Kodaikanal could not adjust to her situation once the Krauses left Bruton.[38]

The Studebakers were succeeded at Wanaparty by the Unruhs, back from furlough. About this time, Unruh sent Hillsboro an article on prayer. All encompassing in its application for the pressing issues of 1955, Unruh pointed to the need for a "proper attitude towards co-workers." He recognized there were times when nerves and strength were "stretched to the limit." While he "did not want to blame or excuse anyone," he made it perfectly clear "that children of God who cannot tolerate their co-workers cannot expect His blessing."[39]

All of this the Studebakers could have accepted, especially since they left having reached some degree of understanding, but they grieved over the attitude of the Dicks for some time. Already unhappy about their first meeting with them at Colombo in 1949, they were hardly prepared for the second. When the Dicks returned from furlough it was obvious they would have liked to return to Wanaparty.[40] Instead they were assigned to Shamshabad and moved the Bible Institute there from Deverakonda. In May 1954 Dick painted a damaging portrait of the Studebakers for the Board. He said they had disqualified themselves, not only from missionary work, but from deputation in the churches, by their "negative attitude in general." He then gave three reasons why their "career as missionaries [had come] to an end": they had not acquired the language and "do not show any interest to do so"; they found it difficult "to work together almost with everybody"; and "their attitude to finances is . . . not as it should be for a missionary." While Dick professed to be sorry to write this "confidential information," he said he felt "obligated to our constituency."[41]

The Studebakers left on a happier note when, "at Wanaparty's request," John Lohrenz bought farewell gifts of silver for them, and Maria Lohrenz had a party for Dilwyn and Mildred at Hughestown on 5 September 1954. Thirty-three persons were present, and Annie Dick and the Sudermans were there to help.[42] When the Studebakers were debriefed at Hillsboro, Janzen wrote Lohrenz that they were "resigning themselves to service here in the homeland" and enjoying the chance to be reunited with Judy, who had been less than happy at Kodaikanal.[43]

### The Wiebes and Schmidts at Mahbubnagar

At Mahbubnagar the Wiebes and Schmidts played out the last episode in a seniority system built up since 1902. Ernest and Evelyn (Straus) Schmidt were assigned to teach at Mahbubnagar. From Hillsboro, A. E. Janzen had insisted that the Schmidts qualify themselves fully for their assignment before going to the field. This they did and, armed with those qualifications, arrived in India in December 1949. The Schmidts completed their first set of language studies before the Hieberts left in November 1951, and were in charge of the station and school when the Wiebes returned.[44] Schmidt was already serving as secretary of the Missionary Council.

What followed was a continuing struggle to determine who was in charge: the Board in Hillsboro or the Missionary Council in India. Hillsboro may have assigned Schmidt to be principal of the Central High School, but in the early 1950s the Missionary Council still determined the question of "stationing." When the Wiebes returned from an extended furlough late in January 1952, the Schmidts did what was expected of them: they followed MC etiquette and invited the Wiebes to return "to any work they would like to do" at Mahbubnagar. Janzen may have assumed a certain division of labor—the Wiebes in evangelization, the Schmidts in education—but he did not follow through to ensure this was understood. To the disappointment of the Schmidts, it was soon evident that the Wiebes also expected to have complete control. At the end of March 1952 Wiebe wrote Janzen: "We realize it would not be right to place full responsibility on a new missionary and since Viola and I are working in this field we realize that we may be called upon to assist with the work."[45] This statement was politically correct, but not entirely guileless, in view of what transpired.[46]

### The Compound Transformed

By comparing Wiebe's letters and Schmidt's subsequent commentary, based on records he preserved, it is evident that the Wiebes requested time to visit the other stations, and were gone about a week while the Schmidts prepared to leave for their last months of language study in the hills. This cleared the way for the Wiebes to move into the position they vacated in 1946,[47] including his reappointment as secretary of the Missionary Council.

When the Schmidts returned from five months at Kodaikanal in early 1952, Wiebe had radically altered J. N. C. Hiebert's plan, which previously had the full support of the Missionary Council and Board. In short, he managed to have an earlier directive from the Missionary Council that Schmidt and Wiebe "carefully study the needs of the school and submit recommendations" displaced by a resolution that the executive of the Missionary Council meet at Mahbubnagar on 30 June "to effect a delineation [a separation] between the Field Evangelistic Station and Highschool compound." Schmidt, as designated principal, was not co-opted for the discussions of this resolution, whereas Unruh at Gadwal was.[48]

In anticipation of the passage of that resolution, the compound was radically transformed and the Schmidts were faced with an accomplished fact. Most importantly, Wiebe managed to persuade the senior missionaries, Hillsboro, and the new medical staff that it would be advisable to sell the old Baptist hospital compound that was part of the greater Mahbubnagar station, especially if half the money (50,000 rupees expected) could be applied to the new central hospital. Thus, as Schmidt discovered, the very building he needed for teacher housing was now up for sale.[49] Second, contrary to the high school's founders, the Wiebes split the high school administratively into boys and girls divisions, the latter to be supervised by the Wiebes. To this Wiebe added the idea of the middle school which he had wanted already in the late 1930s. This threatened the space for the boys' school. Third, other radical physical alterations on campus were completed that impinged on the Schmidt's living quarters and on the operation of the boys' division. Schmidt also lost his budget reserved for science equipment, was three teachers short in July, and found his evangelistic outreach in conjunction with the high school curtailed.[50]

In addition, Wiebe became absorbed in a myriad of Mission property matters, so that very little time, if any, could be devoted to personal touring in the villages.[51] He wrote more than 150 letters to Hillsboro during this last term. His other chief concern was with

169

the creation of the central hospital for Jake Friesen, the new medical doctor and surgeon at nearby Jadcherla.[52]

## The School Strike

All of this must be taken into consideration when one contemplates the "school strike" of August 1952. For this the Wiebes held Schmidt responsible. Whatever else may have been involved, he was responsible to the extent that he tried to work within the food budget.[53] Strapped as this was, he had either to raise fees or cut back on food portions. Other than that, the most serious grievances and actions of the protesters, led particularly by three agitators, several of them "Christian" boys who had come out of the "boardings," were directed against the station missionary. Schmidt, as principal, got the support of the police department because the strike was seen as part of the spreading disaffection of youth over such larger issues as "Mulki" (that is Telengana) hostility against the Andhras.[54] When Wiebe interfered in the contemplated "disciplinary procedures," the police chief and Schmidt were disappointed. As a result, even though the actual school strike only lasted three days (6-8 August), settlement could only be reached once a sub-committee to deal with the high school situation had been appointed. Appointed to it were Wiebe, Dick, and Schmidt. With this wider support, Schmidt adopted procedures used elsewhere: the school was closed for a brief period, students were sent home for fees, and could return only by re-registering. In this way the real troublemakers were screened out.[55]

When the problem in Schmidt's sphere was more or less resolved, the troublemakers singled out the girls' division, which was now the Wiebes' charge. In November 1952 the outside agitators disturbed the girls and "threatened" to assault their boarding matron and teacher. Some high school boys came to her defense and, as a result, there was a considerable fight on Sunday 23 November. The teacher's relatives came to rescue her and she resigned her position. By this time it was hard to isolate the source of the problem because of the spreading agitation, chronicled in the newspapers, which led to the closing of schools throughout the area including Hyderabad city. As difficult as the second half of 1952 was for the Schmidts, they felt little personal animosity. The chief agitator, one Sreehari, actually apologized to Schmidt and Viola Wiebe for creating so much trouble for them.[56] The Schmidts requested reassignment to Gadwal and did not return to Mahbubnagar for a second term. Since taking over from Hiebert their campus had been "shrunk," all the facilities placed under Wiebe's administration, and their spiritual input restricted.[57] The Schmidts moved to Gadwal in 1953, a station vacated by the Unruhs. In spite of the greater distance from the epicenter of the Mission, the Missionary Council in that year made Schmidt chair of a new Education Committee, and again elected him secretary replacing John Wiebe.[58]

During their last year at Mahbubnagar (1958-59), Wiebe became quite distressed by the Board's request that he put all missionary work aside for a "legal assignment." He had already devoted much of his time to property matters, but he and Viola did not want to leave their other work unfinished. He wrote, "Such a complete change in so short a time, at the end of a longer term, which with its joys and victories has also brought severe trials, would continue to bear down heavily upon our spirits and minds."[59]

By the end of 1959, according to their own accounts, the Wiebes had redeveloped the Mahbubnagar compound, including a rebuilding of the church whose roof collapsed in 1954, restructured the high school, and facilitated the building of the Jadcherla medical complex.[60] Even then, they were not asked to return after 1960. Instead, the Wiebes were invited to join the faculty of the Ramapatnam Seminary of the ABMU.[61]

### John and Maria Lohrenz at Hughestown, Hyderabad

The Lohrenzes took a furlough from May 1947 to March 1950. During that time they visited many churches and participated in conference sessions. John taught at Pacific Bible Institute in Fresno in 1947-48. He then filled in for A. E. Janzen as secretary of the mission board when Janzen toured various mission fields in 1948 and 1949. During this time Lohrenz also saw his book, *The Mennonite Brethren Church*, through the press.

Once back in India for their fourth term in May 1950, the Lohrenzes declared their willingness to serve at Hughestown. Maria wrote that "it was the hardest decision we have ever made." They soon found themselves tied down with administrative and treasury duties and hospitality chores for missionary families. Maria had the misfortune almost immediately of falling and badly bruising her left knee. This created much sympathy and brought many missionary well-wishers to Shamshabad, where they lived until the Dicks returned in 1951. Her hospitality for those traveling to Hyderabad or Secunderabad kept her so busy that once everyone had left her diary came to be punctuated with the exclamation: "Now we can do our work!"[62] The visitors kept coming until they left India in April 1957. Once in Hughestown, near the main shopping areas and the hospital facilities in Secunderabad, the burden of company became magnified. Between January and April 1953, for example, she served 418 meals, always having **Zwiebach** and **Perieschkje** for special occasions. On 31 March 1953 she suffered a heart attack. Fortunately Helen Harder was there to assist her.[63]

Administrative problems like those of Maria Lohrenz caught the attention of A. E. Janzen when he visited India. He noted that "our missionaries are not getting out into the 2,000 villages like they should." Janzen blamed this situation on understaffing and being "tied down to station work," especially when a missionary was in charge of two or more stations during furlough times. Those who headed the Bible or high school could not tour during six to nine months of the year, and the hot season took away several more months. "Hence evangelization... becomes less and less."[64]

**The Attack on Lohrenz**

The tensions in this urban Hughestown church dated from the early 1940s, but took on a new life once the Lohrenzes were settled there. In January 1952 a "great row" broke out and "chaos ensued," necessitating intervention of the police. Ironically, one of "six strong but unspiritual leaders" ran for the Lohrenz' house and sought protection there.[65]

A number of problem areas can be isolated. Seemingly, Lohrenz' initiation of a theology class for a dozen students exacerbated the situation. Following their trip to Coonoor and Ootacumund in April/May 1954, John was severely criticized for his work at the school. Nevertheless, with Missionary Council approval, he carried on, teaching "second year subjects." Another problem arose from the presence of D. J. Arthur, a caste Christian,[66] then a young teacher in the Hughestown school. Lohrenz allowed him to teach a Sunday school class in English, but this was opposed. "How can people be so mean?" Maria Lohrenz wrote on 29 January 1954.[67]

Perhaps these problems were minor compared to the direct attack on John Lohrenz' leadership in a letter dated 15 March 1956, directed to A. E. Janzen in Hillsboro. Claiming to speak for the majority of a church of four hundred members, many of whom had comparatively well-paying jobs, the letter charged him personally with the chaos in their church. Lohrenz was "neither constitutional nor scriptural," showed favoritism, never admitted to any faults, and was generally incapable of leading a city congregation. In a letter to Lohrenz personally, signed by forty-five persons and also mailed to Janzen, they used their new nationalism to challenge his continuing leadership. "It is desirable that in this Free India any foreign elements should not dominate over Indian Churches and elect pastors amongst Missionary favorites, as was done elsewhere like Wanaparty, Nagar kurnool, and Deverakonda, where there are still struggles, parties and non-cooperation amongst Missionaries, Pastors, and Church members."[68] Lohrenz had purportedly held an election of this nature on 30 October 1955.

In an annual report for the *Zionsbote* a year earlier, Lohrenz stated that ever since Pastor V. Abraham had gone back to his village, the church had not been able to agree on a successor. He justified his continuing administration of the church by saying that as a result of this circumstance the leadership, organization of services, and officiating at weddings and funerals had fallen on him.[69] Though the Missionary Council and Lohrenz himself were slow in getting copies of these damaging letters, Janzen suggested on 4 April that these divisions at Hughestown were a clear signal that it was time for missionaries to withdraw from direct oversight of the church. In any division the missionary would always be blamed by the losing side.

Lohrenz responded with a complete rationalization of the standoff. The incongruity was great. In one line he asserted that "we love the Indian people and especially God's church here in India." In the very next line, in order to help Janzen "understand our problem better," he characterized the Indian people as "the most quarrelsome people in the whole human race," and proceeded to offer proof from the local scene. His indictment was severe: much immorality was tolerated, including dishonesty in two former headmasters who had issued "false school-leaving certificates." In money matters they were not to be trusted. He took refuge in an identification with the Apostle Paul who had found himself "in danger among false brethren," in "a more difficult place than any pastor in our churches at home."[70]

Janzen, meanwhile, received another letter signed by two Hughestown leaders, thanking the Board for sending them mission- aries like John Lohrenz, for the new plans for self-support, and for the prayers of Americans. On the basis of this "entirely different" kind of tone, Janzen, rather too easily perhaps, accepted Lohrenz' statement as an adequate explanation. Janzen seemed satisfied that this characterization of the "nature and culture" of the Indian peo- ple adequately explained the source of all the problems in the vari- ous congregations. This view was reinforced by a letter from Peter Balzer on behalf of the Missionary Council. Its members resolved unanimously and characteristically that "there was no foundation for the signers . . . and [the complaint] does not represent the Hughestown church."[71]

**Sadness at the End**

Some "newcomers," as Maria Lohrenz called the new mission- aries, saw John Lohrenz in ways that suggested the fault was not all on one side. He was seen as a replica of the British **Raj** (rule), the paternalist who held all the treasuries of the Missionary Council and the India Church in his hands. Lohrenz had serious misgivings about the large construction project to consolidate the medical minis- try at Jadcherla under Jake Friesen.[72] At this time he was most con- cerned to build a much-needed second church in greater Hyderabad. This was also to serve as a memorial to his sister Katharina who died there in 1913, and to the Pankratzes who founded the first congre- gation of the AMBM in 1904. Money for this project, which he saw through to completion, competed with financing for the Jadcherla medical facility.[73] In the villages, by contrast, during the more rapid indigenization of this period, the Mission provided only the roof for any church built with local funds.[74]

To the world outside Hughestown, John Lohrenz seemed quite serene. Maria was less so, even though she had faith that her dear John would "take care of everything." Following the complaint of the forty-five, she reported in her diary that D. J. Arthur "may go away." When the "discontent" letter finally arrived from Hillsboro, she exclaimed on 31 July 1956: "So cruel and really all false." Though she said she was "sick physically" from all this, there was worse to come. The Hughestown opposition took every business meeting opportunity to cast blame on Lohrenz. "O Lord, stop their rudeness and these unrighteous ways," she prayed. The altercations continued in the midst of a ceaseless round of activities–entertaining, saying goodbye to various people–so that in early March 1957 she was completely exhausted, and betrayed her emotional state when she wrote: "My heart is very cold." Their own departure she described as very "painful," though "some wept sorely."[75] This was not what they had expected from their stay in Hughestown.

## CHAPTER 12

# A Time of Tragedies

During the 1950s and early 1960s there occurred a chain of tragic events that almost overwhelmed the mission and for which there was no adequate explanation. Julius Kasper, himself deeply struck by tragedy, captured some of the mystery when he wrote on 25 September 1956: "All our experiences of the past six years–accidents, nervous breakdowns, resignations, strifes, violent deaths . . . seem to increase in momentum, tragedy, and one wonders, asks questions and tries to find the answer."[1]

Tragedy was never far from the door in India. These years, however, threw up more accidents, some fatal, than any other in the mission's history, and most of them are told here for the first time. Though many of these events raised fundamental questions about human error and judgment, decisions about publicity were based on the potential for embarrassment to the mission.

The language used to describe these events was reminiscent of the rationale in the death of Frank Janzen in 1927, when N. N. Hiebert stated that "Wanaparty was where he had been permitted to end his career." Abram E. Janzen called the first accident of this decade "**der schwere Schicksalsschlag in Indien.**" Translated, this meant just a bad stroke of chance, fate, an accident to be explained on the basis of the odds in favor of something happening sooner or later. Margaret Willems, in reference to one of the fatal accidents, stated that God makes no mistakes. If God makes no mistakes, what kind of lessons was he trying to teach others in the Mission or the constituency?[2]

### The Kasper Family

Julius and Eva Block Kasper and two sons Jackie and Julius were among the first missionaries to arrive from Canada after the War. Julius met Eva Block from Nebraska at Tabor College and they married in 1941.[3] They were assigned to Nagarkurnool, the station only recently vacated by the Bergtholds. Though Bergthold had access to a car for years, Julius Kasper started his term at Nagarkurnool in 1947 without a car, a bicycle, or even a team of oxen and cart that he could use for touring in the villages. In retrospect, Janzen's response to this complaint was penny-wise and pound-foolish. Until

177

money was available, "you will have to use the ox cart and gear your patience to the squeal of the axles. The Lord can bless our obedient effort regardless of whether we are working by means of ox carts or automobiles. The main thing is to be in the center of His will." In the very next year Eva Kasper attributed her husband's severe bout with rheumatic fever to his having to walk behind the ox carts. He could not add his weight to the burden of the oxen. When nurse Margaret Willems, doing language study at Wanaparty, came to his rescue, she prescribed six weeks in bed.[4]

Only a few years later the Kaspers met with a fatal accident. On 21 October 1950 they were traveling east from Nagarkurnool to Ongole in the Hieberts' car in search of medical treatment for missionary Julius and for Joanne Hiebert, and undertook to cross the Krishna River using the evening ferry. That day, the only two vehicles on the ferry which allegedly had been accident-free until then, were the Hiebert station wagon and a heavily-laden truck. The truck, not properly centered, caused the ferry to tip, throwing both vehicles and their occupants into deep water. Julius Kasper, standing alongside the car, was thrown into the river but was able to rescue himself. Anna Hiebert, in the middle seat, took one-year old Lois with her and, rising to the surface, was rescued by fishermen. In the back seat, Joanne Hiebert got out safely and swam ashore. Jackie Kasper, eight, the first to see danger, was easily saved. His younger brother Julius and his mother Eva never got out of the car, even though they were in the front with the windows rolled down all the way. Why these two were trapped in the car will ever remain a mystery.[5]

Eva's body was retrieved within a short time, but young Julius was not found until next morning. Those who mourned on the Krishna strand had only wet clothes on their bodies. Once Julius was found, they were taken twenty miles south to the Lutheran Mission at Guntur, where kind missionaries provided food and clothing and made burial preparations. John Hiebert, on receiving the news, left Mahbubnagar (a day's trip away), picked up Herman Warkentin at Kalvakurty, and hastened to the scene of tragedy. They were delayed at the river, and reached Guntur by train too late for the funeral. Abram E. Janzen wrote that Kasper said, "God has given, and now he has translated these two lovely flowers into His kingdom."[6] He was given a brief furlough, and married Mary Doerksen a little over a year later. Janzen was philosophical: "Although time will wash over this occurrence, it will never be forgotten. It looms as one of the unforgettable events in the missionary history of the MB Conference."[7]

## Brother Jacob

The next accident, in 1952, involved Jacob the cook at the Gadwal compound, where Abram and Anna Unruh, Margaret Willems and Edna Gerdes served as missionaries. On 4 December Unruh organized an overnight excursion to the Krishna River, taking Kathryn and Donald Unruh (home from Kodaikanal), nurse Margaret and teacher Edna, and Jacob their cook, a "Christian brother." On the way back to the compound, Unruh detoured to a little lake, called a "tank," not far from the compound. Since he carried a rifle, it was his intention to hunt for ducks. Having succeeded in this quest, it fell to Jacob to retrieve the ducks from the water. Though warned not to get in over his head, Jacob was soon seen to be swimming, but to the opposite shore. After struggling for his life, he disappeared before the eyes of those standing helplessly on shore.[8]

All efforts to retrieve the body were in vain. Donald tied a wash line to his father as he waded in, but this only endangered his life. Unruh wrote: "It would have been a hard blow to our family if the Lord would not have helped us." It certainly was a "hard blow" to Jacob's wife Mariamma and her children. Was this a case of human error or bad judgment? If safer methods of retrieving the ducks were not available, should they have been shot? In his letter to secretary Janzen, Unruh expressed hope that this incident "may not be a hindrance in my service."[9] John A. Wiebe wrote that this drowning "hung like a pall over the Mission." Many years later Donald Unruh suggested that his father lost some degree of confidence as a result of this tragedy. Unruh was not cleared of any culpability in the case until the body was recovered by the police. Unruh and Margaret Willems made some provision for Jacob's widow and her three children, all under four years of age. This incident raised once again the question of the use of guns by Mennonite missionaries. Willems wrote only that she was glad that Ernest Schmidt, who had been assigned to Gadwal to replace the Unruhs, had sold his gun. Apparently Unruh gave up his gun also.[10]

### Herman Warkentin

The third fatal accident occurred at Kalvakurty on 26 March 1953. Herman and Beatrice (Koop) Warkentin had arrived in India in 1947. They were willing to stay at Kalvakurty without furlough for whatever time it took to build up the compound and the MB presence.[11] Until then it had been the training or humbling place for new missionaries. Herman Warkentin had made some converts among caste people, and was invited on that day to the home of a wealthy landowner. First there was a problem to check out in the well that was being dug. Herman thought he had to do it personally. As he began the descent, one side of the rope ladder tore, and he fell, hitting his head on a cross beam, killing him instantly. Present at the site was Herman's father, Henry K. Warkentin, who was visiting and helping on the field, and the young missionary Ted Fast. Though Beatrice never told her children of the suspicion of foul play, Fast believes the rope may have been tampered with by those who resisted Warkentin's success among the caste people.[12]

Once Ted Fast had gone to Kodaikanal to fetch the children, the funeral took place at the Hughestown church, conducted by John Lohrenz.[13] Beatrice, without time even to grieve, returned home with six children, her missionary career over. Later, at a cost of $25,000., Herman's father constructed a memorial prayer chapel on the grounds of Mennonite Brethren Biblical Seminary in Fresno, California.[14]

Another fitting memorial to Herman Warkentin was the dedication of Hebron Bible School at Kalvakurty in 1956. This was brought about by their successors, Henry and Amanda (Lepp) Poetker from Saskatchewan. Taking up the work there following language study, they found that Herman, while making his mark in many ways, had aroused considerable interest in Bible study. With the help of the Warkentin family in California the Poetkers were able to make the influence of Herman and Beatrice Warkentin felt in years to come.[15]

### Other Accidents

Before the Wiebes left on furlough, they and the Unruhs planned a trip to the Ajanta Caves, about 150 miles west of Secunderabad. There were eight persons in the car, one of them a servant named John, and their camping equipment stored in a carryall overhead. Not far from their destination on 28 December 1958, one of the tires blew; they veered four times before the car rolled over on its back, gasoline dripping from the tank. All the windows were broken and their equipment was scattered about. Fortunately, the car did not explode in flames, and everyone was able to crawl out with only minor injuries. Indian people helped them get to a nearby Methodist mission, while Unruh and Wiebe tended to the car. Their insurance did not cover this accident, and they never got to the Ajanta Caves.[16]

Several other accidents involved workers and acquaintances from the various fields. A train crash near Mahbubnagar in 1956 cost 121 lives, not to speak of the many injured. John A. Wiebe was involved in the rescue operation.[17] Closer to the Mission, in 1963, there was a bus accident involving children and teachers from the Gadwal Middle School. A truck laden with logs sideswiped their vehicle near Jadcherla. Among those killed were Kamalamma, wife of headmaster B. A. George, and four girls related to members of the India church community. Others were severely injured.[18]

**The Death of John A. Wiebe**

Though J. A. and Viola Wiebe were happy in their work with the Ramapatnam Baptists, they felt pushed out of their legitimate sphere of service with the American Mennonite Brethren Mission.[19] This made John Wiebe's death in 1963 all the more poignant.

Maurice Blanchard, president of Ramapatnam Seminary where Wiebe had been teaching since September 1961, gave an eye-witness account of the drowning in the Bay of Bengal on 28 December. It was the Christmas season 1963 and the Wiebes had just sent off their Christmas letter filled with news of their children. Their daughter Esther had been accepted as a missionary of the American Baptists and was with her parents at the time. The family and guests were enjoying a picnic on the beach where John Wiebe loved to swim. After giving Esther some lessons, he went out once more alone, giving a wave with raised arms. "It was then that he got caught in one of the currents which swept him out beyond... where any one of us could help." Fortunately for the family, four fishermen were persuaded to rescue him. It took considerable time for them to bring his body in. Though every effort was made to resuscitate him, his spirit had departed.[20]

John Lohrenz, in India at the time, described how the missionaries reacted to the news. "Two large cars with Indian nationals and missionaries immediately left for Ramapatnam." Though the funeral service had taken place, the remains were left in the seminary chapel until the entourage from Mahbubnagar had arrived. Following prayers by those who had worked with him in the plains of the Deccan, his body was laid to rest.[21] There at Ramapatnam Principal Blanchard tried to explain what had happened. In his eulogy he stated that "our chief comfort just now is in the thought that as we stood on this side ... and tried to call him back to us, there seemed to be someone ... standing on the other side of the shore calling him to come over there, and John Wiebe did what he had long been accustomed to doing. He obeyed the voice of the Lord." Blanchard called Wiebe a "skillful and wise teacher... to me a brother, a friend and almost a father."[22]

The eulogies at a memorial service for Wiebe in Mahbubnagar church on 5 January 1964, and in writing, were many. John H. Lohrenz recognized that of their three terms in India, the Wiebes had made their "most abiding" and important contributions while at Mahbubnagar. M. B. John spoke of his "tireless efforts and love for our people." Abram E. Janzen told the Board of his tremendous capacity for work. Except for John H. Voth in earlier decades, Wiebe provided the home office "with more correspondence, reports, [and]... documents... relating to the mission than any other MB missionary on our world-wide fields." His "diplomatic ability" was only exceeded by his "godly boldness" as a witness.[23]

### The Tragedy of Insanity

The greatest tragedies of this period were two events that occurred in 1956: the suicide of John N. C. Hiebert on 20 July 1956 and Helga Dick Upham's murder of her two daughters at Lebanon, Oregon in September. Neither story was ever publicized in the Mennonite press. The constituency was not at that time ready to handle issues of mental illness. Many were more ready to ask: "Who has sinned, this man or his father?" In an exchange at the time between John A. Harder and J. B. Toews, both deeply shaken by these tragedies, it was acknowledged that "this case gives us as a brother-hood much cause for humiliation and cleansing [before God]."[24]

The Helga Dick Upham story is best understood in the context of the Dick family saga. She was the only child with her parents in their daring flight from Russia to India in 1933. The Dicks suffered much in the separation from their children. They gave up Helga to schooling in India in their very first year, and then to Tabor College in 1945. Three daughters married in America without their presence at the weddings.[25]

Helga had learned to know Graham Upham at Ootacumund. They both attended Tabor and later married. Upon completion of medical studies, he set up practice in Oregon. The tragic event there corresponded in time with Paul Dick's accident at Kodaikanal in late August 1956. He had fallen alongside a stream and broken his leg. When news from Oregon first filtered in to Paul, he mistakenly thought it was also an accident that had taken all of the Upham family: Graham, Helga, and the two girls Ruth and Lois. Age 16 , he wrote his parents at Shamshabad that he thought it was about time some members of the Dick family got to heaven "to find out what God is doing." He was not surprised that they had finally been singled out. "Thank God He took the whole family at once. There is a definite plan in all this; I don't think you should get upset about this."[26] The Dick's children at Kodaikanal were not informed of the real facts until well into October.[27]

Apparently Helga Upham had become progressively disoriented in August and September 1956. In a state of extreme depression, she took the life of her two daughters, and then called the police. She was taken to the Oregon State Hospital for examination.[28] After being examined by a number of psychiatrists, she was declared "legally not responsible." Her case was brought before the Grand Jury, where the charge of homicide was dismissed on grounds of insanity. She was committed to an institution, which could not release her until she was "completely well." Had she been charged with murder Helga might have faced deportation to Canada.[29]

Helga recovered surprisingly quickly. She wrote to her sister Helen for the first time on 20 October, and to her parents on 14 November saying: "I do know the Lord has enfolded me in His arms most tenderly especially during the first few weeks after the accident, when at times it seemed as though all hell had broken loose."

She was concerned about her brother Paul at Kodaikanal, about her husband who was bereft of wife and children and barely coping. Graham was allowed to celebrate Christmas with her in the institution.[30]

All of this was too much for Mother Anna Dick to bear. The Dicks had been advised not to rush home, but to stay in India at least until the spring of 1957. At Christmas she collapsed from total nervous exhaustion. By the time they returned in the spring they were able to visit with Helga and Graham.[31] But even as Helga and Graham seemed to be making progress, Anna was slow to gain complete composure. The Dicks, having moved to Vancouver first, were advised to move to Clearbrook where they were given a housing allowance. In 1964 J. J. Dick was able to write of the full restoration to health of "our dear Helga," and stated that Anna was doing her housework with "joy" again.[32] For Anna, however, there were more trials, especially when Graham left Helga in the summer of 1965, and she also found it difficult to permit Jacob to travel to India for a short visit in 1974. By then Helga was seeing Philip Good, whom she eventually married.[33]

**Irony in High Places**[34]

The story of John N. C. Hiebert–his recall, his nervous breakdown while president of Tabor College, and his suicide–can only be understood in the context of what was happening at Tabor during this time. President Peter E. Schellenberg had resigned in 1951 under fierce criticism from fundamentalist elements in the constituency.[35] A call then was made to bring Hiebert home from India to serve as the school's new president. Many believed he would be able to pull Tabor out of the "morass" into which the school was said to have slid.[36]

The challenge placed before P. E. Schellenberg as president from 1942 to 1951 was the creation of a school that could meet both state accreditation and higher spiritual standards than were expected in the home churches.[37] When Schellenberg tried to achieve these conference-approved goals in terms of curriculum and appropriate library resources, he found himself opposed because of three things: he was an academic as opposed to an ordained minister, and his communications were not sprinkled with pious phrases;[38] he was a social scientist, the first MB to hold a doctoral degree in psychology; and, he was seen as a cultural relativist as Tabor gradually adopted more "worldly" standards with respect to gender relations, changing styles for women, and the beginnings of competitive athletics.[39] Criticism first peaked at the MB General Conference of 1943 where Schellenberg was subjected to an examination of his personal faith. In that day, such quizzing was usually reserved for church membership meetings. Many others would have felt humiliated enough to resign. He did, in fact, tender his resignation several times before 1951.[40]

Ironically, Schellenberg's strongest defender was Abram H. Unruh, principal of Winkler Bible Institute and chair of the Education Committee supervising Tabor. In 1944 he lashed out at the "unthinking and unsound criticism" that was floating about, and questioned whether one could expect Tabor's social expression to be of a higher standard than that prevailing in many congregations from which the young people came. In that year Unruh expressed full confidence in Schellenberg as did the General Conference in 1945.[41] Unruh returned to this theme at Mountain Lake in 1948. "The river bed is never higher than the source itself," he argued. He suggested that a former administration was equally to blame. Delegates should remember that "the garment and the bottles [of Tabor College] were given [to us] in such a condition as they were found in 1942 [at the end of A. E. Janzen's presidency]. Our task was to guard and to patch up what was already there."[42]

### The Barrage of Anti-Modernism

In May 1944 and January 1945 Unruh's committee responded to protestations about "symptoms and tendencies" contrary to MB faith principles and "the charge of modernism directed against the school."[43] The Education Committee had an early champion against modernism in the official press. Jacob W. Vogt, editor of the *Christian Leader* during the years of Schellenberg's presidency, took his cues from the recently organized National Association of Evangelicals (NAE), of which the MB Church was a member. In January 1947 Vogt stated boldly that by joining the NAE "we have severed connections in every way with every other fellowship that adheres... to principles of Bible interpretation and doctrines that are not in harmony with the NAE."[44] He published two articles directed against the perceived threat in January to March 1947, one by Elmo Warkentin and the other by Arthur G. Willems. Warkentin took his cue from Carl McIntyre, the most right-wing fundamentalist leader of the day. He blacklisted E. Stanley Jones, much admired by MB missionaries in India, as a "near-communist." He raised questions about George A. Buttrick, a past president of the Federal Council of Churches and a modernist who had written a book on prayer. It was unthinkable to Warkentin that this book should be used by Mennonite Brethren as a "text for study." He also pointed to Harry Emerson Fosdick, the Northern Baptist who was said to deny the deity of Christ. All books by these highly visible liberals were now suspect, and none of them, according to Warkentin, should be in the Tabor Library.[45]

Arthur Willems defined modernists as those who were opposed to "conservatives or fundamentalists" and who try to "satisfy the modern Christian's intellect" by allowing freedom to apply the latest findings in all fields to the Christian faith and life. He concluded by warning that modernism could easily creep into "the ranks of our Mennonite Brethren churches," and pointedly urged constituency members to make certain that Tabor College "remains a strong bulwark of the true faith."[46] Vogt provided space for many more articles related to the theme of modernism in the years 1949 to 1953.[47]

### The Resignation of P. E. Schellenberg

Meanwhile, in January 1946 the Education Committee focused on another chief concern of conservatives: "the deportment of the students." This focused on skirt lengths, cosmetics, and gender relations, even though it was admitted, publicly, that student deportment was generally satisfactory.[48] The way to control this was by a screening process to which Unruh had hinted at Mountain Lake. An early version of this was tried on faculty member Menno S. Harder, who taught biology and English. Harder was critical of oppressive legalism at Tabor. When he seems to have failed to give satisfactory answers to a series of questions, he was fired. Reinstatement came in 1947 only after he wrote a letter of apology, and with the support of board member J. W. Warkentin and President Schellenberg.[49] By October 1947 there were so many rumblings among conference ministers that Schellenberg compared the situation to "a louse gnawing at one's body."[50]

In 1949 the Education Committee presented a statement of "policies and procedures." Present also at the meeting were members of the MB General Conference Board of Reference and Counsel.[51] Their combined purpose, according to Orlando Harms, chair of the Education Committee, was to "render clarification where suspicion... might rest in the constituency toward Tabor College." This was too much for Schellenberg. He wrote his friend J. W. Warkentin, on assignment in Paraguay: "I was rather dumbfounded when faced with these statements and in no mind to accept them." Fearing that such proceedings would fail to instill the confidence that everyone was seeking, he requested, for the third time, to be released from this stressful situation. Ironically, his personal theological position was really not in question. He as much as anyone wondered how to recover theological unity in the Conference.[52]

### The Recall of John N. C. Hiebert

Upon Schellenberg's resignation in January 1949, the Education Committee approached John N. C. Hiebert about taking the presidency of Tabor. Hiebert had been a missionary in India since 1929, and while on an extended furlough had served as principal of Immanuel Bible School and Academy in Reedley (1943-47). He seriously considered the request, but could not be released from his assignment in India until the end of his term (about 1953-54). Failing to get Hiebert released then, the Committee persuaded Schellenberg once again to reconsider his resignation. He did, and continued as president under trying circumstances.[53] Whereas Schellenberg spoke of building students' lives "intellectually, emotionally, and spiritually," the Committee's report, read by J. J. Toews, told of numerous executive meetings, as well as an emergency meeting of the full Board to "bring the school closer to the hearts of our people."[54]

Schellenberg felt he could not carry on in this atmosphere, where declining financial support was linked to Tabor's apparent failure to have sufficient "spiritual impact... on the conference." He resigned one last time in June 1951, but was asked to consider staying on as head of the psychology department.[55] As a result, Hiebert was recalled from the India field with the full advocacy of the Board of Reference and Counsel and the reluctant consent of the Board of Foreign Missions. The Missionary Conference in India officially agreed to the recall, but authorized a committee of three missionaries to challenge the Board's decision on theological grounds. To counter the criticism from that quarter, A. E. Janzen argued that the Board had made provision to replace Hiebert in his role as educator in India with Ernest E. Schmidt and, moreover, that the connection between Tabor and the Mission was so intimate that a negative atmosphere in the school would soon affect the mission fields. Because the MB was "unequivocally... a missionary conference," the academic program could best be "impregnated" with a new spirit by "one who is a missionary at heart." The Board of Foreign Missions, according to Janzen, had done the right thing to support the request of the Education Committee and Board of Reference and Counsel.[56]

Hiebert was inaugurated as President of Tabor College on 3 February 1952. He was welcomed in front page editorials in *The Christian Leader* by J. W. Vogt in January and February 1952.[57] By September 1953, however, the Education Committee was faced with a strange and unexpected dilemma.

### The 'Failed' Presidency

What happened between 1952 and 1956 to make life unbearable for this intelligent and spiritual leader, the heir of the best of the Mennonite Brethren tradition? First, Hiebert's request for six months to rest and take some courses on administration was denied, even though interim arrangements for the administration of Tabor were in place. A review of his myriad involvements in India indicates that such a request was legitimate.[58] Not allowed this release time, Hiebert was also not paid for the month of January 1952. The Board of Foreign Missions apparently terminated his salary in December, and Tabor began payment with his inauguration in February. This lack of consideration, involving a modest sum, created great financial embarrassment for the family at the beginning of his presidency.[59]

Second, the multitudinous demands and the "charge" placed on Hiebert proved too much. In India he had coped with myriad duties and trying circumstances of a different nature, even if the intellectual demands were less onerous there. Regardless of his spiritual and intellectual strengths he could not cope with the stifling atmosphere into which he was thrown. One indication of this may be seen from a discussion of the issue of movies. Hiebert, who had seen many of the latest films in the atmosphere of cosmopolitan Kodaikanal, India, quite innocently asked a long-time secretary: who supervises the showing of movies at Tabor? She replied that movies were not shown at Tabor.[60] This example indicates that, in terms of cultural and theological adjustments to the larger Christian world, the missionaries in India seemed better prepared for the tide of liberalism and "worldliness" being fought by the Education Committee. Each hot season, at various hill stations, the missionaries regularly associated with Christians of many branches of evangelical and more liberal churches.

Given all that Schellenberg had been through, the fear of failure probably lay heavily on Hiebert's mind. At the inauguration he was charged "not to disappoint the confidence placed in you by God, the Conference, and the many parents who are looking to Tabor" and to maintain "the spiritual, moral, social and ethical standards... expected of the school by our brotherhood, by enforcing the Rules of Conduct and by every other means."[61]

Third, by January 1952 Hiebert was troubled by doubts he had not had when first contacted three years earlier. He now acknowledged that he had accepted what he knew would be a very demanding assignment "only after great inward struggles. . . the field of evangelism had [now] filled his vision, and that opportunity was cut short when the conference called him." In 1953 he was still "wrestling with the problem of the divine calling on which he had come to the school and which appeared to terminate in such an unusual way." Hiebert lacked complete assurance that he had done the right thing, without the blessing of fellow missionaries, and this especially in view of his reception in Hillsboro.[62]

## The "Betrayal" and the Crisis at Tabor in 1953

What had appeared most persuasive to Hiebert in 1951 was the assurance of the "unanimous support of the entire constituency." This was for him the overriding call of God. When he got to Hillsboro, however, Hiebert discovered that the Tabor faculty, alumni, many of the students, and the people of Hillsboro saw few reasons why Schellenberg should have been displaced. Even with a master's degree in Asian Studies, some questioned Hiebert's academic qualifications.[63]

Regrettably, Hiebert did "disappoint the confidence" placed in him at his inauguration. Whereas in January 1953 the Board still expressed "unreserved confidence" and assured him that he had "fully met the expectation of the Board," by the summer of 1953 he had to undergo shock treatments in Wichita for a nervous condition that few understood. By September the Committee was completely dismayed, wrestling with what they could only call "the failed presidency," while Hiebert was wrestling with the question of "the failed missionary." Many could only hope that he would recover sufficiently to continue his ministry. Following a stint at manual labor in Minnesota, and after undergoing other treatments, Hiebert was announced well enough by the spring of 1954 to be available as "a Bible expositor and evangelist."[64] Later in July, John B. Toews of the Board of Foreign Missions sought ways and means of having Hiebert and members of his family relocate to Reedley, CA, from Hillsboro, KS. As a result of his meeting with a large committee of concerned persons, Hiebert was placed in the Kings View Home in Reedley in order to aid in his recovery.[65]

Space will not permit full treatment of the way in which the Education Committee resolved the dilemma caused for them by the circumstances of 1953. Its members now turned to Frank C. Peters, age 33, pastor of Kitchener Mennonite Brethren Church.[66] Peters was offered the position of president in succession to John Hiebert, with the proviso that he could complete doctoral studies and thus take up his duties in August 1954. In effect, Peters' request for a delay was accepted whereas Hiebert's had been rejected. During his brief tenure of two years, he would not renew P. E. Schellenberg's contract, even though the former president felt he still had the "confidence of the conference and he [felt] a call to this work [in the field of psychology]."[67] Schellenberg, then about 57, was soon engaged as a professor of psychology at Bethel. From there he went to Bluffton College where Robert Kreider gave him a three-year contract after the age of 65.[68] Peters was replaced by Leonard J. Franz in 1956.[69]

## The Suicide of 1956

Meanwhile, Hiebert had shown some promise of recovery at Kings View. Those who talked with him there in the spring of 1956 thought he was doing quite well. When, however, he discovered that some consideration was being given to shifting him to a state institution in Topeka, Kansas, he took his own life on 20 July 1956.[70]

Hiebert's suicide sent shock waves through the entire North American MB constituency, not to mention the India mission.[71] News filtered out that there had been only a private funeral for the family and a few friends, and that there were difficulties with having the remains laid to rest in the Reedley cemetery. Mennonite Brethren, with their primitive view of mental illness in the 1950s, evidently could not handle the suicide in a redemptive way. How could an ordained minister take his own life unless there was some undisclosed sin in the family? One of Hiebert's daughters told a minister making judgments of this kind that she was glad God would be the judge in these matters, and not he.[72]

Notice of Hiebert's death was couched in the briefest of notices and obituaries.[73] After that, the silence was deafening. Why was his memory so little respected? Why were the normal eulogies made impossible? Was he pushed aside as quickly as possible because of the stigma attached to any suspicion of mental illness?

One of Hiebert's daughters has written frankly on the probable relationship between the stressful situation at Tabor and his subsequent tragic end:

> The question one has to ask is whether the stress caused the mental illness or if [father] would have become ill in any case. This is a problematic question because there is a strong history of depression in the [Hiebert] family. Dad was diagnosed as manic-depressive, a disorder which clearly has some heritable factor. One has to note, however, that this disorder usually has a social trigger, and clearly the unpleasant situation in which Dad found himself was just that–a trigger for depression.[74]

## The Recriminations

Interestingly, the significant discussion of this disturbing event was confined almost entirely to private correspondence and to the files of the Board of Reference and Counsel. Henry R. Wiens, pastor of the Reedley Mennonite Brethren Church and also a member of the Board of Reference and Counsel, emerged as the pivotal person in this discussion. He was the one who had discussed with Anna Hiebert what it would likely mean financially for the family if her husband was taken to Topeka. Until then the conference was supporting the family to some extent. Wiens helped convey the sad news of the suicide to Anna and her daughter Phyllis who were in the area, and he made arrangements for the "closed" funeral in his church, and he looked into the matter of the financial assistance that might be needed at that time.[75]

Anna Hiebert recalled that except for H. R. Wiens, who took a firm stance in favor of the burial in the Reedley church cemetery, and G. W. Peters, who gave "an enlightened and helpful" message at the funeral, hardly any conference leader so much as tried to comfort her and the family. She wrote: "No official group of the conference ever came to see me during [my husband's] sickness (as I recall), or later offered personal condolences." Instead, there was an aloofness as though suicide was unforgivable,[76] as well as a readiness to escape financial responsibilities.

Meanwhile, A. E. Janzen wrote to H. R. Wiens that except for the grace of God "heavy hours of this nature would hold no hope," and that what had transpired was "a grim reality" for both the family and "for us as an entire conference." At about the same time J. B. Toews wrote Board member Harder in Yarrow saying, "How dreadful [to contemplate] what the darkness in the life of a servant of God can do."[77] Wiens wrote P. C. Hiebert in Hillsboro that "it was hard to understand why God permitted such a thing to happen in our midst. We can only humble ourselves and ask God to forgive us where we have not been right with [Hiebert] as individuals and as a conference." Abram H. Unruh in Winnipeg wrote Wiens: "This sad news has shaken us deeply. Would you in confidence share some of the details with me? A brother asked me: 'where was the protecting hand of God in all of this?'.... May the Lord comfort the family... and the missionary workers in India."[78]

### The "Last Straw"

Both A. H. Unruh and P. C. Hiebert asked what the "last straw" might have been for John Hiebert. Had he been told that the Board of Reference and Counsel, of which Unruh was a member, was intending to "discontinue their support"? Wiens assured them that the question had been discussed with Anna Hiebert, but not with her husband. He wrote: "I only told her that in case she moved him to Kansas there would have to be a new resolution passed as to what the Conference would do for them."[79]

Involved in this was another angle. Wiens allowed in his letter of 16 August that his Board was influenced in such discussions by the views of the psychiatrist and staff at Kings View. In their view, support for the family should be withdrawn gradually, "because seemingly they felt that [the patient] and possibly [his] family were feeling too secure with this support and were not willing to be responsible. They felt that if Brother Hiebert knew that his family and brothers and sisters were contributing for his support that he would make a greater effort toward recovery. The Committee's action was taken in view of this wish of the psychiatrist." At the same time, both Wiens and the psychiatrist knew that Anna Hiebert had to work at various low-paying jobs to pay the bills. The conference paid for much of the hospitalization costs and the funeral costs but did not provide enough for living costs. The psychiatrist could not understand why Anna had to work when she had claimed they were part of a "caring community." He had wanted her to participate more in therapy sessions.[80]

**The Conclusion of the Matter**

Whatever the last straw, Wiens was aware that J. N. C. Hiebert was "really disturbed" at the thought of being sent to a state institution in Topeka. He must have known what such confinement could mean. Whether "cheerful and talkative" on the evening before, or leaving behind some incoherent writings on the morning of 20 July 1956, whether manic or depressed, Hiebert knew he did not want to be sent to Kansas.[81]

In the last analysis, while the family was held equally responsible with many others for "something so unwelcome as the passing of our brother [in this way]," one cannot escape from the conclusion that a terrible mistake was made to take this man from his very successful work in India and give him what proved an almost impossible task.

## CHAPTER 13

# The Intervention
# of the Board, 1949-1960

During the 1950s, under rapidly changing circumstances, the Board of Foreign Missions intervened in the affairs of the Missionary Council in order to acquire the authority that always eluded Henry W. Lohrenz and Nicolai N. Hiebert. As the result, the Missionary Council was entirely replaced by 1960. While many in the conference were not conscious of any rippling of the Mission waters, the missionaries and the Board had reached different perceptions of how indigenization was to be carried through. In order to understand why the clash occurred, it is necessary to understand the changes that occurred in the Board of Foreign Missions secretariat beginning in 1945.

### The New Secretary: A. E. Janzen

Abram Ewell Janzen knew "inwardly" he would be asked in 1945 to take the place of Henry Lohrenz as secretary-treasurer of the Mission. Janzen took over the work in his professorial office at Tabor College with a budget of about $172,000. Almost single-handedly until late 1953, except for secretarial assistance, Janzen organized all Board meetings, screened all candidates from a growing number of applications, and carried on a voluminous correspondence with individual missionaries in a growing empire of mission outreach. This correspondence dealt with a whole range of problems, human weakness, matters of principle, and material concerns. His letters usually began with a short homily or what might be termed a "meditorial."[1] These were sometimes in the form of a lecture, if he thought the missionary needed a lesson in humility, or just a restatement of principles.[2] In many ways a consummate bureaucrat, he was able to cope with the financial reports and requests of the Missionary Council in India and bring understandable reports to conferences.[3]

Janzen believed very strongly that the American MB Church had a special mission to evangelize overseas. This view held that its members had left Russia in the 1870s because they had been stifled in their mission outreach. In America, under divine providence, they

195

were especially called to make up for lost time. Janzen once related his belief that those Mennonite Brethren who came to Canada in the 1920s had missed their opportunity and were to be kept in second rank.[4] This may go far toward explaining why Janzen virtually excluded the story of the Russian Mennonite Brethren working with the American Baptists from his writings about the AMBM in India.[5]

## Janzen's Comparative Overview, 1949-1950

Before Janzen undertook a first visit to all the fields in 1948-1949, the Board of Foreign Missions developed its first, long overdue statement of principles. This twenty-three page booklet provided a "criterion" for the Board, as well as a "guide to the missionaries" on how to organize and carry out the mission program. Without indicating any specific indebtedness to the missiological views of Voth and Bergthold, as discussed in Chapter 10, Janzen wrote: "These guiding principles and field policies are based on the Word of God and the half century of experience in foreign missions of our missionaries, the Conference, and the Board of Foreign Missions." This statement did not, however, resolve the long-standing tension over the question of control. In fact, this document permitted the Missionary Council "to frame a Constitution by which it regulates its proceedings and work."[6]

Janzen's visit to India in 1949 gave the Board its first executive appraisal of the total work there. His findings indicated fairly accurately the condition of that field at the beginning of the third generation of effort.[7] There is irony in the difference between his initial amazement at what had been accomplished "in this land of mystery, caste, wealth, poverty and opportunity," and some of his conclusions and recommendations to the Board of Foreign Missions, and also between his report in-camera and to conference delegates. At first Janzen described the India mission as the best of all possible worlds. "Beyond human wisdom," he was certain, God had helped the missionaries to locate their stations strategically so that "each has so many unique features that each is the best and none duplicates the other."[8] Janzen surveyed each station and photographed the two hundred buildings in place, noted developments in education, medical work, zeroed in on the "problems of the indigenous church," and relayed the personal impact of the AMBM's fiftieth anniversary. He fully endorsed J. N. C. Hiebert's plan to move the one central high school to Mahbubnagar from Shamshabad in 1949, and to have three middle schools located in Shamshabad, Deverakonda, and Wanaparty. All stations would have primary schools except Kalvakurty. He noted the hospitals at a time when no central hospital was in prospect.[9]

Janzen was glad the India MB Church could boast over 13,000 Christians in about 180 villages and towns (one-tenth of the number of villages) in a population of 1.5 million for which the AMBM was responsible. But this represented only about .086 percent, or one-third of the national percentage of Christians in relation to the total population of India.[10] He was less happy about the indigenization record. The Bible school graduates were not entering the ministry of evangelism or preaching unless they were guaranteed "a meal ticket for life." They were openly interested in upward economic mobility. Moreover, most missionaries were so busy with station or other institutional work that they spent little time touring in the villages with the Gospel message, and they never moved on, as Bergthold had argued they should. Janzen also realized that the India church was completely "devoid of financial stewardship, and the ministry of giving has not yet been accepted in the Christian concept... To this day there is not one indigenous treasurer who can be trusted with money." Only two churches out of 180 raised enough money to pay their preachers.[11]

Janzen was surprised to hear the requests made by Preacher G. D. Samson in his representative speech at the Jubilee celebrations at Mahbubnagar in February 1949. His perceptions of American wealth were quite different from Janzen's as treasurer in Hillsboro. Samson stated that what was wanted in India, in addition to the Bible school, was a college and a seminary (like other missions). He was quite emphatic in declaring that "the help which the mission workers are getting is quite inadequate... for their social status. We humbly request the Board to increase our salaries viewing the hard situations at present."[12]

Janzen replied that as the church moved towards indigenization, the additional monies would have to come from the local groups. All he promised was that church buildings would eventually be given "to the indigenous church," but that all compounds built "with American mission funds," and therefore a "sacred" investment, "would **not** go to the indigenous church." They would instead be sold and the money reinvested.[13] This principle was not yet adhered to a decade later.

## Evangelization and Indigenization Forecast

While this somewhat disconcerting report moved the Board to initiate changes in the approach to India's evangelization,[14] Janzen gave delegates quite a different impression. He was particularly upbeat at the MB Canadian Conference of 1950, indicating that the work was going forward, "including evangelization in the villages." By the time of the 1951 General Conference at Winkler, the work was progressing "beyond all expectation," though India was not singled out.[15]

John Lohrenz went even farther in his enthusiasm for that Church in 1948. He told delegates: "When we consider that this Telugu MB Church has sprung up in the shadow of the mightiest Mohammedan capital in Asia [a mistaken reference to Hyderabad city], that... the converts come from the degraded and downtrodden outcastes, we can attribute this **phenomenal success** only to the gracious and mighty working of the Holy Spirit."[16] By 1956 Janzen gave out an amazing statistic, suggesting that India now had "23,000 members" and that the church there was taking steps "to become indigenous." This meant that since his visit, the statistic had changed from 13,000 "Christians" to 23,000 **members**.[17] As will be explained, this increase was largely caused by the gratuitous addition of the Makthal/Narayanpet field from Missionary Billington in 1954.

The Board responded in September 1950 by recommending that the Missionary Council deploy an enlarged staff along lines set forth in Janzen's *Survey* so that more evangelization should be accomplished, and specifically involving John N. C. Hiebert.[18] Janzen had predicated this on two couples occupying some stations, perhaps not even aware that no bungalow had been built to house two families. From this stronger emphasis on evangelism it was natural for the Board in October 1951 to re-establish the principle of indigenization. A year later the Board reaffirmed this principle, and began talking of the need for control. Having taken a second look at the *Principles* of 1947, which left the relationship between missionaries and Board ambiguous, the Board wrote a supplement to the 1947 guidelines in 1952. This seriously questioned the legislative strength of the Missionary Council.[19] It was followed up by a more purposeful Board visit in 1957.

## The Acquisition of Makthal/Narayanpet

Only three years before that crucial Board visit, led by J. B. Toews, the Mission took over a field developed by a missionary named C. H. Billington. His Telugu Village Mission covered areas to the west of Mahbubnagar called Makthal and Narayanpet, which he took over from the ABMU in 1909 (just as Frank Janzen received Wanaparty on the east side). He claimed about 6,000 Christians in a population of 200,000, served by forty-five workers. Billington paid John A. Wiebe a visit at Mahbubnagar in July 1953. Having reached the age of seventy-four, he offered the mission to the AMBM, asking only for a pension of two hundred rupees a month for himself and requesting that his Indian associates, among them Caleb Bella, be kept in their positions as leading pastors. The total budget of about 1,400 rupees a month had always been met on a "faith mission" basis through "Friends of the Mission" in America.[20]

This proposal was adopted by the Board, thus adding a ninth field to the AMBM in 1954. When the Balzers returned from their furlough in that year, they were asked to take this field. In many ways it was like pioneering all over again. In order to become acquainted with the workers they initiated Bible training in what they called the "Berean Bible Institute." Before they left Narayanpet they built and dedicated a new church.[21] When the Dicks left India in 1957, the Balzers took their place at Shamshabad and resumed their previous work of supervising the main AMBM training school, Bethany Bible Institute, now located permanently at Shamshabad.[22]

At Narayanpet the Balzers were succeeded by Henry and Alice (Bauman) Krahn from British Columbia. Henry Krahn, a teacher, soon asked for a change in the agreement with the former Billington Mission. Krahn's view of Narayanpet was quite different and perhaps more realistic than the roseate report given by Balzer in 1955. No thought could be given to indigenization here, Krahn argued. He wanted to channel funds from Billington's two long-time sources in America, Missionary Prayer League and Native Preacher Company, into education. Nothing hasty was intended, as Caleb Bella, for example, had already been "hard hit" by the transfer of the field to the AMBM. Needed was an educational program for youth which would require a life's work. To this suggestion Janzen allowed Krahn to continue Bella's support until the transfer of the Billington properties were completed, but steered his educational proposal to the attention of the new Governing Council which was now to take responsibility for education under the New India Plan, the result of the 1957 Board visit.[23]

The educational program to revitalize the Narayanpet field seemed lost in the New India Plan. Ted and Esther Fast continued the work in 1959, and national personnel took over from there.[24] The Krahns moved to Mahbubnagar to replace the Wiebes who went on furlough. Moreover, in the middle of 1958 Krahn turned to the possibilities of radio evangelism and began to ask for large sums of money for equipment. Regrettably, Alice became ill, had to resort to hospital care in Vellore, and their service was cut short by an early furlough in the fall of 1961. They were not able to return.[25]

### The Buildup of Jadcherla as the New Medical Center

By the end of the 1950s, given the constant urging from all quarters to become self-supporting and self-governing, it might not have seemed possible to justify overseas support for the centralization of the medical ministry in India. Yet, increasingly, this ministry came to be seen as the most effective way of bringing the gospel to all caste groups. At the beginning of the decade, it became possible to realize Schellenberg's vision of Jadcherla as an ideal location where surgery would be available.[26] This last big project of the Mission brought the overseas staff into a new concentration of human and material resources. It also meant closing down those hospitals supervised by nurses.[27]

Leadership in the Jadcherla project was provided by the doctor-nurse team of Jake and Ruth (Berg) Friesen from Reedley, California. They came for this purpose in 1951 and had the eager support of John Wiebe. At that time hospitals or dispensaries were in full operation at Deverakonda, Wanaparty, Shamshabad and Nagarkurnool, and Margaret Willems was building one at Gadwal. They were staffed by Canadian or American trained nurses and their Indian assistants, among them a pharmacist (or compounder). All of them, for years, had struggled with cases that required a doctor in any other situation. While on furlough Helen Harder wrote, "our setup has always demanded from nurses the work of a doctor." She did not want to come back to that in 1962.[28]

When Wiebe returned in January 1952 while the Friesens were in language study, he began to seek permission from the authorities for the building of a central hospital, and to get access to the sixty acres of land that were acquired with the purchase of Mahbubnagar/Gadwal from the American Baptists in 1937. One of the drawn-out problems involved in the project was to pry loose a Christian farmer named U. John from this land. He had convinced himself that his long occupancy gave him ownership. While this may have been a traditional Asian concept, Wiebe could not countenance it. But the problem was not wholly resolved until after the Wiebes had left the area.[29] Henry Krahn, given power of attorney in succession to Wiebe, continued to have problems with U. John and came to think of him as one who should be taken to court.[30]

As noted, Wiebe wanted to sell the hospital compound to help pay for the construction costs at Jadcherla. With the help of area authorities, and over much objection from Mahbubnagar church members, who argued that he could not sell **their** property, Wiebe consummated the sale, but not before December 1955, at 55,000 rupees.[31] In the midst of all these transactions, most frustrating in terms of the red tape involved, and in response to Wiebe's somewhat belated argument for greater mission centralization and institution building, A. E. Janzen in Hillsboro gave notice that in 1955 India would have to "do more with less."[32]

As for the Friesens, they were given a warm welcome by the church at Jadcherla in March 1952, and an even more gratifying farewell as they went on their first furlough in the fall of 1958. The Missionary Council and the Board helped to stave off an attempt by the American military to draft Friesen during the Korean War. Between those two dates they managed to build a commodious bungalow as well as a new hospital complex. The main building and the Schellenberg Memorial Ward were dedicated in 1957.[33] The nurses' training institute, under Marie Riediger's direction, did not get underway until 1961. Friesen's particular concern was to staff and equip the hospital adequate to his potential in surgery and other services. Ultimately, this MB Medical Center, accessible to the surrounding population of about 100,000 people, made a significant impact by bringing the gospel to those who came for medical treatment. It also demonstrated to all levels of Mahbubnagar District society, as one India specialist stated, "the real meaning of charity and work as worship." R. S. Aseervadam thought that this "humanitarian aspect" best showed how the MB church "followed the example of Christ."[34]

As George Froese and Peter Block were added to the staff in 1954 and 1961 respectively, it became possible for these medical doctors to serve the outlying "dispensaries," as Friesen called them. George and Annie Froese lived in a second bungalow built at Jadcherla and served Wanaparty, easily accessible by car. Peter and Arlene Block actually took up residence at Deverakonda and tried to bring Maria Wall's hospital up to standard. For the remainder of this decade, the nurses, except Ruth Friesen and Regina Suderman, all had a stint at serving in the outlying hospitals until about 1960-61. At that time Gadwal, Nagarkurnool, and Shamshabad hospitals were closed down, except for daytime clinics which were carried on for some time.

**The Rationale Behind the Board's Intervention**

A surface reason for the Board's intervention was the vast increase in programming since 1943, when the Belgian Congo, Columbia, and China fields were added, and the remarkable increase in recruitment right after the war. Of seventy new workers in 1948, twelve went to India for the first time. The budget was raised from $250,000 to $275,000. Whereas in 1898 a constituency of about 1,200 sent out the first 3 missionaries from America, Janzen reminded delegates that 18,744 members were now sending 123 missionaries abroad.[35]

A deeper reason lay in the conviction that the India Missionary Council had exercised too much legislative power for too long. The Missionary Council had virtually controlled the AMBM between 1914 and 1960. Hiebert and Lohrenz, administrators in the interwar period, had never been satisfied that they had sufficient control of the mission in India. Their service of facilitation carried on under Janzen until the 1950s. As demonstrated, the field perception always was that administrators in Hillsboro were relatively ignorant of the realities in India and were interfering. While in India, Janzen attended a meeting of the Missionary Conference and learned first hand what their "deliberations" meant. He saw how the executive of the Missionary Council paid great attention to proper constitutional procedures, and how issues, once resolved, were considered legislative in force.[36] According to J. B. Toews, the Conference at home was itself to blame for this situation. The Board had exercised some leadership but had never been given adequate authority by the Conference.

The recall of John N. C. Hiebert from the Mission in 1951 created a third reason for intervention. This issue brought the Missionary Council and the Board of Foreign Missions into sharp theological and administrative conflict. Three senior members of the Missionary Council wrote a strongly-worded theological criticism of the Board's action, stating in effect that this was a breach of the missionary call and vocation. While they intended "to further close brotherly relationship and a more harmonious working together between the Home Board and the Missionary," their statement was considered rather provocative. The Board threw back this challenge in two elaborate responses, as noted in Chapter 12.[37]

The strongest reason for intervention was the differing perceptions between Hillsboro and Shamshabad/Mahbubnagar as to how indigenization should and could be achieved. The Board became determined to do something about the institution-building in India. A combination of the seniority system, rather rigidly enforced until this period, and the development of a dependency mentality in the India church, contrary to earlier warnings from Cornelius Unruh, had led to empire-building. This paternalism had to be halted, especially once some Indian voices began to call for the banning of all proselytism from the Republic of India.[38]

Characteristic of the beginning of the post-mission era was a 1957 publication entitled *Revolution in Missions*, in which India's first Governor-General, C. Rajagopalachari, expressed his view on mission work involving deliberate proselytization. Believing that Christianity was not any nearer the truth than any other major religion represented in India, he could not find any justification for convert-making activity.[39] All India missionaries were forced back to the issues raised by a 1931 publication entitled *Rethinking Missions: A Layman's Enquiry*. While the chair of the commission, William Hocking of Harvard, did not at that time question the legitimacy of foreign mission work, he nevertheless doubted "that Christianity was either destined or entitled to displace the other highly developed religions of the world."[40] Though India's evangelicals rejected such extreme views out of hand, nevertheless a complete revaluation of cross-cultural mission was now underway.[41] For all these reasons it seemed imperative to provide stronger board leadership and give it more authority in the indigenization process.

### The Board's New Leadership: Gerhard Wilhelm Peters

Peters first made his mark on the Canadian scene as a generator of ideas, programs, and institutions, sometimes in an irritating fashion. In 1943 he demanded that Colombia be considered as a field for some of his students and colleagues from Saskatchewan.[42] His personal desire to go as a missionary to India never materialized once he was sent to South America on a fact-finding trip in 1945. Henry Lohrenz once acknowledged that Peters was "a man of dynamic power [who had] the strength of two." But there were certain traits in him "that call for caution," such as centralizing power and demanding that things must go entirely his way. Lohrenz did not think the Board would be willing to send him to India.[43] Peters never went to India until about 1964, nor to South America as an early version of a field secretary, when a definite appointment to such a position had been made. This was canceled, leaving Peters hurt and confused. This cancellation, Peters wrote in January 1946, "has cut deeper into our hearts and lives than anything ever has." Fortunately, some like A. H. Unruh told him he was cut out for important tasks at home, and every MB institution of higher education–Tabor College, Pacific Bible Institute and Mennonite Brethren Bible College–wanted him as a teacher in the mid-1940s.[44]

At first Peters' energies were channeled into studies, research, and the writing of history. He completed his doctoral studies at Hartford Seminary. For his thesis he chose *The Growth of Foreign Missions in the Mennonite Brethren Church*. He presented his manuscript to the Board of Foreign Missions in 1947. It was used extensively by A. E. Janzen and John Lohrenz for their histories even before publication in 1952.[45] While at Hartford Peters accepted an invitation to join the faculty of Pacific Bible Institute in Fresno, California, serving as president and dean there from 1947 to 1955, and then as dean of Mennonite Brethren Biblical Seminary from 1955 to 1960.[46]

## John Benjamin Toews

Toews went from Coaldale to Tabor College in 1930 to study Bible under H. W. Lohrenz.[47] While teaching at Bethany Bible Institute in Hepburn, Saskatchewan, beginning in 1932, he pursued further education at various schools. His spiritual mentor Benjamin B. Janz was disturbed that Toews was pursuing doctoral studies in Texas while serving as pastor of the Buhler (Kansas) MB Church. He dissuaded Toews from such a course in 1943. Janz feared that Toews would disqualify himself within the "Brotherhood" by striking out into what was then considered a worldly pursuit or a sign of arrogance. While G. W. Peters had been allowed to pursue doctoral studies at Hartford without criticism, Toews was induced to give up such studies. Two years later Janz and other Canadians came to Toews requesting that he leave Buhler to take the presidency of the new Bible College in Winnipeg. Only three years had gone by, but now it was acceptable to have education for this "higher" Bible school that the Canadians said they needed.[48] As it was, Toews never completed his doctorate.

After three active years as president, Toews followed a call to become pastor of the Reedley (California) MB Church, the largest congregation in the conference. Following five years of gratifying results, Toews was persuaded to leave Reedley in order to strengthen the Board of Foreign Missions' authority for the expanded mission. Going to Hillsboro and staying for nearly ten years, he later recalled, proved to be the most difficult and tiring years of his life. His first election to the Board of Foreign Missions in 1945 was simply to fill out Henry Lohrenz' term. In 1948 he became a full member of the Board, and in late 1953 the full-time deputation secretary, thus taking over some of Janzen's responsibilities.[49] The latter had come to be considered too gentle for the tough decisions that would have to be made with respect to indigenization.

Toews rapidly became aware of the forced changes of the post-War world, especially with the reality of decolonization in British India in 1947. The independence of India, the corresponding formation of the Church of South India in 1947, and the growing nationalist opposition to all mission, in spite of the promise of religious freedom written into India's 1950 constitution, were grounds for taking charge.[50] Toews began to compare how other mission organizations related to their workers abroad, especially in light of the need for rapid indigenization. By the mid-1950s he and others circulated around the congregations preparing them for radical change.[51] Realistically, indigenization in India would allow them to trim the budget so that they could expand elsewhere.[52] For the introduction of such drastic change, the Board wanted a clear mandate from a General Conference delegation similar to the one for the ill-fated recall of J. N. C. Hiebert at the Winkler Conference in 1951. Led by G. W. Peters and J. B. Toews, they sought a comparable vote of confidence at Yarrow in 1957. Named after that conference, the policy statement drafted essentially by Toews gave the Board authority to accelerate indigenization in India.[53]

Toews' appointment as deputation secretary also brought about a fundamental change in news management, one implemented rather abruptly about 1953. Understandable as this was, considering the encroachment of the much expanded mission on the official press, the change seemed drastic. Now missionary letters were compressed, leaving only brief summaries of their news. Quite apart from the lessening of the value of such reporting for the historian, the Board of Foreign Missions took command of the news, filtering to supporters whatever seemed most salient. George Froese, at least, objected to this. Missionaries should have freedom of access to the press, and editing should not be done without permission of the writer.[54] Nevertheless, this trend continued once Toews took over the "deputational" aspect of the Hillsboro office. There was an emphasis on putting an official imprimatur on promotional material.

Janzen made the point in Coaldale in 1955 that Toews was making a difference. The churches, he said, "will surely have noticed" that there have been many more Board-directed mission conferences and visits from the deputation secretary.[55] Among the younger set in India, like Jake Friesen, some thought that Toews did what was necessary, but not without treading on many toes. Vernon Wiebe, in retrospect, thought that Toews was the "blood-letter" to give new life, while others have thought of him as the "driving force of the 1950s" and perhaps for years afterwards.[56] That there was some backlash from this will become evident.

### An Explanation for the Struggle Between Board and Missionary Council

There were two policy trajectories which converged in 1957 and which should have jelled without the sharp clash that ensued.

The Missionary Council, spurred on by changes in India's constitution, as well as by Janzen's 1950 *Survey*, took steps to indigenize as rapidly as they felt possible, so that by 1957 they actually had sponsored a new constitution for mission and church in India before the Board visit in July of that year. Meanwhile, another theoretical trajectory headed in the same direction, but with control of the missionaries in mind, was formed by the more deliberate missiological re-thinking of G. W. Peters and J. B. Toews.

In June 1952 the Missionary Council resolved to find "a united way of procedure in the building up of the Andhra M. B. Churches into a self-supporting indigenous body." Later, in October and in January 1953, the Board in Hillsboro began to speak of a full-time deputation secretary who would bring about greater decentralization of the Mission by indigenization.[57] The Board, more than most missionaries, found in "the rise of nationalism, communism [a growing specter in the USA], and sentiment against foreigners" much cause for pessimism regarding the future of the India field. There was cause for urgency in passing the responsibility to the India church. But evangelization by Indians would not be accomplished without a greater concentration on the training of national workers, nor without having an incorporated body in India into whose hands to place such responsibilities. Hence, in April 1956 the Board approved a recommendation from the Missionary Council that a Governing Council be formed as an extension of the field council of an earlier day.[58]

John Wiebe's letter of 22 February 1957 as secretary confirmed the view that greater direction would have to be taken by Hillsboro. He argued that if England could decolonize in India, surely the MB Mission "should have faith in God and man to also hand over to the Brethren in the East." But then he added his personal misgivings: "[Viola and I] do not find that the Missionary group is ready to really hand over" because they do not see the leaders that are necessary. "I believe that leaders can only become leaders when leadership is delegated to them." Wiebe seemed more willing than others to risk a transfer of responsibility, regardless of the caliber of leadership.[59] These misgivings aside, the Administrative Committee in India worked out a constitution for the transitional stage from Mission to Church in India.

When Janzen received this in April, he was grateful. "These constitutions represent a great deal of hard work and definite planning and counseling with other missionaries and national brethren." The Board, however, found the Missionary Council's constitution too "Presbyterian," too undemocratic.[60] It also lacked a definite timetable for indigenization. In any case, since a visit from J. B. Toews and others was imminent, the Missionary Council was advised to wait for face-to-face discussion about these matters.[61]

To this Unruh, and also Wiebe, responded with the argument that the democratic approach at home "has not proven a success in the East." Unruh allowed that if he were in America he would also look askance at their constitution. But he reminded the Board that they were writing a constitution "for the India churches," with Indian conditions and laws in mind. The India churches simply did not have the organizational strength nor the organic sense of the North American churches. As chair of the Missionary Council Unruh claimed that the India brethren already had reason to feel "that at last the American thorn... was removed" in the constitution the Missionary Council had devised. Wiebe sincerely hoped that their constitution, "drafted and redrafted many times" but now fully accepted by both missionaries and Indians, would be acceptable in Hillsboro. He added: "In our procedures we have always reminded ourselves that greater representation will be delegated to local churches in the subsequent framing of by-laws." (Janzen wrote in the margin of his copy, "Will this ever happen?")[62]

The one thing the Missionary Council was not clear on was how the "direct relationship" between the Board and the Governing Council would involve the Missionary Council. The Missionary Council considered the issue of the transfer and registration of property in the name of a "recognized MB Body, Church or Mission registered in Andhra Pradesh" quite problematic.[63] Time proved them right. If the Missionary Council and the Board of Foreign Missions were so close together in drafting a "new India plan," why was the intervention entirely different from what Unruh and others might have expected?

### The Visit from J. B. Toews in 1957

From the sources, one can only conclude that Toews' visit in 1957 was interpreted by the missionaries as inquisitorial from the outset. A questionnaire had been sent to each missionary in advance and Toews expected compliance. What was even more resented by the seniors was Toews' private meeting with indigenous leaders. They protested that senior missionaries were needed as interpreters. Toews found the India brethren glad to be free for the first time to say what was on their minds. He was told that while the Board assumed there was one mission, in fact there were as many missions as there were senior missionaries. They chafed under this colonial system.[64]

Toews was also criticized for having a private meeting with the single women missionaries. Again, the Missionary Council had no control of this agenda.[65] The women's complaints had opened the door for them to correspond directly with the secretariat and now to talk face to face.

As a result of these experiences, Toews went away resolved to do something much more radical than the gradual transition reflected in Janzen's intervening correspondence. Throughout the visit, however, there was no inkling that the report to be given at Yarrow in October might include anything unusual. In fact, the document known as the "Yarrow Statement" was not written until September 1957. It was drawn from an evaluative report that had been presented to the Board before the conference sessions. It was "prepared jointly" by the four men who made a visit to the fields in that year.

G. W. Peters wrote in 1984 that "the statement, though at first glance quite innocent, was revolutionary. It concentrates all legislative and administrative authority in the Board, removing missionary partnership from both [legislative and administrative power]." He suggested that history dictated this radical step. Then he contradicted that suggestion by allowing efficiency and expediency to override "the spirit of true brotherhood." As Peters admitted, "the Board proceeded unilaterally, contrary to its earlier practices," without consultation with the Missionary Council, and the whole was "not worded cautiously enough to avoid misunderstanding and personal offence."[66] Younger people like Donald Unruh, close enough to observe these events, were left with the feeling that there was in all this "a will to power" at work.[67]

## The Impact of Yarrow

While the missionaries present at Yarrow, especially those from India, grasped the fact that this statement meant significant adjustments for all missionaries on every field, most of the delegates who voted overwhelmingly for change did not realize what impact this would have on India personnel and programs.[68] The seniors especially were taken aback because they had already begun the indigenization process. They were well aware of the needs of the day. Most of them, however, were convinced the India Church was not ready for the accelerated pace demanded by the Board. If the Board of Foreign Missions had studied nineteenth-century missions to India, such a study could have told them that the pattern of "spontaneity" followed by Board intervention–a pattern they had now copied–did not work out well with converts from untouchability.[69]

After that shock had worn off, the implementation of the "New India Plan" of 1958 was slowed down, requiring modification for a variety of reasons, and took at least fifteen years–rather than the three to five years intended. In that sense, the missionaries on the field were largely proven right, quite apart from the paternal and natural tendency to resist any, let alone rapid, change. But even the younger personnel presiding over the institutions, teachers, doctors, nurses, soon faced the realities of dismantling, and questioned whether the Telugus were prepared. Were they really trustworthy with property and money? Hillsboro administrators came to understand the problems better in the late 1960s and the 1970s and in large measure agreed with the missionaries, but under the current Board leadership indigenization had to take its precarious course.

## The New India Plan

The Yarrow statement, as presented in its applied form to the MB General Conference delegates of 1960 and 1963 meant, essentially, that a "new era" had been created, as stated by J. B. Toews: "we have passed from a mission-centered program of world evangelism to an international church-fellowship program" in which the "emphasis falls not on the individual missionary . . . but on the younger churches and our [Board and Conference] relationship to them." The Board of Foreign Missions was to become "an agency to assist the national church to evangelize the people of its own country."[70]

210

With reference to each national church, in this case India, the structural relationship was shown as follows:[71]

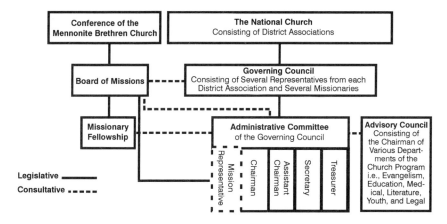

**Organizational Relationship of the Conference of the Mennonite Brethren Church with National Churches Abroad**

This was spelled out more particularly in the new statement of *Principles and Policies*. The "fundamental concept and purpose of missions" was stated as follows: "The permanent aspect of the mission program rests in the national church with its roots in Jesus Christ, its direction in the Holy Scriptures, and its organizational operation adapted to their respective culture."[72] The missionaries were now merely auxiliary. While all this sounded very straightforward and fairly simple to many delegates, the implementation in India was anything but straightforward. The first question had to do with the nature of the Liaison Committee.

**The Liaison Committee**

When members of the Missionary Council first saw the "New India Plan" they returned it with some revisions in September 1958. They wanted the Missionary Council to be the liaison between the Governing Council and the Board of Foreign Missions. Knowing this might prove nettlesome to the Board, John A. Wiebe requested that the Board should send a delegation back to India, very soon, to discuss the whole question of transfer. From hindsight one can say this would have been worth the expense involved. As it was, there was no further Board visit to India until 1961, and endless trouble.[73]

When the Board received Wiebe's suggestion for a strong continuing role for the Missionary Council, they advised Janzen to state that this was a "radical departure from the basic policy of the New Plan." The Administrative Committee of the Missionary Council, meeting in Hughestown, countered by suggesting a five-member liaison committee between the Board and the Governing Council. Assuming that church/board relations henceforth would have mainly to do with finances, they feared the church, which really "has no [loyal] attachment" to Hillsboro, would last only as long as a heavy subsidy was continued. In those minutes, signed by Peter Balzer, the missionaries claimed to be totally devoted to preparing a "completely independent and indigenous church." They ended by requesting an appeal, rather unorthodox, to the Board of Reference and Counsel in this constitutional issue between Missionary Council and Board.[74]

Faced with this firmness in India, the Board in March 1959 seemed to approve of such a five-member Liaison Committee on a three-year trial basis. Whether cause and effect or not, a year later the Board made Toews general secretary, thus giving him the entire administration of the secretariat.[75]

### Abram A. Unruh as Leader of the Opposition

Some missionaries, among them Ernest Schmidt, thought the 1957 statement had very little validity because the delegates who voted for it did not really understand its implications. Certainly A. A. Unruh agreed with him, but he went much further. Unruh took vocal objection to the Yarrow Statement, focusing particularly on certain statements in the document that he perceived as a denigration of the missionaries of his generation in terms of education, missiological inadequacies, and "patterns of work." Unruh, by then a twenty-year veteran of the Mission, was also quite angry about some aspects of the 1957 visit, and his resistance upset the Secretariat very much. He was not alone by any means; he had considerable encouragement. When one compares the correspondence between Toews/Janzen and Unruh, with correspondence from the Missionary Council in India, it was clearly not a winning issue for either side. With the exception of Anna Suderman, Unruh was the only senior to survive this clash of conviction.

Unruh was incensed by a 22 November 1957 letter to India questioning some aspects of his accounts at Wanaparty, which were showing a deficit at this time. He thought his personal integrity was being questioned. "There must be a reason for that question at this time. Only if brethren have full confidence in each other [is] a united work possible."[76] As chair of the new Governing Council, composed of both missionaries and India leaders, Unruh warned the Board that the Governing Council was now as prepared as the Missionary Council to go through any new Hillsboro plan point by point, "changing or refusing it." As though anticipating changes, he raised a host of important points such as "pensions" for the workers, the transfer of the "boardings," and the principalship of the Central High School. To this Janzen replied on the 21st, point by point, before the New India Plan was ready or received.[77] The playing field seemed to be quite level between them.

But meanwhile Unruh had also written Toews a letter on 14 May. The tone here was quite different. The occasion was Toews' request that Unruh shorten a paper for publication on the "Training of Christian Youth." Because he had already translated it for *Suvarthamani,* Unruh was disinclined to cooperate, commenting that "I don't know exactly what for [sic] you want the article in America." He was really more concerned to respond to "all the different statements made in meetings and papers." He would have preferred to meet face-to-face rather than make of these a "controversial question in the home papers [which] would throw up unnecessary dust and bring us into disfavor with the office." While Unruh did not want to go public, he must have made up his mind to do so not long after this. He told Toews that "some of your statements as reported in papers were absolutely uncalled for.... They served no positive purpose but put the motives of the missionaries in question." Unruh said that they all wanted to work towards indigenization, even though they had not yet found full agreement with the Indian church as to methods.[78]

Unruh came to believe he would get somewhere if he could appeal to the whole Board, or to the Conference, or even the congregations. Surely something would be done to caution Toews, Peters, and Janzen on their headlong course of rapid indigenization on the pretext of having authorization from the conference. Did the leading brethren really understand what was going on?

### Resign or Protest!

Unruh's first letter of this kind was a general one in response to the Yarrow Statement itself. He asked, "is the thinking of the Board also the thinking in the churches?" He was convinced that it was not. Unruh was certain that the Yarrow enunciation was "a divergence, infused by a different spirit whose grounds with reference to India were misleading and the conclusion unbiblical." The Statement was "hastily conceived," without consulting with "those who have carried the greatest part of the mission work in the field." Though he was not aware at that moment that some of those on furlough like Lohrenz and Schmidt had been consulted, he felt (as did Kasper) that they in India now ought to have the right to voice their opinions. Unruh at least was not prepared to accept a **fait accompli**. "Do not be surprised, dear Brethren," he continued, "if we cannot keep silent because this involves the work to which we were called of God.... We cannot keep silent when brethren consult **about** us but not **with** us." By slavishly following these directives that stood in conflict with their conscience and understanding of the total mission as a church, they could only "lose our self-respect."[79] For Unruh the only options were to resign or protest.

While he renewed his effort to train leaders for the new course in India,[80] uppermost in Unruh's mind was an appeal to the larger constituency. He chose the *Mennonitische Rundschau,* a paper widely read in Canada but less so in America. He took a chance on bringing himself into "disfavor," just as he had hinted to Toews in May. In this article, entitled "Aufruf" (appeal, proclamation), clearly something more significant than a mere generalization, he wrote: "Today we read much about mission principles, and large conferences are arranged to discuss missionary methods; there are heated debates about the missionary mistakes of the past." He wanted the church to become aware of what was happening. To assert that the evangelization on the India field (as worked for sixty years) was now entirely the responsibility of the India Mennonite Brethren Church "does not absolve us from the responsibility for the million others." Unequivocally, he stated that "a half truth can become a lie which will lead to a terrible awakening when our Lord calls us to

214

account." Did the churches at home realize they were faced with theoretical experimentation, half-truths, and competing voices sending confusing signals? As Jeremiah wrote: "The summer is ended, and we are not saved."[81]

Unruh received powerful support when three other members of the Missionary Council: Balzer, Krahn, and Wiebe, joined him in raising some theological questions about the Yarrow statement. They were fundamentally opposed to its tone and philosophy. Their paper was refined, signed by J. J. Kasper as secretary, and sent to the Secretariat.[82]

The Board became troubled by the adverse feedback regarding Yarrow, and especially by the writings of Unruh, including his use of the *Mennonitische Rundschau* as a vehicle of criticism. They recorded their reaction to Unruh's warnings by asking Janzen to write him, hoping that he could "find an inward release... from prejudice against the Board. The Board concedes that it has made the impression on the India Missionaries of hasty procedure and bears sorrow over this impression."[83]

**End of an Era for the Seniors**

Though no one else raised the opposition to Unruh's level, most had serious misgivings about the readiness of the India Church to take over. Moreover, seniors were disturbed that they were to be set aside in fairly short order. Margaret Suderman, a well-trained Canadian nurse, only fifty-five and in good health, objected strongly to being replaced at Wanaparty by Margaret Willems in 1957. She made it quite clear that she had no intention of leaving her station. "I was called of God and you have no right to order me around. I have to stay here."[84] Nevertheless, she and Anna Suderman were moved to Deverakonda where Maria Wall and Helen Warkentin crowded up in order to accommodate them. Margaret and Anna stayed there until 1962. Anna returned in 1966 for a short term. Margaret also wanted to return, but by the time she had recovered from thirty years of overextending herself she was too close to retirement age.[85]

Peter and Elizabeth Balzer, who had been in India since 1923, went home in 1961. Peter served administratively as chair of the Missionary Council as well as principal of the central Bible school for many years. J. B. Toews was there at Shamshabad on a second visit in that year. He observed Balzer's last months as full-time missionary. Balzer was in the habit of having his preachers report to him before he paid their salary. Toews observed one morning that several preachers were sitting outside on the Shamshabad verandah. Should he not go out to ask what they wanted? Balzer replied, "let them wait, they are being punished because they did not do all I asked them to do." When they were sufficiently remorseful, he would pay them. Balzer's attitude toward his successor, Paul G. Hiebert, only confirmed for Toews that they were right to have taken a firm line against those who could not adjust to change. Though Paul, the son of John and Anna Hiebert, a graduate of Kodaikanal and Tabor College, and holding a master's degree in South Asian studies, had been sent to take over Bethany school at Shamshabad, Balzer stated publicly at their farewell that it pained him a great deal that there was simply no one to take over his position.[86]

After Elizabeth's death in 1966, Balzer married Margaret Willems in 1967. They returned four times between then and the early 1980s for short stays in India. They hoped, like Maria Wall, to reach out to upper-caste people. They did this by investing funds in a Bible institute in the Vijajawada area.[87]

The departure of John H. and Maria Lohrenz from Hughestown in the spring of 1957 has been noted. When Maria Klaassen Lohrenz died in 1962,[88] John married Susie Richert in March 1963 and returned to the field in October for a period of six months. He was particularly concerned to have his latest book in Telugu, *The Doctrinal Teachings of the Bible*, adopted for use.[89]

The veterans Wall and Warkentin, having worked at Deverakonda more or less continuously since 1920, were also not happy about the abruptness of their departure. Maria Wall especially, after forty years of nursing without a doctor to help, wanted to be free to visit former patients, especially caste people, and share the Gospel with them in the villages before she retired. She traveled in a trailer pulled by oxen, taking her Bible women with her. She pursued this for some months, but the Board issued a clear signal that she and Warkentin should return home in the fall of 1957. Later she gave vent to her feelings: "I consider it a great tragedy that experienced workers are being called home at this very critical time." Assigning guilt to those who failed "the many who will not be visited," she ended by saying: "This great need will be before me as long as I live, while I, though strong and able to work as hard as some younger ones, am idling away my time in comfortable America."[90]

The young Deverakonda station missionary, Ted Fast, noticing Wall's distress, warned the Missionary Council that these two veterans were not ready to be shipped home. Had she and Warkentin done something wrong to be treated this way? They wanted to stay at least until the hot season of 1958 in order to wind down their affairs. Fast then tried to appeal directly to board members, asking for a reconsideration. "The idea of their retirement is too sudden to us because physically they are well . . . and their work is carried out most efficiently... This sudden arrangement made by [visitors of 1957] created restlessness among the Christian . . . people in the compound and the field." He was convinced they should be allowed to stay for their own sake and for the welfare of the Mission as perceived by all those whose lives had been touched by these two veterans.[91] This request for an extension was denied and the two women returned in December 1957.

Helen L. Warkentin, very popular with many orphans who treated her as "mother," was obviously not as outspoken as her partner Maria Wall. In 1956 many former students, some of whom served as teachers under her supervision, others in government services, returned to greet her at a reunion of the school founded at Deverakonda thirty-eight years earlier by John H. Voth. Her best known protégé was M. B. John, who visited America as the representative of the new Governing Council in 1960. There were effusive addresses, India-style, in farewell.[92]

**The Musings of Julius J. Kasper**

Another who reflected seniors' feelings was Julius Kasper, who had been serving as secretary to the Missionary Council for some time. Returning from furlough, he was faced with the New India Plan. Kasper tended to join with those missionaries most conservative in their response. He thought they should have been consulted before such drastic measures were to be implemented. He and others had suggestions for making the Yarrow Statement more positive and biblical in tone.[93]

Since he had some cause earlier to be quite pessimistic about the quality of Christians in the church, Kasper was not surprised by the restlessness in the various compound churches when talk of rapid change reached them. An instance of this appeared in Wanaparty where Unruh, chair of the Missionary Council, was asked to vacate Wanaparty and move to Kalvakurty, a lower-profile station. This order mystified Kasper. What Wanaparty needed, he thought, was a new register of believers eligible to vote in church business meetings, thus clearing out all those unregenerate persons pressing to take advantage of any subsidies should indigenization proceed rapidly. Along this line he warned Janzen privately that they should not let certain India brethren travel freely during visits to North America. Some families had wealth enough to make a money-raising trip unnecessary.[94]

At the height of the restlessness in Wanaparty, Hughestown, and Shamshabad congregations, Kasper was relieved of his secretarial duties, as the new liaison committee was introduced. At this time Janzen thanked him warmly for his years of service in the Missionary Council structures and told him: "now do what you went to India to do, preach the Gospel." During his last years of service in India he assisted in the Bible School at Shamshabad. Julius and Mary Doerksen Kasper remained at home after their 1965 furlough in favor of the educational needs of their children.[95]

## CHAPTER 14

# The Mission Administrative Committee

As a result of the difficulties in coming to an agreement on the pace of indigenization, and stung by the criticisms of Unruh, the Board substituted a three-member committee for the earlier suggestion of a five-member liaison between the Board in Hillsboro and the Church in India. After forty-six years and ninety-one such meetings, the legislative power of the Missionary Council was taken away by executive decision in Hillsboro in August 1960. Some of the missionaries deeply resented its makeover into a Missionary Fellowship. It seemed too extreme and too sudden for many and eventually led to requests for the Missionary Fellowship to have a greater voice.

The three-member Mission Administrative Committee (MAC) turned out to be a eight-year micro version of the Missionary Council that did not necessarily ease relations. While the Governing Council of the India Church was to be the key element in the new equation, the MAC largely supervised the transfer, evaluated and placed personnel, and controlled the finances. Some single women especially chafed under this administration. They soon came to think of the new order as a dictatorship.

The Missionary Council had its last meeting in June 1960 under the chairmanship of A. A. Unruh, and the MAC held its first meeting at Jadcherla on 6 October 1960.[1] The Board appointed Ted Fast as chair, Henry Poetker secretary, and Jake Friesen treasurer.

### The First Five Years of the MAC, 1960-1965

Fast's committee was immediately beset by a host of questions, issues, and some serious problems. Fast asked: "Are we . . . consultants or are we able to give our reactions to some of the drastic measures being implemented at home?" He feared that the 1960 Congo crisis, which forced evacuation of all missionaries, was causing hasty decisions to be made in Hillsboro with regard to India.[2] The Governing Council certainly seemed mystified by the constitutional change, found it far too sudden, and tried at first to avoid working through the MAC. Anne Ediger wrote that "the Indian constituency has no voice in the consolidation program."[3] This was comparable to Unruh's complaint that they had no input into the Yarrow Statement. Surely there was a way "toward mutual understanding and cooperation," Janzen wrote reassuringly in response to news of a possible boycott by the Governing Council. Unruh saw the setup as a new colonialism, except now authority was vested in a "colonial secretary" in Hillsboro.[4]

There was another boycott. Within one year Margaret Willems and other single women had come to see the MAC as a new concentration of power using dictatorial methods with respect to personnel. Fast first worried about "a widening gap" in the missionary fellowship, then wrote a few months later of a "definite boycott . . . of this committee" by the single women. Poetker noted a change in Governing Council attitudes by April 1961, stating that at least the MAC was now an acceptable liaison for them, if not for the women. J. B. Toews responded that the committee was kept small not in order to concentrate power, but to "facilitate" liaison and to pinpoint responsibility.[5]

Among the serious questions that arose was a replacement for Henry and Alice Krahn; whether the singles could continue to vacation at Coonoor; and whether promising Shamshabad graduates should go to Ramapatnam or Yeotmal for their theological training.

Though Alice Krahn could not stay in India for health reasons, the Krahns were urged to remain until Toews and Janzen had made their 1961 visit. This merely prolonged the problem. Candidly, Krahn found it difficult to work in an auxiliary capacity and to stay within the high school's budget. Even though he had a very capable headmaster, D. J. Arthur, Krahn seemed determined, like John Lohrenz in Hughestown, to remain in charge and face the consequences "if something fails." In this connection Ted Fast asked whether Ernest and Evelyn Schmidt could be induced to come back to India for the short term. They knew the language and had demonstrated their support for indigenization while working at Gadwal.[6]

Actually, it seemed that Mahbubnagar might again have been open to the Schmidts when J. A. Wiebe was given power of attorney in February 1958 and the Board asked the Wiebes to move out of the bungalow in order to devote their whole time to "the legal assignment" of property management. Though Wiebe was almost wholly engaged in legal matters by this time, he and Viola felt that they could not accept this as an official assignment. They did not want to end their career detached from "other missionary assignments," and argued that they required another year to "round off work according to [our] plan." They valued their strategic position at Mahbubnagar, whose district encompassed seven mission centers.[7]

The Schmidts did not wish to chance any sort of repetition of 1952. At that time the Board had remained passive instead of intervening on their behalf. Another place for them might have been found in Hughestown where a second high school had developed from the middle school begun under the Lohrenz' supervision. They had also observed in 1957 how "self-sacrificing missionaries" could be "turned out to pasture." Given their age in 1958 (he was forty-two), "prudence" made Ernest and Evelyn Schmidt remain in America.[8] That aside, the requests for their return continued from Anna Suderman. This prompted Poetker as MAC secretary to write in April 1962 that the Schmidts would be welcome as long as the "affair" involving the Board, the Wiebes, and Schmidts was settled. He was glad to hear that some kind of "victory" had been achieved.[9] As noted, neither the Wiebes or the Schmidts returned to the AMBM field.

### Coonoor and the Holy Spirit

The question of vacationing in the hills, whether at Kodaikanal or Coonoor, arose in a new form. The MB missionaries had bypassed Ootacumund by this time, and all MB children studied at Kodaikanal.[10] But the single women preferred to vacation at Coonoor because they liked Keswick's spiritual emphasis there. Margaret Willems objected to the "social Christianity and modernism" manifest at Kodaikanal. The preference for Coonoor brought up the question of property for this purpose at that location. It was made clear to her in April 1958 that the Mission could not afford two retreat sites.[11]

The Board was willing to enlarge the facilities at Bruton, Kodaikanal, and make allowances for extra costs "providing that a commitment can be obtained from our missionaries." In this stressful time Janzen wanted all AMBM missionaries in the hills to "meet at one place . . . instead of scattering to different places," as had been the practice for many years. He reasoned that "in order to allow the Holy Spirit to really blend together into a spiritual unity of heart, mind and purpose in the work, **it is necessary that the workers are assembled at one place**." The Board urged the Missionary Fellowship to get a commitment from all to rally at Bruton. Janzen could see the Missionary Fellowship having "a greater voice in arranging evangelical spiritual programs during the summer weeks at Kodaikanal." The MAC also took the occasion to have a scheduled meeting during that time. Ironically, at the first such planned fellowship in June 1961, while all the MB Kodaikanal teachers and Bruton staff were also present, the communion service was spoiled when one missionary walked out.[12]

### Ramapatnam or Yeotmal?

Over the years many potential candidates for the preaching ministry had trained at Jacob Heinrichs' ABMU seminary at Ramapatnam on the Bay of Bengal, at least until the sharp break occasioned by John H. Voth in 1920. Once it became more urgent to staff the training school at Shamshabad and prepare for theological leadership, a consensus was reached that Union Biblical Seminary, Yeotmal (later Pune), south of Bombay, should be favored over the Baptist seminary at Ramapatnam, even when John and Viola Wiebe were assigned there.

In 1961 Wiebe stated that Ramapatnam would welcome more MB students, and invited Toews and Janzen to visit the seminary during their stay in India. He recommended Ramapatnam over Yeotmal on the strength of its historic association with the Russian Mennonite Brethren missionaries.[13] Their presence at the Baptist seminary encouraged its principal to make strong appeals to Shamshabad's graduating students in 1962. When Wiebe met with the Missionary Fellowship at Kodaikanal in June 1963 he confirmed that Ramapatnam also appealed to some of the current Governing Council leaders as a place for them to further their studies. But the Fellowship demurred at this. If an "official commitment had been made to Yeotmal," would the attendance of Governing Council leaders weaken "the unified working of the mission and the church?"[14]

Though the Board at one stage gave the MAC freedom to choose between the seminaries, Toews wanted a clear recommendation in order to facilitate his own negotiations. In Poetker's view, the "devotional life at Ramapatnam remains open to doubt." He disliked its more permissive life-style in areas such as cinema attendance.[15] By the fall of 1963 the Board had hardened its position based on ecumenical considerations. It did not want officially to support theological seminaries like Ramapatnam "which find their ultimate source of authority and finances within the framework of the [World Council of Churches]." Because of this fundamental reservation about liberal ecumenicism, promising candidates like D. J. Arthur and N. P. James were advised to go to Yeotmal even though Wiebe had two scholarships available at Ramapatnam. Actually V. K. Rufus and B. C. John attended Ramapatnam in 1963.[16]

### The Frustrations of These Years

Frustrating situations accumulated as the MAC tried to transfer responsibility for all programs from the Board to the Governing Council. This was no easy task since all three major programs–evangelization and Bible training, the school (boardings) system, and the new centralized medical ministry–were competing for funds while giving at home was in decline. While Fast, Poetker, and Friesen were seen as excessively authoritarian by both the India leaders and the single women, Fast complained that everyone was "throwing burdens on us." He wanted to get out of administration of institutions sooner rather than later. There was some comfort in Toews' expression of deep satisfaction with the MAC's work. "You have performed with deep dedication and efficiency," he told them.[17]

The competition for funds was illustrated by Fast's view that evangelism was being short-changed. He complained about the Board's sending John H. Lohrenz back for a short time in 1963 while "we cannot get our salaries!" During Frank C. Peters' visit in 1964, Fast was so saddened by the heavy board indebtedness that he wrote: "one begins to rethink missions and the call." He seemed ready to quit. When monies kept running late, the Fasts found it almost impossible to manage as a family, quite apart from the distribution of appropriations.[18] In October 1964 he criticized the Board for not providing sufficient money for roofs for church buildings. He argued that

> hospitals and schools can have all the money they need and . . . we in Evangelism barely scrape along paying any gas we need to go touring in villages with our own salaries since it is cut from our budget. The Board will wake up some of these

223

days with only medical and school staff and the rest of us will pray to the Lord to open other doors of service to us.

While he regretted having to write this, Fast reminded the Board that schools and hospitals could be taken over by government, but the programs that must continue, evangelism and church planting, were being shortchanged. To this board treasurer Peter J. Funk responded with some sharpness, stating that it was unfair to "put the piggy on the Board" when he suspected that disputes on the field were causing shifts in the appropriations.[19] There was some truth to that.

In the midst of this frustrating period, Frank C. Peters visited the field for a period of ministry to the missionaries. He found the relations among the workers "disturbing," and sensed a "general feeling of mistrust and suspicions." Alarmed, Peters sent his observations to Henry R. Wiens who had replaced Toews as general secretary in Hillsboro.

> Accusations of mismanagement of funds are rife. Books are not properly audited. . . . The MAC **must** work in a more business-like way. Often two brethren discuss things and one later writes the minutes as he pleases. These have not been formally approved . . . Funds are spent for a project **not** approved by the Council because the secretary happens to be interested in that phase.

Peters wrote that such things are "gnawing at the hearts of some brethren."[20] Paul Hiebert noticed some of the same trends. While he appreciated the MAC, there was still too much individualism. "There has been far too much of 'spheres of influence' in which each has his own project and . . . does what is right in his own sight." Hiebert felt that the difficulties experienced by the Governing Council in proper accounting were reflections of similar problems in the Mission.[21]

In the midst of this turmoil, Peters wrote that he had "never seen so many tired-looking people, and that this could not be from hard work!" Peter J. Funk remarked that this stemmed from "the inability to submit, to adjust, and overlook small grievances." These things caused people "to be worn out and tired."[22]

## The MAC and the Single Women

The New India Plan had vast implications for all, but particularly for the single women. The singles of the post-war period were treated with less respect by their contemporaries than those who labored alongside the American pioneer couples. Many of the singles during this period felt themselves to be "second class."[23] Though never placed "in charge" of a station, or given representation proportionate to their responsibilities in the Missionary Council, the earliest single women missionaries eventually had charge of individual institutions such as hospitals and schools. Like the virtuous woman of Proverbs 29, they undertook to construct wells, hospitals, and bungalows, and yet were often without their own motor vehicles until the 1950s. Though they seldom asserted themselves in earlier decades, they later complained of putdowns, and sometimes refused to bend to directives arising from the New India Plan. When Margaret Willems was once asked to represent the women in India on the Missionary Council, she stated she would serve only if she was considered to be serving as an individual in her own right.[24]

Hardly any of the single women remained entirely out of areas of grievance, and some broke down. Some of them, and married women also, could not handle the combination of circumstances, expectations, heat, pressures of work, and inter-personal relations. Supporters at home and fellow missionaries sometimes found it difficult to accept the possibility that a missionary could break down.[25] Ted Fast and his associates had to help the Board decide whether three or four singles could in fact return to India. Though perhaps wrongly, the MAC declared them unfit for mission work. At the same time, J. B. Toews' meeting with the single women in 1957 had created a freedom to approach the Board directly. While there was no full-scale rebellion by the singles, in numerous instances they went over the heads of the MAC directly to Toews.

## "Doctor" Margaret Willems

In one of her first accounts for the press, Margaret Willems compared the MB medical ministry with the earthly ministry of Jesus. The crippled, the blind, and those with "various fevers . . . and possessed by evil spirits" came to them daily. She surveyed the work of Maria Wall at Deverakonda and Margaret Suderman at Wanaparty, and noted how the Friesens had "answered a great cry for mercy" by coming to build the desperately-needed central hospital at Jadcherla. Meanwhile, Rosella Toews had built up a facility at Nagarkurnool, while Willems, at Gadwal, had been privileged to "build up another one of these hospitals where many come and cry for help daily."[26]

Willems came to be a leader among the single women, especially as the implications of the New India Plan came home to them. When she noticed how the first draft of this plan shook the composure of the teachers, Willems wrote to Toews. She suggest that if Emma Lepp, Katie Siemens, Anne Ediger and Anna Suderman were mere employees of the Mission, this would be the time to look for another job. Whether asked to speak for them or not, Willems seriously questioned the advisability of having these teaching missionaries turn the schools–buildings, accounts, and all–over to a "carnal church." She wrote: "If the sisters are no longer in the plan of the work on the field," why not state it openly? Ediger wrote of her: "Besides giving of herself so unreservedly... she feels the responsibility for things in our mission very heavily."[27]

Willems' heart attack in October 1958 and the perceived male attitudes towards her brought considerable cohesion to the single missionaries. Willems was at Gadwal conducting her girls' camp when she became seriously ill. She was examined by George Froese from the Jadcherla medical staff and tended by Helen Dueck, the nurse at Gadwal. On 8 November Froese wrote that Willems would have to be relieved of her work. Later in the month Ediger told how Willems almost died, but the Christians of Gadwal rallied to the call to prayer. On the 28th she commented: "While there are those who saw in Sister Margaret's sickness an easy way to eliminate the **key sister of our group**, we are claiming complete recovery for her from the Lord." Ediger explained that the heart attack came "after a prolonged strain she has been under [at Wanaparty]." She was not getting the cooperation from other missionaries, nor from the Governing Council, according to Ediger.[28]

Willems recovered and went back to work at Wanaparty,[29] where Froese served on a part-time basis. Between her recovery and her departure in the summer of 1961, Willems continued to focus on weaknesses in the unified medical plan. She also explained to Janzen and Toews the weak position of the women in the new regime. They had "no power in the medical committee." Willems further raised the issue of adequate indigenous medical staffing. The discussions that followed indicated to her that women medical doctors were considered second-rate, and that no Indian male doctor could be placed under a Mission nurse as supervisor, not even during the transitional phase. She had one consolation. "Her boy," the young P. B. Arnold from Wanaparty, was prepared to undertake medical studies. She did what she could to help him get started. Compared with other missions, Willems said, the AMBM had failed to train national staff.[30]

Instead of rejoicing at what had been accomplished, Willems discerned a "closing down and breaking off," an unraveling of the work, and a degree of sabotage. Every program transfer meant that missionary accomplishments were at risk. The transfer of the education program to the Governing Council had been too abrupt, not permitting the principals to say anything in advance to their staff. The preachers had been paid about 20 percent of professional salaries, so the church was in disrepute. Nor could the nationals understand the closing of the hospitals at Nagarkurnool, Shamshabad, and Gadwal.[31]

As a result of this outspokenness on behalf of the singles, Willems was not really welcome to return for a third term unless her attitude changed considerably.[32] By May 1961 the medical doctors considered her a "poor risk" in terms of her health. She had overextended herself in many areas and was not considered well enough physically to carry on.[33]

These criticisms did not stop with Willems' departure. Other issues were raised by other singles which, by 1962, meant a virtual boycott of the MAC. In response, Toews intervened on their behalf twice in that year. Helen Dueck had written in February that the Jadcherla nurses, Regina Suderman, Marie Riediger, and Frieda Neufeld, were all discouraged. Along with Willems, she also criticized the mission's authoritarian structures. Dueck noted that Jake Friesen was treasurer of the MAC, chair of the central medical committee, and director of the Jadcherla Hospital. In practice, he was "not answerable to anyone on the field (though in theory he should be answerable to several bodies)." For these reasons, J. B. Toews asked how the MAC could recover the "general sense of confidence and dedication of the nurses [and teachers]."[34]

## Marie Riediger and the Nurse's Training School

Marie Riediger's first years were hampered by a fundamental misunderstanding about her assignment in India. A graduate of Mennonite Brethren Bible College in Winnipeg and a registered nurse with a diploma in teaching and supervision, she thought she had a clear assignment from the Board to start a nurse's training school. Riediger discovered, however, that the Jadcherla staff did not see the need for such a school, or was not clearly informed of the Board's wishes. Following language study she was assigned to training aids and orderlies, when she wanted to train nationals to a certification level which would open career opportunities for them. After four years had passed, Riediger was given facilities and began the training school on 13 July 1961. During her subsequent furlough she earned a Bachelor of Nursing at McGill in Montreal.

Though her school continued for the next two decades, Riediger's career in India was disrupted by an accident. Six months into her second term, while unloading a jeep, a barrel rolled on her. This injured her back, though she did not notice the effects at the time. About a year later her legs gave out. Urged by Helen Harder, Jake Friesen sent her to the Miraj Medical Center where she was diagnosed, mistakenly, as it turned out, with multiple sclerosis.[35] Riediger knew she did not have MS symptoms, but no one seemed to believe her sore back stemmed from an accidental injury. She went home in February 1966 in a wheelchair.[36]

This was most traumatic. Marie wrote: "I have never been so bewildered and confused about God's will as I was when I came home in a wheelchair." After a period of convalescence and physiotherapy she worked in public health in Manitoba. In 1970 her legs gave out again. She was finally diagnosed in Vancouver with a back injury requiring bone fusion surgery.[37] With the help of surgery again in 1973 she was able to complete six years of teaching at the Royal Columbia School of Nursing and nine years at the B.C. Institute of Technology in Vancouver. After that Marie enjoyed many more years of gratifying service helping others who were in pain or grief. Since 1984 she has served as a lay chaplain and has been "bereavement coordinator" for the Abbotsford Hospice Society."[38]

## Helen Harder: Shamshabad, Shadnagar, and Secunderabad

Helen Harder, who arrived in India with Emma Lepp and the Kaspers in 1946, was glad that she was on furlough when the Shamshabad Hospital was closed. Reflecting on the devotion Katharina Schellenberg had given to this place since the 1920s, and after serving there for fourteen years, Harder described this as a "bitter blow." Between 1947 and 1957 she and her staff gave 130,000 consultations at Shamshabad and Shadnagar, a town to the south, and had treated half of that number. This meant they had also given a Gospel message to thousands. Moreover, they had collected 64,000 rupees in that period.[39] Harder's subsequent assignment between 1962 and 1971, when she left India, was to devote herself to women and children. As she wrote to J. B. Toews, it was time to put soul-winning first. Harder relocated to Secunderabad, where she worked with the Evangelical Nurses Fellowship. This opened doors to Bible studies for nursing students and also to international students who visited her home.[40]

## Helen Dueck

Helen Dueck, from Coaldale, Alberta, had a difficult time in India. She graduated from Coaldale Bible School as well as the missionary course at Mennonite Brethren Bible College and earned her R. N. at Lethbridge, Alberta. Like most AMBM personnel, she had virtually no cross-cultural training and found relations with nationals more difficult than others. Under the circumstances of the time, it was also difficult to pair her with a teacher like the others, though she was at Gadwal with Anne Ediger for some time.[41]

Dueck went back for a second term in 1963 and remained four years. Though she dealt with her "past failures and shortcomings" in her relations with nationals and other missionaries, she was not allowed to return unless the pairing problem could be resolved. In the end she stayed at home in Alberta.[42]

Like others, Dueck had a very rewarding and interesting life at home in spite of feeling under a cloud because she was not invited back to India. She found employment for some years with the Africa Evangelical Fellowship in Zambia and has taken short-term assignments with the Christian Medical and Dental Society in Latin America and the Far East. Closer to home Dueck directed the nursing staff at the Camrose Geriatric Hospital, Camrose, Alberta, worked with the

Victorian Order of Nurses, and served for some time as Director of Home Care in the Lethbridge, Alberta area.[43]

### The Teacher Mildred Enns

The life of Mildred Enns, from Elm Creek, Manitoba, provided an early illustration of the discouragement of some of the single missionaries. She went to India in 1947 and returned home voluntarily in 1954. She seems to have lost confidence in her ability as a missionary, writing to A. E. Janzen in 1953 that "I can see nothing for the future of the work in which I am [engaged]." This was regrettable because Rosella Toews, also at Nagarkurnool, thought of Enns "as a very talented and gifted person." She could not, however, accept those who did not completely share her views. For example, she thought attendance at movies was sin and dismissed indigenous Christian teachers who went to movies.[44] Once she was back in Manitoba, Mildred acquired a B.Ed. degree and taught in Winnipeg schools until 1977. In her last years she published a little booklet, *Through the Lens of Eden*.[45]

### Katie Siemens and Emma Lepp

Katie Siemens, who served as principal at Nagarkurnool, was one of those caught in the new situation and left wondering whether she was wanted. Only four years in India, she willingly cooperated with the 1958 directives to turn her school over to the Field Association. As with Gerdes, she also feared these schools would soon fail because they were not up to the standard for government grants. Besides, having begun alongside Helen Warkentin and witnessing her accomplishments, Siemens did not want to lose the Mission's evangelistic opportunity.[46] When she came back from her first furlough she was assigned to teach English at Kodaikanal and help Peter and Betty Hamm with the missionary children. Peter V. Balzer, as one of his last acts in India, wrote the MAC that he did not think it "the wisest move" to send missionaries who learned Telugu to teach English there when "others could so easily do the work at Kodaikanal."[47] After teaching there one year, Siemens was appointed to teach Bible at Mahbubnagar High School. She taught at Bethany in Shamshabad from 1967 to 1970, and again in the 1970s. Siemens also contributed much to the development of camp work.[48]

Emma Lepp felt much the same about indigenization as did Siemens. She argued that if they could not turn over the schools with the current subsidies, how much less could they do so if they were reduced. Claiming that some "experienced Indian workers are of the same opinion," she asked: was the Board of Foreign Missions prepared to see all five middle schools closed? Did the New India Plan really mean to sabotage what had been built up? This seemed to be a real possibility. Janzen, ever idealistic, prayed that "the teachers will be fine Christians, born-again believers as well as loyal to the MB Church of India, in addition to [having the] necessary training... to meet the requirement" under the new system. In a 1960 article, "Can Christian Schools Survive?," Lepp demonstrated what the transfer had already done to the Shamshabad school. She was now an advisor to a school that the Governing Council had cut back from a thriving middle school to a junior school, while the upper grades were to be transferred to Mahbubnagar, quite a distance away.[49]

### Edna Gerdes

As is evident, Gerdes viewed her difficulties at Wanaparty in much the same light as Siemens and Lepp. In the school situation she had their sympathetic support and that of her closest co-worker, Margaret Willems. Gerdes found it extremely difficult to collect school fees where her predecessor, Anna Suderman, had been too lenient. At Coonoor the single women could agree that the India church was not ready for the transfer of the schools to the Governing Council.

Of these, Edna Gerdes suffered the greatest embarrassment, a personal breakdown. After confessing that 1957-58 had been a "hard year," A. E. Janzen made her feel guilty by writing that they had "not yet succeeded in making the Gospel known to many people and therefore it is our burden... to find ways... to [do this], certainly upon the MB field in this generation."[50] This admonition was hardly necessary when, like others, Gerdes did not want to be assigned to work where she did not have direct contact with Indian children. "I am not willing to teach secular subjects here in India."[51]

Her breakdown began in conjunction with her partner Margaret Willems' heart attack in 1958. Not all other missionaries were sympathetic to her emotional problems. Peter V. Balzer and A.

A. Unruh described Gerdes as "physically aggressive in words and action... against her co-workers." With the support of Friesen's medical opinion, they recommended that she be asked to return home.[52]

During her most stressful time, Margaret Willems managed to get some medication for Gerdes from a Baptist hospital. Once the doctors discovered this, Friesen wrote home to say that the singles "had kept all this covered up so well that hardly anyone knew."[53] When Willems wrote in Gerdes' defense, it became clear to Janzen that the responsibility for the two schools, the additional work connected with handing them over to the nationals, and "above all the critical church situation developed by unspiritual Christians [at Wanaparty] made the load for Sister Gerdes too heavy."[54]

Even though she had done some deputation work at home with Janzen's blessing and was completing a full course load at Tabor College in the spring of 1961, members of the secretariat told Gerdes that she was not fit to return. They based this judgment on Missionary Council perceptions of what had happened in 1959. Her missionary career ended thus on a note of bitterness and with severance pay of $900.[55]

**The Board and Unruh: Fundamental Differences**

One of the questions facing the Board and the MAC was to find an assignment for A. A. and Annie Unruh within the new regime. Because of Unruh's critical attitude, it was necessary to come to an understanding or keep them at home along with other seniors. During 1962 A. A. Unruh appeared before the Board to explain his criticisms of the Yarrow document. Before these appearances, however, Unruh had recorded some private misgivings. In one of these he raised the fundamental issue of "authority." What we have now, he wrote, is "centralized control . . . by strong committees. . . . Many people feel that strong organizational authority will save the church from ruin." Generally fearing a neo-colonialism in Hillsboro, Unruh saw that minds were being "diverted from the only policy & principles revealed in the Word of God. Nobody can claim that he is free from all other influences and has discovered the absolute right and divine plan for the church." While admitting to "shortcomings" of his own, he insisted that long experience on the Board or on the field was "not a guarantee of infallibility in planning for the church."[56] Behind the scenes, Unruh was distressed at the changed relations between missionaries and Board. The former were now being "threatened" in various ways in Board minutes. The secretariat was acting more like an employer, like "a boss," who finds it easier to deal with missionaries as employees but is actually having to overcome "signs of personal weakness."[57]

Of all the senior couples, only the Unruhs returned for a longer assignment, and that was to "nurture pastors and lay leaders in faithful ministry and evangelism through the village churches."[58] Though there was a reconciliation between Board and missionary, and Unruh gave public gratitude to the Board for meeting with them, he hinted at continuing objections to the "different practical and philosophical problems of missions." He objected to evaluative statements of the India situation by J. B. Toews and A. E. Janzen following their 1961 visit. In 1963 he protested the statement that "the changing world situation makes the witness of the Gospel without effect if there is not a greater effort of identification of the missionaries with the nationals." This deeply disturbed him. He asked, "is this what the Board believes?" Had they accepted the "Gospel of Anthropology and Sociology" as the solution to problems of evangelism? For the Board to say that missionaries from abroad have no further place there "is irresponsible."[59]

Obviously, fundamental differences remained between Unruh and Toews. Unruh's son Donald commented that "when all the personal hurt and powerlessness and sense of betrayal [were] removed from the debate, there still remain[ed] a number of points of significant disagreement between my father and [the Secretariat] . . . and some of the other missionaries." The younger Unruh understood his father's attitude of feeling responsible "first to his calling and second to the brotherhood." He thought of the Board as had the American pioneers, "largely as an administrative convenience... I doubt that he ever accorded the Board... with any final legitimacy."[60]

Once A. A. Unruh had been asked by the Board to withdraw from the quarreling Wanaparty church, and was helping Paul Hiebert at the Bible Institute in Shamshabad, he wrote Henry R. Wiens in Hillsboro that they were now promoting evangelism. He believed that current Governing Council leaders realized just how much the emphasis on evangelism had declined among them in favor of "building up institutions." But then he wondered, much as had Ted Fast, whether the Board at home was still interested in evangelism in

India. He challenged Wiens: "Share with the Missionary Fellowship your concern and you will find... brethren... here... who also carry a great concern." He asked how, if the mission had lost interest, could they expect this from the India church.[61] By 1965-66 Unruh was able to report on much greater evangelistic activity, involving D. J. Arthur and R. R. K. Murthy, two upper-strata converts. This led to an effective "evangelism-in-depth" program.[62]

## The Development of Lay Leadership

But how did Unruh's "emphasis on the development of a lay leadership" for village churches turn out? Unruh reported in February 1964 that he had been meeting with preachers and workers for ten days of fellowship, study, and discussion in summer Bible schools, just as John Voth and others had done "since many years." In 1962 and 1963 he had met in retreat with a "chosen group of ministers" from each Field Association for a period of seven days. "We believe it brought many problems and needs to the attention of the ministers, gave them a biblical perspective . . . a group feeling in the Lord, and created a unity in the Spirit."[63]

Frank C. Peters, who observed this activity first-hand in 1964, put a different interpretation on it. Taking a Hillsboro-oriented view, he saw Unruh somewhat more tragically. Unruh's battle with illness at the time had brought him uncertainty. Perhaps because of this he had singled out those pastors who seemed most spiritual into a "special fellowship." Peters' perception was that this special instruction was causing a deep rift in the church, and Unruh's contribution was now sharply minimized. "I really feel that many of his health problems are rooted in his inner conflicts."[64]

Perhaps there were some problems Peters did not recognize. Unruh told Jake Epp in 1965 what Margaret Willems had noticed earlier, that "with the emphasis on Hospital and Education as against Evangelism the leading men were lost to the church. The weaker ministers lost courage." Unruh detected some signs of concern about this among these "leading men." He emphasized that "the presentation of [a plan devised in Hillsboro] leaves the great majority cold." He was convinced that his preachers would act on what they had discovered for themselves on site "with our help." Returning to an earlier position, Unruh stated that what they decided might be "strange to our ways but we must have grace to accept it if is not opposed to God's Word." Acknowledging that his strength was waning, he was encouraged to think that there was a show of interest in "village Churches and Evangelism."[65]

The Unruhs retired in 1967. Unruh, however, continued until 1974 to record his reactions to the many concerns raised in Vernon R. Wiebe's use of the press. While he stressed the need for "greater balance between administration knowledge and practical knowledge in forming our Conference Mission policies," Unruh feared that the "Board has made up its mind," and the missionary is "rated as one among 30,000 members." He suspected that "some of our brethren" wanted to become known as "world leaders" in mission and "use our small denomination as a guinea pig to experiment their ideas." He seriously questioned whether the Board any longer was seeking to be guided by the Holy Spirit and God's Word. Was it not about time, he asked, that every new Board member be examined as closely as every missionary previously?[66]

When Unruh died in 1988, his son Donald J. Unruh tried to make a "dispassionate assessment" of his parents' work in India, and summarized their thiry-one years as missionaries as follows: "Realizing early that it was counter-productive to transplant western forms of church polity and structure into a totally alien Indian context, he worked over a period of years, with his Indian brethren, and sometimes against current wisdom, to build a church consistent with Indian socio-economic and cultural conditions yet grounded firmly in the Bible."[67]

**Bethany Bible Institute**

Following language study, Paul G. and Frances (Flaming) Hiebert went to Shamshabad to assume responsibility for Bethany Bible Institute, even though Peter Balzer had difficulty in 1961 handing over responsibility for the school.[68] They arrived in the midst of a severe power struggle for the compound church. This situation led the Board to separate the Shamshabad bungalows for the use of the Bible school.[69] Assisted at various times by J. J. Kasper, A. A. Unruh, and Emma Lepp, they hoped to have a completely national staff by 1964. Within two more years of "working with a short staff" in order to allow more nationals to complete their training at Yeotmal (or Ramapatnam) they expected to have three men with B.D. degrees, "all of whom show a wonderful Christian spirit and who will work well together." With this degree of success, Paul considered that his short-term objects in India had been largely fulfilled.[70] He returned to Minnesota to complete graduate work.

During their one term in India, 1959-1965, the Hieberts wrote a number of analyses of the mission and church. Their work at Shamshabad convinced them that the biggest mistake of the past had been the "failure to train national leadership." Having worked primarily among the depressed classes could not alone explain this neglect, even though that segment was "given to following and responding to authority more easily." Now it was time to show respect and appreciation for those who were coming forward, to train them for leadership in biblical studies and evangelism theology, and to encourage administrative integrity. It was time to let the "Christian call" that yields to "spiritual needs" override the "professional call" that builds institutions.[71]

The Hieberts did not return for a second term even though he had been assigned to teach at Union Biblical Seminary in Yeotmal. In subsequent years Paul Hiebert contributed his expertise to the Board, and in 1985 published a useful missiology from a Christian anthropological perspective.[72]

In 1962 Emma Lepp faced the challenge of becoming part of Hiebert's staff at Shamshabad. One of her first tasks was to establish the school library on a sound footing. This meant the acquisition of books and training a librarian. Among the first-year students she saw the contrast between what she had given her middle school pupils, about four hundred hours a year of Bible instruction, and the current woeful neglect of the "spiritual welfare" of high schoolers. She noted that "we have no one to blame but ourselves."[73]

Paul Hiebert strongly recommended that Peter M. Hamm return to India and come to Shamshabad to carry on the supervision of the school. Based on his own experience (and perhaps Schmidt's at Mahbubnagar), Hiebert urged Epp in Hillsboro to give the Hamms a "definite assignment" and to support them when things became discouraging.[74]

Peter and Betty Hamm took up that assignment in 1965. His report as principal for the year 1966 named a staff of N. P. James, J. Paranyjothi, V. K. Rufus, Emma Lepp, and himself, as well as five part-time women. He was pleased that these graduates of Yeotmal and Ramapatnam had returned better trained than in the 1950s.

Enrollments had fluctuated between thirty-five and fifty in the 1960s. The semester system and the discipline of re-admission standards had forced a greater degree of seriousness on the student body. Forty of fourty-five students were supported by mission bursaries.[75] By August 1968 Hamm reported a considerable change in staffing now that Bethany was fully transferred to the Governing Council. Arthur was leaving for Yeotmal, and Paranyjothi would become church evangelist. Added to the staff were S. Joseph and Hanna Kampelly (who later married), both Yeotmal graduates.[76] After ten years in India, the Hamms returned to Canada when Peter accepted an offer to teach at Mennonite Brethren Bible College in Winnipeg.[77]

Summing up, one can say that, whereas the "intervention" of the Board largely spelled the end of the seniors, the era of the Mission Administrative Committee led to considerable distress and some pessimism among younger missionaries. The difficulties encountered by the MAC in the path to full indigenization served to lengthen the process of that transition well into the 1970s. The next two chapters will provide a brief portrait of the partners in the new equation between North America and India.

## CHAPTER 15

# "Partnership in Obedience"

The 1947 Whitby Missionary Conference in the United Kingdom gave definition to the new relationship between mission and church in light of the demand for decolonization of empires. While the historical relationships could not be eradicated overnight, and the national church might not be in a position to carry an equal share of the financial burden, all societies could agree that the partners were now to exercise mutual respect and carry equal responsibility for the work entrusted to the Church of Jesus Christ: to carry the Gospel to their people.[1]

### The North American Partner

The Board of Foreign Missions shared in this understanding. Already in 1960, in the discussion surrounding the Yarrow Statement, J. B. Toews focused on the new conference/church relationship as an "international fellowship." Behind his Board stood a General Conference of MB churches that in 1960 celebrated the one hundreth anniversary of its founding and numbered 27,718 members, 52 percent of which belonged to the Canadian Conference. The total giving for foreign missions in that year was $586,003, of which the Canadian conference raised about 62 percent.[2] In 1963 Toews characterized the new relationship of this General Conference with the India Church as a "Partnership in Obedience." This statement, adopted as policy in that year, proposed a "united obedience... in a program of partnership in opportunity and responsibility to extend the message to the multitudes of our generation who have never heard the Gospel."[3]

The Board, Toews stated, had become "an agency to assist the national church" in the primary work of evangelism. In India this meant that the "**permanent** aspect of the mission program" rests with the nationals, while the missionary role was *temporary*, continuing there only to train national leadership for the various avenues of evangelism, including the medical ministry.[4] G. W. Peters, assuming the "mother church" relationship, challenged board and conference to be a spiritual model to lead national churches "into the fuller life of Christ." Their combined work should be carried on at "a deeply spiritual level, in keeping with biblical principles," that the "unity, spiritual intensity and perfect devotion of the brotherhood, as heretofore, be *fostered through our mission program.*"[5] A. E. Janzen, who continued to work much as before in terms of India, expressed great satisfaction that he had been allowed to serve in an area that "constitutes the very spiritual core of the Conference upon which the life and purpose . . . and the unity of our Brotherhood hinges."[6]

In the eleven-member Hillsboro Board of 1960, Lando Hiebert served as chairperson and G. W. Peters as recording secretary. When a traffic accident took the life of Hiebert in July 1962,[7] he was replaced in the chair by Peter R. Lange. J. B. Toews led the secretariat, and the treasury was given to Peter J. Funk, who served in this capacity for the next eight years.

Ironically, in the midst of the rhetoric about partnership, the Board itself did not escape criticism. What happened within that body in 1963 has been described as an "unprecedented leadership crisis."[8] Peters' admonition in that year to maintain high spiritual levels may have been an oblique reference to a shakedown in the Board itself because of the reaction to its strong-willed intervention since 1957. Under the caption "the meeting[s] of the Board," Peters urged that "under no circumstances must we permit a judging spirit to enter our hearts nor suspicion of brotherly integrity to cast a shadow upon another's work."[9] Correspondence shows clearly that opposition from Unruh and complaints from churches seemed to have had a cumulative effect. By April 1962 Lange wrote Peters in Texas that there was "extreme disquietude about our Secretary of Missions in Hillsboro." Lange was then still teaching at Mennonite Brethren Biblical Seminary in Fresno. People were warning him that something should be done "about the Strong Man in the Secretariat."[10]

Toews was succeeded in 1963 by Henry R. Wiens, who struggled with the job. When he was superseded two years later by Jacob H. Epp at the behest of the Board, Wiens resigned. With this and other appointments, and the new division of labor in the Hillsboro office, Epp was the one who particularly related to India.[11] Perhaps because the successive leadership was seen as weaker, the Board in its 1966 revision of *Principles and Policies* proposed a "field secretary" who would replace the liaison in India. This was decidedly rejected by "the India M.B. Missionary brethren" in December. What they and particularly Unruh saw in this was a resurrection of the "colonial secretary" of the past. How could a representative of a subordinate board like the Board of Missions deal directly with a National Conference?[12] Nevertheless, this idea prevailed and in 1970 Jake H. Epp became that secretary.

## The "Identification" Principle Shatters

According to Toews, the new relationship suggested in 1960 was to lead to a "mutual identification which rises above the level of cultural and economic differences." This meant "integrating into the structure of the local fellowship . . . and [removing] all differences in rank and position." Toews stated the Board's conviction that it was time to concentrate on a few people (training Timothys) rather than trying to reach the many. This was to be done at this juncture "without a car even if it takes more time and strength in using trains . . . even the oxcart[!]." We must do our work for the Lord "on the proper level."[13]

Though some tried to apply this guideline, the request to do without a car was totally incomprehensible to Anne Ediger. This carless policy invented in Hillsboro seemed "pennywise and pound foolish," given the purpose of their being in India. She had taken a commercial course during her furlough in order to help with administrative work at Jadcherla/Mahbubnagar. Given this additional demand on her time, as well as teaching and doing evangelistic work in the schools, she reasoned that she needed a "small car." She had tried using the bus, rickshaws, and trains, but found this most frustrating. In a four-page letter she stated her view "without reservation." She had already had sad experiences with concentrating on the training of one "Timothy." She asked whether Toews understood how frustrating it was for a national to keep up with the North American temperament, or equally, how frustrating it could be for a missionary to slow down to the Eastern pace. She stated that her high school students, conscious of India's own advancements, would "mock" her if she was seen in an oxcart. She clinched her argument by saying that identification with nationals is "primarily an attitude of the heart and mind, and only secondarily on outer things that hinges on food, mode of dress, travel or dwelling." She thanked Toews for letting her share her convictions based on experience.

Knowing that she had the support of some colleagues, she went out and bought an India-made Ambassador car from her own savings.[14]

### Stewardship of the Conference

"Obedience in Partnership" seemed an empty slogan without disciplined stewardship. In India, from Daniel F. Bergthold's day until about 1960, hardly any evangelism and church planting, including the training of a well-grounded and spiritual leadership, had taken place without mission funding. At home, even though conference delegates generally applauded the work in India because of its comparatively large numbers,[15] raising funds became more of a vexing question during the 1960s.

There was without a doubt a negative reaction to the New India Plan, because it tended to weed out programs and personnel. Forced retirements, layoffs, and stalling of candidates had a negative effect. If there were cutbacks, was money needed? If J. B. Toews was leaving the Board, was the work finished? Moreover, the Board of Foreign Missions had been very tardy in providing adequate "fringe benefits" for retired missionaries, let alone decent pensions after a lifetime of modest salaries. Some missionary children in their mature years turned away from the MB church, partly because of these realities.[16]

The year 1966 also witnessed the culmination of a significant constitutional change: the merger of the Board of General Welfare and the Board of Foreign Missions to form the Board of Missions and Services, or MBM/S.[17] Incorporating the short-term Christian Service established in 1960 helped to turn the constituency inward and homeward, as eventually reflected in the "Church Growth" movement. There were also changes in the way North American women supported missions, as sewing circles were replaced by MCC-related money-raising activities, involving both old and young women.[18]

For all these reasons there was a downturn of interest, applications, and giving to the mission program. This led to growing indebtedness and the eventual end of the mission to India by 1973.

### The Doctors Stand in the Gap

The MAC, as liaison between Hillsboro and Mahbubnagar, was still a strong force in 1965 and was not weakened by what might be called the "Doctors' Regime." The medical ministry concentrated at Jadcherla was now seen as the pre-eminent evangelistic medium. The three full-time doctors and seven nurses from abroad were assisted by an enlarged indigenous medical staff.[19] George Froese asked in January 1963 whether medical work was being overdone at the expense of evangelism and education. To this Peter Funk replied that, despite all the difficulties, the medical ministry was doing "the best job" in achieving the Mission's only aim: winning souls.[20] Perhaps it was, but many wondered if it was a good idea for the MAC to be comprised of three medical doctors. When Ted Fast took his family on furlough in 1965, he was replaced by George Froese, and Henry Poetker by Peter Block. Fast worried about the lay professionals taking over. He made it plain that there were others eligible for election in 1965. For sheer ability Anne Ediger might have been considered.

As in North America, the status of doctors enhanced their influence and power and diminished the position of the preaching and teaching missionaries. Fast predicted that going to lay persons entirely would have "repercussions" for the future of the work.[21] Froese worried that both he and Block were "novices" in the MAC. For this reason, he told Epp that the Missionary Fellowship should have a greater voice in administration. The MAC was far too unrepresentative and undemocratic. To this Epp simply replied that the MAC now spoke for the Missionary Fellowship too. As doctors went on furlough, Peter Hamm and Dan Nickel filled such vacancies.[22]

This administration soon had as many problems as Fast in 1964. Before his election to MAC, given the troublesome deficit situation, Block had found himself quarreling with Fast and Funk about appropriations for his hospital at Deverakonda. Though everyone was suffering from the cutbacks, Funk's solution was that Jake Friesen's Jadcherla and George Froese's Wanaparty hospitals would have to bail out Deverakonda.[23] Financial questions followed Peter Block home to Saskatoon where he went for more training in 1966. His replacement as secretary, Peter Hamm, asked him to explain the overrun of about 6,400 rupees and why the accounts had not been properly prepared for audit before he left.[24] Though he was asked to return, nevertheless, by 1970 he was disenchanted. His high hopes of 1961 had been dashed and he thought the indifference noted by others had invaded Hillsboro also. Working out of Wanaparty in 1971

Block said they were getting ready to leave and had no plans to return. There was also no successor in sight.[25]

Froese, too, had taken personal funds to buy equipment. Jake Friesen went to a Hindu merchant for a loan in 1967. He was quite blunt in several letters. What made them tired in India was "the apparent indifference [of] so many at home.... [There is] an overtone of materialism [that we] wonder why only missionaries should have to forfeit large earnings, especially doctors, and still be asked to cut expenses to rock bottom while money at home has never flowed so freely." He resented that such people had all their money invested and none available for mission. To this Vernon Wiebe replied with his minority thesis for mission support. The day was gone, he thought, when one could assume the whole conference was interested in mission. We need to appeal "to those frontiersmen in our group who want to take the Word seriously. . . . Our hope is in a smaller minority."[26] By 1971, when the treasury was still down $239,000, Wiebe considered going back to "designated gifts."[27]

David Wiebe, a son of John and Viola Wiebe, came to fill in at Jadcherla for three years while the long-term doctors took furloughs. Not beset by long-term responsibilities, his report could concentrate on some of the interesting cases he was called on to treat. Having experienced life on the plains and in the hills at Kodaikanal, he was even then not quite prepared for the peculiarities of Indian officialdom and the trials of getting supplies through customs, though he was glad for the "absence of malpractice concerns."[28]

**Financial Embarrassments and Successes**

Thrown into the midst of the endless financial questions of this period was Daniel A. Nickel, a trained engineer. Though assigned originally to "Administration and Evangelism" in 1965, for which he studied Telugu, Nickel rarely had time for evangelism. Because he could do administration with a translator, he immediately "plunged" into the business side of the Mission. Having shown his talents for management and accounting by taking on various treasuries, including that of the MAC for some years, Nickel became more and more embroiled in the matter of securing Mission properties in a trust for the India MB Church.

The rather desperate financial situation that Peter Funk seemed powerless to correct led to some serious embarrassments for Nickel.

The shortfall of giving at home coincided with the devaluation of the rupee in 1966, the first year of Indira Gandhi's premiership. In October 1967 Nickel was two months behind (about $12,000) in his payments, so as to affect missionaries and programs. American Express, through whom travel arrangements were made, became upset enough with the Mission's arrears in 1967-68 that it began to charge service fees of up to 5 percent. A master of understatement, Nickel let Funk know more than once he was "a bit embarrassed" at this unwanted situation.[29]

What helped the critical financial situation, but irritated Ted Fast, was Nickel's taking advantage of funds which came to India from the J. W. Friesen estate. This bequest of $80,000, which was to be divided between Ted Fast in India and Ernie Friesen, a missionary in South America, was diverted in ways over which these two had no control. They had turned it over to Hillsboro in order to save on estate taxes, but were promised they would have some determination of its use. Out of this $80,000 bequest Fast at the very least wanted a new car for evangelism. Instead, Dan Nickel was authorized to utilize some of this money to purchase a vehicle for "Bible Training by Extension." The beneficiary in the first instance was Henry Poetker, who, just back from furlough, wanted to get started. Some funds also went into a Christian Communication Center at Mahbubnagar to house the press, radio and literature programs that replaced the earlier work of Suderman and Ediger, also a bookstore and reading room. After failing to get a satisfactory answer from America, Fast was extremely upset.[30] All that he and remaining missionaries were being asked was to cut back. At this point he advocated selling off some of the Bruton property at Kodaikanal just to make ends meet.[31] This was accomplished in 1972 at a considerable profit.

Acquired first in 1949 at a relatively low price, Bruton proved to be an enormously good investment. The buildings and some of the thirteen acres fetched over 900,000 rupees. At 6 percent such an investment could fetch about 55,000 rupees annually. Nickel was thankful to God for having sold at "an optimum price with congenial buyers and being able to invest at the highest rate possible (7 and ¾ percent)." Nickel consulted with Poetker and Lepp at Shamshabad in August 1972 in the matter of investing these funds.

The interest alone, as Henry Poetker had calculated, would maintain the current levels of radio and literature work.[32]

### Ted and Esther Fast, 1966-69

As suggested, the experience of the Fast family reflects how this downturn impacted the mission. They returned in 1966 for a three-year "church and evangelism" assignment auxiliary to the Governing Council. Their campaign called "Penetration Mahbubnagar," was characterized by confrontational evangelism and elicited a counter-campaign from the Hindu opposition.[33] Uppermost, however, was the concern about the continuing shortfall in monies. This was a great source of embarrassment to them personally and as well as to the Governing Council. Like Peter Block's objection to giving money to Yeotmal when they were being shortchanged, Fast objected to $1,000 going outside the Mission when they could not have their full salaries, when gas expenses alone amounted to 300 rupees a month.[34]

Given his experience with the Friesen bequest, Fast's feelings toward MBM/S came through in his response to the request that they come to Hillsboro in 1969 for debriefing. He asked whether the office could not be moved to some central place. "Hillsboro is the most hopeless place to get to, and doubly hopeless to get back out again." By July of that year the romance of mission in India was gone. He was grateful for the pastors they had ordained, the church buildings going up in many fields, and other very positive signs in the field of evangelism in the national church. But the sense of apprehension remained: "there is no mission any more in India, and that means the whole responsibility lies on the church and its related committees."[35]

For Ted and Esther re-entry to the American scene was not easy. They were paid until the end of March 1970. Ted did deputation work while Esther found work as a nurse. When he asked within the conference whether there were any pastoral vacancies he was told "most churches do not want returned missionaries as pastors. What a shock." He found himself trailing, in both training and experience, behind pastoral developments and expectations. He was fortunate to have the Grace Mennonite Church, a General Conference Mennonite congregation in his home town of Dallas, Oregon, offer him an interim position. This lengthened to eight years of pastoral ministry.[36] Ted and Esther Fast returned to India for three short-term assignments after 1980.

The Fasts were also much involved in the conference question of "salaries and pensions." When he became head of the MAC, Ted Fast raised the issue of some security in retirement. The Conference as such had not distinguished itself in the matter of pensions. Missionary salaries in the 1930s were much higher than for the mission administrators and the **Reiseprediger** of the day. They remained fairly constant at $1,000 a year for a married couple until the summer of 1963, when they were raised to $2,200 for a couple, and $1,100 for single women. Jake Friesen shrugged off this continuing modest salary, saying, "I guess austerity is good for us."[37]

Pensions for missionary widows like Elizabeth Janzen were raised from $40 to $60 in 1950. In October 1961 Ted Fast thanked the Hillsboro office "for your definite plans for the missionary personnel and future." This "fine insurance plan" was to be tied into government social security and they were all "breathing a sigh of relief." For the Balzers in 1963 this worked out to a total of $150 monthly for two of them, $38.60 coming from the Mission. But concrete action was delayed. In 1965 the Board of Foreign Missions asked their finance committee to bring recommendations for a pension after twenty years of service.[38] Not until June 1971, however, was a definite policy inaugurated for those who had served before that date. Under this system "anyone who had served twenty years or more prior to 1971 and had reached age sixty-five," would receive the equivalent of $80 per month ($4 x 20 years) as a pension. Any monies over $80 received from insurance companies had to be turned over to the mission. Ted and Esther Fast served for twenty years, 1950-1970, but did not turn 65 until 1989 and 1988 respectively. Hence their pensions, calculated according to that scheme, were only $20 a month combined for their first twenty years of service. Only by entering a conference contributory plan could they hope to increase this amount.[39] Only after the MB Mission to India had run its course did the conference introduce shared contributions to a pension plan over and above government basic plans.

## The Missionary Children, Bruton,[40] and the "School in the Plains"

As long as the missionaries were in India they had to face the question of schooling and recreation in the "hills." The long-established rhythm between mission in the plains and vacation and children's education in the hills seemed threatened in the 1960s. The factors involved were "the school on the plains" and the modernist challenge to the evangelicals at Kodaikanal.

The question of the first and second graders first came up with Peter and Betty Hamm.[41] The burden of caring for these youngest children came to be considered too much for the house mother. Also, everyone agreed they should ideally be in the care of parents. In 1961 J. B. Toews intervened in favor of the Hamm's request and the problem was thrown into the lap of the parents. Involved in the practical outworking of this problem at that time were the Block, Fast, Friesen, Froese, Hiebert, and Poetker families. On the plains day care was not enough; a qualified teacher was needed. Single missionaries were unwilling to become responsible for them, so the duty fell to one of the mothers who was caught between a sense of duty to the mission and to her family.

Around 1961 the Hieberts at Shamshabad decided that Frances would teach their own children for the first three years. This helped to trigger a wider and sometimes heated discussion.[42] Meanwhile, Ruth Friesen and Annie Froese began to teach the early graders at Jadcherla. When the Froeses were transferred to Wanaparty, it was fortunate that Maryann Wall, wife of dentist Ronald Wall, took on this task for two years (1962-64).[43]

The question became controversial in 1964 when the Walls returned to America and Jerry and Nancy Neufeld, the current house parents, were approached about taking "the children below third grade." At a Jadcherla meeting late in 1964 the "parents of the Bruton children" voted to overturn the policy of 1961. Jerry Neufeld wrote H. R. Wiens: "This was done against our will and [we] feel this is . . . too much of a load on Nancy here in the home."[44] George Froese, as chair of the MAC, then explained what the Neufelds' resistance meant in the plains. One boy was missing a year of school as a result, and others either had to be taken from Jadcherla to be kept and taught by Annie Froese at Wanaparty, or someone had to be hired to teach them at Jadcherla. This meant extra transportation expense and curtailment of their mission work. By January 1966 Froese was upset, both with the house parents at Bruton, and with the "dear Brethren half way round the world" who were deciding what was right in India, even for the youngest children of the missionaries. Froese made it clear that they knew what was best for their children, given the demands on them as missionaries.[45] In spite of this provision, Peter and Betty Hamm remained consistent with their earlier conviction about caring for the very young. Betty created a classroom at Shamshabad, as Frances Hiebert had done, and taught Richard and Carolyn using an Alberta provincial correspondence course.[46]

Correspondence between Epp and the Neufelds settled the matter. While Epp did not want to force the issue, the Neufelds agreed in 1966 to take on the first and second graders. As a result they had from 12 to 21 children at Bruton.

**Overcoming the Threat of Liberalism at Kodaikanal**

Earlier misgivings about liberalism were as nothing to the emotions aroused by the perceived modernistic views of Pastor Robert Dewey, who came to Kodaikanal in 1965. He was placed there, as some thought, by the majority United Church of Christ board in order to counteract the strong evangelical influence of such Mennonite teachers as Herb Krause, who served as principal of the school in the 1960s.[47]

Jerry Neufeld alerted Jake Epp to the changed circumstances, raising particular concerns over the possibility that Dewey would teach all the religious education courses. The Neufelds countered this influence by carefully monitoring everything that was taught and then discussing with their missionary children those things conflicting with MB doctrines. Froese and Neufeld thought the deity of Christ and authority of Scripture were under attack. Epp immediately suggested that Bruton children be taken out of such classes and given separate religious instruction during release time.[48] Froese believed that even if Dewey could be removed by evangelicals outvoting the UCC members on the board, a new school might be necessary. He wrote that the "Liberals have been aroused and feel **very** strongly that we have run the school long enough!" Froese predicted that "for this reason Herb Krause's principalship ends in October." Despite his strong feelings in the matter of the schooling of the younger children, Froese appreciated the way in which the Neufelds had stood up to chaplain Dewey.[49]

As it was, Dewey left Kodaikanal in May 1967.[50] In the midst of these worrisome controversies such children as Cathy and Tim Froese, Gordon Nickel, and Alden Poetker found in the house parents the kind of surrogate they needed when young. They came through the Bruton and Kodaikanal experience unscathed theologically and three of these four followed their parents into missionary service overseas.[51] Gordon Nickel benefitted greatly from "specialty courses such as Indian music, religion, geography, history and politics which often meant enjoyable field trips around South India, into the home of Indira Gandhi." He, like the others, had problems "adjusting socially and culturally to Canadian youth culture." Whatever the social problems in re-entry, all found at Kodaikanal a solid academic preparation for further studies, if not for the level of competitive sports in North America.[52]

Unlike Ruth Wiebe Friesen, who had found herself dealing with a great deal of ignorance about India and mission, Alden Poetker in the early 1970s was shocked at the sheer indifference to missionary children from India at the Bible school he attended in Canada. He did not have money to dress in the latest fashions or drive a car. He felt "at a loss as to how to break into their world." Around 1980 he and his wife Katrina went to India to help his parents in their work. After five years there they went to Mennonite Brethren Biblical Seminary in Fresno, and then took an MBM/S assignment in Brazil.[53]

Though Cathy Froese Baerg and her brother Tim Froese found the initial separation traumatic, Bruton provided an "extended family" and real "learning experience." Tim was at Kodaikanal after Bruton dismantled, hence stayed at Longcroft boarding school with John Nickel and Ernest Poetker. Whereas Cathy always "felt ahead" because of her preparation at Kodaikanal, neither of them had difficulties making grades in Canada. Tim was frustrated by the Tamil language classes, whereas Telugu at least put him in touch with Indian playmates at Jadcherla or Wanaparty. He was bothered sufficiently by his biculturalism to feel somewhat disoriented in both Canada and India. This bicultural identity led the families to associate as much as possible with those of like experience.[54]

**Hill Seasons: Pros and Cons**

The Missionary Fellowship in July 1966 found it necessary to rationalize once again the whole question of resorting to the hills at all. Could mission not be carried right through the heat of May with the help of air-conditioning? This idea seemed feasible in theory, saving the mission money and precious time in "these last days." But adequate air-conditioning units for living and working areas would have been prohibitively expensive. Moreover, as all missionaries knew from experience, electric power sources in India were not very reliable.

There were justifiable criticisms of the hill season. It was another source of separation between mission and church, "emphasizing the foreignness of the missionary." There was also the temptation to extend the vacation time to six weeks or more, given that the children were there. But the unalterable fact was that "the main reason for the hill season was and still is to get away from the tremendous heat on the plains [in May]." Another fact was that "very little direct evangelism is being done by missionaries these days, and in the heat not much [of anything] could be done." The Missionary Fellowship could only conclude once more that the advantages of a season of refreshment in the hills far outweighed the drawbacks and appearances of wealth.[55]

**Vernon R. Wiebe, General Secretary, 1968-82**

In 1968 Vernon R. Wiebe took charge of the secretariat. All told, he was probably the most congenial general secretary of them all, forthrightly honest and yet possessing good relational skills. He used the press to advantage, comparable to the BFM's use of the *Zionsbote* before 1955.[56] By taking an intelligent constituency into his confidence he got much feedback in the "letters to the editor" columns of *The Christian Leader* and *Mennonite Brethren Herald*. For example, before bringing the deficit of over $400,000, his first big challenge, to the conference floor, he sent a "Memo to the Brotherhood" in March 1969. He indicated the size of the debt, to whom monies were owed, and revealed clearly how the deficit was accumulated between 1963 and 1968. Budget goals had been unrealistic in view of a decline in giving and bequests, emergencies had intervened, and inflation had taken its toll. The "bottom line" was:

251

"we did not exercise fiscal control... we always hoped the next year would be better."[57]

Subsequent discussions led to some hard decisions. A new strategy was devised for the 1970s that, as Wiebe admitted, was as "dictatorial" as the Yarrow Statement of 1957. "No missionaries were consulted about it," even though his position was "that those who do the work should also... make the decisions." In this connection G. W. Peters remarked at the Winnipeg board meetings in 1970 that the problems lay not with the missionaries, but with "the colonial tendencies of the boards and their officers."[58]

Resorting again to the press, Wiebe forecast full autonomy for national churches, a return of the board to the pre-1953 pattern of facilitation rather than intervention and control, and better training of workers for future assignments. Wiebe also wrote openly about reviewing the performance of missionaries. Why should they go unexamined by fellow missionaries and the board at furlough time when doctors, professors, pastors, and business people are examined annually?[59]

In the "open letter" of June 1970, Wiebe was able to show graphically that the earlier gap between spending and income was being eliminated by systematic debt retirement. What the new strategy meant was a sharp reduction of programs and personnel to keep the budget in balance, and a focus on "high potential" areas for new programs. For India this meant the earliest possible departure, "by the end of 1972." In 1970 Jacob J. Toews and G. W. Peters tried to prepare everyone, including the Governing Council, for "drastic change."[60] As Harold Jantz put it in his accompanying editorial, "it will be difficult to keep a sense of urgency about missions overseas when we begin to feel the impact of the return of a third of our missionary force." He feared that something vital had been lost in a cause that had hitherto provided "the most significant rallying point of our entire brotherhood."[61]

The subsequent discussion forced Wiebe back on his heels. As in the post-Yarrow period, some were offended, and others misunderstood. He had to apologize, explain, and defend the decisions made. Constituents saw "retreat" when in fact MBM/S intended to "reinforce our primary goal of evangelism and church planting," but within the budget.[62] At the 1972 General Conference Wiebe made a "call for Godly optimism" about these goals. He said: "During the past 25 years [since 1947] missions have received a lot of criticism. It became fashionable to discuss the out-dated missionary, the self-seeking national church, and the establishment board apparatus. Some of the criticism was deserved. But much analysis brought an unholy pessimism to the work." He at least did not want to "sink into a negativism that beclouds the fact that we are in the King's business, that He is sovereign, and that His Kingdom will ultimately triumph." He claimed freedom to establish a new playing field with national churches and to renew the mission mandate in the constituency. He lamented the observed phenomenon that for many modern families, given their "changing life styles," mission was a "far-out specialty reserved for a few interested persons." This is what he had tried to explain to Jake Friesen in 1969.[63]

### Nearing the Time for Complete Withdrawal

Whereas the Board of 1957 had wanted a rapid transition to the India Church, all within three to five years, by now the process had taken almost fifteen years and the Missionary Fellowship had resumed a more active consultative role again. Its minutes during these years very much resembled those of the Missionary Council that was scrapped in 1960. By 1970 the missionary membership on the Liaison Committee in India had been reduced to one and missionaries served on various other committees by invitation only. While there was a proliferation of committees, many aspects of the work seemed to be faltering.

As is evident, the thought of packing up and leaving the church members, institutions, and all the programs under the leadership of the Governing Council caused considerable apprehension and uncertainty. What needed to be done before the dateline of 1972-73 was to ensure the continuation of Christian education, to continue support for the most vital programs, to make the final transfer of the Jadcherla medical facility and ministry, and to settle the Mission's properties in a trust.

When Emma Lepp returned in 1970, charged with the continuation of the Bible institute, she decided that a concerted effort needed to be made in Christian education. She and Henry Poetker seemed to be witnessing the collapse of Bible teaching in the schools and the consequent weakening of the Sunday school also. Though Lepp was grateful for an adequate teaching staff of nationals at

Shamshabad, she also wanted Katie Siemens to return. What Lepp proposed was that she and Siemens divide their time between assisting the national staff at BBI and developing a strong Christian education program, meaning Sunday school and Daily Vacation Bible School workshops.[64] This they did, and with departure from the field looming, the two women concerned themselves particularly with the development of graded materials in Telugu. During the cool season of 1972-73 Siemens and Lepp visited ninety-four churches in the interest of Sunday school, and expressed some hope of its continuity.[65]

Henry Poetker devoted his weekends to preaching in the churches in the various fields, while weekdays were taken up with Bible Training by Extension. Along with D. J. Arthur, Poetker spent fourteen hours a week giving instruction in Bible, but his 137 students, mostly teachers, were scattered from Hughestown to Gadwal, with Mahbubnagar, Jadcherla, and Wanaparty in between. Emma Lepp wrote: "I don't know how he keeps going at such a pace." In addition, as they traveled to these areas, they found themselves "involved in church matters" and many "problems to wrestle with."[66]

The dateline of 1973 for departure also brought up the matter of continuing subsidies. Poetker was particularly concerned about the support for radio and literature work, as well as some of the work beyond Mahbubnagar district as a result of the upheaval in 1969, to be discussed in Chapter 16. Epp, however, had some reservations about subsidies for the radio and literature programs developed after 1969. He was clear about continuing the Bible institute at Shamshabad, but felt evangelism should be wholly self-sustaining.[67] The Missionary Fellowship strongly recommended that "extension evangelism" beyond Mahbubnagar should be supported. This involved Y. E. (Yalla) John, who was edged out of the literature program in 1969. By this time he had forty centers of believers as a result of his evangelistic endeavors in the Godavari Delta.[68]

If subsidies were to continue, would there be requests for short-term assignments? With this possibility in mind, Lepp and Siemens concerned themselves with decisions about what to sell off, and what to keep in India. By decision of the Missionary Fellowship, they sold "the major portion of all our Mission furniture and household articles, keeping [only] household articles and furniture for two single ladies and for one couple." As suggested by Lepp and

Siemens, the Ladies' Bungalow at Shamshabad was retained for storage of mission property and as a residence for short-termers and visitors.[69]

### Jadcherla left to P. B. Arnold

As is evident, the transitional medical team from 1971 to 1973 went away worrying about the future, though they had great hopes for P. B. Arnold. Jake and Ruth Friesen, Frieda Neufeld, and Regina Suderman remained until 1972. Regina assisted Jake Friesen in surgery during her twenty years in India. Rosella Toews carried forward the training school initiated by Marie Riediger until 1971. Frieda Neufeld continued as the nurse in charge until 1972, while George Froese provided a transitional supervision in 1972-73.[70] Frieda Neufeld and Rosella Toews were appointed to work in Bangladesh in 1973.

When George and Annie Froese returned for a short time at Christmas 1972 to bridge the gap between the Friesens' leaving and Arnold's arrival, he found that the Indian medical staff seemed too eager to take risks. They would rather operate than "lose face" in cases that Froese knew should be referred to Hyderabad. Froese had faith that Arnold would "do well," but was glad to be able to work with him for some months.[71] Though Froese thought the hospitals should be run as long as possible before being given over to government, he could not help but notice in 1972-73 how many opportunities there were for quarrels, embezzlement, favoritism, and patronage because "we have over-institutionalized our church."[72]

### Property and the Church

The problem of property arose in part from a change in policy triggered by events in the Belgian Congo. Before 1960 it had been A. E. Janzen's stated policy to turn over the church buildings, but retain other properties. These had been "built with **American** funds," and would "remain sacred" until sold and the money reinvested in the "propagation of the Gospel **at other places.**"[73] The Board allowed events elsewhere to override that policy. The revolt of the Zairois against the Belgians in 1960[74] told Janzen that "the transfer of mission responsibility and property to the national church is very imperative and urgent." He now suggested that all missionaries should be removed from compounds, live "in separate residences away from the compounds," and that their bungalows be used "for institutional purposes."[75] This panic resolution was moderated only with respect to the medical staff at Jadcherla and the Bible Institute personnel at Shamshabad. There the bungalows were fenced off. A house was purchased for missionary use in Hyderabad. This was separated from the old Hughestown bungalow, which was used for the high school that developed there.[76] This also meant a policy different from the earlier use of compound church buildings. Toews and Fast told the Governing Council at Mahbubnagar in 1961 that "the Board of Missions does not recognize any organized church groups in Mission compounds." These houses of worship could be attended by people living off compounds, but they were there primarily "for the benefit of the Institutions," were owned by the Board of Missions, and worship services were to be conducted under Mission direction.[77] Undoubtedly this had the effect of adding to the restlessness that surfaced earlier.

For the future it was most important to place all the remaining compound properties in trust. This task fell to Dan Nickel, who served on the Mission Properties Committee. In 1971 he wrote Epp in Hillsboro how "very time consuming" these matters had become, when he really wanted to turn, finally, to evangelism. But he "understood this to be [his] duty" to the Missionary Fellowship, the Church, and the Board. Property matters kept choking off precious time from his first love.[78] He had actually begun looking into property matters in 1967. He benefitted greatly from the preliminary work done by John A. Wiebe, Henry G. Krahn, and others. They had prepared the way by "collecting the sale deeds, property tax receipts, and other documents which might constitute proof of ownership." Even then Nickel almost despaired at some of the difficulties encountered. Proof of ownership was not easy to obtain where missionaries, not being able to own any property officially in the early years, had registered acquisitions in the name of Indian Christian families. Once these were being held by "the third generation" such families were loathe to sign them away as belonging to the Mission. Nickel "struggled with this dilemma for some years."[79] Even if the Mission had wanted to give all Mission properties freely to the Church, the state would have taken about $15,000 in "stamp fees" alone.[80]

## The Final Disposition of the Institutions

When it became difficult to find a suitable existing trust, the Governing Council asked Nickel in 1972 to proceed with the formation of a trust, later named the MB Property Association. Nickel then advised M. B. John of the Governing Council to come to an agreement with the Hillsboro Board in this matter. "It is certainly not the prerogative of the GC only to decide the issue."[81]

He finally found a way around the question of establishing ownership in some "hard" cases by securing the services of an experienced Hyderabad lawyer. His premise was an old one: "possession is 90% of ownership." On this basis, Nickel proceeded to list all properties of the Mission in preparation for placing them in trust. As the time of departure from India (May 1973) rapidly approached, he saw for the first time that his job could actually be completed within a specified time.[82] As it was the India Church held its first annual general meeting of the MB Property Association of India Private Limited on 13 December 1974. It was registered in the state of Madras with the mediation of Louis F. Knoll of the American Baptists.[83]

When Knoll presented his report in 1978, before taking a new posting in California, he showed an investment of about 10,00,000 (or 10 lakhs of) rupees being held in Madras. The gross income for the year was 20.8 percent, about 250,000 rupees. This amount was disbursed for various Governing Council programs and expenses.[84] These were the trust funds turned over to Advocate Devadason who replaced Knoll in 1979.[85]

Even though these properties and monies were placed in a secure trust, it was evident only five years after the departure of the Mission that competition for control over these material possessions would detract the GC from its main mission, that of providing leadership in the evangelism of their own people. This sort of struggle had been predicted by Henry Poetker, as well as by Dan Nickel at the 1973 Conference.[86]

## "The Family of God" in the 1970s

Meanwhile, the financial picture in Hillsboro had improved enormously. In January 1974 Wiebe stated that "four years ago we were four months behind in payments... now we are five months ahead." He explained that their strategy of 1969 had paid off, so to speak. Constituents had responded to the debt crisis, as well as to the new opportunities, by giving 2 to 3 percent beyond the inflation rate of personal incomes. Wiebe naturally was delighted, but warned against any kind of moratorium-thinking. There was still a tremendous need, but all missionary candidates needed to be de-westernized in order to satisfy those who had cause to complain about continuing paternalism.[87]

During the previous year Wiebe had quite courageously opened himself to a barrage of questions and criticisms by his discussion of salaries, "designated gifts," furloughs (now structured for short-term missionaries), and even the possibility of "moonlighting" while at home from the field. Salaries now ranged from $7,350 to $9,450. Wiebe compared these with two-family incomes received by many in the constituency, and with the income opportunities of the secretariat and staff in Hillsboro. He urged a responsible treatment of special gifts so that "the disciplined plan of the whole missionary family" would not be subverted.[88]

Wiebe carried the theme of the larger international MB church family to the conference of 1975 in Winnipeg. The challenge to North Americans in that "more with less" decade was to simplify their lifestyles for the sake of mission in its true sense of "God's mission,"[89] so that MBM/S could realize a doubling of their budget. For India the family of God concept meant that the India Church was now totally responsible, though not without subsidies, nor without short-term help from various missionaries. In fact, Henry and Amanda Poetker, Dan and Helen Nickel, Ted and Esther Fast, Anne Ediger, Emma Lepp, and Katie Siemens did return to India to work "in non-administrative spiritual ministries within and without the MB church."[90] All were technically auxiliary to the Governing Council, whose chairmen corresponded directly with Jake Epp, the secretary for India in Hillsboro under Vernon R. Wiebe.

In summary, it was obvious that full indigenization took much longer than first considered possible by the forceful intervention of the Board in 1957. This intervention was certainly decisive, but proved more divisive than anticipated. The transfer of responsibility to the India Church seemed premature and many programs seemed to unravel as a result. And the subsequent attempt to implement a significant new partnership remained largely rhetorical[91] and relatively disappointing to both partners, as the next chapter will show.

## CHAPTER 16

# The India Partner

For some years before 1957, and increasingly after, there were frequent and perhaps surprising statements of misgivings about the readiness of the India Church for its share in the partnership with the North American MB Church. As the programs were gradually turned over or jointly run, the vitality of the India Church seemed totally threatened by the Telengana/Andhra struggle, which came to a head in 1969. A decade later there was an even more crippling split within the Governing Council. The one led to a fragmented church and the other to a fractured leadership. The church had some vitality underneath, but seemed paralyzed at the top. While the inside story of that church has distressed many, there is a much brighter side. The Gospel seed that has been sown has not all fallen on stony ground. The evangelistic thrust of the India Church continues with encouraging results.[1]

What follows is at best a cursory review of the India partner in the equation of 1963. But before providing that review of the India MB Church, it is relevant to chart the changing world of India into which North Americans had taken the Gospel and to look at the data. These figures do not include the Christians in the three areas served earlier by those from Russia.[2]

### The Changing World of India[3]

| British India | Muslim Hyderabad | Majority Hindu | Republic of India |
|---|---|---|---|
| (1760-1947) | (1801-1948) | (Caste System) | (1950-   ) |
| Government in Council | The Nizam's Government | Brahmans (Twice Born) | P. M. Nehru |
| | | | Lok Sabha |
| British India Army | British Resident | Warrior Caste | Military forces |
| Covenanted services: | Talukdars | Merchants and | Administrative services: |
| 1) Political | Administrative services | moneylenders | Commerce/industry |
| 2) Civil Collector | Professions | | Professions |

259

| Uncovenanted services | Tahsildar | Farmers | Agriculture |
|---|---|---|---|

[Christians in Mahbubnagar]◄─┐

|  | the Muslim faithful | Untouchables: | Scheduled Castes |
|---|---|---|---|
|  |  | 1) Madigas | "Depressed Classes" |
|  |  | 2) Malas |  |

## The Configuration of the MB Church[4] Within the Indian Context

| Year | All India | | Andhra Pradesh | | Mahbubnagar District | |
|---|---|---|---|---|---|---|
|  | Population | % Christian | Population | % Christian | Population | % Christian |
| 1951 | 351,980,860 | 2.55% | 31,115,289 | ? | ? | ? |
| 1961 | 349,301,771 | 2.44% | 35,938,447 | 3.97% | 1,437,564 | 0.90% |
| 1971 | 547,949,809 | 2.60% | 45,932,708 | 4.19% | 1,735,855 | 1.30% |
| 1981 | 683,329,000 | ? | 53,550,000 | ? | ? | ? |
| 1991 | 843,931,000 | ? | 66,305,000 | ? | ? | ? |

## India MB Church Membership

|  | 1939 | 1950 | 1970 | 1978 |
|---|---|---|---|---|
| Deverakonda | 3,500 | 3,000 | 1,877* | 2,637 |
| Gadwal | 4,000 | 4,000 | 9,369 | 10,648 |
| Hughestown | 907 | 1,100 | 887 | 1,378 |
| Kalvakurty | 553 | 800 | 1,028 | 889 |
| Mahbubnagar | 728 | 1,200 | 2,030 | 2,584 |
| Nagarkurnool | 119 | 1,200 | 1,041 | 943 |
| Maknal/Narayanpet |  | 6,000 | 1183* | 857 |
| Shamshabad | 565 | 800 | 512 | 627 |
| Wanaparty | 1,000 | 1,134 | 1,006 | 782 |
| Bombay | 0 | 0 | 0 | 221 |
| Total | 12,443 | 13,234 | 18,993 | 21,566 |

## Census, Converts, and Conversion

Some anomalies* appear in these findings. Until Peter Hamm published his 1970 study of church membership, most people thought India had 25,000 members. Until then Deverakonda had inflated figures, and Billington in 1954 had claimed 6,000 members for Narayanpet/Maktal.[5] According to Henry Krahn Billington's figures were inflated.

Peter Hamm has left an account of how he did his field work in 1970. Over a period of four months he and his team visited 8,500 families in 666 villages and towns. Besides being involved in half of these interviews, Hamm interviewed sixty-nine groups of elders and fifty-three pastors. He wrote: "The intent was to have a more accurate account of active church membership, as well as a better understanding of the nature of that membership." Much the same method was used by V. K. Rufus of Shamshabad in 1978. He added Bombay, where evangelists began to work among the Telugus who moved into industrial areas of that Maratta-speaking megalopolis.[6] As a result of an active evangelistic thrust, despite all the troubles in the church, the India Mennonite Brethren Church in 1990 claimed 65,314 baptized members.[7]

When asked in 1970 how many of these members were truly born again, Peter Hamm suggested a figure of about 25 percent.[8] If Hamm's calculations for 1970 still applied in 1990, there would have been 16,328 born-again MB members in India in 1990. But how could it be that only a small percentage of the India MB church membership was considered genuinely converted when the personnel of the AMBM (and ABMU) were as much concerned about this test of validity as any other Mission? Had John H. Voth been too quick to baptize? If he was so successful, why are the final statistics for Deverakonda (which had many Malas) so meager compared with the impressions he gave in 1939 and in all his reports?

South Asian scholars agree that conversion means much more than a person moving from Hinduism to Islam or Christianity. It means a directional change with respect to beliefs and behavior. G. A. Oddie sees three stages in conversion: 1) a period of struggle under conviction of unworthiness; 2) a climax involving surrender; and 3) a sense of sins forgiven and feeling one with God. Oddie, however, reminds us that "no conversion ever occurred without a history."[9] Whatever the depth of the individual experience, D. B.

Forrester has pointed to the impact on the "depressed classes" of the British in India generally, and the Gospel that came with them since 1813. The upper castes may have feared they were all to be forcefully converted, but it was the untouchables who turned to Christianity after the Mutiny of 1857.[10] The Madigas and Malas found new patrons in the American Baptist John E. Clough, in the Russian Mennonite Brethren with the ABMU, and in the AMBM and other missions. No one else had offered them such self-worth through education, medical services, and employment.

**A Brief Overview of the India Mennonite Brethren Church**

From the beginning, the India Church was an unequal partner in mission. John H. Pankratz organized the first fledgling AMBM congregation on 27 March 1904 at Malakpet. For the next ten years the pioneer Americans seemed content to attend the annual meetings of the Deccan Telugu Association of the Baptist Union. Only in 1918 did the AMBM organize the Telugu Convention, an annual meeting of their churches. In 1949 Janzen helped to celebrate the fiftieth anniversary of the AMBM and in 1954 he edited a volume commemorating fifty years since the founding of what he called the Andhra Mennonite Brethren Church.[11]

The India Church took a different starting point for its jubilee in 1968. It was in 1918 that the AMBM organized the Telugu Convention, an annual meeting of their churches. At that time there were about 2,000 Christians. J. Paranjyothy called that first "faith convention" of 1918 "the starting light of life which has increased steadily for 50 years." While the succeeding conventions were intended to meet the "spiritual needs of the believers" in community, a more structured body representing the entire church, numbering about 13,000 Christians, met as a Field Council in 1946. "It became a dynamic force which made a spiritual impact on individual believers and on church life and practice."[12]

This jubilee statement of 1968, as rhetorical as any conference statement at home, must be balanced by the findings of A. E. Janzen during his 1949 visit and the subsequent criticism of G. W. Peters, who visited India in 1964.[13] Yet there was great hope for the future as seen in the ordination of ten preachers in early 1967, among them N. P. James, J. Paranjyothy, D. J. Arthur, and R. R. K. Murthy.[14]

## Devolution on the Governing Council

In post-war political terms, devolution meant the transfer of sovereignty, authority, assets, if not liabilities, to a national entity that had been subordinate. In this case, devolution meant the transfer of administrative responsibility for all programs to the India Church, but in practice to the Governing Council. This body was made up of representatives, about fifty in all in 1962, from the congregations, organized into nine districts called Field Associations. Decisions with respect to church planting, education, and eventually the medical ministry, devolved on that central body. Not all programs were transferred at once, nor were subsidies wholly withdrawn during this entire period. In practice the whole process took fifteen and more years.

In 1968 Ted Fast reviewed the process to date: We began by "turning over the church building, both spiritual as well as physical." Next came the educational program, then evangelism, and last, the medical program which, at that time, was still under the Mission. But in all areas "boards were set up with both national and missionary personnel working together." Chairmanships were given over to nationals. "The missionary continues to work as a fraternal worker and colleague of the national church."[15]

From the beginning there was considerable concern about a carnal element infiltrating the Governing Council. When M. B. John as chair showed Henry Poetker the membership list in 1961, the latter pointed to the "mixed crowd in the leadership," confident that he could name all those who should be disqualified. He did not think that any property should be transferred to such a group.[16] Margaret Willems wrote J. B. Toews in the initial stages of the transfer that he should come and "straighten out the Governing Council," that he should "separate the spiritual from the carnal," especially in Wanaparty. Such misgivings had a sobering effect on Toews. Had they been too hasty in the drive to transfer authority to the Church? During a conversation with the Home Minister in Hyderabad, Toews was told not to place "national churches on their own without being assured that they were capable of offering consistent leadership." Toews admitted a degree of failure to Fast: "We did not give them a structure of operation and their spiritual premise of personal relationship is proving inadequate to work these out by themselves."[17]

George W. Peters expressed some of the same fears during his Board visit in 1964. He found the Governing Council hardly prepared for the transfer of responsibility. As a constitutionalist, he now thought the Board's New India Plan too idealistic and the relational lines of the MAC to the Governing Council not clear. By then it was clear that in 1958 the Board in Hillsboro had not been listening to the missionaries. He saw "heavy losses," evangelism "bogging down," and the teaching program "sadly lagging." What seemed most important to the Governing Council was the administration of institutions and properties.[18]

One of the weaknesses in India's Governing Council showed up in a dramatic fashion in 1965 when M. B. John, the India leader with the highest profile at the time, was exposed by an audit. He was entrusted with the treasury in succession to Henry G. Krahn, though he seems not to have known how to keep books. Though he was not alone in this, he could not account for the sum of 5,222.48 rupees and refused, at first, to take responsibility. Many irregularities showed up in the matter of monies spent for the Wiebe Memorial Building. When the MAC had no choice but to recommend that M. B. John be relieved of all offices in the Governing Council and to request that he repay what he owed, he eventually agreed to repay this amount over the next five years.[19] Unruh counseled this leading brother that he should begin to repay at once to "prove that you are willing to correct your fault" lest you find it "difficult to [re]establish the confidence in the brotherhood." Make sure, he counseled John, that "the integrity of the GC and yours personally will be preserved."[20]

Paul Hiebert, teaching at Shamshabad, did not hold the Mission blameless in the matter of accountability. Serving on the Medical Committee gave him some insights into administration at this time. He confirmed F. C. Peters' view of this when he suggested that there was still too much of the old individualism and the carving out of "spheres of influence," where "each works independent of others with each acting according to what is right [as in Judges] in his own sight." In connection with the 1965 audit he wrote to Peter Funk: "Clearly there has been poor accounting and misappropriation of funds.... We in the mission too must set an example with open books and audits."[21]

**Signs of Immaturity**

Having seen how Lohrenz and Unruh fared at Hughestown and Wanaparty, respectively, before their retirements, it was to be expected that congregational factions, fueled by nationalistic feelings, would surface once the transfer of property was anticipated. It was this increasing restlessness in nearly every location that met the delegation when it arrived from Hillsboro in 1961.[22] This had only increased when John and Susie (Richert) Lohrenz requested a return visit in 1963. The MAC told them they were welcome, but they should not plan to be involved in two stations, Hughestown and Shamshabad, where he and his first wife Maria had worked for so long. He would be "deeply distressed" at the spiritual conditions prevailing. "Forces have arisen" that are prepared to "destroy" these places. Actually, matters did not turn out that badly, for they received many signs of welcome in both places. Bethel Church members wrote: "There were times when you had to face hardships, reproaches and disheartening circumstances and shed tears. But by God's grace you... went on with the Lord's work."[23]

One view from India matched the concern expressed by Poetker, Willems, Ediger, and Peters. Whatever their spiritual qualifications, D. J. Arthur told MB General Conference delegates at Corn, Oklahoma in 1966, many church members still needed considerable nurture, leadership training, and ecclesiological education. Instead, "there came a cut in the number of missionaries... and in financial help... in many phases of the work." Indigenization was introduced "rather suddenly with too little time for adjustment, the morale of the preachers was badly affected, and the ministry received a setback. Many . . . turned for their security to a secular occupation in the absence of any alternative help from the national church."[24]

Though the concept of preachers turning to self-employment in various trades such as weaving, sewing, cobbling, or holding land would have been most welcome to the Corn delegates, Arthur pointed to the reality: in India they were hoping to raise a mere 20,000 rupees (under $3,000) annually. Two years later he projected a total of 47,700 rupees annually, from all sources, without subsidies. M. B. John, the India representative at the 1960 MB General Conference, had told the constituency in 1957 that self-support had not been taught or emphasized from the beginning. Ted Fast, from his position at Deverakonda, confirmed the neglect to teach giving. As far as he could see, teaching them to give had "absolutely not" been done. This may not seem so strange when one recalls that J. H. Voth, at Deverakonda for three decades, had probably weakened his own teaching of self-support by creating a dependency on North American funds.[25]

### Partnership in Radio and Literature

One of the significant areas of partnership focused on radio and literature outreach. By 1969, however, this appeared too missionary-controlled and too dominated by Andhras to escape a revolution. This had serious implications for the persons working with Anna Suderman and Anne Ediger in literature and radio. One came from a Brahman family, and the others were mostly Andhras. When the ethnic agitation flared in 1969, most of these persons were forced out with the help of such leaders as M. B. John. He would drop in to the press headquarters and embarrass Anna Suderman's literature secretary Y. E. John by asking: "What have the Andhras to do among the Telenganas?"[26]

Some political history is required to understand the critical situation that developed in 1969. Not long after the State of Hyderabad was coerced into the Union in 1948, the Telugu-speaking Andhras in northern Madras demanded their own linguistic province; they no longer wanted rule by Tamil-speaking people. Under threat from the leader of the Andhra movement in December 1952, Nehru created the Andhra state. (Some notice was taken of this agitation surrounding the Mahbubnagar school strike of 1952.) In 1956 Andhra and the old state of Hyderabad, the other half of Telugu country, were joined to form Andhra Pradesh. Over many protests, the hitherto Muslim-dominated city of Hyderabad was retained as the capital city of the new state.[27]

This created many political and socio-economic problems. The Andhras, with the purer Telugu,[28] began to move north and west looking for positions in government and schools, and bringing their superior culture with them. This increasingly upset the people, now called Telenganas, who inhabited the Mahbubnagar district where the Mennonite Brethren were found. Most Mennonite Brethren, in fact, came to think of themselves as ethnic Telenganas. Peter Hamm at Shamshabad wrote David Ewert that the agitation of about nine months resembled a "civil war."[29]

Anna Suderman had been permitted to return for a three-year term in 1966 to develop the literature ministry, headquartered with the radio work at Mahbubnagar. Two of the most gratifying results from her last stint were a successful Bible correspondence course and the organization of a first workshop for writers. The Andhra couple responsible for the correspondence course were Y. E. John and his wife Mary. They were not from Mahbubnagar district but from the southeast, and not of MB background. But while attending Bethany Bible Institute in Shamshabad they were baptized into the MB Church.[30]

It was through Suderman's writings that the constituency heard about these evangelistic efforts and of the developments in the radio work.[31] After Henry Krahn left in 1961, Anne Ediger took over the radio interest. In charge of teaching English at the central high school in Mahbubnagar, she began to draw together some persons for a high quality radio ministry. One of these was a fellow-teacher, G. Bhagvandos, who was keen to become the radio technician, and the other was R. R. K. Murthy. The former was an Andhran and not a MB member at the time; the latter was one of the few Brahman converts. He was baptized by Henry Krahn and began to serve the church in various capacities, even as secretary of the Governing Council in 1960-61. By the time of her furlough in 1965, Ediger was prepared to leave teaching and enter the radio ministry full-time. She and Murthy had been told at a Far East Broadcasting Company conference held in Bangalore in 1964 that their Gospel programs "were the best of the lot in Telugu in that our approach to the Educated Hindu Elite is the right one." Because of this Murthy felt led to give himself fully to this ministry because so many Hindus were turned off by so much that was called Christian. Another factor in his decision was the manifest change in attitudes among Governing Council and pastoral leaders as a result of the visit by F. C. Peters and G. W. Peters in 1964, though there was still a greater concern to protect institutions and places of power than to focus on evangelism.[32] It was clear by 1965 that Murthy, the ablest of them all, had become the pivotal person for both literature and radio evangelism.[33]

Though Ediger's fixed purpose by August 1965 was radio ministry and she intended to take a course in journalism and scriptwriting while on furlough, she actually had great difficulty getting permission to return. She had been quite critical of the Governing Council and her return to head up the radio work was for some time conditional upon her living off the Mahbubnagar compound. She was therefore glad to be quite warmly welcomed upon returning from furlough in 1967.[34]

### The Drastic Shakeup of April 1969

This was how matters stood when the Telengana struggle against the Andhras broke up the group they had gathered about them. It was disillusioning for Suderman and saddening for Ediger. Neither could have anticipated such a drastic shakeup.

The reaction from the Telenganas came after Ediger wrote Epp in February 1969 that she thought G. Bhagvandos, who was proving helpful and adept in the radio ministry, should get more technical training in radio. This became a triggering element. Some, like M. B. John, took alarm at the prospect of having this Andhran from an American Baptist background take work away on their very doorstep.[35] In April the Governing Council "refused to endorse" Bhagvandos; he must be replaced by a Telengana. They accused the technician of neglecting his school teaching in favor of radio ministry. This also happened to Y. E. John and to B. Aseervadam in the literature program. Both Ediger and Suderman were vulnerable too. If Ediger was known to be critical of the Governing Council, it was even more injudicious for Suderman to be administering the financial aspect of the literature ministry during this ethnic tension. The political reality in 1969, as Dan Nickel confirmed, was that the agitation frequently meant the harassment of anyone who supported Andhras. This meant that Anne Ediger and Anna Suderman would be seen as disloyal to Telenganas and therefore out of favor.[36]

While the missionaries could not be dismissed, they could not save their chosen personnel. Murthy, who had just been ordained to the MB ministry in the Calvary Church at Mahbubnagar, and B. Aseervadam, a veteran of twenty years at the press, resigned rather than work under the new management. The missionaries, severely shaken by this turn of events, naturally gave vent to strong feelings. Suderman stated that the person replacing Aseervadam "knew noth-

ing about the press operation" and the new committee, which included Dan Nickel, was surprisingly "unsympathetic to the Christian printing ministry."[37] She pleaded with Jake Epp for assistance
for Aseervadam and his family, who hoped to stay in the area. He
was a man who had "given his all for the press" for several decades.
She stated that Aseervadam "cannot work under people whose quest
is prestige and power." Could her protégé be assisted to set up a
"parallel press" as a reward for his service? Murthy too was asked by
various persons to stay and perhaps set up a "parallel MB church."
Anna Suderman was realistic enough to know that Jake Epp could
not endorse anything like this.[38] But the very fact that she drew this
scenario suggests the severity and emotion of the moment.

At first Ediger too was dismayed that the new committee
seemed content to broadcast for local Telugu consumption. Ediger
and Murthy were actually aiming for "high quality work" to reach
beyond Andhra Pradesh, to all Telugus. Anne allowed that radio
programming would surely continue, but at a "mediocre" level, with
"neophytes" as technicians. She could not see herself continuing
under the new leadership in the long run, though she was willing
to help train those who were now to be installed. She saw the attack
coming from "unspiritual laymen," mostly government workers, who
dominated the Governing Council, some of whom, in Ediger's view,
were "drunkards and chain smokers." In her mind Murthy, a Brahman convert with his family, and Bhagvandos, a technician "who
knows the tastes and language, as well as the music of the educated
Hindu," were God's gifts to the MB Church.[39] It was clear that Ediger,
Bhagvandos and Murthy were "overqualified" or, as some thought,
too elitist for radio work in Mahbubnagar.[40]

Ironically, Paul Hiebert had stated only two years earlier that
God had given "our India field... some of the finest leaders in the
total MB conference [in many ways] surpassing any of us on the
missionary staff."[41] But at this critical point, Peter Hamm and Dan
Nickel supported the Governing Council. Hamm actually took
Murthy to task for his "unspiritual" criticism of the "church, its committees, and its leaders." He was quite severe: "What surprises me...
is that you are at the same time, while criticizing your brethren,
seeking their support morally and for prayer in your evangelistic
ministry." He told Murthy he could not be a representative of the
church and be censorious at the same time. He had gone to the

lengths of using *Suvarthamani* in order to "misrepresent both the national church and most missionaries." Why "take along the whole radio project" in order to reach the Telugu beyond Mahbubnagar?[42] Meanwhile, Jake Epp in Hillsboro was being assured that "the radio work is making good progress, although it did receive a *bit of a setback in July*. It is more indigenous now than it has ever been before."[43]

Meanwhile, between 1966 and 1969 Yalla John and Mary had enrolled 14,000 in correspondence and saw good results in "signed decision cards." They proved effective in planting churches by following up those enrolled in the correspondence school, especially in the Godavari Delta. As the Mission was winding down in Mahbubnagar, MB-related churches were multiplying in Godavari. A considerable number of upper strata conversions were reported.[44] In this way an alternate church developed to some extent.

### Anne Ediger's Alternative Service

For her 1969 vacation Ediger went to the northern hill station of Mussourie. There she found spiritual refreshment through visiting speaker Myron Augsburger and met representatives from other Mennonite missions in India, as well as Allen and Leoda Buckwalter of the Far Eastern Broadcasting Association (FEBA). They found Ediger "very distraught" over what was happening in Mahbubnagar.[45] As indicated, they were already aware of the radio broadcasts prepared by Murthy and Ediger. As a result of this contact, Ediger formulated a proposal to shift Murthy's radio ministry either to Yeotmal or to New Delhi, so that the jealousies that were aroused during the Telengana agitation might not weaken this signal opportunity. She saw the fundamental cause for the breakup as Telengana jealousy of "our Andhra brethren." They would not be allowed to work in Mahbubnagar. Ted Fast was supportive of her suggestion as a "way out of this dilemma."[46]

In July Allen Buckwalter of FEBA requested that the MBM/S second Anne Ediger to them to operate their New Delhi studio as a replacement for someone who was leaving. Anne followed this request with a personal plea for the Board to make a decision soon. She explained that J. Paranjyothy was "doing his best [at Mahbubnagar] as new script-reader and writer" for Christians as the main target, while Nickel was supervising the technical work.[47]

Four months later, Ediger gave her more mature reflections on the events of April 1969. In consideration of the process of indigenization, initiated legislatively in 1958, Ediger admitted that the Governing Council did not ask for an advanced program of literature and radio. "We, the Home Board and the missionary body here, have imposed it on them." Rather bluntly she wrote that they could not expect a "people of an oxcart economy to think intelligently and progressively in terms of electronic evangelism, let alone minister to higher strata of society." She realized that the church was not ready "to shoulder the challenge of radio and literature." She would however give her support where she could.[48]

Before the matter of her seconding to FEBA[49] could be finalized, Ediger required medical attention and surgery. This was done successfully during a furlough. She began her work with FEBA out of New Delhi in 1971 and continued in this service until her untimely death from bone cancer in St. Catharines, Ontario, on 26 September 1981. During those years she worked in Manila with FEBA International, then in New Delhi, as well as with several other evangelical broadcasters. In contrast to the emotional drain caused by her experiences in Mahbubnagar, her last terms in radio work were marked by a renewal of her spiritual strength.[50]

### R. R. K. Murthy and Caste Differences

This 1969 incident pointed up one of the fundamental problems in the India Church: caste differences, which could not be broken down at that stage.[51] From the days of Abraham J. Friesen in the 1890s to the 1950s, supporters at home were promised that many caste conversions were just around the corner. Not many upper strata converts, however, showed up in the MB census of 1970. There were a mere 213 upper-caste members out of about 20,000 total members. This was just over 1 percent.[52] It had come home to one of them, Murthy, that "to many [Madigas] a Mennonite was necessarily a Telenganite." He did not want to accept that kind of thinking, though he understood the historical and political reasons for it. Over this issue and Telengana jealousy manifested in the Governing Council came the parting of the ways. Its leaders were not interested in any kind of ministry among Brahmans.[53]

Murthy was brought up in a middle-class Brahman family with potentially negative attitudes towards depressed classes. While he did not think this way, his lawyer father could not see how anyone of his class could ever become a Christian without, at the first contact with a Christian from an outcaste background, being "stamped for ever as Harijans." His father thought this applied to missionaries also. Following his baptism at the hands of Henry Krahn, the young Murthy served the India Church in various capacities. Eventually he came to see that his father had been right. Many Brahmans who see the truth in Christ would prefer to remain secret believers rather than be identified with an organized church dominated by harijans.[54]

Henry Poetker came to see this also and predicted in 1972 that the Mahbubnagar-centered Church would prove to be even less effective with the upper classes than the Mission. "It is doubtful," he wrote, "whether the Christians here from the scheduled caste background [depressed classes–former untouchables] will ever become a missionary church, at least beyond its borders." If revival should come, much could change, but he feared that persons of Brahman lineage like Murthy would be "edged out" after the missionaries were gone.[55]

In theory India's constitution of 1950 reshaped the caste system, outlawed untouchability, guaranteed religious freedom and should have made it easier, as Ted Fast hoped, for caste people to make that very sharp cultural break. In practice, however, it was ironic that, at the very moment of R. R. K. Murthy's ordination and with endless possibilities for upper strata evangelism through radio, he should be edged out.[56]

**The Madiga Mindset**

On mature reflection, even Ediger thought it more realistic to keep the evangelization of the Telenganas in the hands of a church whose membership was 99 percent of untouchable background. Its members had enough trouble relating to differences within the "depressed classes," let alone between them and the upper strata. It became clear that Christian Madiga or Mala castes did not want to convert higher caste people because, even if educated, they still feared Brahman social and political domination. In Mahbubnagar Madigas (reinforced by the Telengana element) were jealous of upper caste persons like Murthy. If those who had moved up the ladder into secure positions in municipal and government services feared this, it stands to reason that the 80 percent who had remained low on the socio-economic scale would not want such leadership either.[57]

These caste realities were confirmed by D. J. Arthur, who claimed to be from the upper strata.[58] He has already appeared in this story as a teacher in Hyderabad and Mahbubnagar. Further schooling at Yeotmal and Fresno prepared him for leadership in the India Church. He served as director of evangelism and as chair of the Governing Council before he too was edged out, as will be demonstrated. In an interview with Marie K. Wiens in Hillsboro he only confirmed what Murthy had said. "To become a Christian, caste is definitely a hindrance. Caste carries with it levels of social status," and even caste Christians cannot marry beneath their social status.[59] Intermarriage was a problem between Madigas and Malas. Madiga Christians were mostly Baptist and Malas Lutheran, but not both. In Voth's Deverakonda, where there were some of both, Madigas and Malas tended to worship in different village congregations. In the 1960s Madigas and Malas still did not mix very well nor intermarry, and seemed almost to need separate conferences.[60]

In 1968 Arthur explained that family traditions and caste still had a very strong hold on outcaste Christians. It was difficult for a "former untouchable to approach a Brahman," and the church as such found it difficult to "provide evangelists to get a hearing among the higher castes."[61] While he did not change his mind on this point, Poetker discovered that when Arthur was in America during 1972-73, he "talked caste work" because he knew it would "strike a tender cord in the heart of the Board." Back in India he wanted to move away from Mahbubnagar because "the India Church is not interested in caste evangelism." When Poetker asked why, Arthur responded, "once caste people are in the church, they invariably assume places of leadership. Furthermore, because caste people are not interested in intermarriage, we are also not interested in them." Arthur told Poetker he was exploring the possibility of launching a ministry elsewhere.[62]

Arthur felt the Telengana antipathy in 1972. During the Church Convention of March 1972, attended by both Epp and Wiebe from Hillsboro, an attempt was made to remove Arthur from the Chair. As Poetker reported: "Each day taxi loads of observers came to make sure that he would not be removed bodily from leading the G. C.

meetings." On the pretext that Arthur's name could not be found in a 1936 church register, he was not to be permitted to speak at the convention.[63]

### "God Has Spoken" Ministry

For these reasons, it seemed wise, as well, to direct Murthy's ability and experience in radio work away from Mahbubnagar district. Based in Secunderabad since 1973, the Poetkers joined forces in 1976 with Murthy in a new radio outreach called "God Has Spoken Ministries." When invited to air their fifteen-minute gospel broadcasts over Trans World Radio, based in Sri Lanka in 1978, they were potentially able to reach all Telugu-speaking people, about fifty million in all. In 1980 the Secunderabad office received 46,000 letters. When it is considered that the literacy rate is only about 30 percent, this suggests a very wide listening audience in the 27,000 villages and towns of Andhra Pradesh. Claims were made that these broadcasts had influenced judicial decisions, virtually closed temples in some areas for lack of worshipers, and inspired the formation of prayer groups and house churches. According to this view, R. R. K. Murthy had found a large and effective ministry or, as the Poetkers put it, "radio had opened doors for outreach of which they could never have dreamed."[64]

### Henry Poetker's View of the Situation

Poetker's composite portrait of the church, given by one on the scene in the early 1970s, was not flattering. His view echoed the repeated misgivings about the genuineness of the India church. In his correspondence Poetker focused especially on the Governing Council on whom such high expectations had been placed. Was the Governing Council as totally unrepresentative of the Church in 1973 as it was made out to be?

Poetker wrote G. W. Peters in March 1972 that it was time to "decentralize," to separate the Church from the Governing Council. In Gadwal, for example, the preachers might be "fighting for office" but the Christians were responsible, constructing worship places and "waiting for roofs."[65] More and more he wondered "whether the GC is the voice of the Church or the voice of a group within it. So much is done by even one or two in the name of the GC." And yet it was the Governing Council that was getting all the money from Hillsboro. All that the Governing Council members lived for was to have control of these funds and properties, if possible, for their own agenda. Just before the final transfer point was reached (May 1973) Poetker wrote that the Governing Council was unrepresentative of the Church "in practice and reality. The GC is an imported transplant organization that functions as an institution and is wholly funded by foreign funds. When these funds will cease, the GC will cease to function.... The church and the GC are incompatible. The GC structure constitutes Saul's armour, an impressive, well intentioned gift of the king [MBM/S], but which hinders more than it helps."[66]

While on furlough in Clearbrook, British Columbia (1973-75), Poetker kept challenging the Board to eliminate "the financial props for the foster child [the Governing Council]," and subsidize only radio, literature, and extension evangelism led by Murthy. He was quite certain that Murthy would never receive support from Mahbubnagar if money for him was sent through the offices of the Governing Council. In the fall of 1973 Poetker seemed somewhat more pleased with the elections to the Governing Council. In the executive, replacing Arthur as chairman was the familiar M. B. John, while M. C. Emmanuel of Malakpet was secretary, and P. B. Richard treasurer.[67]

### Conflicts at the Top

Overshadowing the genuine work of the Gospel in the churches and radio were bureaucratic struggles for power and position, money and monopoly. Why did matters turn out this way? Must the missionary and the board at home be held in any way responsible for this failure? Or were such power struggles endemic to the Madiga Christian culture, including the patron/client relationship?

It is clear from the official files that the power struggle came to a head in 1978, when B. A. George from Gadwal, then serving as headmaster of the Hughestown High School in Hyderabad, challenged P. B. Arnold for the leadership of the Governing Council. As Paul Wiebe observed at the time, behind the conflict were fundamental "regional, family, and other social considerations play[ing] a part in the organization of the church's leadership." He pointed out that other India national churches have featured similar power struggles. Gadwal, the home of the largest, most self-supporting, though not the wealthiest MB concentration, was pitted against Wanaparty, but the struggle centered on control of Mahbubnagar and Jadcherla.[68] At that time George had the strong support of M. B. John. This challenge coincided somewhat with the consolidation of the MB Property Association under the direction of Louis F. Knoll. Various letters followed during the next months, capped by an "open letter" from the Governing Council detailing suit and counter-suit in various levels of the law courts.[69]

Peter Hamm, the Asia secretary for MBM/S and Henry Poetker, the resident missionary in Secunderabad, tried to bring about a reconciliation between the warring factions, but totally in vain.[70] Both of these men were considered too prejudiced against the India leadership. The latter also were not happy with the attitudes of the Board at the time.[71] Vernon Wiebe and Bill Wiebe in Hillsboro tried to bring some "understanding" of this situation to the North American constituency.[72]

After 1982 MBM/S, led by new Executive Secretary Victor Adrian, continued to support the Governing Council under the headship of P. B. Arnold. A vigorous challenge was made in 1991 by the "Governing Council" of the opposing MB Laymen Evangelical Fellowship.[73] Before and since then numerous attempts have been made, mostly unsuccessful, to bring about a reconciliation between the rival groups.[74]

Underscoring the continuing disappointment and even sorrow for the conflicts within the India MB community, conference leaders in Fresno in March 1994 asked the international MB community for continuing prayer "on behalf of our sister conference in India.... We are deeply saddened by this progression of events that so obviously is hindering the mission of the church and is bringing dishonour to the name of Christ."

Finding it "difficult to intervene" in an "indigenous conference," they hoped that "the credibility and accountability of the leadership of the India MB Conference can be restored... Pray much for our over 800 India churches and pastors who struggle daily with this spiritual crisis."[75]

## CHAPTER 17

# The Legacy of the Mission

What began as a vision and a plan in the mind of Abraham J. Friesen a century earlier had become reality. The work among the Telugu-speaking people to which the Mennonite Brethren were once called had come to fruition. As Daniel Bergthold would have said: this story resembles that of Paul and Barnabas and their first missionary journey as told by Luke in the Book of Acts. Just as that journey resulted in exceedingly difficult faith and cultural questions, leading to serious discussions between Antioch and Jerusalem, so the Russian and North American MB journey in Andhra Pradesh resulted in some right decisions as well as some severe disappointments for both missionaries and India Christians.

If, as stated earlier, the Mennonite Brethren church in India seems fragmented and the leadership fractured, what can one say positively about a legacy? Legacy is what remains and is handed to the next generation who take up the torch. Fortunately, the whole work is greater than the sum of its parts. One can point to various positive aspects of the legacy and give at least faint praise to many parts that seem distressing for the moment.

### The Legacy in the Church

The greatest legacy lies in the people who were touched by the gospel. In 1973 the favorite Scripture of the leaders and converts was "once we were not a people, but now we are the people of God" (I Peter 2:10). This declaration could be made by converts who were once outcaste, enserfed into degrading occupations, and living in segregated **pallems**.[1]

In the early days missionaries invariably sent home pictures of themselves surrounded by their preachers, Bible women, and students. As the numbers grew to around 20,000 about 1970, the media showed large numbers congregating for annual faith conventions. But in the 1960s and 1970s the India Church came to be identified with certain protégés of missionaries who were brought along as potential leaders. Perhaps that recollection seems patronizing today, but M. B. John came from Helen Warkentin's Deverakonda boarding school, Delevai J. Arthur found a sponsorship with John H. Lohrenz in Hyderabad, and P. B. Arnold with

277

Margaret Willems at Wanaparty. Many others found their way to Bethany Bible School, a "school for prophets" begun by the pioneering American missionaries in 1920. Among these leaders of promise were N. P. James, M. A. Solomon, S. J. Joseph and Hannah Kampelly, V. K. Rufus, who began in Hughestown school with Lohrenz, and the R. S. brothers: Lemuel, Aseervadam, and Victor. Some of these attended Yeotmal or Ramapatnam also, and some furthered their studies in North America. These are only representative of hundreds more. The most outstanding Brahman was R. R. K. Murthy, who converted while he served as language teacher to Henry and Alice Krahn. Many continued as workers in the India Church, while others like Joseph and Hannah started their own ministry just outside Shamshabad. As M. C. Emmanuel, an active lay evangelism leader, wrote recently, there are many others "who have not bowed the knee to Baal." The Elijahs are not the sole defenders of truth.[2]

The majority of MB church people are found in village churches shepherded by persons like K. E. Paul. He was born in 1905, went to school in Malakpet under Katharina Lohrenz and became a Christian at the age of eighteen. He and his first wife were guided into Christianity by John and Maria Lohrenz. Though suffering persecution, they persevered and Paul was still serving faithfully as pastor in 1976 at Shahabad in the Shamshabad field. He had a congregation of 179 members which met in a church built in 1971 which seated about 200 on a mud floor.[3]

The greatest number of congregations, also those manifesting the greatest degree of self-support of their programs, reside in the Gadwal area served longest by Abram A. Unruh. In 1978 Gadwal had as many members as all the other fields put together. Evangelism and church planting has been carried on by lay people even when there was conflict among the leaders above them.[4]

Perhaps there is more than one MB Church in India. Another church owing much to the MB Mission may have branched off in 1969 with the breakup of the literature and radio group focused around Anna Suderman and Anne Ediger. Many converts from Murthy's radio ministry and Yalla's earlier correspondence work are perhaps not registered with the official Mennonite Brethren Church. They are scattered eastward and southward of Mahbubnagar and many may have gone interdenominational. No one knows how many congregations may be adhering to a rival governing council, or what numbers this alternative church has. Many are working faithfully in the Gospel, "some from inside the MB fold and some from without."[5]

One of the latter is R. R. K. Murthy who still airs "God Has Spoken" over Trans World Radio, "adding daily those who [are] being saved" (Acts 2:47, NIV). He now works out of a studio at the Bharat Bible College in Hyderabad. In 1981 the written responses averaged 40,000 a year and the results in changed lives and the impact on society were indeed impressive.[6]

Though quantification and qualification are difficult in the present circumstances, R. S. Lemuel claimed in 1990 that "by the grace of God," there were 810 churches in 3,000 villages of Andhra Pradesh and, with extensions into Bombay and Karnataka, more than 65,000 "baptized M. B. Members in India."[7]

**The Written Legacy**

As J. B. Toews recognized in 1975, A. E. Janzen wrote or edited more books about the India Mission than anyone else. These included several *Missionary Albums* which are of great value. Frequent reference has been made to all of these works.[8] A more significant written legacy has been given by members of the John A. Wiebe family. Reference has been made to John's master's thesis on the Madiga while on furlough in the 1940s. Perhaps inspired by this example, son Paul went into sociology and in 1988 produced the first critical analysis of the India Church in a book that has been very helpful: *Christians in Andhra Pradesh: The Mennonites of Mahbubnagar*. He, with his sister Marilyn, also helped his mother Viola publish a remarkably fine legacy in pictures and prose: *Sepia Prints: Memoirs of a Missionary in India*. This covers much of the early life and work of the Bergtholds as well as that of the Wiebe family.

While I am grateful for the opportunity to have been present at the celebration of 100 years of Mission and Church at Mahbubnagar in October 1990,[9] I could not venture to write the full history of the India Church. Even if there were sufficient resources to draw a composite picture of the Church, as there are for the Mission, justice could not be done without extensive work in the nine fields of the Mission. I hope India readers will, however, appreciate the openness with which this story of the Mission has been told, and that someone will be inspired to do an in-depth analysis of the India Church by asking Asian as well as Western questions of the sources.[10]

The India Church has also contributed some significant items to the written record. *Suvarthamani*, a periodical initiated by John H. Voth in 1920, has continued to this day under the successful editorship of E. D. Solomon and Karuna Shri Joel.[11] Even more helpful as memorials are the anniversary books that have been published. These celebratory volumes have been determined by differing perspectives on the past. A. E. Janzen edited the first such book in 1954, taking the founding of the first AMBM church in 1904 under Pankratz as the significant anniversary. The India Church in 1968 took 1918, the founding of their Telugu Convention, as more important. In 1975 however, wanted to remember the initiation of the AMBM under N. N. Hiebert in 1899. But only 15 years later the Governing Council thought better of this and decided that the 100th anniversary belonged to the memory of Abraham J. Friesen who went to Nalgonda district in late 1889. While the 1968 volume was in English, the last two featured as much Telugu as English. [12]

**The Legacy in Memory and Memorials**

In North America the legacy of the India Mission is a fading memory. In about 1969 Vernon R. Wiebe stated that mission had become the interest of a shrinking minority. Nevertheless, the memory will linger in that minority who were strong supporters as long as they live, as well as among children of those missionaries who had a long-term commitment [13]

When A. E. Janzen found himself on that first field visit to India, he photographed the more than 200 buildings constructed "with American money," as he wrote.[14] Most of them are being used in some capacity to this day, listed under the MB Property Association. As long as they are standing, India people will associate them with the missionaries who built them. Though some of the bungalows seemed too ostentatious during the period of decolonization, they will remain longest as a legacy of the West's missionary age.

Not all the memorials can be mentioned. As noted, John Lohrenz was concerned to build Bethel Church in Hyderabad in memory of his sister Katharina, who died there in 1913. His building program at Shamshabad in the 1920s and 1930s is wonderful to contemplate even to this day: the main bungalow, the ladies' bungalow, reserved today for guests from abroa[15] the hospital building for Katharina Schellenberg, the church, and numerous outbuildings, and two wells. Very central today on that campus is the Bergthold Memorial Building which houses Bethany Bible Institute and College under the supervision of R. S. Lemuel. In Fresno, on the campus of the Mennonite Brethren Biblical Seminary, there are two significant memorials: one built by the Warkentin family in memory of Herman Warkentin who lost his life at Kalvakurty in 1953, and apartments for students as a memorial to the Daniel Bergtholds.[16]

## The Legacy in Ministries

P. B. and Sharada Arnold are correct in pointing to the medical work as the most pervasive, visible, popular, and helping ministry still carried on. In this respect the MB Hospital at Jadcherla joins the many other hospitals contributing to India's medical work by Christian missionary societies since the 19th century. In 1975 Dr. N. S. Isaiah reviewed the entire MB medical ministry in India, highlighting the work at Nagarkurnool, Deverakonda, Wanaparty, Shamshabad, Gadwal, and Jadcherla. He emphasized that this ministry "removes barriers of caste and untouchability."[17] As no other ministry, it provides unique opportunities to witness, and sets guidelines for hygiene and nutrition.

Educational work is being carried forward at all levels up to the Bible institute and Bible college level at Shamshabad. According to R. S. Lemuel all of these schools, in addition to the facets of the work coming under the evangelism department, are in fact contributing to evangelism to this day.

It was encouraging in 1990 to encounter students at Shamshabad's Bible Institute going out to the villages on weekends to bring the Gospel, and looking forward to a more extensive outreach following graduation. The evangelistic outreach of the India Church has been expanding for the past 15 years, even to Bombay and Karnataka, in spite of the apparent breakdown at the top.

## The Colonial Legacy

One of the inescapable conclusions of this study is that, in varying degrees, a colonial legacy pervaded the Mission and Church. The following unsolicited comment,[18] suggests what others have said, that the district collector and the missionary "in charge" of his station and field, and the Governing Council leadership as a "boss-type" are somewhat analogous.

> India was under the British boot for two centuries. The majority of the Indian masses including the intelligentsia were happy to toe the line of the powers that be. The same mentality prevailed in terms of the missionaries and their administration. In the eyes of the poor national Christians, the missionaries were a fortunate race, rich, resourceful and powerful. Their word was law. Now the national leaders, with power and pelf, expect the same kind of submission. . . He who chooses to differ with the status quo in their policies and programs is branded as the enemy of the church and the leadership. This strange phenomenon is beyond the comprehension of the Mission Board.... The leadership thinks that administration and the institutions are the church. They are not bothered about the local congregations which are the real church.

The English collector was beholden only to a distant commissioner who related to the lieutenant-governor, who answered to the governor-general who, in turn, answered to London. The more the collector kept things together and everyone beholden to him in his place, and the revenue increased every year, the more he could hope to rise to even higher positions. He was paid about as much as all others in his establishment put together.[19]

John H. Voth, missionary in charge of Deverakonda for 30 years, used his appropriations and all those designated gifts to build up a Christian establishment that somewhat resembled the administrative structure of the collector, one of the proconsuls of empire. Voth worked very hard at training a large coterie of young people who would evangelize the field of Deverakonda. For many years he also worked hard in the villages himself. For those who could not go to the Bible school that Bergthold ran at Nagarkurnool, he held hot-weather in-station training sessions for weeks on end. They all needed financial support, and he saw that they got it. He agitated for the system of designated gifts, even soliciting funds while on furlough at the height of the depression, right under the nose of the mission administrators at home, who were grieving the need to cut back appropriations and salaries. By the mid-1930s he claimed 3,000 converts when the whole AMBM had only 4,000 in 9 fields.

The heavy-handed intervention of the Board in 1957 did not change this colonial system. According to Abram A. Unruh it merely shifted the authority from the missionary "in charge" to the colonial secretary seated in Hillsboro, the "London" of the MB empire abroad. A new crop of younger missionaries readily accepted the new regime and willingly served in the Mission Administrative Committee of the 1960s as the extension of this new force to bring about change. As noted, the MAC was largely boycotted by the single women as too dictatorial. When the doctors filled these powerful positions and Jake Friesen, the leading doctor, also held the treasury of the Mission and built a bungalow on the old scale, this modeled an enviable lay leadership style. By this time the medical ministry had the highest billing; it was seen as the most effective way to achieve the one thing "we had gone to India for, to win souls." Evangelism and the church were second-ranked.

All of this was grist for the mill of the well-understood patron-client system that prevailed in India. This legacy of dependence and too much institutionalism opened the road for corruption. The compounds, these earlier lighthouses, centers of refuge for the ostracized, and source of livelihood for the talented poor, became centers of power-seeking.[20] It was only a matter of time before someone from within the India Church saw an opportunity to take control of all resources: personnel, institutions, and finances. That person turned out to be P. B. Arnold of Wanaparty. Arguably multi-talented, and having the high profile of a competent surgeon/healer, he seems to have grasped control only a few years after being given "charge" of the Jadcherla hospital. His Governing Council came to manage the entire Church, its administration, its medical and educational institutions, its properties, as well as the distribution of all funds that accrued to that Council. This became patronage writ large. In order to strengthen his position, he also sought ordination to the gospel ministry, so that he could add that aura of sacred ministry to his personality. At the Centenary in 1990, in an eighty-minute oration, he gave a complete rationalization for his conduct, basing it on God's leading in his life since childhood.[21]

This new system took such control in Mahbubnagar/Jadcherla that the inevitable challenge came by 1978. Resort was taken to the courts to expose alleged embezzlement and corruption, to dislodge and replace those in positions of power.[22] What departing missionaries feared had now come to pass. Yet in the early 1980s MBM/S felt it had no choice but to work through the legally-constituted Governing Council. It seemed then that this was the lesser of several evils and the only way through the present crisis.[23]

P. B. Arnold, who was now operating as the India boss type out of Jadcherla, claimed that the Mission had only itself to blame. In 1986 he declared that the church system brought to India was always seen as foreign in its "patterns of worship, modes of thought, church architecture," and too dependent on Western assistance. Instead of planting the gospel seed in Asian soil, and letting it germinate and bear fruit there, the whole Western tree was transplanted, root and branches. He called this a "purely self-serving community."[24]

**The Credibility Gap**

Quite apart from the embarrassment of the fractured leadership, a greater problem enveloping even the village churches persists. Paul Wiebe discussed this in conjunction with the theory of "plausibility structure."[25] That is to say, from the perspective of the political, social, and economic leaders of the Hindu majority, who were rarely asked whether they wanted this Gospel intrusion, there is a large degree of implausibility.

What this means is that the India Mennonite Brethren, largely identified as Telenganas centered in Mahbubnagar, could not appear convincingly believable to attract the strong support for their endeavors from those leaders quite apart from caste considerations that alone are sometimes insuperable. How could essentially "**harijan**" types become leaders? Upper-strata people may wish to hear the gospel, but cannot respect the evangelist. Some leaders whom they might have respected were driven out in 1969. And the fact that a whole array of pre-1978 MB leaders and former missionaries were not even invited to the Celebration of 1990 could by no stretch of the imagination strengthen the Church's credibility.

That a Telengana Church is ill-fitting in the social/cultural scene is one thing. According to Wiebe, the strength of Hinduism is not diminished nor is Christianity "considered a serious threat" to regional Hindu leaders. Hinduism remains "extraordinarily capable [of] absorbing and neutralizing" alternative "penetrating messages" from the outside. Besides, reconversion to Hinduism is a strong temptation because to be identified as a Christian apart from the

Scheduled Castes is to lose out on "preferential treatment" in government programs and job opportunities. This latter is crucial because everyone with some education wants to experience upward mobility. The fact is, that most rural churches are buffeted by these realities, and in many cases are not much better off than they were before the missionaries came.[26]

Then there are the family and caste considerations. Missionaries often discovered that family solidarity, held in clans, dictated how money and positions were disbursed, how church discipline was treated, and how whatever promoted the family's well-being was paramount. Nor has Christianity shaken caste distinctions. For this neither the Governing Council nor the missionaries are directly to blame, though by not knowing how to achieve a breakthrough among leading people, and exulting too much in large numbers from the lower ranks, they tied themselves to those who, while they needed the Gospel, could not pass it on except to their children.[27]

## Conclusion

There is, unfortunately, a legacy of some irony. As is evident from this account, the intervention of the Board in 1957 led by J. B. Toews, did not have the anticipated results. What was needed, as Vernon Wiebe was told more than once, was a solid partnership with trusted missionaries continuing in service. The India Church in the 1960s wanted partnership, real partnership, not "freedom" to be cut loose.[28] In his written legacy of the 1990s, Toews looked back on "Partnership in Obedience" as largely rhetorical, the North American partner still too dominant, prolonging economic paternalism, while identification was marginal and cross-cultural understanding minimal.[29]

The ironic cannot shade the heroic. As explained elsewhere, the Russian Mennonite Brethren were from the first drawn to one of the bleakest and least productive areas of India: the Deccan, for the simple reason that this is where the "needy" Telugu-speaking peoples lived and where they had responded to the Gospel in large numbers at Ongole in the 1870s. When one thinks of the extent of illiteracy among the Madigas, their general poverty, and the many obstacles and difficulties encountered, one cannot dispute the considerable achievement. Any North American group would have found the culture and climate difficult. But the problems of making a Christian breakthrough in an all-pervasive Hindu culture were not sufficiently appreciated.

Looking positively and optimistically beyond the statistical analyses, however, the influence of Mennonite Brethren in India must be seen as incalculable. Given the large numbers that have been added during the last two decades, the potential for evangelism among the depressed classes, at least, is enormous. Jesus came to "preach good news to the poor."

# APPENDIX

## 1) The Three Generations of Missionaries, 1885-1975

While the text and the photographs included in this work provide much biographical data, the portrait would not be complete without the following lists: 1) all those who worked "down in the plains" (those working at Bruton or teaching at Kodaikanal did not consider themselves missionaries in the sense of working out of a station in the Deccan); 2) a summation (with endnotes) of the educational qualifications; and 3) those working in the secretariat (mainly Hillsboro, Kansas) with reference to India.

The asterisk* indicates marriage in retirement: M. Enns, first to Robert G. Deacon, second to Helmut Toews; H. Harder to Peter Loewen; E. Lepp to Reuben Baerg; Aganetha Neufeld to Heinrich Hamm; Elizabeth S. Neufeld, first to Peter Wall, second to Carl Wichert; K. Siemens to Abe Esau; and M. Willems to P. V. Balzer.

## 1) List of India Missionaries

| Name | Birth date | Years of Service | Education | Death date & Place |
|------|-----------|------------------|-----------|--------------------|
| Balzer, Peter V. | 22 May 1891 | 1923-68, 4 terms, 1 short | AB, ThB, MA | 6 July 1995, CA |
| Balzer, Elizabeth Kornelsen | 2 January 1901 | 1923-61, 4 terms | Bible school | 4 Dec. 1966, KS |
| Bergthold, Daniel F. | 12 January 1876 | 1904-46, 4 terms, 2 short | AB | 25 Oct. 1948, CA |
| Bergthold, Tina Mandtler | 16 December 1878 | 1904 | | 20 Nov. 1904, India |
| Bergthold, Anna Epp | 30 April, 1878 | 1904-15, 2 terms | Nurse's training, Russia | 5 Sept. 1915, India |
| Bergthold, Anna Suderman | 26 December 1875 | 1899-1946, 4 terms, 1 short | Bible school, nurse's training | 11 March 1957, CA |
| Block, Peter J. | 17 Sept. 1933 | 1961-71, 2 terms | MD | |
| Block, Arlene | 13 April, 1934 | 1961-71, 2 terms | | |

| Name | Birth date | Years of Service | Education | Death date & Place |
|------|-----------|------------------|-----------|--------------------|
| Dick, Jacob J. | 19 April 1904 | 1934-57, 3 terms | Bible schools | 9 Aug. 1980, BC |
| Dick, Anna Berg | 18 Sept. 1905 | 1934-57, 3 terms | | 2 Dec. 1976, BC |
| Dueck, Helen | 6 January 1925 | 1956-67, 2 terms | Bible, 6 years; RN, BSc | |
| Ediger, Anne L. | 20 November 1920 | 1953-81, 2 terms + 5 short terms | BRE, Teaching Certificate | 26 September 1981, ON |
| Enns, Margaret | 6 May 1926 | 1981-87, 2 terms | Bible School, Teacher | |
| Enns, Mildred* | 27 November 1921 | 1947-54, 1 term | Bible, 2 years, BEd | 24 June 1986, MB |
| Fast, Ted H. | 8 March 1924 | 1951-92, 2 terms + 5 short terms | BS, ThG | |
| Fast, Esther | 11 October 1923 | 1951-92, 2 terms + 5 short terms | Bible School Teacher | |
| Friesen, Abraham J. | 15 May 1859 | 1889-1914, 2 terms + 2 short | ThB equivalent [1] | 18 November 1920, Russia |
| Friesen, Maria Martens | 15 June 1860 | 1889-1908, 2 terms + 1 short | | 19 April 1917, Russia |
| Friesen, Jake | 19 March 1920 | 1951-73, 3 terms | Bible, 2 years, MD | |
| Friesen, Ruth Berg | 24 January 1923 | 1951-73, 3 terms | Bible, 2 years, RN | |
| Froese, George J. | 10 October 1922 | 1954-73, 2 terms + 1 short | Bible, 1 year, MD | |
| Froese, Annie Bergman | 11 January 1928 | 1954-73, 2 terms + 1 short | Bible, Teaching Certificate | |
| Gerdes, Edna | 10 December 1919 | 1946-60, 2 terms | Bible, 5 years, Teaching Certificate, ThG | |
| Hamm, Peter M. | 26 August 1930 | Bruton (1958-63), 1965-70, 1 term | ThB, BD, MA, PhD | 16 August 1993, BC |
| Hamm, Betty Hildebrand | 29 June 1929 | Bruton (1958-63), 1965-70, 1 term | Bible, RN | |
| Hanneman, Anna | 28 November 1890 | 1915-40, 3 terms | AB, Teaching Certificate | 21 February 1943, KS |
| Harder, Helen* | 20 February 1919 | 1946-71, 2 terms + 2 short terms | Bible, 1 year, RN | |
| Hiebert, J. N. C. | 5 March 1904 | 1929-51, 3 terms | ThB, BA, MA | 20 July 1956, CA |
| Hiebert, Anna Jungas | 2 August 1906 | 1929-51, 3 terms | Bible | |
| Hiebert, Nicolai N. | 29 July 1874 | 1899-1901, 1 short term | Bible | 14 September 1947, KS |

| Name | Birth date | Years of Service | Education | Death date & Place |
|------|-----------|------------------|-----------|---------------------|
| Hiebert, Susie Wiebe | 19 July 1880 | 1899-1901, 1 short term | | 1 January 1963, KS |
| Hiebert, Paul G. | 13 July 1932 | 1959-65, 1 term | BA, MA, PhD | |
| Hiebert, Frances Flaming | 22 August 1934 | 1959-65, 1 term | Arts, PhD | |
| Huebert, Abram J. | 22 July 1866 | 1898-1936, 3 terms | ThB equivalent | 8 May 1949, India |
| Huebert, Katharina Penner | 1873 | 1898-1936, 3 terms | Nursing studies | 12 April 1948, India |
| Janzen, Frank A. | 30 June 1880 | 1910-27, 2 terms | BA, ThB | 8 October 1927, India |
| Janzen, Elizabeth Dickman | 9 March 1889 | 1910-46, 3 terms | Bible studies | 12 September 1960, KS |
| Kasper, Julius J. | 6 February 1915 | 1946-65, 3 terms | Bible, ThG | |
| Kasper, Eva Block | 23 December 1918 | 1946-50, 1 term | Arts | 21 October 1950, India |
| Kasper, Mary Doerksen | 24 November 1912 | 1951-65, 3 terms | RN | 27 November 1993, BC |
| Klahsen, Jacob P. | 28 May 1899 | 1930-53, 3 terms | BD, MTh | |
| Klahsen, Katie Huebert | 26 December 1899 | 1930-53, 3 terms | Bible | 1973, ON |
| Krahn, Henry G. | 7 July 1923 | 1956-61, 1 term | BRE, BA, MA, PhD | 9 Dec. 1985, MB |
| Krahn, Alice Bauman | 17 July 1925 | 1956-61, 1 term | Bible, Arts, RN | |
| Lepp, Emma* | 14 February 1917 | 1946-78, 3 terms + 3 short terms | Bible, 4 years, BA, MA | |
| Lohrenz, John H. | 2 March 1893 | 1920-64, 4 terms, 1 short | AB, BD, MA | 5 Mar. 1971, CA |
| Lohrenz, Maria Klaassen | 28 November 1892 | 1920-57, 4 terms | AB, BD | 19 July, 1962, CA |
| Lohrenz, Katharina | 11 March 1882 | 1908-1913, 1 term | Teaching Certificate | 5 September 1913, India |
| Neufeld, Aganetha* | July 1880 | 1913-23, 1 term | Nurse's training, Russia | 7 May 1963, Brazil |
| Neufeld, Elizabeth S.* | 15 September 1872 | 1899-1906, 1 term | Teacher | 1 May 1952, CA |
| Neufeld, Frieda | 11 January 1918 | 1951-65, 2 terms + 2 short terms | Bible, 4 years, RN | |
| Nickel, Daniel A. | 3 October 1928 | 1965-74, 1 term, 1 short term | Bible, MA, | |

| Name | Birth date | Years of Service | Education | Death date & Place |
|---|---|---|---|---|
| Nickel, Helen Martens | 11 Sept. 1929 | 1965-74, 1 term, 1 short term | | |
| Pankratz, John H. | 14 January 1867 | 1902-26, 1938-41, 3 terms + 1 | ThB | 19 July 1952, CA |
| Pankratz, Maria Harms | 11 March 1880 | 1902-26, 1938-41, 3 terms + 1 | Bible, 1 year | 25 January 1941, India |
| Penner, John A. | 31 January 1885 | 1913-50, 4 terms | ThB equivalent | 7 Jan. 1977, ON |
| Penner, Anna Nikkel | 17 November 1888 | 1913-50, 4 terms | RN | 28 June 1970, ON |
| Peters, Anna | 10 August 1882 | 1911-12, 1 term | Teacher, Russia | 14 Jan. 1939, ON |
| Poetker, Henry | 17 March 1918 | 1952-86, 3 terms + 4 short terms | Bible, 3 years, AB, MA | |
| Poetker, Amanda Lepp | 2 June 1918 | 1952-86, 3 terms + 4 short terms | Bible, 5 years | |
| Reimer, Catharine | 14 January 1900 | 1930-37, 1 term | RN | 23 Feb. 1958, CA |
| Reimer, Katharina | | 1905-08, 1 term | Teacher, Russia | Russia |
| Riediger, Marie | 28 October 1924 | 1957-63, 1 term + 1 short term | RN, BRE, BNursing | |
| Schellenberg, Katharina L. | 28 November 1870 | 1907-45, 3 terms | MD | 1 January 1945, India |
| Schmidt, Ernest E. | 12 November 1916 | 1949-57, 1 term | Bible, 2 years, BA, MA, Teaching | |
| Schmidt, Evelyn Straus | 21 May 1923 | 1949-57, 1 term | Bible, 1 year, MA, Teaching | |
| Siemens, Katie* | 18 January 1923 | 1954-87, 3 terms + 7 short terms | Bible, 5 years, AB, Teaching | |
| Studebaker, Dilwyn B. | 21 October 1918 | 1949-54, 1 term | AB, BD | |
| Studebaker, Mildred Heinrichs | 5 October 1923 | 1949-54, 1 term | Arts | |
| Suderman, Anna | 9 April 1902 | 1938-69, 3 terms, 1 short | Bible, 1 year, ThB | 27 June 1983, FL |
| Suderman, Margaret | 10 April 1902 | 1929-62, 4 terms | Bible, 2 years, RN | 23 May 1991, MB |
| Suderman, Regina | 18 April 1920 | 1951-72, 2 terms + 2 short terms | Bible, 3 years, RN | |
| Toews, Rosella | 25 March 1920 | 1946-71, 4 terms | Bible, 3 years, RN | |
| Unruh, Abram A. | 20 October 1903 | 1936-67, 4 terms | ThB, BA | 7 Sept. 1988, MB |
| Unruh, Annie Elias | 17 March 1900 | 1936-67, 4 terms | Bible, 1 year | 13 Aug. 1982, MB |

| Name | Birth date | Years of Service | Education | Death date & Place |
|------|-----------|------------------|-----------|--------------------|
| Unruh, Cornelius | 8 April 1873 | 1904-39, 4 terms | ThB equivalent | 9 Dec. 1941, ON |
| Unruh, Martha Woltman | 27 March 1879 | 1904-39, 4 terms | RN, Germany | 14 Nov. 1956, NY |
| Unruh, Heinrich | 4 October 1868 | 1898-1912, 2 terms | ThB equivalent | 13 October 1912, India |
| Unruh, Anna Peters | 24 December 1875 | 1898-1913, 2 terms | | 13 October 1923, Russia |
| Voth, John H. | 23 December 1879 | 1908-42, 4 terms | BA, ThB | 29 July 1943, OK |
| Voth, Maria Epp | 1 January 1881 | 1908-42, 4 terms | | 16 September 1968, CA |
| Wall, Maria C. | 5 September 1885 | 1915-57, 4 terms | Bible, RN | 22 Mar. 1968, CA |
| Wall, Ronald | 24 November 1936 | 1962-64, 1 term | Dentist | |
| Wall, Maryann Peters | 13 November 1936 | 1962-64, 1 term | Teacher | |
| Warkentin, Helen | 25 November 1887 | 1920-57, 4 terms | Bible, 1 year, Teaching Certif. | 25 June 1975, MB |
| Warkentin, Herman | 30 June 1917 | 1946-53, 1 term | BA, BD, MTh | 26 March 1953, India |
| Warkentin, Beatrice Koop | 17 November 1922 | 1946-53, 1 term | Bible, 1 year, Teaching Certif. | |
| Wiebe, David | 20 August 1937 | 1966-68, 1 term | MD | |
| Wiebe, Lorma | 9 June 1937 | 1966-68, 1 term | | |
| Wiebe, John A. | 29 March 1900 | 1927-59, 3 terms + 1 term, ABMU | AB, BD, MA | 28 December 1963, India |
| Wiebe, Viola Bergthold | 17 August 1903 | 1927-59, 3 terms + 1 term, ABMU | AB | 10 September 1996, KS |
| Wiens, Franz J. | 23 November 1880 | 1909-14, 1 term | ThB equivalent | 31 July 1922, CA |
| Wiens, Marie Warkentin | 27 March 1883 | 1909-14, 1 term | RN equivalent | 3 December 1970, CA |
| Wiens, Johann G. | 3 August 1874 | 1904-10, 1 term | ThB equivalent | 2 Jan. 1951, MB |
| Wiens, Helene Hildebrandt | 19 October 1877 | 1904-10, 1 term | Nursing studies | 29 May 1967, MB |
| Willems, Margaret* | 9 December 1907 | 1946-68, 2 terms, 1 short | Bible, 4 years, RN | 19 May 1994, SK |

291

## 2) The Summary of Educational Attainments

Not having had access to personal missionary records, the following measurements or levels for the **ninety-six missionaries** involved cannot be wholly accurate. The high school certificate or its equivalent[2] is assumed.

### Certificates and Diplomas

| | | |
|---|---|---|
| Teaching Certificates[3] | 15 | 16.60 % |
| Registered Nurses | 18 | 18.70 % |
| Married Women: education unknown | 10 | 10.40 % |
| Bible school as highest level | 33 | 34.40 % |
| Summer Linguistic and Medical courses | 3 | 3.12 % |
| Engineering | 1 | 1.04 % |

### College and University Degrees[4]

| | | |
|---|---|---|
| BRE, ThB, GTh as highest level | 17 | 17.70 % |
| BA (or AB) as highest level | 8 | 8.30 % |
| Bachelor of Nursing of Science | 2 | 2.08 % |
| BD as highest degree | 2 | 2.08 % |
| MA as highest degree | 7 | 7.20 % |
| MTh as highest degree | 2 | 2.08 % |
| PhD as highest degree | 3 | 3.10 % |
| MD | 5 | 5.20 % |
| Dentistry degree | 1 | 1.04 % |

# 3) The Secretariat

| Secretariat, India, Name | Birth date | Years of Service | Office | Death date and Place |
|---|---|---|---|---|
| Adrian, Victor | 23 May 1927 | 1983-1992 | General Secretary | |
| Braun, Heinrich J. | 30 April 1873 | 1889-1918 | Finance, Rückenau | 24 June 1946, Germany |
| Epp, Jake H. | 22 June 1910 | 1964-1975 | Secretary for Asia | 12 January 1993, KS |
| Epp, Siegfried | 9 February 1931 | 1975-1996 | Finance | |
| Funk, Peter J. | 25 September 1914 | 1960-1969 | Finance | |
| Hamm, Peter M. | 26 August 1930 | 1980-1989 | Administrator | 16 August 1993, BC |
| Hiebert, Nicolai N. | 29 July 1874 | 1902-1936 | Secretary | 14 September 1947, KS |
| Janzen, Abram Ewell | 22 November 1892 | 1945-75 | Secretary, Historian | 2 December 1995, KS |
| Kliewer, Marion | 27 August 1928 | 1955-1970 | Publicity | 2 June 1986, KS |
| Lohrenz, Henry W. | 2 February 1878 | 1936-1945 | Secretary Treasurer | 16 March 1945, KS |
| Pauls, Henry | 29 November 1943 | 1969-1977 | Finance | |
| Toews, John Bernard | 24 September 1906 | 1953-1963 | General Secretary | |
| Wiebe, Vernon R. | 7 November 1926 | 1968-1982 | General Secretary | 28 January 1997, KS |
| Wiebe, William | 21 March 1919 | 1974-1980 | Associate Gen. Sec. | |
| Wiens, Henry R. | 16 July 1904 | 1963-1967 | General Secretary | 20 August 1996, KS |
| Wiens, Marie K. | 9 July 1921 | 1970-1980 | Publicity | |

# ABBREVIATIONS

| | |
|---|---|
| ABAC | American Baptist Archives Center, Valley Forge, PA |
| ABFMS | American Baptist Foreign Missionary Society |
| ABMU | American Baptist Missionary Union |
| AMBM | American Mennonite Brethren Mission in India |
| BFM | Board of Foreign Missions, Hillsboro, Kansas |
| BORAC | Board of Reference and Counsel |
| CC Yearbook | *Canadian (also Northern District) Conference Yearbooks (also those with German titles from 1910 to 1960)* |
| cf. | compare |
| CL | *Christian Leader* |
| CMBS/F | Center for MB Studies, Fresno |
| CMBS/H | Center for MB Studies, Hillsboro |
| CMBS/W | Centre for MB Studies, Winnipeg |
| ff | and following pages |
| GC Yearbook | *Yearbooks of the General Conference of MB Churches of North America (including those with German titles before 1943)* |
| JMS | *Journal of Mennonite Studies* (Winnipeg) |
| MAC | Mission Administrative Committee, India |
| MBBC | MB Bible College, Winnipeg |
| MB | Mennonite Brethren |
| MBBS | MB Biblical Seminary, Fresno |
| MBH | *MB Herald* |
| MBM/S | MB Missions and Services |
| MC | Missionary Conference (Council), India |
| MF | Missionary Fellowship (1960), India |
| ML | *Mennonite Life* (North Newton, KS) |
| MO | *Mennonite Observer* (Winnipeg) |
| MQR | *Mennonite Quarterly Review* (Goshen, IN) |
| MR | *Mennonitische Rundschau* |
| Rooms, The | The Secretariat of the ABMU |
| Zionsbote | Note: when missionaries did not have titles for their reports, the editor simply entitled them "Aus Indien (out of India)." |

# A Bibliographical
# Note on Primary Sources

As is evident, this book is based almost entirely on primary sources. They come essentially from two archival sources–the American Baptist Archives Center at Valley Forge, Pennsylvania, and the three Centers for Mennonite Brethren Studies (Fresno, California; Hillsboro, Kansas; Winnipeg, Manitoba)–and from correspondence and interviews generated by the author.

From Valley Forge we now have, in hard copy, the collections of correspondence of the Russian Mennonite Brethren who worked among the Telugu-speaking peoples of Hyderabad State, 1889 to the 1950s in conjunction with the American Baptist Missionary Union (ABMU) of the American Baptist Foreign Missionary Society (ABFMS) of the Northern Baptist Convention: Abraham J. Friesen, Abram J. Huebert, Heinrich H. Unruh, Cornelius H. Unruh, Johann G. Wiens, Franz J. Wiens, John A. Penner, and Jacob P. Klahsen.

These collections include letters to the missionaries from the Secretariat of the American Baptist Foreign Mission Society, headquartered in Boston until 1920, and then in New York. These also are available on microfilm, including the correspondence of Jacob Heinrichs who played a large role at Ramapatnam, in the Archives of Colgate Historical Library, Rochester, N.Y. This archive also houses a major collection of secondary sources, as referenced in the endnotes.

The major deposits used for this work are found in the Center for Mennonite Brethren Studies at Fresno. Crucial to our understanding of the Mennonite Brethren Mission to India have been the **Files** of the various conference boards, Mennonite Brethren Missions and Services and its Secretariat, the Missionary Council and Mission Administrative Committee in India, and of the missionaries who served in India. Other files donated to the Fresno Center by families of key persons in the story are catalogued as **Papers**. Of premier importance are those of Henry W. and John H. Lohrenz. A significant collection not found in Fresno are the Papers of Abram A. Unruh. These are available in the Centre in Winnipeg.

Many more collections which are still in private hands will come to the Fresno Center in due course. These are all referenced in the endnotes. In due course the Peter Penner Collection will be added there. This collection includes many items sent the author on request: pictures, family memoirs and biographical sketches, copies of collections having to do with India, and other material.

Included in this collection is correspondence with the following persons: Leoda Buckwalter (Elizabethtown, Pa.); Elizabeth (Hiebert) Dahl (Omaha, Nebr.); William Dick (Kitchener, Ont.); M. C. Emmanuel (Malakpet, Hyderabad, A.P.); Robert and Sarah (Voth) Ferris (Tulsa, Okla.); Ted Fast (Dallas, Ore.); Edna Gerdes (Alamo, Tex.); Philip C. Good (Blaine, Wash.); Peter M. Hamm (Winnipeg, Man. and Abbotsford, B.C.); Helen Harder (Loewen) (Waterloo, Ont.); Orlando Harms (Hillsboro, Kans.); M. B. John (Hyderabad, A.P.); Anna (Jungas) Hiebert (Mountain Lake, Minn.); Paul G. Hiebert (Deerfield, Ill.); Arnold Janzen (Ponte Vedra Beach, Fla.); William Johnson (Hillsboro, Kans.); Julius Kasper (Abbotsford, B.C.); Jacob P. Klahsen (London, Ont.); A. J. Klassen (Abbotsford, B.C.); Marie (Unruh) Krocker (Canim Lake, B.C.); Emma Lepp (Baerg) (Saskatoon, Sask.); Jacob A. Loewen (Abbotsford, B.C.); Dan Nickel (Abbotsford, B.C.); Hulda Penner (Kitchener, Ont.); Waldo Penner (Guelph, Ont.); Henry P. Poetker (Edmonton, Alta.); Santosh Raj (Vancouver, B.C.); Margaret "Peggy" (Unruh) Regehr (Winnipeg, Man.); Marie Riediger (Abbotsford, B.C.); Ernest E. Schmidt (Fresno, Calif.); M. A. Solomon (Mahbubnagar, A.P.); Dilwyn B. Studebaker (Modesto, Calif.); Margaret (Penner) and Herb Swartz (Harrisonburg, Va.); Isaak Tiessen (Strathroy, Ont.); Rosella Toews (Glasgow, Mont.); Maryon (Schellenberg) Troyer (Meadville, Pa.); Donald Unruh (Winnipeg, Man.); Cornelius C. Unruh (Pittsford, N.Y.); Henry C. Unruh (Singer Island, Fla.); John C. Unruh (Abbotsford, B.C.); Theodore Voth (Platteville, Wis.); David Wiebe (Kearney, Nebr.); Paul D. Wiebe (Kodaikanal, India); Vernon R. Wiebe (Hillsboro, Kans.); Viola (Bergthold) Wiebe (Hillsboro, Kans.); Carolyn (Mrs. John) Wiens (Winnipeg, Man.).

There are also notes made at the time of Interviews, as shown in the following list: Peter and Arlene Block (February 1989); Allen and Leoda Buckwalter (May 1989); Katie (Friesen) Davidson (by phone, September 1988); Helen Dueck (September 1992); Anne L. Ediger (February 1973); M.C. Emmanuel (October 1990); Margaret

Enns (September 1992); Jake H. Epp (February 1989); Jacob and Linda Ewert (May 1989); Ted and Esther (Heinrichs) Fast (September 1992); Anna Frantz (November 1992); Jake and Ruth (Berg) Friesen (October 1988); George and Annie (Bergmann) Froese (September 1988); Peter and Betty (Hildebrandt) Hamm (September 1988; July 1990; September 1992); Marvin Hein (1988-89); Paul G. Hiebert (November 1988); Waldo Hiebert (December 1988); Helen Harder (Loewen) (November 1990); Abram E. Janzen (May 1989); M. B. John (February 1973); S. J. Joseph and Hannah (Kampelly) (October 1990); the late Roy Just (December 1988; November 1992); Julius J. and Mary (Doerksen) Kasper (November 1988); George Konrad (November 1988, November 1992); Herb and Rose Krause (November 1992); Werner Kroeker (October 1994); Emma Lepp (Baerg) (February 1989); Frieda Neufeld (November 1988); Nancy Neufeld (November 1992); Dan and Helen Nickel (February 1973; September 1992; Fresno, January 1993; September 1994); Hulda Penner (26 August 1989); Henry and Amanda (Lepp) Poetker (February 1973); B.A. Prasangi (October 1990); Martha (Bergthold) Pullman (December/January 1992-93); Susan Reimer (September 1988); Cornelius J. and Marguerite (Baerg) Rempel (June 1991); Marie Riediger (September 1992); Ernest and Evelyn (Strauss) Schmidt (January 1989, May 1989, January 1993); Katie Siemens (Esau) (November 1988); M. A. Solomon (October 1990); Dilwyn and Mildred (Heinrichs) Studebaker (November 1992); Regina Suderman (November 1992); Margaret (Penner) and Herb Swartz (February 1993); John B. Toews and Paul Toews (1988-89; 1992-93); Betty Unruh and Henry Unruh (sister and brother) (November 1988); Cornelius C. Unruh (August 1990, June 1991); Donald Unruh (July 1990); John A. Voth (January/February 1993); John Wall (June 1991); Beatrice (Koop) Warkentin (November 1992); Vernon R. Wiebe (April 1989); Viola (Bergthold) Wiebe (April 1989); Delbert Wiens (December 1988); Frank and Marie Wiens (May 1989); Jake and Susie Wiens (April 1989); Margaret Willems (Balzer) (February 1989).

This Penner Collection also includes a file of 5 x 8 cards that list all the letters noted in the missionary files, and all the letters or articles by missionaries in the *Zionsbote, Mennonitische Rundschau* and other periodicals, and articles relevant to the India Mission. This Collection includes many slides of MB Missionaries (1889-1970s) shown at the Centennial Celebration of the India MB Church,

Mahbubnagar (October 1990). These are reproductions from archival collections, personal collections, and from official papers; also a collection of prints (and negatives) of MB Missionaries (1889-1970s), reproduced from various sources.

The Fresno Center has copies of other primary sources and significant materials: the relevant conference yearbooks from all levels with their official reports, the printed reports for special anniversaries, and much more. It has copies of all the particularist books dealing with India, those published in North America as well as in India. The Center has obtained copies of the theses relevant to the India Mission.

The adjacent Hiebert Library on the campus of Mennonite Brethren Biblical Seminary houses a large collection of secondary sources: books and periodicals whose insights contributed to the understanding of this story.

Some of the above materials, primary and secondary, are duplicated in varying degrees in Hillsboro and Winnipeg.

As to secondary sources–books and articles–these are fully referenced in endnotes.

# INTRODUCTION

1. By "mission" is meant the sending constituency, its home boards, the missionaries sent to India, and the institutions they built. Though there are many references to it, this account does not include the full story of the Church that emerged from Telugu converts.

2. John A. Lapp, *The Mennonite Church in India (1897-1962)* (Scottdale, Pa.: Herald Press, 1972); James C. Juhnke, *A People of Mission: A History of the General Conference Mennonite Overseas Mission* (Newton, KS: Faith and Life Press, 1979): William Hoke, *Each One Win One* (Allahabad: Allahabad Biblical Seminary, 1972).

3. J. Herbert Kane, *A Global View of Missions: From Pentecost to the Present* rev. ed. (Grand Rapids: Baker Book House, 1975), 103.

4. Herb Giesbrecht, "The Mennonite Brethren and Archives," *Mennonite Brethren Herald* (hereafter *MBH*), 15 June 1973, 4-5; "A Dream Come True," 1 October 1976, 17.

5. J. B. Toews, *A Pilgrimage of Faith: The Mennonite Brethren Church, 1860-1990* (Winnipeg: Kindred Press, 1993); Paul D. Wiebe, *Christians in Andhra Pradesh: The Mennonites of Mahbubnagar* (Bangalore: Christian Institute for the Study of Religion and Society, 1988).

6. Peter Penner, "Mennonite Brethren in India (1): the American Mennonite Brethren Church in India," and (2), "The India Mennonite Brethren Church," *Mennonite Reporter*, 28 May 1973, 2; 11 June 1973, 2.

7. A. E. Janzen, *Foreign Missions: India: The American Mennonite Brethren Mission in India, 1898-1948* (Hillsboro, Kans.: Mennonite Brethren Board of Foreign Missions, 1948); John H. Lohrenz, *The Mennonite Brethren Church* (Hillsboro: MB Board of Foreign Missions, 1950); Gerhard Wilhelm Peters, *The Growth of Foreign Missions in the Mennonite Brethren Church* (Hillsboro: MB Board of Foreign Missions, 1952); Anna W. Hiebert (Mrs. H. T.) Esau, *First Sixty Years of M. B. Missions* (Hillsboro: The MB Publishing House, 1954); A. H. Unruh, *Die Geschichte der Mennoniten-Brüdergemeinde: 1860-1954* (Hillsboro: General Conference of the MB Church, 1955); Phyllis Martens, *The Mustard Tree: The Story of Mennonite Brethren Missions* (Fresno: MB Board of Christian Education, 1971); John A. Toews, *A History of the Mennonite Brethren Church: Pilgrims and Pioneers* (Fresno: Board of Christian Literature, General Conference of MB Churches, 1975); G. W. Peters, *Foundations of Mennonite Brethren Missions* (Winnipeg: Kindred Press, 1984).

8. Peter R. Toews, "On Publications," *Canadian Conference of MB Churches Yearbook* (hereafter *CC Yearbook*), (1971) 40-42; E. L. Unrau, "Unpleasant Details of Truth," *MBH*, 22 June 1979, 7; Wally Kroeker, "Telling the Truth in Love: the Dilemma of the Church Press," *The Christian Leader* (hereafter *CL*), 15 February 1979, 2 ff.; Katie Funk Wiebe, "That Church Press Release," *CL*, 25 May 1979, 36.

9. Ted Fast to Peter Penner, 22 September 1991, Peter Penner Collection.

10. Myth is used here largely as a "mistaken belief", see J. Herbert Kane, *Understanding Christian Missions* (Grand Rapids: Baker Book House, 1986), 16 ff.

11. Anna Suderman, "Aus Indien,"*Zionsbote*, 16 January 1952, 6; J. A. Loewen, former MB missionary, used this term "massaging the truth" in "Culture, Culture Change, and Truth and Objectivity," an Address to the Annual Meeting, Mennonite Publishing Service [*Mennonite Reporter*], Richmond, BC, 8 February 1986, 2-3, Peter Penner Collection.

12. John H. Lohrenz, *CC Yearbook* (Hepburn, 1928), 39; *GC Yearbook* (Mountain Lake, 1948), 31.

13. J. B. Toews, *A Pilgrimage of Faith*, 261; the American missiologist, Rufus Anderson, said in 1845 that only the 'great commission,' Matthew 28, will make people go, make people return, and make supporters give year after year. See "The Theory of Missions to the Heathen, a Sermon on the Ordination of Mr. Edward Webb as Missionary...." in *Imperialism*, ed. Philip Curtin (New York: Harper and Row, 1970), 209-227. Mennonite Brethren dwelt on "the love of Christ constraining us," II Cor. 5: 14, and other passages such as Romans 10:14-17.

14. Gerhard W. Peters, *Foundations of Mennonite Brethren Missions* (Hillsboro: Kindred Press, 1984), 44-45.

15. See Herbert Kane, "The Making of the Missionary," and "Matters Relating to Recruitment," *Understanding Christian Missions*, 27 ff., 51 ff.

16. For a reference to Heinrich Voth, Minnesota leader, wrestling over the question of sending out N. N. Hiebert, see J. A. Froese, *Witness Extraordinary: A Biography of Elder Heinrich Voth* (Winnipeg: Kindred Press, 1975), 40 ff.

17. *GC Yearbook* (Henderson, 1927), 4-5.

18. Abram E. Janzen was concerned in 1964 with a "lag in doing research in Mennonite Brethren history and its heroic personnel." He wanted someone to prepare materials by "which our young people can be challenged...," Janzen to Henry R. Wiens, 12 December 1964, H. R. Wiens Papers, CMBS/F.

19. Peter Penner, "When Paternalism was Unavoidable: The Anglican Mission in North India" (unpublished paper based on Church Missionary Society primary sources, presented to the Humanities Association of Canada, Sackville NB Branch, 1980), Peter Penner Collection; cf. the popular survey by Julian Pettifer and Richard Bradley, *Missionaries* (London, BBC Series, 1990); Duncan B. Forrester "The Depressed Classes and Conversion to Christianity," in *Religion in South Asia: Religious Conversion and Revival Movements in South Asia in Medieval and Modern Times*, ed. G. A. Oddie, (New Delhi: Manohar, 1977), 41-42; and Paul D. Wiebe, *Christians in Andhra Pradesh*, 126.

20. For a social configuration of Mahbubnagar district, see Paul Wiebe, *Christians in Andhra Pradesh*, 53, 90.

21. Cf. Daniel F. Bergthold, "Die freiwillige Verkuendigung des Evangeliums," in *Unsere Mission in Indien: Achtzehn Berichte von Arbeitern*, ed. Henry W. Lohrenz (Hillsboro: Amerikanische Mennoniten Brueder Mission, 1936), 9.

22. Jacob Heinrichs, "Ein Versuch zur Erklaerung," *Zionsbote*, 26 August 1903, 2-3; John H. Voth, "Die christliche Mission wird angefochten," *Zionsbote*, 13 December 1916, 2-4; "Aus Indien," 26 March 1919, 3-4.

23. R. Pierce Beaver, *American Protestant Women in World Mission: A History of the First Feminist Movement in North America* (Grand Rapids: Baker Book House, 1980); cf. Ruth A. Tucker, "Women in Mission: Reaching Sisters in 'Heathen Darkness' in *Earthen Vessels: American Evangelicals and Foreign Missions, 1880-1980*, ed. J. A. Carpenter and W. Shenk (Grand Rapids: Eerdmans, 1990), 251-280.

24. One exception was the American Baptist women whose society, the American Baptist Women's Missionary Society, had its own existence alongside the American Baptist Foreign Mission Society (ABFMS); cf. Joseph C. Robbins to Cornelius H. Unruh, 7 July 1928, C. H. Unruh Collection, ABAC.

25. Ruth Tucker, "Women in Mission," in *Earthen Vessels*, 252. In summary, the AMBM in India fielded two women for each man in the whole ninety years. Without counting the couples on short-term assignments at Bruton, Kodaikanal, (five) or as medical doctors/dentist (three), there were 32 men and 62 women. Of these women 32 were married, one returning as a widow; of these 13 were nurses, 19 teachers (though their training is not always clearly delineated); 30 were single; of these 17 were nurses, 13 teachers.

26. Board of Foreign Mission Resolutions, "Ordaining and Commissioning of Missionaries" (1945-1965), I., 191-192. The reference is to the conference action which separated single missionaries from those ordained to "minister the Word" see *GC Yearbook* (Yarrow, 1957), 106.

27. J. B. Toews, "Report from the Secretariat," *GC Yearbook* (Winnipeg, 1963),63.

## CHAPTER 1

1. Ken Reddig, "Abraham and Maria Friesen: Trailblazers of Mennonite Brethren Missions," *Mennonite Brethren Herald* (hereafter *MBH)*, 27 July 1984, 18-19.

2. Peter M. Friesen, *The Mennonite Brotherhood in Russia (1789-1910)*, translated from the German, ed. J. B. Toews, et al, (Fresno: Board of Christian Literature (hereafter BCL), 1978,) 686; cf. J. J. Toews, "The Missionary Spirit of the MB Church in Russia," *The Church in Mission: A Sixtieth Anniversary Tribute to J. B. Toews*, ed. A. J. Klassen (Fresno: BCL, 1967), 148.

3. Walter Quiring and Helen Bartel, *In the Fullness of Time: 150 Years of Mennonite Sojourn in Russia,* 3rd ed. (Waterloo: Aaron Klassen, 1974), 21 ff.; see James Urry, "Through the Eye of a Needle: Wealth and the Mennonite Experience in Imperial Russia,"*Journal of Mennonite Studies* 3 (1985), 7-35.

4. Cornelius H. Unruh, "A. J. Friesen, a Tribute," n. d., C. H. Unruh Collection, American Baptist Archive Center (hereafter ABAC).

5. P. M. Friesen, *Mennonite Brotherhood,* 686; for a general view, see Adolf Ens, "Mennonite Education in Russia," in *Mennonites in Russia: Essays in Honour of Gerhard Lohrenz,* ed. John Friesen (Winnipeg: CMBC Publications, 1989), 75 ff.

6. Abraham J. Friesen, "Pfingsttage in Indien," *Das Erntefeld.* September 1906, 121-128; the Missionary Register, ABAC; concerning the adoption of their two children, see Chapter Two.

7. W. Cathcart, *The Baptist Encyclopedia* (Philadelphia, 1881), 448-450; John A. Toews, *A History of the Mennonite Brethren Church: Pilgrims and Pioneers* (Fresno: BCL, 1975), 72.

8. P. M. Friesen, *Mennonite Brotherhood,* 675; Carl Schneider, ed., *Jubilaeumsschrift anlaesslich der Feier des 25 jaehrigen Bestehens des Predigerseminars der deutschen Baptisten zu Hamburg-Horn (1880-1905) (*Hamburg: Predigerseminar, 1905), 10 ff., 21-27.

9. P. M. Friesen, *Mennonite Brotherhood,* 674-675.

10. Ibid., 676; cf. Gerhard W. Peters, *The Growth of Foreign Missions of the Mennonite Brethren Church.* (hereafter *Growth*) (Hillsboro: Board of Foreign Missions, 1952), 58.

11. Robert G. Torbet, *Venture of Faith: The Story of the American Baptist Foreign Missionary Society and the Women's ABFMS, 1814-1954* (Philadelphia: Judson Press, 1955), 253 ff.; John E. Clough, *Social Christianity in the Orient: The Story of a Man, a Mission and a Movement,* recorded by his wife, Emma Rauschenbusch Clough (New York: MacMillan, 1914), 294 ff. "The Rooms" referred to the secretaries with whom the missionaries corresponded.

12. Secunderabad was the seat of the English Resident, who essentially guided the Nizam's foreign policy. The Residency of British India usually included the "civil lines" as well as the military cantonment. In this case there was also an English-run hospital, frequented by Mennonite missionaries.

13. A. J. Friesen, "Aus Indien, Nalgonda," *Zionsbote.* 15 April 1891, 1. **Note:** the Friesens did language study in Secunderabad, not Madras as stated in Reddig's biographical notice, Endnote # 1.

14. A. J. Friesen, "Bericht ueber unsere erste Reise nach Nalgonda,"*Zionsbote.* 28 May 1890, 2-3.

15. A. J. Friesen, "Aus Indien," *Zionsbote*. 15 April 1891, 1; "Ein offner Brief," *Zionsbote*. 24 February 1892, 2-3; A. J. Friesen to Samuel W. Duncan, Boston, 29 September 1893, A. J. Friesen Collection, ABAC.

16. Henry Yule and A. C. Burnell, *Hobson-Jobson: A Glossary of Anglo-Indian Colloquial Words and Phrases* (London: Routledge and Kegan Paul, 1968), 240-243.

17. A. J. Friesen, *Zionsbote*. 17 January 1894, 2; Samuel W. Duncan, Boston, to A. J. Friesen, 29 September 1893, A. J. Friesen Collection, ABAC.

18. Herbert Kane, *Understanding Christian Missions*. 156-157; **comity** referred to mutual recognition of mission society jurisdictions.

19. Anna W. Hiebert (Mrs. H.T.) Esau, *First Sixty Years of MB Missions* (Hillsboro: Mennonite Brethren Publishing House, 1954), 91 ff.

20. Paul D. Wiebe, *Christians in Andhra Pradesh: the Mennonites of Mahbubnagar* (Bangalore: Christian Institute for the Study of Religion and Society, 1988), 43.

21. Katharina Huebert, "Unterschiede zwischen Christentum und Heidentum," *Das Erntefeld*. December 1901, 1-3; A. J. Friesen, "Anzeigen und Bemerkungen," *Das Erntefeld*. January 1902, 6-8; "Ein Bericht aus Indien (on the Parsis of Bombay and Secunderabad)," *Zionsbote*. 29 June 1892, 4.

22. A. J. Friesen to The Rooms, 10 May 1890, A. J. Friesen Collection, ABAC.

23. A. J. Friesen to The Rooms, 20 June, 29 September 1893; 5 March 1894, A. J. Friesen Collection, ABAC.

24. S. W. Duncan to A. J. Friesen, 20 December 1893; 24 January 1895, A. J. Friesen Collection, ABAC.
To have "charge" of a station had very specific connotations. Such supervisory responsibility was given by the ABMU Reference Committee, Ramapatnam, and gave the male missionary control over all aspects of the station for the time of his appointment. The American Mennonite Brethren adopted the same structured role for male missionaries throughout their time in India.

25. A. J. Friesen to S. W. Duncan, 14 December 1894, A. J. Friesen Collection, ABAC; cf. D. Downie, "The Specific Donation," *Baptist Mission Review*. 11 (May 1896), 164-167.

26. Abraham and Maria Friesen, "Aus Indien," *Zionsbote*. 10 April, 2; 17 April 1895, 2.

27. A. J. Friesen to S. W. Duncan, 7 September 1895, A. J. Friesen Collection, ABAC.

28. A. J. Friesen, "Aus Indien," *Zionsbote*. 3 June 1891, 1; A. J. Friesen to "The Rooms," 21 November 1894, A. J. Friesen Collection, ABAC; A. J. Friesen to Joseph Lehmann, "Aus Indien," *Zionsbote*. 12 December 1894, 2.

29. *Konferenzbeschluesse der Mennoniten Bruedergemeinde.* (hereafter *GC Yearbook* (in one volume, 1883-1919), 104, 139, 165; cf. A. J. Friesen to The Rooms, 10 May 1890, A. J. Friesen Collection, ABAC; cf. G. W. Peters, *The Growth of Foreign Missions in the MB Church* (Hillsboro: MB Publishing House, 1952), 73-74. For articles on the famine of 1900 and the Boer War, where Thomssen ministered to Boer prisoners of war, held in India, see G. N. Thomssen, "Rueckblick aus Indien," *Zionsbote*. 14 November 1900, 4; and "Allerlei aus Indien," 11 June 1902, 2-3.

30. See Abram E. Janzen, "Father of the American Mennonite Brethren Church," *MBH.* 31 October 1969, 4-6; cf. David Schellenberg, "Meine letzte Erfahrungen auf meiner Besuchsreise in Amerika," *Zionsbote.* 16 September 1908, 7; for more information on David Schellenberg and his fall from his strong position in Rückenau, see Leona W. Gislason, "Rückenau" (a manuscript in progress shown to the author).

31. A. E. Janzen, "Father,"; J. A. Froese, *Witness Extraordinary: A Biography of Elder Heinrich Voth* (Hillsboro: BCL, 1975), 40 ff.; Peter Penner, *No Longer at Arm's Length: Mennonite Brethren Church Planting in Canada* (Winnipeg: Kindred Press, 1987), 10-11, 15.

32. *Ein Heide* was translated "heathen," usually meaning an idolater, a worshiper of other gods in a country having a different culture. The heathen Amerindians were also unconverted and far away socially. Cf. the General Conference Mennonite mission to Hopi Indians, in James Juhnke, *A People of Mission: A History of General Conference Mennonite Overseas Missions* (Newton: Faith and Life Press, 1979), 9, 24; *GC Yearbook* (1883-1919), 87, 120, 132.

33. G. W. Peters, *Growth*, 75, 77-8, 81-2.

34. *GC Yearbook,* (1896), 186-190; cf. G. W. Peters, *Growth*, 79.

35. G. W. Peters, *Growth*, 77 ff.; cf. John F. Harms, "Eine schoene Missionsgabe," *Zionsbote.* 30 November 1898, 4; and A. J. Friesen, "Ein Wort der Erklaerung," *Zionsbote.* 22 March 1899, 3-4.

36. *GC Yearbook* (1898), 207-8; G. W. Peters, *Growth*, 83-84.

37. *GC Yearbook* (1896), 188; cf. Anna Hiebert (Mrs. H.T.) Esau, "Mission Study Lesson," *Christian Leader* (hereafter *CL)*, April 1939, 11.

38. G. W. Peters, *Growth*, 83-84.

39. Katharina Penner was born in Sagradowka colony, and not in Rückenau as her obituary stated. Abram J. Huebert was born in Rückenau, Molotschna. Obitu-

ary, "Katharina Huebert," *Mennonitische Rundschau.* 19 May 1948, 7; and *The Watchman Examiner.* 22 July 1948, 774; "Abram J. Huebert," 30 June 1949, 647.

40. *American Baptist Telugu Mission.* (1898-1899), 89 ff; A. J. Huebert, "Von Ruszland nach Nalgonda, Indien," *Zionsbote*, 18 May 1899, 3; 25 May 1899, 3.

41. A. J. Huebert, "Wie Gott zu mir redet," *Das Erntefeld*, July 1904, 54.

42. Maria Friesen to the *Baptist Mission Review* 14 (June 1899), 233.

43. *Ibid.*

44. S. W. Duncan to A. J. Friesen, 19 January 1898, A. J. Friesen Collection, ABAC.

45. John F. Harms, "Die schoene Missionsgabe," *Zionsbote*, 30 November 1898, 4; Orlando Harms, *Pioneer Publisher: The Life and Times of J. F. Harms* (Winnipeg: Kindred Press, 1984), 39-40. The amount was about 1,800 rubles.

46. J. F. Harms, "Die schoene Missionsgabe," *Zionsbote*, 30 November 1898, 4.

47. A. J. Friesen, "Ein Wort der Erklaerung," *Zionsbote*, 22 March 1899, 3-4.

48. *Ibid.*

49. *Ibid.*

50. J. F. Harms, "Bericht ueber die Verhandlungen der Missionsbehoerde," 11 April 1899, *Zionsbote*, 12 April 1899, 4.

51. Elizabeth S. Neufeld Wall, "Great is Thy Faithfulness," *Greetings* (Hillsboro: BFM, May 1943), 34-7; Obituary, "Elizabeth S. Neufeld (Wichert, Wall)," *Zionsbote*, 20 May 1953, 14-15.

52. Heinrich H. Unruh, "Unsere Reise nach Nalgonda," *Zionsbote*, 20 December 1899, 1-2.
The family tells the following story that at Odessa Nicolai Hiebert ran into difficulty with his passport. Because his wife Susie was not named in the passport, she was not allowed to embark. But she's my wife! No matter; you can go, she stays! Hiebert therefore had no choice but to remain behind with Susie. The steamer pulled away without them. Shortly, however, they noticed that the steamer had dropped anchor and a small vessel came back to the dock–not to pick up the Hieberts, as they expected, but to get some baggage the captain had forgotten on shore. By this time the Hieberts had managed to persuade some officials of the validity of their travel papers. Anyway, how could they as American citizens be left stranded on Russian soil when their destination was British India? In this way they were able to rejoin their party–a lifeboat rescue indeed!
Paul G. Hiebert, interview by author, Fresno, CA, 6 November 1988, Peter Penner Collection.

53. Kipling's poem appeared in the London *Times* (4 February 1899), and contained this stanza:

Take up the White Man's burden -
Ye dare not stoop to less -
Nor call too loud on Freedom
To cloak your weariness;
By all ye cry or whisper,
By all ye leave or do,
The silent sullen peoples
Shall weigh your Gods and you.

Rudyard Kipling, "The White Man's Burden," in John Beecroft, ed., *Kipling: Stories and Poems* (New York: Doubleday, 1956), 444-445; see Charles Carrington, *Rudyard Kipling* (Harmondsworth: Penguin Books, 1970), 336-337.

54. A. J. Austin, *Saving China: Canadian Missionaries in the Middle Kingdom, 1888-1959* (Toronto: University of Toronto Press, 1986), 76, 106.

55. Glyn Williams and John Ramsden, *Ruling Britannia: A Political History of Britian, 1688-1988* (London: Longman, 1990), 334-335.

G. N. Thomssen, from Kansas, saw many resemblances between the Boers and the Mennonites he knew. He said they looked "just like my beloved Mennonite Brethren look. Their manner, their singing, their prayers, their weeping is just like your own, because these men in truth are your brothers."; Thomssen, "Allerlei aus Indien," *Zionsbote*, 11 June 1902, 2-3; cf. Anna Suderman, "Aus Indien," *Zionsbote*, 20 August 1902, 2.

56. Irving Hexham, *The Irony of Apartheid: The Struggle for National Independence of Afrikaner Calvinism Against British Imperialism* (Niagara Falls, N.Y.: Edwin Mellen Press, 1981), 46 ff.

57. Among books critical of Viceroy Curzon's policies at the time were:

1) Romesh C. Dutt charged British rule with such a narrowing of the sources of national health that India's poverty "is unparalleled in any civilized country." He asked why fifteen million people had perished under British rule in the famines of 1877-78, 1889, 1897, and 1900, in R.C. Dutt, *The Economic History of India*, 2 vols. 1901 and 1903 (New Delhi: Government of India Reissue, 1960), xxiv ff.

2) William Digby claimed that each of the most recent famines had resulted in "a money loss to the people of India of at least 120,000,000. [pounds sterling]," *'Prosperous' British India*, 1901 (reprinted Calcutta: Sagar, 1969), 539.

58. Stanley Wolpert, *A New History of India*, 3rd. ed. (New York: Oxford University Press, 1989), 267; William Brough, "India's Famine and its Cause," *Arena*, 24 September 1900, 299-312; J. T. Sunderland, "The Cause of Indian Famines," *New England Magazine* 23 (September 1900), 56-64.

These famines at the end of the century occasioned world comment and brought India's plight to the attention of the Mennonite Church in America. See John A. Lapp, *The Mennonite Church in India* (Scottdale: Herald Press, 1972), 27 ff.

59. "Wer ist Schuld?" *Zionsbote*, 3 May 1916, 3-5; P. Schulze, "Auesere Armut in Teluguland," *Zionsbote*, 14 October 1916, 3-4. More at fault than the exploitive moneylender was the economically regressive impact of British India on India as revealed during the famine debate at the turn of the century.

60. Abram J. Huebert, "Einige Tage in Secunderabad," *Das Erntefeld*, May 1901, 2; John H. Lohrenz, *The Mennonite Brethren Church* (Hillsboro: Mennonite Brethren Publishing House, 1950), 231; A. J. Friesen, from Nalgonda, "Notizen," *Das Erntefeld*, September 1900, 4.

61. Elizabeth (Neufeld) Wall to G. W. Peters, 19 December 1945, G. W. Peters Papers, CMBS/F. Ironically, it was not long after this that John N. C. Hiebert wrote openly of his father's *"Nervenleiden* (nervous illness)" and that he had been taken to a sanitorium in Lincoln, Nebraska; John N. C. Hiebert, "Mitteilungen,"*Zionsbote*, 4 September 1946, 10.

The family acknowledges that Nicolai Hiebert was plagued with weak nerves all his life. Yet he was kept in the office of secretary to the Board of Foreign Missions from 1906 until 1936.

62. When G. W. Peters once asked Abram H. Unruh about going to India as a missionary, the latter wrote him: "It makes no sense that N. N. Hiebert went to India ill [not entirely well] and had to return very quickly," 8 April 1944, G. W. Peters Papers, CMBS/F; cf. N. N. Hiebert's own reservations in a letter about his educational qualifications for missionary work. He admitted he was "bloede und aengstlich von Natur" (by nature shy and somewhat fearful), "Brief," *Zionsbote*, 6 July 1898, 2.

63. N. N. Hiebert, "Aus Indien," *Zionsbote*, 3 April 1901, 2; *N. N.* Hiebert, "Auf dem Schiffe *Arcadia*," 15 May 1901, 1.

64. J. A. Froese, *Witness Extraordinary*, 41.

## CHAPTER 2

1. Jacob Heinrichs, "Ein Versuch zur Erklaerung," *Zionsbote*, 26 August 1903, 2-3; Note: the article from the *Baptist Missionary Review* is enclosed in this reference.

2. *Ibid*.

3. This was William Bambrick Boggs (1842-1913), a Canadian Baptist who switched to the ABMU when still quite young. His son was William E. Boggs. Both served as president of Ramapatnam Seminary: father (1887-1893), and son (1917-1932). See John Craig and Helena Blackadar, "A Sketch of the Origins and Development of our Mission Stations in India," *Beacon Lights* (Toronto: Canadian Baptist Foreign Mission Society, January, 1922), 11-14. A third missionary with this sur-

name, Wheeler Bogg(e)s, itinerated as an evangelist, even in Mennonite Brethren stations.

James D. Mosteller, "Ramapatnam: Jewel of the South India Mission," *Foundations: A Baptist Journal of History and Theology* (October-December 1968), 308-325.

4. Jacob Heinrichs, "Ein Versuch zur Erklaerung," *Zionsbote*, 26 August 1903, 2-3; The Canadian Baptists worked with the ABMU from 1866 to 1873. See John Craig and Helene Blackadar, *Beacon Lights*, 15-6.

This concept of all working together was a sound one. Heinrich's hint that they would never be able to evangelize all the areas of their field turned into a prediction, for in 1937 a very large area was sold to the American Mennonite Brethren.

Jacob Heinrichs revealed his Mennonite derivation in "Missionsglocken aus Indien," *Zionsbote*, 26 July 1911, 3-4; for additional biographical details see John H. Voth, "Meine Eindruecke von unserm herrlichen Amerika nach meiner Rueckkehr von Indien," *Zionsbote*, 5 May 1937, 2-3.

5. See *GC Yearbook* (1900), 226-227.

6. *Ibid.*

7. Abraham J. Friesen to H. C. Mabie, Boston, 28 June 1901, Abraham Friesen Collection, ABAC.

8. A. J. Friesen, A. J. Huebert, and H. H. Unruh to The Rooms, Boston, 22 October 1902, Friesen Collection, ABAC; cf. *GC Yearbook* (1901), 240-244; Jacob Heinrichs, "Ein Versuch zur Erklaerung," *Zionsbote*, 26 August 1903, 2-3.

In this matter Peter M. Friesen, the Russian Mennonite Brethren historian advised John F. Harms to maintain an independent position because American MB could easily be swallowed up by the giant Baptist denominations, whereas in Russia there was little danger of that occurring. P. M. Friesen to John F. Harms, "Ein Brief," *Zionsbote*, 14 May 1902, 2-3.

9. Tina Mandtler, the daughter of Peter and Katie Mandtler, Dalmeny, Saskatchewan, married Daniel Bergthold in June 1902. Bergthold had preached there during his time of preparation for missionary service; see Viola Bergthold Wiebe and Marilyn Wiebe Dodge, *Sepia Prints: Memoir of a Missionary in India* (hereafter Viola B. Wiebe. *Sepia Prints*) (Winnipeg: Kindred Press, 1990), 2.

10. *GC Yearbook* (1901), 241-242; (1902), 260; (1903), 289.

11. Henry W. Lohrenz, ed., *Our Mission among the Telegus* (Hillsboro: Board of Foreign Missions (hereafter BFM), 1939), 4; John H. Lohrenz, *What God Hath Wrought* (Hillsboro: BFM, 1949), 6 ff.; M. A. Solomon, *Joy for Mourning: Life and Ministry of D. F. Bergthold* (Mahbubnagar: B. Aseervadam, 1980), 4 ff.

12. Anna Suderman went to Gujarat, India, with the Alliance Mission in 1898, and came to the AMBM once they had launched a work in Hughestown. See Viola

B. Wiebe, *Sepia Prints*, 33; and "Anna Suderman Bergthold," *Christian Leader*, 1 June 1957, 8-9; G. W. Peters, *The Growth of Foreign Missions in the MB Church* (Hillsboro: MB Publishing House, 1952), 166-172.

13. Carl Schneider,*Jubilaemsschrift ... des Predigerseminars der deutschen Baptisten zu Hamburg-Horn*, 17-18.

14. Thomas S. Barbour to A. J. Friesen, 5 January 1903, Friesen Collection, ABAC

15. A. J. Friesen to Samuel Duncan, 28 February 1895, Friesen Collection, ABAC.

16. P. M. Friesen, *Mennonite Brotherhood*, 1916; Abram H. Unruh, *Die Geschichte der Mennoniten=Bruedergemeinde, 1860-1954 (*Hillsboro: Board of Reference and Council (BORAC), 1954), 317, 326 ff.; Unruh gives the constitution of the Russian mission, but does not identify the committee members. See A. J. Friesen to Thomas Barbour, 18 January 1905, Friesen Collection, ABAC.

17. P. M. Friesen,*Mennonite Brotherhood*, 835 ff. See Abraham Friesen (Santa Barbara) *History and Renewal in the Anabaptist/Mennonite Tradition*, being the 1992 Menno Simons lectures (North Newton, 1994), 1-5.

18. Cf. Clarence Hiebert, "The Development of Mennonite Brethren Churches in North America - Some Reflections, Interpretations and Viewpoints," and John B. Toews (Fresno), "Mennonite Brethren Identity and Theological Diversity," in *Pilgrims and Strangers: Essays in Mennonite Brethren History*, ed. Paul Toews (Fresno: CMBS, Mennonite Brethren Biblical Seminary, 1977), 123 and 141, respectively.

19. Orlando Harms, *Pioneer Publisher: The Life and Times of J. F. Harms* (Winnipeg: Kindred Press, 1984), 27; Harms attended the Evangelical Bible Institute, Naperville, Illinois.

20. John H. Lohrenz, "Henry W. Lohrenz." *ME* III (1957), 386.

21. A. J. Friesen, "Monatliche Berichte ueber Saat und Ernte in Haiderabad, Deccan, Indien [monthly report of sowing and harvesting in the Deccan]," *Das Erntefeld*, 1900, 1. Friesen served as editor, assisted by his wife Maria, and sometimes by Heinrich H. Unruh. *Das Erntefeld*, printed by Raduga Press in Neu-Halbstadt, has various series and corresponding changes in format and pagination; the CMBS/F has copy which is more or less complete.

22. (Katharina Huebert), "Unterschiede zwischen Christentum und Heidentum," *Das Erntefeld*, December 1901, 1-3.

23. See J. Edwin Orr, *Evangelical Awakenings in India* (New Delhi: Masihi Sahitya Sanstha, 1970), 109 ff.

24. A. J. Friesen, "Der Buddhismus und die Frau," *Das Erntefeld*, March 1904, 24 ff.; C. H. Unruh, "Reisebericht," *Das Erntefeld*, February 1905, 12.

25. A. J. Friesen to H. C. Mabie, 10 March 1899, Friesen Collection, ABAC.

26. A. J. Huebert, "Altes und Neues aus dem Tagebuch," *Das Erntefeld*, January 1901, 4; A. J. Huebert to Boston, 12 March and 8 June 1901; Thomas S. Barbour to Huebert, 1 August 1902, Huebert Collection, ABAC.
Many Muslims were mercenary troops in the ranks of the British. Huebert implied that this had a moderating effect on Muslim attitudes.

27. A. J. Huebert to Thomas Barbour, 19 May and 13 July 1903; Barbour to Huebert, 27 July 1903, Huebert Collection, ABAC.

28. Cf. George B. Huntingdon to A. J. Huebert, 29 June and 26 September 1906, Huebert Collection, ABAC.
This bungalow, a very large one built of heavy stone blocks, remains on the Suryapet Baptist compound (1990) as a blackened dinosaur of another age.

29. A. J. Huebert to Thomas Barbour, 9 November 1903 and 23 August 1904; Barbour to Huebert, 27 October 1903 and 4 February 1904, Huebert Collection, ABAC.

30. H. H. Unruh, "Anzeigen und Bemerkungen," *Das Erntefeld*, March 1904, 27; "Ein offner Brief," *Das Erntefeld*, April 1904, 30, 34.

31. H. H. Unruh, "Jangaon," *Baptist Missionary Magazine*, 93 (1906), 236-7.

32. Thomas Barbour to A. J. Friesen, 5 January 1903, Friesen Collection, ABAC.

33. A. J. Friesen, A. J. Huebert, and H. H. Unruh to Thomas Barbour, 22 October 1902, Friesen Collection, ABAC.

34. Thomas Barbour to A. J. Friesen, 1 August 1902; Friesen, Huebert, and Unruh to Barbour, 22 October 1902, Friesen Collection, ABAC.

35. A. J. Friesen to Thomas Barbour, 15 April 1903, Friesen Collection, ABAC.

36. A. J. Friesen to Thomas Barbour, 21 March 1904, Friesen Collection, ABAC.

37. Thomas Barbour to A. J. Friesen, 24 July 1903 and 12 May 1904, Friesen Collection, ABAC.

38. A. J. Friesen, "Aus Indien," *Zionsbote*, 10 April 1895, 2; Maria Friesen, *Das Erntefeld*. August 1900, 2; A. J. Friesen, "Notizen," *Das Erntefeld*, September

1900, 4; Maria Friesen, "Auf der Heimreise," *Das Erntefeld*, July 1904, 55 ff.; P.A. Penner, regarding his visit to Nalgonda, *Das Erntefeld*, January 1908, 20.

39. A. J. Friesen, "Zerstreute Palmblaetter aus Nalgonda, 11 *Das Erntefeld*, March 1904, 27; Friesen to T.S. Barbour, 21 March 1904, Friesen Collection, ABAC; "Report of Mr. Friesen," *Baptist Missionary Magazine* 91 (1904) , 139; H. H. Unruh, "Allerlei vom Missionsfelde," *Das Erntefeld*, April 1904, 34.

40. A. J. Friesen to T. S. Barbour, 15 April 1903; Barbour to Friesen while in Russia, 12 May 1904, Friesen Collection, ABAC.

41. Susan Reimer, Vineland, Ontario, to Peter Penner, 30 January 1990, Peter Penner Collection; G. W. Peters, "Friesen, Abraham," *ME* II (1956), 404.

42. Aron Martens Friesen's descendants live mainly in Western Canada; Susan Reimer, Vineland, ON, to Peter Penner, 30 January 1990, Peter Penner Collection. Cf. Paul G. Hiebert, *Anthropological Insights for Missionaries* (Grand Rapids:Baker Book House, 1985), 279.

43. Cf. Ken Reddig, "Friesen, Maria Martens," *ME* V (1990), 312-313. Regrettably, this article says nothing about this adoption. Other corrections are also required: Maria took language training in Secunderabad; she became ill enough in 1904 to warrant a furlough on medical grounds, and retired in 1908 owing to ill health.

44. A. J. Friesen, from Chortitza, to T. S. Barbour, 27 May 1904, A.J. Friesen Collection, ABAC.

45. T. S. Barbour to A. J. Friesen, 6 July 1904; Friesen, from Rükenau, to Barbour, 25 July and 29 August 1904, A. J. Friesen Collection, ABAC.

46. A. J. Friesen to T. S. Barbour, 21 March 1904, A. J. Friesen Collection, ABAC.

47. T. S. Barbour to A. J. Friesen, 12 May 1904, A. J. Friesen Collection, ABAC.

48. T. S. Barbour to A. J. Friesen, 3 October 1904; Friesen to Barbour, 25th October 1904 and 18 January 1905, Friesen Collection, ABAC; see G. W. Peters, "Plan of Cooperation (1904)," *The Growth of Foreign Missions in the MB Church* (Hillsboro: MB Publishing House, 1952), 59-60.

49. G. W. Peters, *Growth*, 59-60.

50. A. J. Friesen to T. S. Barbour, 25 October 1904, A.J. Friesen Collection, ABAC.

51. A. J. Friesen to T. S. Barbour, 18 January 1905, A. J. Friesen Collection, ABAC

52. T. S. Barbour to A. J. Friesen, 24 March 1905, A. J. Friesen Collection, ABAC.

53. A. J. Friesen to T. S. Barbour, 29 August 1905 and 14 November 1906, Friesen Collection, ABAC.

54. A. J. Friesen to T. S. Barbour, 28 August 1907, Friesen Collection, ABAC.

# CHAPTER 3

1. MB missionaries in India prior to World War I were the following:

Russian
Abraham J. & Maria Martens Friesen, 1889
Abraham J. & Katharina Penner Huebert, 1898
Heinrich H. & Anna Peters Unruh, 1898
Anna Epp, 1904, second wife of D. F. Bergthold
Cornelius H. & Martha Woltmann Unruh, 1904
Johann G. & Helena Hildebrandt Wiens, 1904
Katharina Reimer, 1905
Anna Peters, 1909
Franz J. & Maria Warkentin Wiens, 1909
Aganetha Neufeld, 1913
John A. & Anna Nikkel Penner, 1914

American
Anna Suderman, 1898, third wife of D. F. Bergthold
Nicolai N. & Susie Wiebe Hiebert, 1899
Elizabeth S. Neufeld, 1899
John H. & Maria Harms Pankratz, 1902
Daniel F. & Tina Mandtler Bergthold, 1904
Katharina L. Schellenberg, 1907
Katharina Lohrenz, 1908
John H. & Maria Epp Voth, 1908
Frank A. & Elizabeth Dickman Janzen, 1910

2. Gerhard W. Peters, *The Growth of Foreign Missions in the Mennonite Brethren Church* (Hillsboro: MB Publishing House, 1952) (hereafter *Growth*), 82-83, 167, 169-172; John H. Lohrenz, *The Mennonite Brethren Church* (Hillsboro: MB Publishing House, 1950), 230 ff.; Anna Hiebert (Mrs. H. T.) Esau, *First Sixty Years of Mennonite Brethren Missions* (Hillsboro: MB Publishing House, 1954), 138 ff.; Peter Penner, "Baptist in all but name: Molotschna Mennonite Brethren in India," *Mennonite Life* 46 (March 1991), 17-22.

3. Katharina Reimer, "Teure Eltern u. Geschwister [a travelogue]," *Das Erntefeld*, April 1906, 42-43.

4. Peter M. Friesen, *The Mennonite Brotherhood in Russia (1789-1910)* (Fresno: Board of Christian Literature, 1978), 627; David MacKenzie and Michael W. Curran, *A History of Russia and the Soviet Union*, 3rd. ed. (Chicago: Dorsey Press, 1987), 514 ff.

5. Abraham J. Friesen to Thomas S. Barbour, 22 March 1905, A. J. Friesen Collection, ABAC.

6. Henry C. Unruh (Florida), "Memoir" [c. 1977], 2, in Peter Penner Collection.

7. Cornelius H. Unruh to T. S. Barbour, 18 September 1907, C. H. Unruh Collection, ABAC. Edward Chute built up the Palmur station (Mahbubnagar) in 1898. It was sold to the American Mennonite Brethren Mission in 1936-37.

8. Abraham L. Schellenberg, the editor of the *Zionsbote*, agreed with C. H. Unruh's viewpoint about assigned gifts. Schellenberg thought that supporters were all too human when it came to giving and distributing. Unruh stated that "bad blood" was avoided among the Russian missionaries by allowing the ABMU Reference Committee, which always had a Russian Mennonite Brethren member, to disburse the incoming monies equally. See Unruh, "Ueber das Verteilen [dividing] der Missionsgelder," *Zionsbote*, 19 July 1911, 3-4.

9. C. H. Unruh to The Rooms, 19 October 1909, C. H. Unruh Collection, ABAC.

10. Carl Schneider, *Jubelaeumsschrift ... des Predigerseminars ... Hamburg-Horn* (Hamburg: Predigerseminar, 1905), 38; Johann G. Wiens, "Unsere erste Eindruecke in Nalgonda," *Das Erntefeld*, February 1905, 15-17.

11. George Pries, *A Place Called Pniel: Winkler Bible Institute, 1925-1975* (Altona: D. W. Friesen, 1975), 19; cf. Eingesandt (contributed), "Die goldene Hochzeitsfeier der Geschwister Wiens," *Konferenz=Jugendblatt* 2 (December 1946), 6-7.

There is no biographical information on Helena Wiens. One must assume that she, as with every missionary's wife, had the care of her family, the responsibility for the servants and the entire station in her husband's absence. As Paul Hiebert has suggested, some missionary wives remained without "any added rewards and without feeling directly a part of the work herself. She must be content to hear her husband's exciting reports and gain a vicarious sense of worth through his achievements," in Paul G. Hiebert, "The Missionary and his Wife," *Anthropological Insights for Missionaries* (Grand Rapids: Baker, 1985), 278.

12. J. G. Wiens to T. S. Barbour, 17 September 1907; 21 January 1908; 1 September 1909; J. G. Wiens' Annual Report, 1909, in J. G. Wiens Collection, ABAC; Wiens, "Ein Notschrei aus Indien," *Das Erntefeld*, 1910, 51-4.

13. C. H. Unruh, "Indien," *Das Erntefeld*, 1910, 140-1; J. G. Wiens, "Eine gezwungene Europareise [a forced trip to Europe]," *Das Erntefeld*, 1910, 187-192; *American Baptist Telugu Mission* 107 (Boston, 1910), 87-8; (1911), 70.

14. J. G. Wiens modeled this school on his alma mater in Hamburg-Horn, and then he and his associates, Abram H. Unruh and Gerhard Reimer, used Tschongraw as a model for the founding of Winkler Bible School in 1925; see John A. Toews, *A History of the Mennonite Brethren Church: Pilgrims and Pioneers* (Fresno: Board of Christian Literature, 1975), 113-114.

15. *Ibid.*; see C. H. Unruh, on behalf of J. G. Wiens, to Joseph C. Robbins, New York, 14 and 15 May 1922; and Robbins to Unruh, 11 July 1922, in C. H. Unruh Collection, ABAC.

16. See Katharina Reimer, "Teure Eltern," *Das Erntefeld*, February 1906, 13-16; May 1906, 55-58; June 1906, 69-74, 84-90.

17. According to Marie (Unruh) Krocker, the eldest daughter of Heinrich Unruh, Reimer was her teacher at Gnadenfeld, Molotschna, once she and her siblings were left in the financial care of Heinrich J. Braun; Marie Krocker, Canim Lake, to Peter Penner, 20 December 1988, Peter Penner Collection. Cf. William Schroeder and Helmut T. Huebert, *Mennonite Historical Atlas* (Winnipeg: Springfield Publishers, 1990), 97.

18. Katharina Huebert, "Etwas aus der Arbeit," *Das Erntefeld*, 1911, 7; Anna Peters; "Indiens Frauen," *Das Erntefeld*, 1911, 196-6; "Meine letzten Tage in Suriapett," *Das Erntefeld*, 1911, 242-244; Anna Peters died in Vineland, Ontario, in 1939, Missionary Register, ABAC.

19. Aganetha Neufeld, "Ein Bericht von der Reise in die 'blauen Berge'," *Das Erntefeld*, 1914, 141-142. See two letters to *Das Erntefeld*, 1914, 153-154; and 185-186; *Missionary Album 1889-1963: Mennonite Brethren and Krimmer Mennonite Brethren Conferences* (Hillsboro: Board of Foreign Missions, 1963), 115; A. J. Huebert, "Auf der See," *Mennonitische Rundschau* (hereafter *MR*), 30 May 1923, 6-7; cf. A. Neufeld, "Lieber Bruder Winsinger," *MR*, 10 October 1923, 8. Like her Russian missionary colleagues, Neufeld went to California hoping to get American citizenship. She transferred to Vancouver, Canada, with the Hueberts on 10 September 1923. She remained in Canada until 1930 when she joined her immigrant parents, the Gerhard Neufelds, in Santa Catarina, Brazil. Handicapped by an accident, she married widower Heinrich Hamm in Curitiba in 1939. Following his death in 1941 and that of her parents in the next year, she lived on but in ill-health until 1963; Jak. Kasdorf, "Aganetha Neufeld Hamm,", *MR*, 12 June 1963, 9.

20. Maria Klaassen Lohrenz, "Katharina Lohrenz," in *Foreign Missions: the American Mennonite Brethren Mission in India* (hereafter *India*, 1948) ed. Abram E. Janzen (Hillsboro: BFM, 1948), 133-141. Her parents, Heinrich and Elizabeth Lohrenz, members of the Ebenfeld Church in Marion County, KS, also gave two sons to the mission: Henry W. as a Board member and John H. as missionary.

21. A. E. Janzen, *India* (1948), 138; Katharina Lohrenz, "Aus Indien," *Zionsbote*, 14 February 1912, 1-2.

22. A. E. Janzen, *India* (1948), 140; K. Lohrenz, "Aus Indien," *Zionsbote*, December 1912, 2; [Maria Pankratz], "Einiges ueber die Krankheit unserer Schwester Tina Lohrenz," *Zionsbote*, 10 September 1913, 2; John H. Pankratz, "Kurze Nachrichten von Hughestown," *Zionsbote*, 22 December 1915, 2-3.

23. Ruth Tucker, "Women in Missions," in *Earthen Vessels: American Evangelicals and Foreign Missions*, eds. J. A. Carpenter and Wilbert Shenk (Grand Rapids: Baker, 1990), 250-280.

24. A. J. Huebert, "Einige Tage in Secunderabad," *Das Erntefeld*, May 1901, 2.

25. Neoma Jantz, "[Katharine L. Schellenberg:] Continuously on Call for God," *Mennonite Brethren Herald*, 22 June 1984, 23.

26. Nettie Berg, "[Schellenberg's] 37 Years of Missionary Service in India," *Mennonite Observer*, 13 August 1960, 7; Katie Funk Wiebe, "Schellenberg, Katharina Lohrenz," *ME* V (1990), 795.
If Schellenberg ever had prospects of marrying Daniel Bergthold, as mooted by family, these disappeared when he married Tina Mandtler, a Canadian from Dalmeny instead, and again when he married Anna Epp in India in 1905. Though Schellenberg worked at Nagarkurnool for a number of years, she never attained her father's wish, even if it was hers also. Daniel married Anna Suderman in 1915 at Nagarkurnool as his third wife. Viola Bergthold Wiebe, interview by author, Hillsboro, KS, 3 May 1989, Penner Collection.

27. K. L. Schellenberg, "Das Leben der mohammendanischen Frauen," in *Licht und Schatten: Achtzehn Berichte von Arbeitern*, ed. D. F. Bergthold (Nagarkurnool: Amerikanische M. B. Mission in Indien, 1931), 7-10.

28. Elizabeth S. Neufeld, *Missionary Album* (Hillsboro: 1951), 15; though with the American Mennonite Brethren Mission, she worked at the Russian MB/American Baptist station, Nalgonda, most of her time in India (1899 to 1906); see A. J. Friesen, Report to *Baptist Mission Magazine* 94 (1904), 139; E. S. Neufeld, "An die Schwestern der Rueckenauer Gemeinde in Ruszland," *Das Erntefeld*, October 1905, 82-84; Obituary, "Elizabeth S. Neufeld [Wall, Wichert]," *Zionsbote*, 20 May 1953, 14-15.

29. Cf. Viola B. Wiebe, *Sepia Prints: Memoirs of a Missionary in India* (hereafter *Sepia Prints*) (Winnipeg: KP, 1990), 33.

30. Daniel F. Bergthold, "Missionsstation, Nagarkurnool, Indien," *Zionsbote*, 21 August 1907, 2; G. W. Peters, *Growth*, 172-3; Viola B. Wiebe, *Sepia Prints*, 14 ff.; Viola, the only daughter of the first marriage, was joined at Nagarkurnool by Lydia (1907), Bertha (1908), Martha (1909) from the second marriage.

31. D. F. Bergthold, touring with J. H. Pankratz, "Aus Indien," *Zionsbote*, 24 and 31 January 1906, 2; *Ibid.*, 14 and 21 March 1906, 2.

32. J. H. Pankratz, "Allerlei vom Aufenthalt in Nagarkurnool," *Zionsbote*, 8 and 15 April 1908, 2.

33. See N. N. Hiebert and J. H. Pankratz, "John H. Voth," *Greetings* (October 1943), 20-29; for a picture of the young men's association of Mountain Lake area (1898), see *Christian Leader*, February 1939, 4. This included Henry S. and John H. Voth, and the two brothers, Nicolai N. and Cornelius N. Hiebert.

34. Elizabeth Hulda, the first child, was joined in India by Sarah Elsie (1910), Menno John (1912), and Theodore Henry (1916). Mathilda Mary was born in 1917, and Hugo Ernest in 1920. Hugo died in 1944. *Missionary Album* (Hillsboro: 1951), 18.

35. In 1915 the Voths were still searching for an adequate house in Deverakonda itself until they could build their own bungalow. When the Unruhs were on furlough, or detained in Germany at the beginning of the War, the Voths were "at home in Nalgonda," see J. H. Voth, "Tagebuch," *Zionsbote*, 14 April 1915, 1-2.

36. John H. Voth's articles, letters, reports as printed in the *Zionsbote* and in conference yearbooks far exceed 400, probably as many as all the other pioneers put together.

37. John H. Voth, "Geschichtlicher Anfang der Missionsarbeit in Deverakonda," in *Licht und Schatten*, 20-22.

38. J. H. Voth, "Auf der Reise," *Zionsbote*, 9 February 1910, 2-3; "Deverakonda," *Zionsbote*, 13 April 1910, 2-3; "Geschichtlicher Anfang," *Licht und Schatten*, 20-22.

39. Frank J. Wiens (China), "Stadtmissions=Arbeit in Rochester, New York," *Zionsbote*, 23 January 1902, 2.

40. [A. E. Janzen], "Frank A. Janzen, 1880-1927," in *India* (1948), 143-152. The Janzens had three sons, Leander, Edwin and Arnold.

41. D. F. Bergthold, "Aus Indien," *Zionsbote*, 25 August 1909, 2; cf. Anna (Mrs. John. N. C.) Hiebert, "Auf den Nilgiri Bergen," in *Licht und Schatten*, 86-88.

42. Maria Friesen, "Aus Indien," *Das Erntefeld*, August 1900, 4; May 1901, 2-3.

43. John H. Pankratz, "Eine Gemeinde in Malakpet," *Zionsbote*, 4 May 1904, 22.

44. J. H. Pankratz, "In Nalgonda und Suriapett gewesen," *Das Erntefeld,* May 1904, 42-44; June 1904, 45-46.

45. Cf. J. H. Pankratz, "Telugu Convention in Palmur," *Zionsbote*, 27 March 1903, 2; and Elizabeth S. Neufeld, "Telugu Convention in Nalgonda," *Das Erntefeld,* March 1905, 21-22.

46. J. H. Pankratz, Obituary: "Schwester D.F. Bergthold," *Zionsbote*, 4 January 1905, 2.

47. *Ibid.*

48. Viola B. Wiebe, *Sepia Prints*, 13; cf. Vadala Samuel Willard, "Sketch of the Missionary Life of Daniel F. Bergthold," typescript (Hyderabad: Private, 1989), 3.

49. Anna (Epp) Ens, ed., *The House of Heinrich: The Story of Heinrich Epp (1811-163): Rosenort, Molotschna, and his Descendants* (Winnipeg: Epp Book Committee, 1980), 106-109; Anna Epp, the daughter of Abraham and Katharina Epp, did not travel to Russia alone, as Ens states. She was chaperoned by the C. H. Unruh and J. G. Wiens couples in 1904.

50. C. H. Unruh, "Reisebericht," *Das Erntefeld*, February 1905, 8-14.

51. D. F. Bergthold, "Deccan Convention at Suriapett," *Das Erntefeld*, January 1906, 1-3.

52. C. H. Unruh, "Einiges ueber die Jahreskonferenz," *Das Erntefeld*, March 1906, 25 ff.

53. Leoda Buckwalter, *Silhouette: Colonial India as We Lived It* (Nappanee: Evangel Press, 1988).

54. Peter Penner, *The Patronage Bureaucracy in North India: The Robert M. Bird and James Thomason School* (Delhi: Chanakya Publications, 1986), 216-217, 234, note 18.

55. Marie (Warkentin) Wiens, "Nachricht aus Jangaon," *Das Erntefeld*, 1912, 297-298.

56. Henry C. Unruh (Florida), "Memoir" [c. 1977], 8, in Peter Penner Collection.

57. A. J. Friesen, *Das Erntefeld*, 1910, 40; Viola B. Wiebe, *Sepia Prints*, 24-5.

58. See J. Edwin Orr, *Evangelical Awakenings in Asia in the Early Twentieth Century* (New Delhi: Masihi Sahitya Sanstha, 1970), 89-90. Essentially this was an extension into India of the revival that began in Wales in 1904.

59. See Peter Penner, "The Holy Spirit and Church Renewal," *Direction* 20 (Fall 1991), 135 ff.

60. Katharina Huebert, "Etwas aus meiner juengsten Erfahrung," *Das Erntefeld,* November 1906, 154-155; this paper, from August 1906 to April 1907, was replete with stories of revival blessings which these participants took with them back to the Plains.

61. J. H. Pankratz, "Die Erweckung auch in Mulkapett," *Das Erntefeld,* January 1907, 1-5; D. F. Bergthold, "Segenstage in Indien," *Zionsbote,* 12 December 1906, 2, 8.

62. J. H. Voth, "Geschichtlicher Anfang," in *Licht und Schatten,* 20-22.

63. *GC Yearbook* (1912), 435.

64. H. S. Voth, brother to John H. Voth, was paid $35 a month as a conference-appointed *Reiseprediger* during this time; see Peter Penner, *No Longer at Arm's Length: MB Church Planting in Canada* (Winnipeg: Kindred Press, 1987), 158; on the subject of "Finance as Power," see Michael Hollis, *Paternalism and the Church: A Study of South Indian Church History* (London: Oxford University Press, 1962), 58 ff.

65. For an early missiological example of this criticism, see Peter Penner, *Robert Needham Cust: A Personal Biography* (New York: Edwin Mellen Press, 1987), 293 ff.

66. Maria Friesen, "Aus Indien," *Das Erntefeld,* August 1900, 2-3; Paul Hockings, "British Society in the Company, Crown, and Congress Eras," in Paul Hockings, ed., *Blue Mountains: The Ethnography and Biogeography of a South Indian Region* (Delhi: Oxford University Press, 1989), 334-359.
Shirley Truscott has described the "Nilgiri Passenger" train which, pushing up and pulling down, "climbs 1,877 meters, crosses 250 bridges, and chugs through sixteen tunnels," over a 46 kilometer route between Ootacumund and Mettupalaiyam, in "Passage Through India," *Calgary Herald,* 13 May 1995, Section H, 8.

67. For impressions and some history of these schools, see Viola B. Wiebe, *Sepia Prints,* 29; Anna (Jungas) Hiebert, "Auf den Nilgiri Bergen," in *Licht und Schatten,* 86-8; Henry C. Unruh, 'Memoir," 21 ff., and 38 ff.; Waldo Penner, son of John A. Penner to Peter Penner, 19 June 1990, Peter Penner Collection.

68. A. J. Huebert to the Rooms, 14 February 1909, A. J. Huebert Collection, ABAC; in 1912 Anna Unruh went to stay with Anna, daughter of Heinrich Unruh; Marguerite (Baerg) Rempel, interview by author, Kitchener, Ontario, 25 June 1991; cf. N. N. Hiebert, *Missions=Album aus der Mission der Mennoniten Bruedergemeinde* (Hillsboro: MB Publishing House, 1914), 25.
We have already referred to Katharina Reimer as a teacher for the kind of school Friesen may have had in mind.

69. Marguerite Rempel, interview with author, Kitchener, 25 June 1991, Peter Penner Collection.

70. Henry C. Unruh, "Memoir", 21 ff, 38 ff.; his view is reinforced by his brother: C. Cornelius Unruh to Peter Penner, 27 January; 16 March 1992, Peter Penner Collection. These brothers were at Ootacumud during the lower grades and up to Sixth Form before 1930. Both thrived on the experience and had successful careers.

71. Viola B. Wiebe, *Sepia Prints*, 32-33.

72. Martha Bergthold Pullman, interview with author, Fresno, CA, 1 December 1992, Peter Penner Collection.

73. Arnold Janzen to Peter Penner, 15 September 1990, Peter Penner Collection.

# CHAPTER 4

1. P. A. Penner, "Ein Besuch in Indien," *Das Erntefeld*, February 1908, 18-22; cf. James Juhnke, *A People of Mission: A History of General Conference Overseas Missions* (Newton: Faith and Life Press, 1979), 17 ff.; and Samuel T. Moyer, *They Heard the Call* (Newton: Faith and Life Press, 1968), 12-33.

2. John H. Pankratz, "Eine Gemeinde in Mulkapet [31 March 1904]," *Zionsbote*, 4 May 1904, 2; G. W. Peters, *The Growth of Foreign Missions in the Mennonite Brethren Church* (Hillsboro: Mennonite Brethren Publishing House, 1952), 166-172.
John and Maria (Harms) Pankratz came to India with one daughter Rubina Leona, born in 1900. During their first term they had three more children: John, Ernest, Linda; Waldo was born in the USA; *Missionary Album* (Hillsboro: Board of Foreign Mission, 1951), 16.

3. J. H. Pankratz, "Kurze Mitteilungen aus Mulkapet," *Zionsbote*, 6 July 1904, 2; "Reisenotizen," *Zionsbote*, 15 February 1905, 2; E. S. Neufeld, "Aus Indien," *Zionsbote*, 5 April 1905, 2.

4. C. H. Unruh, "Komm herueber und hilf uns," *Das Erntefeld*, March 1906, 58-60; J. H. Pankratz, "Die Telugu Assoziation zu Hanamakonda," *Das Erntefeld*, January 1908, 2-4.

5. In the city of Hyderabad, though called a Muslim city, the Hindus dominated in a ratio of about 5 to 4; in Mahbubnagar, by comparison, about 9 to 1; see Paul D. Wiebe, *The Christians in Andhra Pradesh: The Mennonites of Mahbubnagar* (Bangalore: Christian Literature Society, 1988), 60-1.

6. C. H. Unruh, "Indien," *Das Erntefeld*, 1910, 128-129; Anna Sudermann, "Aus Indien," *Zionsbote*, 30 March 1910, 1-2.

7. J. H. Pankratz, "Der Mensch denkt und Gott lenkt," *Zionsbote*, 8 June 1910, 2; J. H. Voth, "Zum Abschied [farewell]," *Zionsbote*, 31 August 1910, 2-3.

8. *GC Yearbook* (1912), 435-436.

9. Abram E. Janzen, *Foreign Missions: The American Mennonite Brethren Mission in India* (hereafter *India*, 1948) (Hillsboro: BFM, 1948), 147; cf. F. A. Janzen, from Nagarkurnool, to N. N. Hiebert, 30 June 1914, F. A. Janzen File, CMBS/F.

10. N. N. Hiebert was appointed recording secretary to the BFM in 1902, *GC Yearbook* (1902), 264.

Given all the difficulties the Missionary Council had with Hiebert as secretary, one must ask: was it necessary to appoint him secretary of the Board because he was the only person in the Conference with 'international experience'? Though he was a logical choice, the position was such a constant source of anxiety for him, that one questions the wisdom of the choice.

11. It became a clearly-formed conviction that no missionary bungalow was big enough for two families, unless designed that way. No one on the field expected to accommodate another family for longer than the normal Christmas exchange visits, or in an emergency. For the Janzens the only short term alternative was the Rajah's guest house.

12. F. A. Janzen to N. N. Hiebert, 30 June 1914, F. A. Janzen File, CMBS/F; cf. A. E. Janzen, *India* (1948), 146-147. Note: there is nothing in Frank Janzen's June 1914 letter about the Rajah of Wanaparty, but his generosity was drawn to the attention of the *Bundeskonferenz*, and Janzen sent a message to the 1915 Conference that he had received permission to build Wanaparty station, see *GC Yearbook* (1912), 435-6; (1915), 453.

13. A. J. Friesen to Thomas S. Barbour, 28 August 1907; George B. Huntingdon extended sympathy to the Friesen family in this time of illness and disappointment, 2 October 1907, A. J. Friesen Collection, ABAC.

14. A. J. Friesen to T. S. Barbour, 18 March and 28 August 1907, Friesen Collection, ABAC.

15. A. J. Friesen from Rückenau to T. S. Barbour, 16 May 1908; Barbour to Friesen, 24 July 1908, Friesen Collection, ABAC.

16. A. J. Friesen from Rückenau to T. S. Barbour, in reply to G. B. Huntingdon, 20 July 1909, Friesen Collection, ABAC.

17. A. J. Friesen to T. S. Barbour, 23 April, 21 June, and 20 July 1909; Huntingdon to Friesen, 24 June and 27 August 1909, Friesen Collection, ABAC.

18. A. J. Friesen to T. S. Barbour, 18 March 1910, Friesen Collection, ABAC; Abram H. Unruh, *Die Geschichte der Mennoniten=Bruedergemeinde, 1860-1954* (Hillsboro: Board of Reference and Counsel, 1954), 322.

19. G. B. Huntingdon to A. J. Friesen, 14 March 1910, Friesen Collection, ABAC.

20. Thomas S. Barbour Collection, Colgate Historical Library, Rochester.

21. C. H. Unruh, "Nalgonda," *Das Erntefeld*, 1911, 43-46. Unruh enjoyed the opportunity for some sarcasm when writing about Barbour's visit. What was to be a whirlwind tour of the Deccan stations, American style, by car, ended in a slow progress by oxcart.

22. Heinrich H. Unruh, "Eine Woche auf Missionsreisen," *Das Erntefeld*, December 1904), 93-96; "An die Jahressitzung der Mennonitenbrueder in Suedruszland," *Das Erntefeld*, 1912, 151.

23. H. H. Unruh, "An die Jahressitzung....," *Ibid*; "Programm zur Jahressitzung der Vereinigten Christlichen Taufgesinnten Mennoniten=Bruedergemeinde in Ruszland," *Das Erntefeld*, 1912, 127.

24. **Typhus** is a fever marked by eruption of purple spots, great prostration, and unusual delirium, as distinct from **typhoid** fever, which is an infectious fever with eruption of red points on the chest and abdomen and severe intestinal irritation, enteric, causing depressed vitality, and occurring in many acute diseases, *The Concise Oxford Dictionary*.
    The dreaded illness was finally accompanied by pneumonia, see Marie (Warkentin) Wiens, "Liebe Geschwister (31 October 1912)," *Das Erntefeld*, 1912, 280-281; the Unruhs had left four children in Russia; in India they still had "the chubby healthy Cornelius (later renamed John C.)," and little Anna who died in infancy. Elizabeth, their youngest, was born after Heinrich died, see *Das Erntefeld*, 1912, 21-23.

25. Marie W. Wiens, "Von dem Tode unsres lieben Bruder Heinrich Unruh," 31 October 1912, *Das Erntefeld*, 1912, 280-283; John C. Unruh, Abbotsford, BC, to Peter Penner, 3 January 1989, Peter Penner Collection, CMBS/F.

26. Marie Wiens, "Nachricht aus Jangaon, Indien (for the Friesens in Russia)," *Das Erntefeld*, 1912, 297-298.

27. C. H. Unruh, "Was sagen unsere eingeborenen Christen in Indien ueber unsren Heinrich Unruh?" *Das Erntefeld*, 1913, 55-56; see A. H. Unruh, *Geschichte*, 318; despite the provision, the children experienced many hardships, John C. Unruh to Peter Penner, 6 August 1993, Peter Penner Collection.

28. Franz J. Wiens, "Unseres heimgegangenen Bruders letzte Worte an uns," *Das Erntefeld*, 1912, 298-301.

29. Johann G. Wiens, "Indische Echo," *Das Erntefeld*, 1909, 3-8.

30. See Hans Kasdorf, *Gustav Warneck's missiolocrisches Erbe: Eine biographische=historische Untersuchuncr* (Basel: Brunner Verlag Giessing, 1990).

31. C. H. Unruh, "Unsere Reihen lichten sich" (idiomatically this means "Our ranks are thinning out)," *Das Erntefeld*, 1914, 76-78.

32. A. J. Friesen, from the Crimea, to the Rooms, 26 November 1912, Friesen Collection, ABAC.

33. Arthur C. Baldwin to A. J. Friesen at Nalgonda, 2 June 1914, Friesen Collection, ABAC.

34. F. J. Wiens, "Wohl 'zerschlagen' - aber doch 'froehlich' (crushed, but joyous anyway) gemacht," *Das Erntefeld*, January 1913, 4-7.

35. Cf. F. J. Wiens, "Von den missionsstationen Nalgonda und Jangaon, Indien", *Das Erntefeld*, 1913, 147; and A. J. Friesen, "Aus Briefen (to Maria in Russia) meines lieben Mannes," *Das Erntefeld*, September 1914, 144; see also G. B. Huntingdon to Franz J. Wiens, 2 April 1913, F. J. Wiens Collection, ABAC.

36. G. B. Huntingdon to F. J. Wiens, 26 December 1913, F. J. Wiens Collection, ABAC. There is nothing about this cause for dismissal and disappointment in the files kept by his son. See Jacob F. Wiens, "Our Heritage from our Parents . . . " (an unpublished paper of 17 pages, 1979), Peter Penner Collection. Jacob thought it strange in retrospect that his parents would have chosen California when they had income from property in Siberia. This income helped them to acquire land in California.

37. Cf. F. J. Wiens, analysis of his nervous illness in "Brief aus Indien," *Zionsbote*, 24 December 1913, 2-3 (copied from the *Friedensstimme*); and his "Wohl 'zerschlagen'- aber doch froehlich," *Das Erntefeld*, January 1913, 4-7; C. H. Unruh wrote in 1914, while on furlough, that Franz Wiens had a "weak heart," in "Unsere Reihen lichten sich," *Das Erntefeld*, May 1914, 76.
The references to the degree of illness afflicting Franz and Marie Wiens are admittedly contradictory. After the fatal shooting in 1922 (told in Chapter Seven), Marie Wiens stated that "after five years our health had deteriorated, and we could no longer carry on," in "Unser Leben faehrt schnell dahin, als floegen wir davon," *Zionsbote*, 15 November 1922, 9-11.

38. A. J. Friesen from Rückenau to T. S. Barbour, 24 September 1911, Friesen Collection, ABAC; A. J. Huebert to G. B. Huntingdon, 12 May 1913, Huebert Collection, ABAC.

39. A. J. Friesen to The Rooms, 4 October 1911, emphasis added, Friesen Collection, ABAC.

40. A. J. Huebert to G. B. Huntingdon, 12 May 1913; Arthur Baldwin to A. J. Huebert, 20, 25, and 30 November, and 18 December 1914, Huebert Collection, ABAC.

41. A. J. Friesen to A. C. Baldwin, 1 January 1915, Friesen Collection, ABAC.

42. A. S. Baldwin, "A Statement Concerning Needs of the Mennonite Work in South Russia." (n. d., probably early 1915, 3 pages), A. J. Huebert Collection, ABAC.

43. *Ibid.*

44. A. J. Friesen to A. S. Baldwin, 9 February 1915, Friesen Collection, ABAC. It is not clear when Baldwin's "statement" reached Friesen.

45. In these letters A. J. Huebert related that he had some news from Katie, that he had no further hope of getting funds out of Russia, that H. J. Braun had written to say his son Abram was lying wounded in a Tiflis (Tbilsi) hospital, and things in Russia looked hopeless; Huebert to G. B. Huntingdon, 30 September 1915, 20 January and 25 August 1916, Huebert Collection, ABAC. After that there are no more letters from Russia.

46. A. H. Unruh, *Geschichte*, 316-318; part of the family lore is the belief that Treasurer Braun misappropriated funds meant for the children, perhaps before Anna returned home in 1912 with her two youngest children. Marguerite Rempel, interview by author, Kitchener, ON, 25 June 1991, Peter Penner Collection.

47. See Ben Doerksen, "Mennonite Brethren missions: History, Development, Philosophy and Policies" (D. Ministry thesis, Fuller School of missions, Pasadena, 1986); and Peter Penner, "'Baptist in all but name:' Molotschna Mennonite Brethren in India," *Mennonite Life* 46 (March 1991), 17-23.

48. C. H. Unruh, from Altona Germny, to A. C. Baldwin, 12 August 1914; Fred P. Haggard, ABFMS, to W. T. Bryan, Secretary of State, Washington, 27 November 1914, the C. H. Unruh Collection, ABAC; cf. Theo. F. Hahn, "Das Los der deutschen Missionare in Indien (the fate of the German missionaries in India)," *Zionsbote*, 5 January 1916, 5-6; and an anonymous "Zionspilger," who wrote: "Deutsche missionen in englische Kolonien," *Zionsbote*, 30 May 1917, 3-4.

49. J. H. Pankratz to H. W. Lohrenz, 13 June 1922, Henry W. Lohrenz Papers, CMBS/F.

50. This statistic comes from Arthur C. Baldwin, in his "Statement Concerning Needs of the Mennonite Work in South India," (1915), A. J. Huebert Collection, ABAC.

51. J. G. Wiens, Annual Report from Jangaon to The Rooms, 1909, 1-2, J. G. Wiens Collection, ABAC.

52. See F. Kurtz, "The Influence of the Mission Station on the Town," *Baptist Missionary Review* 30 (March 1914), 84-87.

53. J. H. Voth, "Aus Indien," *Zionsbote*, 26 May 1915, 1; cf. *CC Yearbook* (Herbert, 1917), 23.

54. *GC Ibid* (1915) , 452.

55. Arthur C. Baldwin, "A Statement Concerning Needs of the Mennonite Work in South India," (1915), 2, A. J. Huebert Collection, ABAC.

## CHAPTER 5

1. Missionary Council (hereafter MC), Minutes, 13 December 1914, CMBS/F. There were 93 such numbered sessions between this date and June 1960. See J. H. Voth, *Ein Jahr unter den Telugus* (Hyderabad: M. B. Mission, 1929), 20. For a constitution of the MC, see Gerhard W. Peters, *Foundations of Mennonite Brethren Missions* (Hillsboro: Kindred Press, 1984), 208 ff.

2. J. H. Pankratz to H. W. Lohrenz, 10 January 1922, H. W. Lohrenz Papers, CMBS/F. The General Conference constitution, if not weak, was ambiguous about the relationship between the Board at home and their missionaries in India. For the various constitutions and general explanations for the changes and their motivation, see G. W. Peters, *The Growth of Foreign Missions in the Mennonite Brethren Church* (Hillsboro: MB Publishing House, 1952), 289 ff.; and *Foundations of Mennonite Brethren Missions,* 92, 207 ff.

3. He viewed his role as "eine Vermittelung," facilitating, mediating, not directing, the work of the Mission, see N. N. Hiebert, "Ein oeffentliches Wort vom Missionskomitee," *Zionsbote*, 31 October 1934, 3-4.

4. See J. A. Froese, *Witness Extraordinary: A Biography of Elder Heinrich Voth, 1851-1918* (Winnipeg: Board of Christian Literature, 1975), 51 ff.

5. N. N. Hiebert to J. H. Voth, 18 March 1919, J. H. Voth Papers, CMBS/F; cf. Hiebert, "Ein kurzes Wort vom Missionskomitee," *Zionsbote*, 25 December 1918, 3.
According to John B. Toews, N. N. Hiebert "had a life-long struggle for survival." His energies were dissipated by teaching in a local Bible school and running a dairy assisted by his sons. For all that he remained relatively poor. He might have wished that he was back in India and receiving $1,000. a year as a missionary. He received the wages of a **Reiseprediger** (about $35 a month) when he had time to travel in that capacity. John B. Toews, interview by author, Fresno, 18 January 1993, Peter Penner Collection.

6. *GC Yearbook* (Reedley, 1921), 6.

7. Henry W. Lohrenz to N. N. Hiebert, 18 December 1914, Lohrenz Papers, CMBS/F. Perhaps Hiebert's 40-page publication, *Missions=Album aus der Mission der Mennoniten Bruedergemeinde* (Hillsboro: MB Publishing House,1914) was the result of that prompting.

8. Frank A. Janzen to N. N. Hiebert, 30 June 1914, F. A. Janzen File, CMBS/F.

9. Jacob W. Wiens carried on a voluminous, regular, and timely correspondence, even though his German spelling was atrocious. He was apparently well liked since he lent a ready ear to problems.

10. Cf. J. H. Voth to J. W. Wiens, 6 February 1919, Voth File; and Voth, "Aus Indien," *Zionsbote*, 2 April 1919, 3-5. This is the same letter, except for the **omission** of an offensive reference to Hiebert in the press copy. See also Wiens to Voth, 3 April 1919, Voth Papers; Wiens to Voth, 24 November 1919, Voth File; Wiens to Voth, 20 April 1920; Voth to Wiens, 20 April 1920, Voth Papers; N. N. Hiebert to Wiens, 30 March 1920, H. W. Lohrenz Papers, CMBS/F.

11. J. H. Voth to J. W. Wiens, 30 June 1930, Voth File, A 250-6-2, CMBS/F.

12. N. N. Hiebert to the MC, India, 12 March 1923; Hiebert to H. W. Lohrenz, 20 and 24 October 1924, H. W. Lohrenz Papers, CMBS/F.

13. N. N. Hiebert to H. W. Lohrenz, 27 May 1921, Lohrenz Papers.

14. N. N. Hiebert to J. W. Wiens, 30 March 1920, Lohrenz Papers; J. H. Voth to J. W. Wiens, 10 June 1920, Voth File, CMBS/F.

15. N. N. Hiebert to H. W. Lohrenz, 19 March 1925, Lohrenz Papers, CMBS/F.

16. Anna Hanneman to H. W. Lohrenz, 27 October 1925, Lohrenz Papers, CMBS/F.

17. H. W. Lohrenz to J. H. Lohrenz, 11 February 1923, H. W. Lohrenz Papers, CMBS/F.

18. H. W. Lohrenz to J. H. Lohrenz, 10 October 1925; Anna Hanneman to H. W. Lohrenz, 3 November 1925, H. W. Lohrenz Papers, CMBS/F.

19. H. W. Lohrenz to N. N. Hiebert, 29 March and 10 October 1925, Lohrenz Papers, CMBS/F. Hiebert's discouragements during the 1920s brought him close to resignation at least three times.

20. *GC Yearbook* (1919), 477; (1921), 12; (1924), 28. Monies listed as "spezielle Missionsgaben" for specified persons were listed in the *Zionsbote* periodically; for donations given in October 1919, see *Zionsbote*, 19 November 1919, 13.

21. Though John Voth outranked all others in support received, he worried when North American monies began to go to the China mission, or were siphoned off for relief of Mennonites in Russia. He admitted later that much of his Deverakonda 'success' had been accomplished with money from designated gifts, "Kurze Erzaehlungen vom 'Gottesberg'," *Zionsbote*, 3 August 1938, 2-3; he kept the question of such gifts controversial until his last years; see John A. Wiebe to H. W. Lohrenz, 22 September and 6 October 1943, J. A. Wiebe File, CMBS/F.

22. J. H. Voth denied any **Prahlerei** but boasted of 2,600 members in Deverakonda alone when the combined total was not much over 3,000, in "Aus Indien," *Zionsbote*, 14 February 1923, 2-3.

During John H. Lohrenz's first years in India, treasurer Jacob W. Wiens explained the difference between general, special and relief funds to him and added: "Special gifts are not the best for the India Mission." Cf. J. W. Wiens to J. H. Lohrenz, 21 February 1922, John Lohrenz File; and Wiens to H. W. Lohrenz, eight years later, 20 February 1930, Henry Lohrenz Papers, CMBS/F.

23. J. H. Pankratz, "Kurz und Abgerissen," *Zionsbote*, 27 May 1914, 2-3; "Missionsstation in Hughestown erworben und eingeweiht," *Zionsbote*, 24 February 1915, 2-3.

24. J. H. Pankratz, "Aus Indien," *Zionsbote*, 27 December 1916; and 25 July 1917, 4; a later chapter indicates that Shamshabad was not entirely free of the plague either.

25. G. W. Peters, *Growth*, 179; A. Hanneman, "Aus Indien," *Zionsbote*, 9 February 1916, 3-4.

26. J. H. Pankratz, "Aus Indien," *Zionsbote*, 11 June 1919, 3-4.

27. J. H. Pankratz, "Aus dem Krankenzimmer," *Zionsbote*, 1 January 1919, 3-4; "Aus Indien," 7 May 1919, 4-5; for the extended travelogue, see 17 September 1919, 3-4, and subsequent issues until into October.

They visited P. S. Goertz at Foochow, then a missionary to China (1918-26). Later he taught at Tabor College (1926-30), *ME* V (1990), 348. They also visited F. J. and Agnes (Harder) Wiens at Shonghong, see *Missionary Album, 1889-1963: Mennonite Brethren and Krimmer Mennonite Brethren* (Hillsboro: BFM, 1963), 34. This may have been the Board's answer to F. J. Wiens' request for an executive visit to India and China.

28. Maria Pankratz, "Aus Indien," *Zionsbote*, 9 November 1921, 1-2; "Missionsglocken," 26 April 1922, 3-5.

29. J. H. Pankratz, "Zwei Monate in Indien," *Zionsbote*, 4 January 1922, 1-3; "Unsere Bibelschule in Shamshabad," 19 July 1922, 2-4; "Jahresbericht aus Shamshabad, 1921-22," 1 November 1922, 4-7.

30. Martha Bergthold Pullman, interview by author, Fresno, CA, 1 December 1992, Peter Penner Collection.

31. J. H. Voth, "Aus Indien," *Zionsbote*, 14 July 1920, 3-4; "Jahresbericht von Deverakonda," 9 February 1921, 2.

32. J. H. Voth, "Die christliche Mission wird angefochten (the mission is under attack)," *Zionsbote*, 13 December 1916, 2-4. In this article Voth found support from Methodist Bishop Frank W. Warne, who took the trouble to look into the career of a critic, supposedly from Benares, who had been interviewed in America and widely quoted, and found that he was unknown in Benares; H. H. Unruh made the same point in 1907: "Allerlei aus Jangaon," *Das Erntefeld*, September 1907, 141-143.

33. J. H. Voth, "Aus Indien," *Zionsbote*, 22 September 1920, 2-3; 30 March 1921, 2-3.

34. *GC Yearbook* (1921), 12; F. A. Janzen to J. W. Wiens, 1 April 1922, F. A. Janzen File, A 250-6-2, CMBS/F.

35. Cf. G. W. Peters, *Growth*, 174; A. E. Janzen, "Frank A. Janzen," in *India* (1948), 147.

36. Viola B. Wiebe, *Sepia Prints: Memoirs of a Missionary in India* (Winnipeg: Kindred Press, 1990), 59; cf. Dilwyn B. Studebaker (missionary on the Wanaparty field from 1949 to 1954), interview by author, Modesto, CA, 10-11 October 1992, Peter Penner Collection.

The author visited Wanaparty in company with Missionary Dan Nickel on 3 February 1973. There he heard the stories about the plaster mix and the exceptional life and mysterious death of Frank Janzen; Peter Penner to Justina Penner, London, UK, 3 February 1973, Peter Penner Collection.

37. K. L. Schellenberg, "Aus Indien," *Zionsbote*, 8 September 1926, 5.

38. J. H. Lohrenz, "Aus Indien," *Zionsbote*, 21 September 1927, 2-3; J. H. Lohrenz to H. W. Lohrenz, 14 August 1927, Lohrenz Papers, CMBS/F; *CC Yearbook* (1928), 39.

39. One may conjecture that the missionary's natural endowments such as character and training, education, and the finishing school of family, community, and experience were not being impregnated with the spiritual empowerment of the Holy Spirit and the power of prayer. See R. S. Troup, "Why do missionaries 'crack up'?" *Prairie Harvester* (Three Hills, October/December 1961), 15; and J. Herbert Kane, *Understanding Christian Missions* (Grand Rapids: Baker Book House, 1978), 76 ff.

40. K. L. Schellenberg, "Aus Indien, 11 *Zionsbote*, 3 April 1918, 5. A. L. Schellenberg was prepared to expose hypocrisy. In 1922 he set up the rule that he alone would decide when "controversial material . . . would shed light on the truth;" see Daniel Born, "From 1904 - a story of service," *Christian Leader*, 27 January 1979, 5-6.

41. J. H. Pankratz to the Board of Foreign Missions, 2 May 1918, Pankratz File, CMBS/F.

42. D. F. Bergthold to Heinrich Voth, 23 August 1918, Bergthold File; Bergthold to Heinrich Voth, 10 January 1919, John H. Voth Papers, CMBS/F. Heinrich Voth died in late December 1918 at Vanderhoof, British Columbia.

43. Cf. *GC Yearbook* (1903), 289; and D. F. Bergthold, "Geschwister Bergthold's Abfahrt," *Zionsbote*, 3 August 1904, 2.

44. F. A. Janzen to D. F. Bergthold, 20 February 1919, Bergthold Papers; D. F. Bergthold to J. H. Voth, 18 February 1919, Voth File, CMBS/F.

45. Missionary Council, Minutes, # 6, 24 January 1917, CMBS/F; K. L. Schellenberg, "Aus Indien," *Zionsbote*, 29 November 1916, 6.

46. Maria C. Wall, "Jahresbericht," *Zionsbote*, 13 November 1918, 10-11; 8 April 1919, 4-5.

47. J. H. Voth complained about losing one-third of his salary or appropriations in the exchange; J. H. Voth to J. W. Wiens, 20 April 1920, Voth Papers, CMBS/F.

48. *GC Yearbook* (1919), 483.

49. G. W. Peters, *Growth*, 199-200.

50. Cf. Peter Penner, *No Longer at Arm's Length: Mennonite Brethren Church Planting in Canada* (Winnipeg: KP, 1987), 15.

51. W. E. Boggs to J. H. Voth, from Coonoor, 1 June 1920; Voth to Boggs, from Ootacumund, 7 June 1920; Boggs to Voth, 10 June 1920, Voth Papers, CMBS/F.

52. W. E. Boggs to J. H. Voth, 10 June 1920, Voth Papers.

53. D. F. Bergthold to J. H. Voth, 20 June, 19 and 22 July, and 12 August 1920, Voth Papers, CMBS/F. The corresponding Voth letters seem to be missing. Bergthold suggested that they might utilize the work of James M. Gray, Rueben A. Torrey, William Evans, and Heinrich F. Toews. For an indication of how widely such authors were used, see J. B. Toews, *Pilgrimage of Faith: The Mennonite Brethren Church in Russia and America, 1860-1990* (Winnipeg: Kindred Press, 1993), 173, 353.

54. D. F. Bergthold to J. H. Voth, 22 September 1920, Voth Papers, CMBS/F; see J. H. Lohrenz, "Die Heranbildung der eingeborenen Arbeitern," in *Licht und Schatten: Achtzehn Berichte von Arbeitern* (Nagarkurnool, 1931), 50-53; J. H. Lohrenz, *The Mennonite Brethren Church* (Hillsboro: BFM, 1950), 242-243.

About this time Voth wrote a "dialogue between husband and wife,, entitled "Entmutigendes (discouraging elements) aus dem Missionsleben," *Zionsbote*, 21 August 1921, 2-3.

55. N. N. Hiebert's "fourth letter" to the MC, 12 March 1923; to J.W. Wiens, 30 March 1920; to H. W. Lohrenz, 27 May 1921, Lohrenz Papers, CMBS/F.

56. N. N. Hiebert to the MC, 12 March 1923, Lohrenz Papers, CMBS/F.

57. J. H. Lohrenz to J. W. Wiens, 22 October 1922, John Lohrenz File, CMBS/F.

58. J. H. Pankratz to H. W. Lohrenz, 10 January 1922; cf. "Protokol der 17ten Sitzung (Minutes of the MC)," 31 December 1922 to I January 1923, CMBS/F; John Lohrenz also thought that Hiebert had written "incautiously," though he faulted Pankratz for blowing the intervention out of all proportion; J. H. Lohrenz to H. W. Lohrenz, 3 January 1922, H. W. Lohrenz Papers, CMBS/F.

59. N. N. Hiebert to J. W. Wiens, 30 March 1920; Hiebert to H. W. Lohrens, 25 December 1921, Lohrenz Papers, CMBS/F; like the Board at home, the Missionary Council began to ask: shall we send home only those items that "really concern the Board?"

60. N. N. Hiebert to the Missionary Council, 12 March 1923; J.H. Lohrenz to H.W. Lohrenz, 4 March 1923, H. W. Lohrenz Papers, CMBS/F.

61. J. H. Pankratz to J.W. Wiens, 26 September 1923, Pankratz File, CMBS/F.

62. J. H. Pankratz to H. W. Lohrenz, 21 November 1923, Lohrenz Papers, CMBS/F.

## CHAPTER 6

1. John H. Lohrenz to Henry W. Lohrenz, 8 September 1921, John Lohrenz File, CMBS/F.

2. Stanley Wolpert, *A New History of India* (New York: Oxford University Press, 1990), 286 ff.

3. *Ibid,* J. H. Lohrenz to J. W. Wiens, 12 October 1922, Lohrenz File, CMBS/F.

4. J. W. Wiens to J. H. Lohrenz, 21 February 1921, Lohrenz File; Lohrenz to Wiens, 6 February 1925, H. W. Lohrenz Papers, CMBS/F.

5. J. H. Lohrenz to H. W. Lohrenz, 24 March 1923, H. W. Lohrenz Papers, CMBS/F.

6. J. H. Lohrenz to H. W. Lohrenz, 14 December 1925, H. W. Lohrenz Papers, CMBS/F.

7. H. W. Lohrenz to J. W. Wiens, 26 April 1927, Lohrenz Papers, CMBS/F.

8. J. H. Lohrenz to H. W. Lohrenz, 14 August 1927, H. W. Lohrenz Papers, CMBS/F; J. H. Lohrenz, "Aus Indien," *Zionsbote*, 16 November 1927, 4-6; *GC Yearbook*, (1928), 39.

9. *Missionary Album*, ed. A. E. Janzen (Hillsboro: BFM, 1951), 21.

10 Peter V. Balzer, "Beobachtungen waehrend des Studiums der Telugu Sprache," *Zionsbote*, 15 October 1924, 4; "Aus Indien," 29 July 1925, 2-3,

11. P. V. Balzer, "Aus Indien," *Zionsbote*, 10 November 1926, 2-3; 9 March 1927, 5; 27 July 1927, 2.

12. P. V. Balzer, "Aus Indien," *Zionsbote*, 11 April 1928, 3.

13. P. V. Balzer to H. W. Lohrenz, 6 February 1928, Lohrenz Papers, CMBS/F; Balzer, "Aus Indien," *Zionsbote*, 29 February 1928, 3-4; 11 April 1928, 3.

14. Anna Hanneman to J. W. Wiens, 7 January 1919, Hanneman File, CMBS/F.

15. K. L. Schellenberg, "Jahresbericht ueber die aertzliche Hilfe," *Zionsbote*, 15 October 1913, 3-4.

16. A. Hanneman, "Aus Indien," *Zionsbote*, 7 December 1927, 3-4.

17. By "whites" she meant, rather crudely, her fellow missionaries. The Telugus, being Dravidian, were quite dark-skinned; K. L. Schellenberg, "Aus Indien," *Zionsbote*, 17 July 1917, 4; A. Hanneman to J. W. Wiens, 31 May 1920, Hanneman File, CMBS/F; cf. Nettie Berg, "37 Years of Missionary Service in India," *Mennonite Observer*, 19 August 1960, 7 ff.

18. K. L. Schellenberg, "Jahresbericht, Hughestown," *Zionsbote*, 13 November 1918, 8-9; "Aus Indien," 1 October 1919, 4-5.

19. Anna Hanneman, "Eine Beleuchtung der Krankenarbeit auf unsern Feldern," *Licht und Schatten: Achtzehn Berichte von Arbeitern* (Nagarkurnool, 1931), 70-76; cf. A. E. Janzen, *Foreign Missions: The American MB Mission in India* (Hillsboro: BFM, 1948), 72.

20. H. W. Lohrenz to K. L. Schellenberg, 19 August 1925, Lohrenz Papers, CMBS/F. This letter reveals that J. H. Pankratz wanted Anna Hanneman back, but not K. L. Schellenberg.

21. A. Hanneman to H. W. Lohrenz, 16 October 1930, Lohrenz Papers, CMBS/F.

22. K. L. Schellenberg, "Aus Indien,"*Zionsbote*, 4 April 1928, 2-3; "Seelenheil unter den Kranken," 10 July 1929, 2-4.

23. Among Anna Hanneman's first experiences with the missionary family were the death and funeral of Anna Epp Bergthold, and then the happier circumstance when Daniel Bergthold married Anna Sudermann who had been in India since 1898. The wedding took place at Ootacumund on 20 June 1916. Hanneman, "Aus Indien," *Zionsbote*, 1 December 1915, 1-2; 9 August 1916, 3.

24. H. W. Lohrenz to P. V. Balzer, 5 July 1925, Lohrenz Papers, CMBS/F; Lohrenz, "Sister Anna Hanneman, a short biography," *Greetings* (May 1943), 4-14.

25. For a survey of education provided in the elementary, middle, and high schools of the AMBM, see A. E. Janzen, *India* (1948), 53-68; A. Hanneman, "Aus Indien," *Zionsbote*, 14 February 1917, 2-3; 5 September 1917, 4-5.

26. A. Hanneman, "Jahresbericht unsrer Missionsschule in Shamshabad," in J.H. Voth, ed., *Ein Jahr unter den Telugus* (Hyderabad: M. B. Mission, 1929), 71-72.

27. A. Hanneman, Mission Report, *CC Yearbook* (Brotherfield, Saskatchewan, 1925), 30.

28. Maria Pankratz, Mission Reports, *CC Yearbook* (Gnadenau, Saskatchewan, 1920), 25; Anna Suderman Bergthold (Winkler, Manitoba, 1921), 6; K. L. Schellenberg (Main Center, 1923), 21.

29. Maria C. Wall, "Aus Indien," *Zionsbote*, 10 November 1915, 1-2.

30. M. C. Wall, "Jahresbericht,"*Zionsbote*, 13 November 1918, 10-11; 9 April 1919, 4-5; 23 June 1920, 3; 12 January 1921, 4-5.

31. Peter Penner, "By Reason of Strength: Johann Warkentin, 1859-1948," *Mennonite Life*, 33 (December 1978), 4-9.

32. H. L. Warkentin to J. W. Wiens, 27 May 1931, Warkentin File, CMBS/F.

33. M. C. Wall to J. W. Wiens, 18 October 1930, Wall File; cf. Maria Klaassen Lohrenz, Diary, vol. 1, 20 October 1931, 85, John Lohrenz Papers, CMBS/F; M. C. Wall, "The Ministry of Health and Healing in Hospital," *The Andhra Mennonite Brethren Church of India: Fifty Years in Retrospect, 1904-1954*, ed. , A. E. Janzen (Hillsboro: BFM, 1954), 26-27.

34. John A. Penner, "A Brief Memoir of My Life," (1971), translated into English by Catharina Thiessen, 6 pp., Peter Penner Collection

35. J. A. Penner helped to prepare the gravestone for H. H. Unruh; he recalled meeting Unruh at Hamburg-Horn four years earlier; see J. A. Penner, "Indien," *Das Erntefeld*, 1914, 205.

36. *Ibid.*

37. Peter Klassen, Rueckenau, "Aussendungsfeier [Commissioning Service]," *Das Erntefeld*, 1913, 243-244.

38. J. A. Penner, "Unsere Reise nach Indien," *Das Erntefeld*, 1913, 277-279; 1914, 39-42. There were other instalments.

39. John and Anna (Nikkel) Penner, Annual Report (1918) ; Anna suffered a "nervous breakdown" in February of 1920. Her husband took her to Ootacumund and then hurried back to the work. She recovered within five months, Penner, Annual Report (1920), and J. A. Penner to Joseph C. Robbins, 31 May 1920, John A. Penner Collection, ABAC.

40. Waldo Penner, son of John Penner, to Peter Penner, 19 March 1990, Peter Penner Collection.

41. J. A. Penner, "Report of the Agricultural and Industrial Work," 15 January 1921; J. C. Robbins to J. A. Penner, 20 June 1921, John Penner Collection, ABAC.

42. For a brief account of the Leninist Revolution and the Civil War lost by the White forces, see John B. Toews (Vancouver), "In Response to Anarchy," in *Czars, Soviets, and Mennonites* (Newton: Faith and Life, 1983), 79 ff.

43. Following the period of 'War Communism' (1918-1921), the full-scale relief effort of the new Mennonite Central Committee led by P. C. Hiebert, Hillsboro, Kansas, meant a phenomenal drain on mission resources; cf. Mission Report, *CC Yearbook* (Main Center, 1923), 18-20.

44. See Gerard Colby and Charlotte Dennett, "The Baptist Burden," in *Thy Will be Done: The Conquest of the Amazon: Nelson Rockefeller and Evangelism in the Age of Oil* (New York: HarperCollins, 1995), 9 ff.

45. J. A. Penner, Annual Report (1919); J. C. Robbins to J. A. Penner, 11 July 1919 and 22 April 1920, John Penner Collection, ABAC; Robbins to C. H. Unruh, 18 July 1919; 23 July 1920; 7 June 1921, C. H. Unruh Collection, ABAC.

46. C. H. Unruh, A. J. Huebert, and J. A. Penner to J. C. Robbins, 14 June 1920; Penner to Robbins, regarding the devastations wrought by Nestor Makhno, the anarchist, in the Molotschna and Sagradowka villages of South Russia, 8 September 1920, John Penner Collection, ABAC.

47. J. C. Robbins to J. A. Penner, 20 January 1921, John Penner Collection, ABAC.

48. J. A. Penner to J. C. Robbins, 14 June 1920, 25 June 1921, 14 July 1921, 21 April 1922, and 7 August 1923, John Penner Collection, ABAC.

49. C. H. Unruh to J. C. Robbins, 8 and 21 August 1923; 8 February 1924, C. H. Unruh Collection, ABAC.

50. C. H. Unruh to J. C. Robbins, 30 June 1923, 8 and 21 August 1923, C. H. Unruh Collection, ABAC.

51. C. H. Unruh to J. C. Robbins, 14 December 1912; 12 July 1913; 26 April 1922; 20 June 1924, C. H. Unruh Collection, ABAC.

52. Donald J. Unruh at his father's funeral, "A Tribute to Abram A. Unruh," Winnipeg, September 1990, in Peter Penner Collection.

53. C. H. Unruh to J. C. Robbins, 10 April 1929; Annual Report, 1930, Unruh Collection, ABAC.

54. A. J. Huebert, Annual Report, 1930; J. A. Penner, Annual Report, 1929, ABAC.

55. J. H. Voth, *Ein Jahr unter den Telugus* (Hyderabad: M. B. Mission, 1929), 22; cf. Peter M. Hamm, *India: Mennonite Brethren Church Statistical Report* (Shamshabad: M. B. Mission, 1970) 26, 65; and H. W. Lohrenz, *Our Mission Among the Telugus* (Hillsboro: BFM, 1939), 18.

56. A. Hanneman, "Aus Indien," *Zionsbote*, 13 March 1929, 2-4; Hanneman to H. W. Lohrenz, 16 October 1930; J. H. Lohrenz to H. W. Lohrenz, 11 July 1938, Henry Lohrenz Papers, CMBS/F.

57. H. W. Lohrenz, ed. *Our Mission Among the Telugus*, 18.

## CHAPTER 7

1. Jacob F. Wiens, "Our Heritage from our Parents and Forefathers," a brief unpublished memoir (1979), in Peter Penner Collection.

2. "Fresno Firemen Open Fire When Car Speeds Away," *The Fresno Morning Republican (FMR)*, 1 August 1922, 1, 6; John A. Penner to J. C. Robbins, 4 August 1922, John Penner Collection, ABAC.
Herbert Swartz, son-in-law to John A. Penner, typescript copy (made about 1981) of the sensational press coverage in *The Fresno Morning Republican* and the *Reedley Exponent*, August and September 1922 (henceforth Herbert Swartz typescript), Peter Penner Collection.

3. Jacob F. Wiens, "Our Heritage," 16-17; Marie Warkentin Wiens, "Unser Leben faehret schnell dahin, als floegen wir davon," *Zionsbote*, 15 November 1922,

9-11; J. A. Penner to J. C. Robbins, 4 and 18 August 1922, John Penner Collection, ABAC.

4. *Fresno Morning Republican*, 2 August 1922, Herbert Swartz transcript, 3, Peter Penner Collection.

5. *FMR*, 4 August 1922, 1,8, Herbert Swartz transcript, 8-12, 14, 18.

6. *FMR*, 5 August 1922, 13, Swartz transcript.

7. *Reedley Exponent*, 11 August 1922, Swartz transcript, 16-17.

8. *Reedley Exponent*, 29 August, 8 September 1922, Swartz transcript, 18-19.

9. Jacob J. Wiens, "Henry Warkentin Wiens (1910-1968)," one page biography of the diplomat, and "Mrs. Marie H. Wiens," one page; Marie received $9,000. from an insurance company; Frank and Marie Wiens, Hillsboro, to Peter Penner, 7 February 1994, Peter Penner Collection.

10. John H. Pankratz, when support for Johnny was cut off, to J. W. Wiens, 26 September 1923; J. H. Pankratz to H. W. Lohrenz, 19 July 1924, J. H. Pankratz File, CMBS/F.

11. J. H. Pankratz, "Aus Indien," *Zionsbote*, 5 November 1924, 3-5; see "Fuenfundzwanzig=jaehriges Jubelaeum in Hughestown/Shamshabad," *Zionsbote*, 26 November 1924, 3-5. K. L. Schellenberg's name was omitted from these expressions of gratitude; cf. H. W. Lohrenz to A. Hanneman, 19 August 1925, Lohrenz Papers, CMBS/F.

12. J. H. Pankratz to the Board of Foreign Missions (BFM), 7 February 1924; D. F. Bergthold to the BFM, 19 January 1924, H. W. Lohrenz Papers, CMBS/F; Samuel was taken to Secunderabad for emergency help but his life could not be saved. There was nothing in the *Zionsbote* about this fatal shooting.

13. J. H. Pankratz to H. W. Lohrenz, 7 February 1924; N. N. Hiebert to H. W. Lohrenz, 3 March 1924, Lohrenz Papers; cf. Missionary Council, Minutes, 21 January 1925, CMBS/F.

14. J. H. Pankratz to H. W. Lohrenz, 21 February 1924, Lohrenz Papers, CMBS/F; "Vom Geiste durchdrungen," *Zionsbote*, 20 August 1924, 3-4; "Wunderbare Gebetserhoerungen," 24 September 1924, 2-3.

15. H. W. Lohrenz to N. N. Hiebert, 29 March 1925, H. W. Lohrenz Papers; J. H. Lohrenz to H. W. Lohrenz, 1 June 1925, John Lohrenz File; J. H. Voth to J. W. Wiens, 1 December 1925, John Voth File, CMBS/F.

16. Maria Pankratz, "Aus der Shamshabad Missionsschublade ("mission drawer)," *Zionsbote*, 18 July 1923, 3; cf. the J. F. Harms and Jacob Heinrich ex-

change under the title, "Ein Versuch zur Erklaerung," *Zionsbote*, 26 August 1903, 2-3. See Chapter Two.

17. Maria Pankratz, "Allerlei aus der Missionsschublade," *Zionsbote*, 18 July 1923, 2-3; "Nur kurz ueber Missionsarbeit," 18 September 1923, 3-4.

18. J. H. Pankratz, from Ootacumund, to H. W. Lohrenz, 13 June 1922, Lohrenz Papers, CMBS/F.

19. C. H. Unruh, "Lieber Bruder (Hermann) Neufeld," ed., *Mennonitische Rundschau*, 8 April 1925, 8-9.

20. C. H. Unruh had received about $4,000. during the period under discussion. Most of that came for famine relief **before** their furlough in 1922-4; cf. lists of money contributions, in *Zionsbote*, 10 September 1919, 14; and 22 September 1920, 14.

21. C. H. Unruh to Herman Neufeld, *MR*, 8 April 1925, 8-9.

22. *Ibid.*; J. H. Pankratz backed away from his criticism when he discovered that some field preachers were more to blame than Cornelius Unruh; cf. J. H. Pankratz to "Liebe Geschwister," 26 May 1923, and 13 July 1925, Pankratz File, Box 12; J. H. Lohrenz to H. W. Lohrenz, 1 June 1925, H. W. Lohrenz Papers, CMBS/F.

23. K. L. Schellenberg to Helen L. Warkentin, at home in Winkler, Manitoba, 31 October 1927, Warkentin File; J. H. Lohrenz, "Aus Indien," *Zionsbote*, 16 November 1927, 4-6.

24. N. N. Hiebert, "Bruder Missionar Franz A. Janzen in Indien heimgegangen," *Zionsbote*, 26 October 1927, 3.

25. J. H. Lohrenz, "Aus Indien," *Zionsbote*, 16 November 1927, 4-6.

26. According to regulations, the remains needed to be buried the next day, on Sunday, the 9th; K. L. Schellenberg to Helen L. Warkentin, 31 October 1927, Warkentin File, CMBS/F.

27. D. F. Bergthold, "Aus Indien," *Zionsbote*, 21 December 1927, 4.

28. D. F. Bergthold, "Aus Indien, 11 *Zionsbote*, 28 March 1928, 2; Ed. B. Montgomery, "Aemtliche Bestaetigung des Todesfalles (official confirmation of the cause of death) von Missionar Janzen," *Zionsbote*, 4 April 1928, 3.

29. M. C. Wall to H. L. Warkentin, 12 November 1927; K. L. Schellenberg wrote Helen Warkentin that Frank Janzen had told his wife Elizabeth: "Ich habe alles durchgekaempft (I have been victorious in my struggles)," 31 October 1927, Warkentin File, CMBS/F.

30. The Wanaparty Church, "Ein Anerkennungschreiben zu Ehren des Rev. Janzen," *Zionsbote*, 18 April 1928, 2-3.

31. J. H. Lohrenz also pointed to the compounder (mixer of medicines) as "the most bitter enemy the Janzens had" and that he may have been guilty; J. H. Lohrenz to H. W. Lohrenz, 1 November 1927, H. W. Lohrenz Papers.

32. *Ibid.*

33. K. L. Schellenberg to H. L. Warkentin, 31 October 1927, Warkentin File, CMBS/F.

34. Anna Jungas Hiebert told the author this story at Jadcherla in 1973 when he visited the Canadian missionaries on site. She named "Sukko Paul" as the cook. Viola B. Wiebe, who arrived in India in 1927, two years before Anna, confirmed that "months later, the Janzens' cook admitted that the compounder had given him poison to put into the *dora's* (master's) food," in *Sepia Prints: Memoirs of a Missionary in India* (Winnipeg: Kindred Press, 1990), 58.

35. Cf. Elizabeth Janzen, Mission Report, *CC Yearbook* (Herbert, 1928), 39; N. N. Hiebert, Mission Report, *GC Yearbook* (1933), 15.

36. N. N. Hiebert, *Missions=Album aus der Mission der Mennoniten Bruedergemeinde* (Hillsboro: MB Publishing House, 1914, 25; Pankratz felt the covert criticism for taking their children back to India in 1920, when the Bergtholds had just done the same; J. H. Pankratz to H. W. Lohrenz, 13 June 1922, Lohrenz Papers, CMBS/F.

37. J. H. Voth, "Auf der Reise," *Zionsbote*, 7 March 1928, 2-3; "Versdhiedenes aus Indien," 12 June 1929, 2-3; "Auf der Reise," 18 April 1934, 3-4; Theodore Voth to Peter Penner, 10 April 1992, Peter Penner Collection.

38. V. B. Wiebe, "Little Missionaries," in *India* (1948), ed. A. E. Janzen, 127.

39. Waldo Penner to Peter Penner, 19 June 1990; Hulda Penner to Peter Penner, 12 June 1990; Hulda and Erna Penner, interview by author, Kitchener, 26 August 1989, Peter Penner Collection.

40. Henry C. Unruh to Peter Penner, 2 February 1992, Peter Penner Collection.

## CHAPTER 8

1. John A. Wiebe to J. W. Wiens, 12 February 1933, John A. Wiebe Papers, M 185; N. N. Hiebert to J. W. Wiens, 5 October 1929, J. W. Wiens File, 250-6-2, CMBS/F.

2. A. E. Janzen, "Missionary Dynamic Develops in America," in T*he Church in Mission: A Sixtieth Anniversary Tribute to J. B. Toews*, ed. A. J. Klassen (Hillsboro: Board of Christian Literature, 1967), 156, 162.

3. J. W. Warkentin, "Die Schulsache," *CC Yearbook* (1931), 48; (1932), 49.

4. Cf. the positive accounts in J. H. Voth, ed., *Ein Jahr unter den Telugus* (Hyderabad, 1929); D. F. Bergthold, ed., *Licht und Schatten: Achtzehn Berichte von Arbeitern* (Nagarkurnool, 1931); H. W. Lohrenz, ed., *Unsere Mission in Indien: Berichte von Arbeitern* (Hillsboro, 1939); and Bergthold's inference that the missionaries being sent out were not filled with the Holy Spirit, but with "*Eifersucht u. Eigenwill*" (extreme individualism and self-will); Bergthold to Heinrich Voth, 10 January 1919, Bergthold File, CMBS/F.

5. A. E. Janzen, *Foreign Missions: The American Mennonite Brethren Mission in India, 1898 to 1948* (Hillsboro: BFM, 1948), 168.

6. J. H. Pankratz was not engaged to teach. There seemed to be questions raised about his qualifications and his temporary disorientation from the Mission; J. H. Pankratz to H. W. Lohrenz, 7 August 1930, Lohrenz Papers, CMBS/F.

7. (N. N. Hiebert), "Die Tabor Bibel=und Missionsschule fuer 1931-1932", *Zionsbote*, 29 July 1931, 3-4.

8. Open letter from "Das Direktorium von Tabor College," *Zionsbote*, 4 October 1933, 10-11; J. H. Lohrenz, "Lohrenz, Henry W. (1878-1945)," *ME*, III, 386.

9. H. W. Lohrenz to J. N. C. Hiebert, 23 March 1931, Lohrenz Papers, CMBS/F.

10. H. W. Lohrenz to J. H. Lohrenz, 14 May 1930 and 15 February 1931, Lohrenz Papers, CMBS/F; H. W. Lohrenz wrote K. L. Schellenberg in India that "what had taken years to build some persons could tear down in short order," 14 May 1930, Henry Lohrenz Papers, CMBS/F.
Lohrenz was caught between those who held the "liberal arts ideal with its cultural connections" and those who wanted at best a "fundamentalist College and Bible School." See Paul Toews, "Henry W. Lohrenz and Tabor College," *Mennonite Life* 38 (September 1983), 11-19; and "Fundamentalist Conflict in Mennonite Colleges: A Response to Cultural Transitions?" *Mennonite Quarterly Review* 57 (July 1983), 241-256.

11. Cf. N. N. Hiebert, "Eine Missions= und Bibelschule;" H. W. Lohrenz, "Einige Grundzuege zur Einrichtung einer Bibel= und Missionsschule," and "An den werten Bundesgemeinden," *Zionsbote*, 6 August 1930, 2-4; H. W. Lohrenz to A. E. Janzen, 15 March 1932, Lohrenz Papers, CMBS/F.

12. Instead, the pattern of administration established seemed to have everything to do with seniority and pride of place in India, and a struggle for control

between Mountain Lake/Hillsboro and Shamshabad/Deverakonda. Personalities seemed more important than policies and issues.

13. D. F. Bergthold to H. W. Lohrenz, 24 March and 17 July 1933, Lohrenz Papers, CMBS/F.

14. D. F. Bergthold to H. W. Lohrenz, 24 March and 27 April 1933, Lohrenz Papers, CMBS/F; N. N. Hiebert, "Bericht vom Missionskomitee," *Zionsbote*, 12 April 1933, 2-3; Bergthold, "Nach dem fernen Osten," *Zionsbote*, 2 August 1933, 4.

15. D. F. Bergthold to J. W. Wiens, 20 March 1934, Bergthold File; cf. Bergthold to H. W. Lohrenz, 24 March, 17 April and 17 July 1933, Lohrenz Papers, CMBS/F. The word **geistig** used by Bergthold has two possible meanings: mental or spiritual. Since one could hardly think of Nicolai Hiebert as unspiritual, Bergthold may have been expressing a feeling current for some time that Hiebert's weak nerves made him less than competent to deal with the issues of the Mission.

16. N. N. Hiebert, "Ein Bericht vom Missionskomitee," *Zionsbote*, 12 April 1933, 2-3; D. F. Bergthold to (H. W. Lohrenz), 27 April 1933, Lohrenz Papers, CMBS/F.

17. D. F. Bergthold, "Nach dem fernen Osten: Indien," *Zionsbote*, 2 August 1933, 3-4.

18. N. N. Hiebert, "Einige Missionsfragen," *Zionsbote*, 27 September 1933, 2.

19. N. N. Hiebert, "Ein oeffentliches Wort von der Heidenmission," *Zionsbote*, 14 August 1935, 2.

20. N. N. Hiebert, "Ein oeffentliches Wort der Teilnahme [sympathy]," *Zionsbote*, 15 May 1935, 2; this concerned the terrible dust storm which engulfed Kansas, Oklahoma, and Texas.

21. *GC Yearbook* (Hepburn, 1930), 17.

22. The following amounts were paid out from the General and Specifics Fund, but not including the Trust Fund:

**1915-1930**

| | | |
|---|---|---|
| 1914-1915 | $23,702 X 3 = | $71,106 |
| 1918-1919 | 80,743 X 3 = | 242,229 |
| 1920-1921 | 81,037 X 3 = | 243,111 |
| 1921-1924 | | 245,446 |
| 1924-1927 | | 215,400 |
| 1927-1930 | | 200,120 |
| | | |
| 1915-1930 | | $1,217,412. |

**1930-1945**

| 1930-1933 | 161,839 |
|---|---|
| 1933-1936 | 120,268 |
| First mention in 1936-9 of a "Pension Fund" (4,216) | |
| 1936-1939 | 139,039 |
| 1939-1942 | 195,405 |
| 1942-1945 | 444,665 |
| | |
| 1930-1945 | $1,061,216 |

Source: *GC Yearbooks* (1915-1945), varying pagination for the Financial Statement of the Board of Foreign Missions, Hillsboro.

23. H. W. Lohrenz to N. N. Hiebert, 23 March 1931; and Hiebert to Lohrenz, 26 August 1931, Lohrenz Papers, CMBS/F.

24. N. N. Hiebert, "Ein kurzer Bericht vom Missions komitee," *Zionsbote*, 23 September 1931, 2; "Ein oeffentliches Wort ueber unsere Heidenmission," 23 March 1932, 2-3; ""Ein Wort vom Missionskomitee," 8 June 1932, 2-3; also 10 August 1932, 2; *CC Yearbook* (Herbert, 1932), 29.

25. *GC Yearbook* (Hillsboro, 1933), 17, 46; (Corn, 1939), 23-24.

26. J. H. Voth, "Eine Angelegenheit," *Zionsbote*, 13 June 1934, 2.

27. J. H. Voth, "Zum Abschied," *Zionsbote*, 18 January 1928, 3; N, N. Hiebert, "Ein Bericht vom Missionskomitee," *Zionsbote,* 12 April 1933, 2-3. His position on this was almost heroic in light of his family circumstances. He believed that God had said a decided 'NO' to pensions; see "Einige Missionsfragen," *Zionsbote*, 27 September 1933, 3.

28. H. W. Lohrenz, "Bericht vom Missionkomitee," *CC Yearbook* (Winkler, 1937), 13.

29. D. F. Bergthold's criticisms in 1933 and 1934 may have helped to induce this resignation; cf. Bergthold to "das Missionskomitee," 27 April 1933, H. W. Lohrenz Papers; and Bergthold to J. W. Wiens, 20 March 1934, Wiens File CMBS/F.

30. *GC Yearbook* (Reedley, 1936), 12-14; (Corn, 1939), 6-7; cf. N. N. Hiebert, "Ein oeffentliches Wort bezueglich unserer Heidenmission," *Zionsbote*, 30 December 1936, 3-4.

31. J. H. Lohrenz to H. W. Lohrenz, 11 April 1931, J. H. Lohrenz Papers, CMBS/F; cf. James Juhnke, *A People of Mission: A History of General Conference Mennonite Overseas Mission* (Newton: Faith and Life Press, 1979), 102-103.

32. John H. Voth and Anna Hanneman, eds., *Ein Jahr unter den Telugus* (Hyderabad: M. B. Mission, 1929); see J. H. Voth, "Aus Indien," *Zionsbote*, 7 May

1930, 6; D. F. Bergthold, *Licht und Schatten: Achtzehn Berichte von Arbeitern* (Nagarkurnool: Amerikanische M. B. Mission, 1931).

33. J. N. C. Hiebert to H. W. Lohrenz, 31 August 1931, John Hiebert File, A 250-6-2, CMBS/F.

34. J. N. C. Hiebert to H. W. Lohrenz, 31 August 1931; Catharine Reimer was at Nagarkurnool when John Hiebert managed to get *Harvest Field* started: Reimer to H. W. Lohrenz, 6 August 1936, Catharine Reimer File, CMBS/F; Elizabeth Balzer, ed., *Harvest Field* 2 (June 1937), 2.

35. H. W. Lohrenz to J. N. C. Hiebert, 19 December 1939, 21 October 1940, 17 July 1941; Hiebert to Lohrenz, 20 January 1942, Lohrenz Papers, CMBS/F; cf. H. W. Lohrenz's comment about *Harvest Field*, in *Greetings* (1941), 16.

36. H. W. Lohrenz, ed., *Unsere Mission in Indien: Berichte von Arbeitern* (Hillsboro: BFM, 1936), 5-13; cf. J. H. Lohrenz to H. W. Lohrenz, 18 April 1939, John Lohrenz File, CMBS/F.

37. J. H. Lohrenz to H. W. Lohrenz, 12 January 1940, Henry Lohrenz Papers, CMBS/F.

38. J. N. C. Hiebert to Anna Hiebert (Mrs. H. T.) Esau, 11 June 1940, Hiebert File, CMBS/F. Even if a sub-editor was involved, Henry Lohrenz was responsible for the sentences which spoke of the "temperate climate," and "the same cereal grains" in fields "neither barren nor poor," nor "many handicaps to a life of health and happiness" in India. This was a portrait which he would not have painted had he visited India, in *Our Mission Among the Telugus* (Hillsboro, 1939), 8.

39. Missionary Council, Minutes, 3-5 January 1940; H. W. Lohrenz, having received encouragement from J. A. Wiebe to make revisions, had hoped he would be "forgiven for making considerable changes." He wasn't!. Cf. J. A. Wiebe to H. W. Lohrenz, 17 August 1939 and 1 and 3 March 1941; Lohrenz to Wiebe, 5 October 1939 and 1 February 1941, John A. Wiebe File, CMBS/F.

40. See H. W. Lohrenz, "Sister Anna Hanneman," in *Greetings* (May 1943), 4-14; "Memorial to John H. Voth," in *Greetings* (October 1943), 15-35; J. H. Lohrenz, "Henry W. Lohrenz," in Memorial Number, *Greetings,* ed. A. E. Janzen (March 1946).

41. Cf. the advertisement for a booklet by John H. and Maria Lohrenz, *Glaubenshelden (Heroes of Faith) in der christlichen Heidenmission* in *Zionsbote,* 3 September 1919, 15; and J. H. Lohrenz, Introduction to his *The Mennonite Brethren Church* (Hillsboro: MB Publishing House, 1950), 11.

42. A. E. Janzen to H. R. Wiens, 12 December 1964, H. R. Wiens Papers, M 59, CMBS/F.

43. Peter Penner, "Guardian of the Way: The Farmer-Preacher H. S. Voth, 1878-1953," *Mennonite Life,* 37 (September, 1982), 8-13.

44. John B. Toews, interview by author, Fresno, 17 January 1989; cf. J. B. Toews, *The MB Church in Zaire* (Fresno: BCL, 1978), 60-1. H. W. Lohrenz could not have full confidence in this **Verein** because there were too many 'Allianz' people (those MB not strict about baptism by immersion) in it; H. W. Lohrenz to J. H. Lohrenz, 14 November 1938, John Lohrenz File, CMBS/F.

45. See *Missionary Album* (Hillsboro: BFM, 1951), 28.

46. A. A. Unruh to H. W. Lohrenz, 25 July 1939, Unruh File, CMBS/F; A. A. Unruh, "Aus Indien," *Zionsbote*, 12 October 1938, 2-3.

47. While the Dicks were grateful that Helga, with her Russian and German, was able to begin her schooling in English, they found the nine-month separation "terribly hard." Jacob J. Dick, "Aus Indien," *Zionsbote*, 3 October 1934, 2; 23 January 1935, 2. The Dicks were immediately exposed to Hindi, Telugu, and English languages; J. J. Dick, "Teure Geschwister (blood relatives in Coaldale, Alberta)," 16 April 1934, J. J. Dick Papers, M 173, CMBS/F. He began to serialize their story in Canada: "Erlebnisse: Von Geschwister J. Dueck, Indien," *Mennonitische Rundschau*, 11 September 1935, 8 (five instalments); cf. *From Exile in Russia into Mission Work in India* (Gretna: Private, 1940, complete with map).

48. J. J. Dick, "Aus Indien," *Zionsbote*, 3 October 1934, 2-3.

49. N. N. Hiebert, "Ein oeffentliches Wort vom Missions komitee," *Zionsbote*, 30 May 1934, 2-3; Maria Lohrenz, "Aus Indien," *Zionsbote*, 26 September 1934, 2. H. W. Lohrenz to J. W. Wiens, 24 May 1935, Lohrenz Papers, CMBS/F.

50. J. J. Dick to William Dick, Ontario, 17 June 1936; Helga did very well at Breeks Memorial during these years, standing at the head of her class in 1938; J. J. Dick to H. W. Lohrenz, 30 July 1939, Dick File, CMBS/F.

51. J. J. Dick to H. W. Lohrenz, 4 November 1937, 20 January and 14th April 1939, Dick File, CMBS/F.

52. J. J. Dick to H. W. Lohrenz, 16 November 1942, Dick File, CMBS/F.

53. J. J. Dick to A. E. Janzen, 17 July 1945, Dick File.

54. Jacob P. Klahsen, "Memoir" (1979), 24 pages, in Peter Penner Collection; for a reference to Katie Huebert en route to Canada, see A. H. Neufeld, ed., *Hermann and Katharina (Neufeld), Their Story* (Winnipeg: CMBS, 1984), 152.

55. J. P. Klahsen to Peter Penner, (Spring 1990), Peter Penner Collection.

56. Board of Foreign Mission, Minutes, 21 March 1945, A 250-0-2, CMBS/F; A. A. Unruh, "Aus Indien," *Zionsbote,* 3 July 1946, 3-4.

57. J. A. Wiebe, "Report from India," *Christian Leader,* July 1945, 6-7.

## CHAPTER 9

1. The union-like seniority ranking which these first American missionaries established dictated that junior missionaries were upstaged only through apprenticeship and then journeyman years until the mid-fifties.
The term "in station" comes from the life of the English 'district collector' who, when not touring his district or away 'in the hills,' was available at his **kutcherry** (**office**) or bungalow for consultation.

2. Paul G. Hiebert, interview by author, Fresno, 6 November 1988, Peter Penner Collection.

3. John and Maria Pankratz, "Zur Erklaerung [in explanation of our long stay in America]," *Zionsbote*, 3 September 1930, 6-7; cf. J. H. Pankratz to H. W. Lohrenz, 7 August 1930, H. W. Lohrenz Papers, CMBS/F.

4. J. H. Pankratz, "Nur voran," *Zionsbote*, 9 November 1938, 2-3; cf. Board of Foreign Missions, Minutes, 9 April 1938, A 250-0-2, CMBS/F. Leaving their children in America was more traumatic than ever. Regarding Hughestown, see J. H. Pankratz to the Board, 24 January 1940, Pankratz File; Pankratz, from Los Angeles, to H. W. Lohrenz, 6 January 1943; J. H. Lohrenz to H. W. Lohrenz, 27 February, 1 May and 2 July 1943, H. W. Lohrenz Papers, CMBS/F.

5. J. H. Pankratz and Children, "Maria Pankratz," *Zionsbote*, 16 April 1941, 2-5; Elizabeth D. Janzen to Anne and Marie Harder, Buhler, 15 October 1940; Maria C. Wall to Anne and Marie Harder, 26 November 1940, M. C. Wall File, CMBS/F.
Gerhard W. Peters, "Das Abend=und Morgenrot unsres Missionaren J. H. Pankratz," *Zionsbote*, 24 September 1952, 5-6; Peters, "John H. Pankratz's Contribution to our Mission Cause," *Christian Leader*, 1 December 1952, 8-9.

6. Elizabeth D. Janzen to Anne and Marie Harder, 15 October 1940; to H. W. Lohrenz, 14 August 1942 and 9 March 1943, Elizabeth D. Janzen File, CMBS/F; Arnold Janzen to Peter Penner, 1 November 1993, Peter Penner Collection.

7. H. W. Lohrenz to E. D. Janzen, 12 January 1943; Janzen to Lohrenz, 31 May 1944; Janzen to Herwanna Chapter, Buhler, 9 December 1944; Janzen to Abram E. Janzen (who replaced Henry W. Lohrenz as secretary of the Board of Foreign Missions), 17 October 1945, E. D. Janzen File, CMBS/F.
Elizabeth Janzen, "Aus Indien," *Zionsbote*, 25 July 1945, 3; "Work and Experience in the City [of Hyderabad]," in *Foreign Missions: The American Mennonite Brethren Mission in India*, ed. A. E. Janzen (Hillsboro: BFM, 1948), 93-96.

8. A. R. Epp, Obituary Notice for Elizabeth Janzen, *Zionsbote*, 6 December 1960, 8. Her sons inherited the land their mother had owned and rented out to a Buhler farmer; Arnold Janzen to Peter Penner, 1 November 1993, Peter Penner Collection.

9. Cf. J. H. Voth, "Reisenotizen und Missionsgedanken," *Zionsbote*, 6 January 1943, 2-3; "To the Readers of the Christian Leader," *Christian Leader*, September 1937, 5-6.

10. J. H. Voth to N. N. Hiebert, 9 February 1933, John H. Voth Papers, M 204, CMBS/F; Voth, "Auf Missionsreisen hierzulande," *Zionsbote*, 26 September 1934, 3-4.

11. J. H. Voth, "Kurze Missionsnachrichten," *Zionsbote*, 6 March 1935, 3-4; Voth, "Missionsnachrichten," 14 April 1937, 2-3.

12. J. H. Voth, "Meine Eindruecke von unserm herrlichen Amerika nach unsrer Rueckkehr von Indien [translated: what has happened to our wonderful America?]," *Zionsbote*, 5 May 1937, 2-3; he took aim at tobacco use, a sinking of the moral tone and language; for Mabel Lossing, see "Eli Stanley Jones," *Current Biography* (1940), 438-440.

13. J. H. Voth, "Aus Indien," *Zionsbote*, 12 November 1930, 2-3.

14. J. H. Voth, "Aus Indien," *Zionsbote*, 15 April 1931, 3; 4 April 1934, 2. Elizabeth and Sarah, honors graduates from Breeks Memorial school, were teaching in Kansas; Menno was at Tabor College; Theodore, Mathilda, and Hugo were studying at Ootacumund. Voth rated Ootacumund very highly; "Verschiedenes aus Indien," Zionsbote, 12 June 1929, 2-3. The last separation in 1937 was the most difficult. "If only we could have had our work as well as our children with us," Voth wrote. He thanked those in the constituency who understood the nature of the sacrifices made by the children; "Missionsprobleme," *Zionsbote*, 25 June 1941, 2-3.

15. J. A. Wiebe to H. W. Lohrenz, 20 July and 10 August 1939, Wiebe File; Wiebe to Lohrenz, 3 August 1939, Lohrenz Papers, CMBS/F.

16. In 1939 Voth objected to lumping church statistics together. He wanted the fields 'individualized' so that his achievements would look good; J. A. Wiebe to H. W. Lohrenz, 3 August 1939, Lohrenz Papers; cf. J. H. Voth, *Ein Jahr unter den Telugus* (Hyderabad: M. B. Mission, 1929), 22; Peter M. Hamm, *India: Mennonite Brethren Church Statistical Report, 1970* (Shamshabad: M. B. Mission, 1970), 26, 65; and H. W. Lohrenz, ed., *Our Mission Among the Telugus* (Hillsboro: BFM, 1939), 18; cf. J. H. Lohrenz to H. W. Lohrenz, 12 January 1940, H. W. Lohrenz Papers; and John N. C. Hiebert to Anna Hiebert, Herwana Chapter, Buhler Mennonite Brethren Church, 11 June 1940, John Hiebert File, CMBS/F.

17. H. W. Lohrenz to J. A. Wiebe, 16 July 1943; Wiebe to Lohrenz, 6 October 1943, Lohrenz Papers, CMBS/F.

18. J. A. Wiebe to H. W. Lohrenz, 22 September 1943, Wiebe File, CMBS/F; P. C. Hiebert, "Zum Andenken an Missionar J. H. Voth," *Zionsbote*, 18 August 1943, 3-4; (Theodore Voth, Platteville, WI), "Mrs. J. H. [Maria Epp] Voth," in *Mennonite Brethren Herald*, 4 October 1968, 9.

19. A. E. Janzen, "Bergthold Memorial Press Building in India," *Morning Light*, 1 July 1954, 2-3, CMBS/F; the most recent Bethany Bible Institute building at Shamshabad is also named after Daniel F. Bergthold.

20. Daniel F. and Anna Suderman Bergthold to Martha Bergthold (Pullman), 7 July 1935, in Peter Penner Collection.

21. D. F. Bergthold, "Dear Fellow Believers," *Zionsbote*, 24 April 1946, 3.

22. J. H. Lohrenz and J. A. Wiebe, "In Memoriam: D. F. Bergthold, 1876-1948," *Christian Leader*, 1 December 1948, 7-8, 11-12; Viola Bergthold Wiebe, "Zum Andenken an Anna Suderman Bergthold (1875-1957)," *Zionsbote*, 12 June 1957, 5.

23. K. L. Schellenberg to H. W. Lohrenz, 16 October 1930 and 10 August 1941; to Miss K. Schellenberg, 12 March 1931; Lohrenz to Schellenberg, 5 August 1936, Lohrenz Papers, CMBS/F.

Margaret Suderman and Anna Suderman, co-workers at Wanaparty, observed the physical decline of Katharina L. Schellenberg. Though often "in agony" she "still keeps going;" Margaret Suderman to the Board of Foreign Missions, 10 August 1944, Margaret Suderman File, CMBS/F.

Dr. Schellenberg's life inspired a number of eulogies: J. H. Lohrenz, "The Home-Going of Katharina L. Schellenberg (1870-1945)," *Christian Leader*, March 1945, 5; Nettie Berg, "37 Years of Missionary Service in India," *Mennonite Observer*, 19 August 1960, 7; Naoma Jantz, "Continuously on call for God," *Mennonite Brethren Herald*, 22 June 1984, 23.

24. K. L. Schellenberg, "Aufgaben u. Pruefungen des Lebens," *Zionsbote*, 19 July 1939, 2-3.

25. K. L. Schellenberg, "From India," *Zionsbote*, 25 August 1943, 4.

26. A. Hanneman to H. W. Lohrenz, 6 January 1938, 8 June 1939, and 21 February 1940; Lohrenz to Hanneman, 12 July 1939, Lohrenz Papers, CMBS/F.

27. A. Hanneman to H. W. Lohrenz, 6 January 1938, Lohrenz Papers, CMBS/F; J. H. Voth, "Aus Indien," *Zionsbote*, 7 May 1930, 6-7.

28. K. L. Schellenberg to Miss K. Schellenberg, 12 March 1931, H. W. Lohrenz Papers, CMBS/F.

29. A. Hanneman to H. W. Lohrenz, 3 December 1936, 6 September 1937, 3 August 1939, Lohrenz Papers, CMBS/F; Anna Hanneman, "Aus Indien," *Zionsbote*, 8 May 1935, 2-3; H. W. Lohrenz, "Sister Anna Hanneman: a short biography," in *Greetings*, May 1943, 4-14.

This search for a renewal experience compares with that of Johann G. Wiens at Coimbatore, 1906.

30. H. W. Lohrenz, "Sister Anna Hanneman;" and J. H. Voth, "An Appreciation of Sister Anna Hanneman," in *Greetings*, May 1943, 4-14 and 15-18, respectively.

31. J. H. Lohrenz to J. W. Wiens, 1 December 1930 and 18 April 1932; on the rate of exchange there were five letters between May and July 1940 in the John Lohrenz File; J. H. Lohrenz to H. W. Lohrenz, 2 December 1941 and 16 July 1943, Henry Lohrenz Papers, CMBS/F.

32. J. H. Lohrenz, "Aus Indien," *Zionsbote*, 11 September 1935, 2-3; see index on **famines** in India.

33. Peter V. Balzer, "Aus Indien," *Zionsbote*, 17 October 1937, 2.

34. J. H. Lohrenz to J. W. Wiens, 1 July 1931. J. H. Lohrenz File; J. H. Lohrenz, "Aus Indien," *Zionsbote*, 8 March 1933, 2-3.

35. J. H. Lohrenz, *A Life for Christ in India: Mrs. Maria Lohrenz, 1892-1962* (Hillsboro: BFM, 1963), 28-29.

36. Maria Klaassen Lohrenz, Diary, vol. 1, 1 September 1929, 54; 22 April 1933, 103; 13 August 1935, 131; the 1935 surgery involved, as she wrote, a "fibroid-tumor in my uterus." Only a few days later she was diagnosed with typhoid fever, 2 September 1935, 132, in J. H. Lohrenz Papers, CMBS/F.
In 1933 the Canadian conference delegates at Dalmeny were told that Elizabeth Balzer needed time to recuperate, preferably in a dry climate like Arizona; *CC Yearbook* (Dalmeny, 1933), 53.

37. In 1947, with respect to "married missionaries" (this term referred only to wives) it was stated that "the Board will consider the educational requirements met when the husband meets the standards herein set forth." The wife should accept the clauses on "responsibility" equally with her husband, and "acquire as much other training as family circumstances allow." Abram E. Janzen, ed., *Foreign Missions: Guiding Principles and Field Policies* (Hillsboro: BFM, 1947), 4.

38. N. N. Hiebert, *GC Yearbook* (1933), 23, 25; P. V. Balzer to H. W. Lohrenz, 4 April 1933; Lohrenz to Balzer, 13 April 1933), Lohrenz Papers, CMBS/F; P. V. Balzer, "Nach langem Schweigen [after a long silence]," *Zionsbote*, 25 July 1934, 2-3.

39. PVB, *Zionsbote*, "Vom Missionsfelde in Indien", 52/45 (4 November 1936), 3; 53/36 (4 September 1937), 2

40. Helen. L. Warkentin, "School Boardings," *India* (1948), ed. A. E. Janzen, 110-113.

41. M. C. Wall to J. W. Wiens, 18 October 1930; to H. W. Lohrenz, 24 February 1938, Maria Wall File; Board of Foreign Mission, Minutes, "Ueber die Beschuldigungen (about the charges against Warkentin)," 9 April 1938, M. C. Wall File, CMBS/F.
Isaac Voth (brother of John H. Voth), "Abschiedsfest der Schwester Helena Warkentin," *Zionsbote*, 16 November 1938, 3.

42. M. C. Wall to Maria and Ann Harder, 26 November 1940, Maria Wall File, CMBS/F; M. C. Wall, "Aus Indien," *Zionsbote*, 26 May 1943, 3-4; 4 July 1945, 2-3.

43. H. L. Warkentin, "Kostschulen [Boarding Schools], oder Kinder, die der Mission zur Erziehung uebergeben sind," in *Licht und Schatten*, ed. D. F. Bergthold, 1931, 53-7; A. S. Joshua, *Mother Helen Leena Warkentin of Deverakonda* (Hyderabad: MB Philadelphia Church, 1975); M. B. John, *A Brief Story of the Life of Rev. and Mrs. M. B. John, from 1908 to 1983* (Mahbubnagar: Calvary MB Church, 1983), 6.

44. See H. W. Lohrenz correspondence with J. C. Robbins of the ABMU, January 1936 to February 1940, CMBS/F.

45. J. H. Lohrenz to H. W. Lohrenz, 9 March 1927, Henry Lohrenz Papers, CMBS/F.

46. *Ibid*.

47. J. A. Wiebe to J. W. Wiens, 31 October 1930 and 14 July 1931, J. A. Wiebe File, CMBS/F.

48. How Kalvakurty was shortshrifted because of understaffing and niggardly appropriations during the depression years becomes quite clear in A. E. Janzen's *India* (1948), 36; cf. J. A. Wiebe's seven-page letter to H. W. Lohrenz 15 June 1937, Wiebe File, CMBS/F.

49. J. A. Wiebe to H. W. Lohrenz, 12 October 1933, Lohrenz Papers, CMBS/F.

50. J. A. Wiebe to H. W. Lohrenz, 15 February 1939, Wiebe File, CMBS/F.

51. J. N. C. Hiebert to H. W. Lohrenz, 20 January 1942, Hiebert File; J. A. Wiebe to H. W. Lohrenz, 4 February 1942, Wiebe File, CMBS/F.

52. J. A. Wiebe to J. W. Wiens, 9 July 1933, Wiebe Papers, CMBS/F.

53. To the writer's knowledge this is the only suggestion that single men could, should, be employed in overseas mission; J. A. Wiebe to H. W. Lohrenz, 1 July 1942, Wiebe File. For Wiebe's account of the 1942 crisis, see "Sein auserwaehltes Ruestzeug (his chosen vessel]," *Zionsbote*, 26 August 1942, 7-8.

54. J. H. Voth, "Missionsnachrichten," *Zionsbote*, 19 April 1937, 1.

55. J. A. Wiebe to J. W. Wiens, 12 February 1933, Wiebe Papers; to H. W. Lohrenz, 28 October 1937, Wiebe File, CMBS/F.

56. D. F. Bergthold to H. W. Lohrenz, 20 May 1937, Bergthold File; Bergthold, "An Unevangelized Field," *Chistian Leader*, October 1937, 8-9.

57. J. A. Wiebe to H. W. Lohrenz, 25 March 1938, Wiebe File; Wiebe's posses-siveness in all aspects of the Mahbubnagar/Jacherla station becomes more appar-ent in 1952.

58. J. N. C. Hiebert to H. W. Lohrenz, 18 July 1935, Hiebert File, CMBS/F.

59. Maria K. Lohrenz, Diary, vol. 1, 9 December 1940, 233, John Lohrenz Papers, CMBS/F.

60. J. N. C. Hiebert, "Aus Indien," *Zionsbote*, 3 February 1932, 4-5; 19 De-cember 1934, 2; "Ein Wort der Teilnahme [sympathy extended to Viola and her son Paul]," 3 July 1940, 2-3; "Mitteilungen [news] aus der Arbeit," 28 May 1941, 2-3; "Mitteilungen aus Kalvakurty," 4 February 1942, 2.

61. C. A. Reimer, "Auf der Reise nach Indien," *Zionsbote*, 21 January 1931, 2-3; 25 February 1931, 2; 30 March 1932, 3-4.

62. C. A. Reimer to H. W. Lohrenz, 29 July 1937; Reimer to the missionary Council in India (bypassing the BFM), 26 May 1939, Catharine Reimer File; J. H. Lohrenz to H. W. Lohrenz, 31 May 1939, and 1 February 1940, John Lohrenz File; John and Maria K. Lohrenz went to Reimer's funeral; J. H. Lohrenz to H. E. Reimer, 17 April 1962, John Lohrenz Papers, CMBS/F.

63. Margaret Suderman, "Von einer Krankenpflegerin (from a nurse)," *Zionsbote*, 16 May 1928, 2-3; "Aus Indien," 3 December 1930, 2-3.

64. M. Suderman, "Witwen u. waisen," in *Licht und Schatten*, 67-70; "The Ministry of Healing," in *India* (1948), 117-119; M. Suderman to H. W. Lohrenz, 12 February 1936, M. Suderman File, CMBS/F.

65. Anna Suderman, "En Route to India," *Christian Leader*, January 1939, 78; "Dear Christian Friends", May 1939, 8-9.

66. Anna Suderman, "Greetings from India," *Zionsbote*, 8 February 1939, 23; 26 April 1939, 3; "The American Mennonite Brethren Mission Station, Wanaparty," *Christian Leader*, September 1941, 6-7; Laurene Peters, ed., "Memoirs of Anna Suderman, 1902-1981," 1983, CMBS/F.

67. A. Suderman, "Greetings from India," *Zionsbote*, 24 May 1944, 3-4.

68. A. Suderman to H. W. Lohrenz, 25 June 1944, A. Suderman File, CMBS/F.

## CHAPTER 10

1. J. B. Toews, "Mennonite Brethren Identity and Theological Adversity," in *Pilgrims and Strangers: Essays in Mennonite Brethren History*, ed. Paul Toews (Fresno: Center for MB Studies, 1977), 141.

2. See C. Peter Williams, *The Ideal of the Self-Governing Church: A Study in Victorian Missionary Strategy* (Leiden: E. J. Brill, 1990). According to Williams the ideal approach was first defined by Henry Venn, then expanded, threatened, undermined, replaced and compromised. cf. J. Herbert Kane, *Understanding Christian Missions* (Grand Rapids: Baker, 1978), 282.

3. Rufus Anderson, "The Theory of Missions to the Heathen, A Sermon for the Ordination of Mr. Edward Webb as a Missionary to the Heathen," Boston, 1845, in P. D. Curtin, ed. *Imperialism* (New York: Harper and Sons, 1971), 209 ff.; S. F. Pannabecker, "Missions, Foreign Mennonite," ME III, 712; cf. Wilbert R. Shenk, "Missiology," V, 590; *Henry Venn - Missionary Statesman* (Maryknoll: Orbis Books, 1983), 44-6; Alwyn J. Austin, *Saving China: Canadian Missionaries in the Middle Kingdom, 1888-1959* (Toronto: University of Toronto Press, 1986), 336.

4. William R. Hutchison, *Errand to the World: American Protestant Thought and Foreign Missions* (Chicago: University of Chicago Press, 1993).

5. James Patterson, "The Loss of Protestant Missionary Consensus: Foreign Missions and the Fundamentalist-Modernist Controversy," in *Earthen Vessels: American Evangelicals and Foreign Missions, 1880-1980*, ed. J. A. Carpenter and Wilbert Shenk (Grand Rapids: Eerdmans, 1990), 73-90; cf. William E. Hocking, Chair, *Rethinking Missions: A Layman's Inquiry After One Hundred Years* (New York: Harper and Sons, 1932).
Joel A. Carpenter, "Propagating the Faith Once Delivered: The Fundamentalist Missionary Enterprise, 1920-1945," in *Earthen Vessels*, 92-132.

6. Orlando Harms, *Pioneer Publisher: The Life and Times of J. F. Harms* (Winnipeg: Kindred Press, 1984) 87; Peter Penner, *No Longer At Arm's Length: Mennonite Brethren Church Planting in Canada* (Winnipeg: Kindred Press, 1987), 14.

7. See George David Pries, *A Place Called Pniel: Winkler Bible Institute, 1925-1975* (Altona: D. W. Friesen, 1975), 59-60. About twenty of its graduates went into mission work during the years 1925 to 1950, 55-56.

8. See the testimony of Peter Esau, in Peter Penner, *No Longer At Arm's Length*, 25.

9. See J. H. Lohrenz, *The Mennonite Brethren Church* (Hillsboro: BFM, 1950), 144, 158, 172; also Vernon R. Wiebe, *Come Let Us Stand United: A History of the Corn Bible Academy, 1902-1977* (North Newton: Mennonite Press, 1977).

10. David Ewert to Peter Penner, 10 January 1992; this was the general conclusion from a dozen other responses to a questionnaire, in the Peter Penner Collection.

11. G. D. Pries, *A Place Called Pniel*, 37 ff.; *CC Yearbook* (1945), 74-78; for a discussion of Bible schools in Canada, see Peter Penner, *No Longer At Arm's Length*, 24-26.

12. Stephen Neill, *The Story of the Christian Church in India and Pakistan* (Madras: Christian Literature Society, 1972), 149.

13. J. H. Voth, "Verschiedenes aus Indien," Zionsbote, 12 June 1929, 2-3; 6 April 1932, 2.

14. See Eric H. Erikson, *Gandhi's Truth: On the Origins of Militant Nonviolence* (New York: Norton, 1969), 265-277.

15. For "the impact of World War One" on India, and "Toward Independence," see Stanley Wolpert, *A New History of India* (New York: Oxford University Press, 1989), 286-328; the movie *Gandhi* by Richard Attenborough gives a convincing portrait of this period.

16. J. H. Voth, "Probleme im Missionsleben," *Zionsbote*, 9 June 1926, 4-5.

17. Cf. J. H. Voth, *CC Yearbook* (Herbert, 1929), 46-8; Eric Erikson, *Gandhi's Truth*, 265-278. Jacob A. Loewen wrote that Gandhi taught him more about the Anabaptist path to a position of non-resistance than his church peers: "My path to peace," *Mennonite Life* 48 (September 1993), 11-14; cf. Stephen Neill, *The Story of the Christian Church in India*, 149.

18. Andrews, an Anglican clergyman, probably the most widely respected Christian in India, was one of Gandhi's strongest supporters and an early interpreter of what Gandhi's movement meant. See Benarsidas Chaturvedi and Marjorie Sykes, *Charles Freer Andrews: A Narrative* (London: George Allen and Unwin, 1949), 151.

19. J. H. Voth, "Missionsnotizen," *Zionsbote*, 6 January 1937, 2.

20. J. H. Lohrenz, "Aus Indien," *Zionsbote*, 30 March 1938, 2-3; cf. Stephen Neill, *The Christian Church in India*, 129 ff.

21. The great Baptist forerunner in this approach in India was John E. Clough, *Social Christianity in the Orient: The Story of a Man, a Mission, and a Movement*, recorded by his wife, Emma Rauschenbusch Clough (New York: Macmillan, 1914).

22. John H. Voth, *Zionsbote*, 3 May 1925, 2-3; Herbert Kane, *Understanding Christian Missions*, 278 ff., 351 ff.

23. C. H. Unruh to J. H. Voth, 14 January 1917, John Voth Papers, CMBS/F; cf. Franz J. Wiens, "Wohl 'zerschlagen' - aber doch 'froehlich' gemacht," *Das Erntefeld*, January 1913, 4 ff.

24. J. H. Voth, "Prakitsche Fragen auf dem Missionsfelde," *Zionsbote*, 13 April 1927, 3; 15 April 1932, and 5 April 1933, 4; "Einigkeit in der Evangelization," 12 October 1938, 2; 5 April 1939, 2-3; "Ziele u. Aussichten unsrer Missionstaetigkeit," 22 November 1939, 2-3.

25. J. H. Voth, "Ziele u. Aussichten unsrer Missionstaetigkeit," *Zionsbote*, 22 November 1939, 2-3.

26. John C. B. Webster, *The Christian Community and Change in Nineteenth Century North India* (Delhi: Macmillan Company of India, 1976), 227 ff.

27. Peter Penner, "When Paternalism was unavoidable: the Anglican Mission in North India," (paper presented to Humanities Association of Canada, Sackville, New Brunswick Branch, 1980); J. H. Voth, "Einigkeit in der Evangelization," *Zionsbote*, 12 October 1938, 1-2.

28. Cf. David Kopf, *British Orientalism and the Bengal Renaissance: The Dynamics of Indian Modernization, 1773-1834* (Berkeley: University of California Press, 1969); and Daniel E. Potts, *The British Baptist Missionaries in India, 1793-1837: The History of Serampore and Its Missions* (London: Cambridge University Press, 1967).

29. Stanley Wolpert, *A New History of India*, 214. See chart at beginning of Chapter 16.

30. Michael Hollis, *Paternalism and the Church: A Study of South Indian Church History* (London: Oxford University Press, 1962), 51 ff.

31. J. H. Voth, "Praktische Fragen bezueglich Verhaeltnisse im Werk der Mission in Indien," *Zionsbote*, 2 March 1927, 4.

32. See Abram A. Unruh, reporting on a Missionary Council meeting, in "Aus Indien," *Zionsbote*, 8 March 1939, 2-3.

33. J. H. Lohrenz, "Das Zusammenarbeiten (working together) der Missionare mit den eingeborenen Mitarbeiter," *Zionsbote*, 12 November 1930, 3-6.

34. Euthanasia has a different connotation today, but Henry Venn used this term freely to mean withdrawal of support from the emerging church, see Wilbert Shenk, *Henry Venn*, 46, 111, 119.

35. D. F. Bergthold to H. W. Lohrenz, 28 October 1936, 20 May 1937, Bergthold File, CMBS/F.

36. D. F. Bergthold, "Die freiwillige Verkuendigung des Evangeliums," in *Unsere Mission in Indien: Achtzehn Berichte von Arbeitern*, ed. H. W. Lohrenz (Hillsboro: BFM, 1936), 5-13.

37. D. F. Bergthold to H. W. Lohrenz, 7 August 1931, Henry Lohrenz Papers, CMBS/F; Bergthold, "Wieder nach dem fernen Osten," *Zionsbote*, 5 April 1933), 3.

38. D. F. Bergthold, "Die freiwillige Verkuendigung," 9-10; Bergthold to H. W. Lohrenz, 28 October 1936, 22 May 1937, Lohrenz Papers, CMBS/F.

39. N. N. Hiebert, "Einige Missionsfragen," *Zionsbote*, 27 September 1933, 2; cf. Vidyasagar Narimalla, "Does India still need missionaries from North America?" *Mennonite Brethren Herald*, 20 February 1987, 26-27.

40. C. H. Unruh, "Nalgonda," *Mennonitische Rundschau*, 26 August 1936, 5-6.

41. D. F. Bergthold to H. W. Lohrenz, 24 June 1938, Lohrenz Papers, CMBS/F.

42. P. V. Balzer to H. W. Lohrenz, 15 November 1939, Balzer File, CMBS/F.

43. P. C. Hiebert, "Zum Andenken an Missionar J. H. Voth," *Zionsbote*, 18 August 1943), 3-4; J. H. Pankratz, "J. H. Voth, the Unforgettable," in *Greetings* (October 1943), 26.

44. J. H. Lohrenz, "In Memoriam: Daniel F. Bergthold, 1876-1948," *Christian Leader*, 1 December 1948, 7-8, John Lohrenz Papers, CMBS/F; for a reference to Bergthold's "prophet's chamber" on the roof of the Nagarkurnool bungalow, see Viola Bergthold Wiebe, *Sepia Prints: Memoirs of a Missionary in India* (Winnipeg: Kindred Press, 1990), 19.

45. With some encouragement John H. Voth could have been the George Lapp of the AMBM. See John A. Lapp, *The Mennonite Mission in India* (Scottdale: Herald Press, 1972), 138, 145-148. The (Old) Mennonites were more oriented toward social reconstruction, even going so far as to purchase an entire village and act as the traditional **malguzar** (landlord), see "The Mission and Economic Uplift," *Ibid.*, 136 ff.

46. N. N. Hiebert, "Our Foreign Mission Fund," *Christian Leader*, June 1942, 9-10.

47. *Constitution of the Conference of Mennonite Brethren Church of North America* (1936), 27.

48. *GC Yearbook* (Hepburn, 1930), 19, 37.

49. *GC Yearbook* (Reedley, 1936), 23, 25-26.

50. *GC Yearbook* (Buhler, 1943), 10, 17.

51. Paul G. Hiebert, *Anthropological Insights for Missionaries* (Grand Rapids: Baker Book House, 1985), 141 ff.
For Jacob A. Loewen's series on the 'missionary role,' published first between 1964 and 1967, see *Culture and Human Values: Christian Intervention in Anthropological Perspective* (Pasadena: William Carey Library), 349 ff.

52. J. H. Voth, "Reminiscences of and Observations in India," *CL*, March 1943, 5-6. After only two years in India (1909) they accompanied others of the AMBM on

a journey to northern India. At Agra Voth heard Charles F. Andrews speak. To the writer's knowledge Voth never made this trip public until thirty years later.

53. Jacob P. Klahsen to J. C. Robbins, 13 July 1937, J. P. Klahsen Collection, ABAC.

54. J. P. Klahsen to R. L. Howard, New York, 26 February and 1 October 1943; Klahsen Collection, ABAC. The Klahsens remained in India throughout the "Quit India" crisis, not leaving until 1945.

55. See Peter Penner, *No Longer At Arm's Length*, 24, 63-64; cf. *North Saskatchewan District Conference* (May 1940, September 1941).

56. Helen Dueck, interview by author, Coaldale, Alberta, 17 September 1992; see *The Rainbow* (Winnipeg: MBBC Yearbook, 1949).

57. Vernon R. Wiebe to Peter Penner, 9 February 1994, Peter Penner Collection.

58. Helen Harder, "Answers to Questions, [posed by Marie K. Wiens, Hillsboro]," n. d. [early 1970s], Helen Harder File, CMBS-F; Helen Harder, "Shamshabad, India," *Christian Leader*, 1 August 1947, 3-4.

59. Henry G. Krahn, "Reflections on Telugu Language Study," CL, 1 August 1957, 6; cf. P. V. Balzer, "Beobachtungen waehrend des Studiums der Telugu Sprache," *Zionsbote*, 15 October 1924, 4; Peter M. Hamm was probably the only one to study Telugu at university, in his case the University of Wisconsin, see his *Reflections on My Journey* (Abbotsford: Private, 1993), 131, 142-143.

60. *Guiding Principles and Policies* (Hillsboro: BFM, 1961), 19, 32; (1963), 21; (1977), 16 ff.

## CHAPTER 11

1. A. A. Unruh, "Report of my experience at the time of Police Action (September 1948)," 16 pp. longhand, Unruh File, CMBS/W; cf. J. N. C. Hiebert, "Behind the Hyderabad Blockade and Out by Plane (Shamshabad, 1948)," 3 pp., Hiebert File, CMBS/F.

2. Emma Lepp to Abram E. Janzen, 13 September 1948, Emma Lepp File, CMBS/F.

3. A. A. Unruh, "Report of my experience. . . ."; P. V. Balzer to A. E. Janzen, 22 September 1948, Balzer File; J. N. C. Hiebert, 12 August and 15 September 1948, Hiebert File; Jacob J. Dick, 14 and 25 September 1948; Janzen to Dick, 29 September 1948, Dick File, CMBS/F.

The various actions taken raise the question: does the missionary stay with his 'children,' as the Christians from outcaste background were still considered, or does he cut and run in a crisis? If the compound was intended as an enclave, a refuge for the sheep (The Gospel of John, 10), what was it without the shepherd?

4. J. J. Dick, from Kurnool (on the border) and Ootacumund, to A. E. Janzen, 14 and 25 September 1948, Dick File; Julius J. Kasper to A. E. Janzen, 21 September 1948, Kasper File, CMBS/F; J. P. Klahsen to Dr. Smith, 7 October 1948; and to Mr. De Trude, New York, 20 October 1948, Klahsen Collection, ABAC.

5. Stanley Wolpert, *A New History of India*, 3rd. ed. (New York: Oxford University Press, 1989), 351 ff.

6. Theodore H. von Laue, "The Bandung Generation," *The World Revolution of Westernization: The Twentieth Century in Global Perspective* (New York: Oxford University Press, 1987), 239 ff; see Tariq Ali's reference to "Pakistan as a Trojan horse of the Pentagon," in *An Indian Dynasty: The Story of the Nehru-Gandhi Family* (New York: G. P. Putnam's Sons, 1985), 100.

7. John A. Toews, *History* (1975), 438; see the Appendix for a list of all missionaries.

8. John A. Wiebe in a "Personal Letter" to A. E. Janzen, 24 August 1956, and to Janzen, 22 February 1957, "Washington's Birthday," Wiebe File, CMBS/F. Was this a holdover from the *Amerikaner/Russlaender* feelings which surfaced in an earlier decade?

9. J. N. C. Hiebert to H. W. Lohrenz, 22 May 1939, Hiebert File, CMBS/F; Hiebert, "Die Missionskonferenz in Gadwal," *Zionsbote*, 2 April 1941, 2-3; Phyllis H. Martens to Peter Penner, May 1990, Penner Collection.
The cool-season vacations on the plains, when children and parents came together at Missionary Council meetings at one station and had a chance to play with Indian children on the compounds were very meaningful; cf. Ruth Wiebe Friesen, taped response to the author's questionnaire, 1992; cf. Peter M. Hamm, *Reflections on My Journey* (Abbotsford: Private, 1993), 143 ff.

10. Viola B. Wiebe to H. W. Lohrenz, 29 November and 7 December 1943, Lohrenz Papers, CMBS/F; V. B. Wiebe, *Sepia Prints: Memoirs of a Missionary in India* (Winnipeg: Kindred Press, 1990), 98-99.

11. J. N. C. Hiebert to A. E. Janzen, 12 January and 3 March 1948, Hiebert File, CMBS/F.

12. Rose and Herbert Krause, interview by author, Fresno, CA, 12 October 1992; Linda and Jacob Ewert, interview by author, Hillsboro, 1 May 1989, Peter Penner Collection.

13. J. N. C. Hiebert, "A Missionary Home in Kodaikanal," *Christian Leader*, 1 September 1949, 14-15.

14. Ruth Wiebe Friesen, taped response to author's questionnaire, 1992; Penner Collection.

15. J. P. Klahsen to R. L. Howard, New York, 26 February 1943 and 19 October 1943; to C. C. Roardarmel, 10 February 1947, Klahsen Collection, ABAC.

16. Donald J. Unruh, interview by author, Winnipeg, 25 July 1990, Penner Collection.

17. V. B. Wiebe, *Sepia Prints*, 29, 98; from various responses, 1990-1992, Peter Penner Collection.

18. Ted Fast to Peter Penner, 22 September 1991, Penner Collection.

19. Board of Foreign Mission, Minutes, 4 July 1958, 37, CMBS/F.

20. Margaret Willems Balzer told the author she was used to being treated with more respect than she received at Gadwal, interview by author, Saskatoon, February 1989, Penner Collection; A. E. Janzen to Margaret Willems, 30 March 1953, Willems Files; Mary Willems, "Margaret (Willems) Balzer, a Story of Resilient Faith," *Mennonite Brethren Herald*, 19 February 1988, 31-32.

21. Mary Willems, "Margaret (Willems) Balzer, a Story of Resilient Faith;" M. Willems, "TB Wards Dedicated," *Christian Leader*, 15 October 1957, 6-7; the author met Lois and Eunice, now married, in October 1990.

22. Edna Gerdes to Peter Penner, September 1990; this is confirmed by Margaret Willems Balzer, interview by author, Saskatoon, February 1989; and by Rosella Toews who wrote of feeling 'second class,' to Peter Penner, 4 January 1994, Penner Collection.

23. They were also switched from San Francisco to New Orleans as a point of embarkation. Having landed in one place, Colombo, where they met the Dicks going home, they had a most difficult time getting their baggage from another off loading point.

24. Dilwyn B. Studebaker to Peter Penner, 26 July 1991, Penner Collection.

25. Dilwyn and Mildred Studebaker, interview by author, Modesto, CA, 10-11 October 1992; Anna Suderman to A. E. Janzen, 2 April 1953, Suderman File, CMBS/F.

26. A. Suderman to A. E. Janzen, 8 October 1951, Suderman File, CMBS/F.

27. Dilwyn and Mildred Studebaker, interview by author, Modesto, October 1992, Penner Collection; D. B. Studebaker to A. E. Janzen, 3 March and 24 June 1951, Studebaker File, CMBS/F.

28. A. E. Janzen to D. B. Studebaker, 18 January 1951, Studebaker File, CMBS/F.

29. Though R. R. K. Murthy was their **munshi** (teacher), according to their own admission, Mildred never passed the examinations but easily picked up the "bazaar Telugu," whereas Dilwyn finished the language training but was never very fluent in formal Telugu; interview by author, Modesto, CA, 10-11 October 1992, Penner Collection.

30. A. Suderman to A. E. Janzen, 24 May and 29 November 1949, 4 January 1950; Janzen to Suderman, 15 September 1949, Suderman File, CMBS/F.

31. D. B. Studebaker to A. E. Janzen, 13 November 1951, Studebaker Personal File, Peter Penner Collection.

32. A. Suderman, "Ox-Carts or Motor Cars? or Missionary Travel in India," *Christian Leader*, 1 January 1951, 6-7; "Memoirs of Anna Suderman, 1902-1980," 1983, 36-37; A. Suderman to Janzen, 2 January 1952, A. Suderman File; Margaret Suderman to A. E. Janzen, 4 June 1951, M. Suderman File, CMBS/F.
Margaret Suderman "badly bruised" the top of this car when she rolled it over the first time out, see Maria K. Lohrenz, Diary, vol. 3, 26 February 1952, 233.

33. Examples were Helen Harder's 1956 Studebaker from Manitoba young people, see Harder to A. E. Janzen, 24 July 1956; Janzen to Harder, 17 May 1956, Harder File; and Henry G. Krahn's 1957 station wagon from the South Abbotsford congregation; most of the $6,000. for this car came from the Krahn family, Krahn to Janzen, 3 March and 14 July 1958, Krahn File, CMBS/F.

34. D. B. Studebaker, "We Built a House on Wheels," *Christian Leader*, 15 January 1953, 6-7; the Building Committee of the Missionary Council visited Wanaparty in August 1952 and reported that "the four missionaries ... find it very difficult to work together. . . ." John A. Wiebe to A. E. Janzen, 1 September 1952 and 1 April 1953, Wiebe File, CMBS/F.

35. A. Suderman to A. E. Janzen, 12 March and 2 April 1953, A. Suderman File, CMBS/F.

36. A. Suderman to A. E. Janzen, 2 April and 14 June 1953, Suderman File; D. B. Studebaker said that having "fellowship" on the station was "well-nigh impossible," interview by author, Modesto, CA, October 1992, Peter Penner Collection.

37. A. Suderman to A. E. Janzen, 14 June 1953; Janzen to Suderman, 24 July 1956, Suderman File, CMBS/F.

38. A. E. Janzen wrote Anna Suderman that he was being informed about Wanaparty by P. V. Balzer, Helen Harder, Emma Lepp, and A. A. Unruh, 28 August 1953, Suderman File; Jake Friesen reported to the Board on the illnesses plaguing the Studebaker family, 6 May 1954, Friesen File, CMBS/F.

Mildred was very candid with the Sisters Suderman, admitting that Judy was very disturbed. "We cannot leave her here, that is all there is to it." Mildred to Sudermans, 25 May 1954, Studebaker File; cf. Studebakers, interview by author, Modesto, October 1992; Rose Krause, interview by author, Fresno, 12 November 1992; Jake and Linda Ewert, interview by author, Hillsboro, 1 May 1989, Peter Penner Collection.

39. A. A. Unruh, "Das Gebet fuer den Missionsarbeiter," *Zionsbote*, 16 November 1955, 3-4.

40. Upon visiting, Dick requested return of the dining room set. While there were good reasons for wanting to remove that furniture from Wanaparty to Shamshabad, it seemed totally inappropriate to ask for Rupees 100 as a rental charge. See Maria K. Lohrenz, Diary, vol. 3, 29 January 1952, 228, J. H. Lohrenz Papers, CMBS/F; Studebakers, interview by author, Modesto, November 1992, Peter Penner Collection.

41. J. J. Dick to A. E. Janzen, 31 July 1954; he wrote they were "geistlich bankrott [spiritually bankrupt]," Dick to J. B. Toews, 26 September 1954, Dick File; this was a harsh judgment when it is known that the Dicks somehow asked for money from the Studebakers on both occasions.

42. Maria K. Lohrenz, Diary, vol. 4, 31 August and 5 September 1954, 159-160, J. H. Lohrenz Papers, CMBS/F.

43. A. E. Janzen to J. H. Lohrenz, 9 November 1954, Lohrenz File, CMBS/F; Dilwyn and Mildred Studebaker had rewarding careers in teaching and travel agency work, while Judith eventually went into corrections work and today is a police officer; interview by author, Modesto, November 1992, Penner Collection.

44. J. N. C. Hiebert, "Mitteilungen von der Arbeit in Mahbubnagar," *Zionsbote*, 5 December 1951, 6.

45. J. A. Wiebe to A. E. Janzen, 29 March and 1 May 1952, Wiebe File, CMBS/F.

46. On this point J. B. Toews wrote recently: "In the missionary pecking order, older workers dominated the program and the younger missionaries and single women were relegated to secondary roles. Seniority had to be earned over a period of years," in his *JB: The Autobiography of a Twentieth-Century Pilgrim* (Fresno: Center for MB Studies, 1995), 160; cf. Paul Wiebe, in Preface to Viola Bergthold Wiebe, *Sepia Prints*, xiv.

47. Ernest Schmidt's perception was that "motivation [in this case] seemed rooted in 'seniority' where missionaries gradually obtained more prestige, eventually getting a turn at the top," Schmidt, "M. B. Central High School, Mahbubnagar, Hyderabad, India," typescript, 39 pp., submitted to the author, 9-11; interview by author, Sanger, CA, January and May 1989, Peter Penner Collection.

48. Missionary Council, Minutes of Meeting # 75, 25-28 June 1952, CMBS/F; E. E. Schmidt, "M. B. Central High School," 15; J. A. Wiebe to A. E. Janzen, 7 July 1952, Wiebe File, CMBS/F.

49. It may be questioned whether selling the old hospital compound, which Wiebe accomplished after years of trying, was at this time authorized by either the Missionary Council or the BFM, Schmidt, "M. B. Central High School," 11.

50. E. E. Schmidt, "M. B. Central High School," 11-17, Penner Collection; while Janzen believed there was "enough work for two," Wiebe was saying that the bungalow was not built for two families, J. A. Wiebe to A. E. Janzen, 25 February and 19 July, 22 March, and 10 May 1952, Wiebe File, CMBS/F.
   With reference to this situation, M. B. John's comment was: "two missionary families cannot work at one place for want of residential and also ministry problems [sic]," M. B. John to Penner, 9 September 1991, Penner Collection.

51. There is some indication that new church buildings were erected in the hinterland villages in this period, J. A. Wiebe, *Great Things God Hath Done, 1884-1959* (Mahbubnagar: Private, 1959), 12; cf. A. E. Janzen to Wiebe, 22 March 1952, Wiebe File, CMBS/F.

52. J. A. Wiebe to A. E. Janzen, 13 March 1952, and 19 February 1953, Wiebe File, CMBS/F.

53. J. A. Wiebe to A. E. Janzen, 1 September 1952, Wiebe File, CMBS/F; cf. Viola B. Wiebe, interview by author, Hillsboro, April 1989; Ted Fast to Peter Penner, 22 September 1991, Penner Collection.

54. This ethnic struggle between the Telenganas of Mahbubnagar and the Andhras moving in from the south-east was very serious in 1952, but an explanation of it is left to the 1969 situation found in Chapter Sixteen.

55. E. E. Schmidt, "The Beleaguered School against a Backdrop of Political and Social Unrest," in "M. B. Central High School," 21-27; pages of the *Deccan Chronicle* attached, Peter Penner Collection.

56. Cf. Schmidt, "M. B. Central High School," 19; and Wiebe, *Sepia Prints*, 134.

57. In short, John Hiebert's work had been "undone," and the Schmidts felt shortchanged in terms of their assignment, Schmidt, "M. B. Central High School," 19, Penner Collection.

58. Schmidt explained that, by moving away, some of the "negative energies" could be turned into "positive ones," "M. B. Central High School," 29 ff.; when Schmidt was reappointed secretary, A. E. Janzen told J. A. Wiebe, in response to Wiebe's "confidential letter" of 19 February 1954, which is missing, that the requisite Missionary Council files should also go to Schmidt; Janzen to Wiebe, 6 March 1954, Wiebe File, CMBS/F.

59. J. A. Wiebe to A. E. Janzen, 15 and 17 April 1958, Wiebe File, CMBS/F; cf. V. B. Wiebe, *Sepia Prints*, 142.

60. V. B. Wiebe, "The Central High School, and Training Youth," in *The Andhra MB Church of India: Fifty Years in Retrospect, 1904-1954* ed. A. E. Janzen (Hillsboro: BFM, 1954), 22-23; J. A. Wiebe, *Great Things God Hath Done, 1884-1959: Mahbubnagar* (1959), 19 pages; cf. R. S. Aseervadam, "The Mennonite Brethren Church in Andhra Pradesh: A Historical Treatise" (Ph. D. diss., Osmania University, Hyderabad, Andhra Pradesh, 1980), 182-183.

61. Board of Foreign Mission, "Mission News," *Christian Leader*, 25 July 1961, 7. This item stated that the Board "made provision" for the Wiebes to go to Ramapatnam, "felt inwardly led to release" them from the AMBM, and that the Wiebes had "responded with joy" to this alternative service; cf. V. B. Wiebe, *Sepia Prints*, 142, where she revealed a continuing feeling of disappointment twenty years later.

62. J. H. Lohrenz to A. E. Janzen, 16 December 1951, Lohrenz File; Maria Klaassen Lohrenz, Diary, Six Volumes covering the period from June 1918, before India, to December 1960, J. H. Lohrenz Papers, CMBS/F.

63. Maria Lohrenz, Diary, vol. 4, 31 March 1953, 70.

64. A. E. Janzen, *Survey of Five of the Mission Fields . . . India [1949]*, typescript bound, pictorial (Hillsboro: BFM, 1950), 25.

65. Maria Lohrenz, Diary, vol. 3, 1 January 1952, 224; cf. J. H. Lohrenz, from Coonoor, to A. E. Janzen, 18 April 1956, Lohrenz File, CMBS/F.

66. For the further controversy surrounding D. J. Arthur, see Chapter Sixteen, endnote # 57.

67. There is some suggestion that Jacob Dick at Shamshabad may have resented Lohrenz' theology classes, as though they detracted from his work at Bethany Bible School, cf. Maria Lohrenz, Diary, vol 4, 18 January, 10 February, 20 June, and 14 November 1954, Lohrenz Papers; and J. H. Lohrenz to A. E. Janzen, 21 July 1954, Lohrenz File, CMBS/F; Lohrenz, "Von der Missionsarbeit in Hughestown," *Zionsbote*, 22 June 1955, 5-7.

68. "Your loving Brethren in Christ [the Hughestown signers]," to A. E. Janzen, and John Lohrenz, 15 March 1956, Lohrenz File, CMBS/F.

69. J. H. Lohrenz, "Von der Missionsarbeit in Hughestown, Indien," *Zionsbote*, 22 June 1955, 5-7.

70. A. E. Janzen to J. H. Lohrenz, 4 April 1956; Lohrenz to Janzen, 18 April 1956, Lohrenz File, CMBS/F.

71. A. E. Janzen to J. H. Lohrenz, 31 May 1956, Lohrenz File; P. V. Balzer to Janzen, 13 October 1956, Balzer File, CMBS/F.

72. Jake Friesen had serious reservations about Lohrenz' paternalistic attitudes, interview by author, Reedley, 30 October 1988, Peter Penner Collection; Maria recorded the many (anxious) trips made by her husband to Jadcherla in May 1953 with reference to the Friesen/Wiebe building projects, which included a spacious bungalow for the Friesens, Maria K. Lohrenz, Diary, vol. 4, 9 and 23 May 1953, Lohrenz Papers, CMBS/F.

73. For this $6,400. project he appealed particularly to his family in America, J. H. Lohrenz to family, 10 June 1955, Lohrenz Papers, CMBS/F; Lohrenz, "Einweihung [Dedication] der Bethlehem MB Kirche, Malakpet, Hyderabad, Indien," *Zionsbote*, 28 December 1955, 4-5.

74. Ted Fast to Board of Missions, 19 October 1964, Fast File, CMBS/F.

75. Maria K. Lohrenz, Diary, vol. 4, 29 January 1954; vol. 5, 4 March, 16 April, 4 May 1954, 30-31 July, 18 September, and 10 October 1956, John Lohrenz Papers, CMBS/F.

## CHAPTER 12

1. Julius J. Kasper to Jacob J. Dick, 25 September 1956, J. J. Dick Papers, CMBS/F.

2. Abram E. Janzen, "Der schwere Schicksalsschlag [fateful happening] in Indien," *Zionsbote*, 15 November 1950, 3-4; Margaret Willems to A. E. Janzen, 7 May 1953, Willems File, CMBS/F.

3. J. J. Kasper, "On the Way to India," *Christian Leader*, March 1946, 3.

4. A. E. Janzen to J. J. Kasper, 14 March 1947; Eva Kasper to Janzen, 28 January 1948, Kasper File, CMBS/F.

5. J. N. C. Hiebert, "Aus Indien," *Zionsbote*, 22 November 1951, 2-4; the Block Family, "In Memoriam to Mrs. J. J. Kasper and son, Julius, Jr.," *Christian Leader*, 15 December 1950, 11-12.
6. A. E. Janzen, "Der schwere Schicksalsschlag in Indien," *Zionsbote*, 15 November 1950, 3-4.

7. A. E. Janzen to Anna Suderman, 1 February 1951, Suderman File, CMBS/F. Many questions were left unanswered. Was the ferry safe for anyone? Did the state authorities investigate the accident and suggest improvements in safety standards? It seems that only Maria K. Lohrenz at Hughestown recorded the conviction that the accident was caused by "overloading and negligence," Diary, vol. 3, 24 October 1950, 116.

8. John A. Wiebe wrote the Board a detailed report, based on his visit to the site and A. A. Unruh's statement of 9th December; Wiebe to Janzen, 13 December 1952, Wiebe File, CMBS/F.

9. A. A. Unruh to A. E. Janzen, 13 December 1952, Unruh File, CMBS/F.

10. A. A. Unruh, 1 February 1953, Unruh File. Following the scheduled meeting of the Missionary Council at Gadwal, the "brethren" missionaries decided behind closed doors against publicity in the case of Jacob, Edna Gerdes to Peter Penner, September 1990; Donald Unruh, interview by author, Winnipeg, July 1990, Peter Penner Collection. Cf. J. A. Wiebe to A. E. Janzen, 12 January 1953, Wiebe File; Margaret Willems to Janzen, 6 March 1953, Willems File, CMBS/F.

11. J. H. Lohrenz, "Herman H. Warkentin, 1917-1953," *CL*, 17/8 (15 April 1953), 6-7; the Warkentin Family, "India," *CL*, 17/10 (15 May 1953), 5-6.

12. Beatrice Warkentin, interview by author, Fresno, 4 November 1992; Ted Fast, interview by author, Dallas, OR, 28 September 1992, Peter Penner Collection.

13. J. J. Kasper told how three Warkentin children were taken from Kodaikanal by train to Bangalore, and then by plane to Hyderabad, "An account of the death and burial of Herman H. Warkentin," *Konferenz=Jugendblatt*, March-April 1953, 31.

14. Beatrice Koop Warkentin trained as a teacher and taught in Reedley and Fresno high schools for twenty-eight years. She and her son John also have a successful business, and all of her children are well placed; Beatrice Warkentin, interview by author, Fresno, 4 November 1992, Penner Collection.

15. Henry P. Poetker, "Hebron Bible School Dedicated," *Christian Leader*, 15 November 1956, 6.

16. J. A. Wiebe to A. E. Janzen, 3 January 1959, Wiebe File, CMBS/F.

17. J. A. Wiebe, "Das Mahbubnagar Eisenbahnunglueck [train accident] hat 120 Leben gekostet," *Zionsbote*, 10 October 1956, 5-6. A Gadwal teacher named Reuben was rescued by clinging to a tree floating in the river.

18. Ted Fast to "Dear Friends," 16 March 1963, Fast File, CMBS/F.

19. V. B. Wiebe, *Sepia Prints: Memoirs of a Missionary in India* (Winnipeg: Kindred Press, 1990), 142, 145 ff.

20. Maurice Blanchard's eye-witness account of the drowning, and the Editor, "More About the Death of John A. Wiebe," *Christian Leader*, 21 January 1964, 7; cf. Viola B. Wiebe, *Sepia Prints*, 154-155.

21. J. H. Lohrenz, "In Memoriam: John A. Wiebe - in Service for Christ in India," *Mennonite Brethren Herald*, 24 January 1964, 10.

22. Editor, "More About the Death of John A. Wiebe," *Christian Leader*, 21 January 1964, 7.

23. J. H. Lohrenz, "John [A. Wiebe], the Beloved Missionary," with encomiums, 7 pp., Lohrenz Papers, CMBS/F.

24. J. B. Toews to John A. Harder, 21 July 1956; Harder to Toews, 14 September 1956, Board Members' Files, Box 12, CMBS/F. There was, however, no call for a public catharsis in 'dust and ashes,' as an Old Testament prophet might have called for.

25. A. E. Janzen, regarding Helga at Tabor College, to J. J. Dick, 15 January 1946; regarding Margaret's wedding, Janzen to Dick, 28 July 1955, Dick File, CMBS/F.

26. Paul Dick, at Kodaikanal, to Jake and Annie Dick, 15 September 1956, Dick Papers, CMBS/F.

27. Rose Krause, Kodaikanal, to J. J. Dick, 2 October 1956, Dick Papers, CMBS/F.

28. Margaret (Dick) and Mike Wiebe, Kansas, 27 September 1956; and Helen (Dick) and Walter Friesen to J. J. Dick, Shamshabad, 13 October 1956, Dick Papers, CMBS/F.

29. Walter Friesen to J. J. Dick, 13 September 1956; Graham Upham to Dick, 15 November 1956, Dick Papers, CMBS/F. Most helpful have been William Dick, Ontario, a cousin and a psychologist, to Peter Penner, 6 August 1991; and Helga's second husband Philip C. Good, 10 August 1992, Penner Collection.

30. Helga to her parents, regarding her treatment, 14 November and 28 December 1956, Dick Papers, CMBS/F.

31. J. J. Dick to A. E. Janzen, 30 December 1956; to George Roberntz, Stockholm (Spring 1957), Dick Papers; J. A. Harder to J. B. Toews, 14 September 1956, Board Members, Box 12; Board of Foreign Missions, Minutes regarding the Dicks, 26-29 March 1957, 32, CMBS/F.

32. J. J. Dick to A. E. Janzen, 16 November 1959; Board of Foreign Missions, Minutes, February 1960, 39-41, CMBS/F; Dick's letter to editor, *Mennonite Brethren Herald*, 10 January 1964, 2.

33. Anna Dick to Graham Upham, 7 July 1965; Anna to Jacob, for example, 24 March 1974; Helga to her father, 6 March 1974, Dick Papers, CMBS/F.

34. The case involving P. E. Schellenberg and J. N. C. Hiebert shows up the Niebhurian sense of 'humane irony' where, clearly, the consequences of human actions were totally contrary to the original intention of those taking the action,

and were also greatly responsible for the discrepancy. See Richard Reinitz, *Irony and Consciousness* (Lewisberg, Pa.: Bucknell University Press, 1980), 19-26.

35. Wesley J. Prieb and Don Ratzlaff, *To a Higher Plane of Vision: Tabor College - The First 75 Years* (Hillsboro: Tabor College, 1983); cf. two articles by Paul Toews: "Fundamentalist Conflict in Mennonite Colleges: Response to Cultural Transitions?," *Mennonite Quarterly Review* 57 (July 1983), 241-256; and "Henry W. Lohrenz and Tabor College," *Mennonite Life* 38 (September 1983), 11-19.

36. B.B. Janz, Coaldale, wrote to P.E. Schellenberg about "dieser stinkende moralische Sumpf," giving voice to "eine schreckliche Anklage [frightening charge]" about the alleged moral decline at Tabor, 20 January 1945, in H. S. Voth Collection, File 15, CMBS/W.

37. Cf. P. R. Lange, "Konferenzschule," *GC Yearbook* (Buhler, 1943), 41; P. E. Schellenberg, "Tabor College" (Dinuba, 1945), 48 ff.; A. H. Unruh, "Tabor College" (Mountain Lake, 1948), 69 ff.; and A. H. Unruh, "Bericht . . . ueber TC," *CC Yearbook* (Coaldale, 1944), 13-14. One detects an unusual degree of sarcasm in Unruh's 1948 statement about expecting higher spiritual standards at TC than in the home congregations.

38. All former presidents since 1908 had been ordained men. Whereas the most recent one, A. E. Janzen (1935-1941), had worked hard to preclude criticism, Schellenberg wanted a more "open" atmosphere comparable to H. W. Lohrenz' day (1908-1930). This was reflected in his language: there was no imitation of piety, no hypocrisy. Roy Just, interview by author, Fresno, 6 December 1988 and 16 November 1992, Peter Penner Collection.

39. See P. E. Schellenberg, "Tabor College," *GC Yearbook* (Dinuba, 1945), 48 ff. His Ph. D. was from the University of Minnesota. George Dyck suggested that psychology's threat lay in suggesting other ways of understanding human nature and bringing about behavioral change than only through Jesus Christ as the fundamentalists asserted, "Psychology and Psychiatry," *Mennonite Encyclopedia* 5 (1990), 730. Interestingly, TC had a director of athletics and coach as early as 1926 and the "roaring 'twenties" were reflected in women becoming "more daring" in their styles, in Prieb, *To a Higher Plane of Vision*, 14-15.

40. For the statement regarding Schellenberg's "personal testimony," and the "clear tone" to be maintained at all times, see "Konferenzschule," *GC Yearbook* (Buhler, 1943), 32-42. Some Schellenberg supporters urged him to state more openly that he believed in the fundamentals of the faith according to the Mennonite Brethren Confession, and his many supporters in California, Tabor College alumni, tried to counteract the "undermining attitude" of the day; see R. C. Seibel to P. E. Schellenberg, 11 January, and 7 March 1945, Maryon Schellenberg Troyer Collection.

41. A. H. Unruh, "Bericht ueber Tabor College," *CC Yearbook* (Coaldale, 1944), 13-14; *GC Yearbook* (Dinuba, 1948), 90.

42. Cf. *GC Yearbook* (1945 and 1948), 48 ff. and 69-75, respectively.

43. Education Committee, Minutes, 26-27 May 1944, 15 January 1945, A 280, CMBS/F

44. J. W. Vogt, Editorial: "God forbid that we should ever compromise with or tolerate liberalism in our schools and churches," *Christian Leader*, 1 January 1947, 1.

45. Elmo Warkentin, age 30 in 1942 when he began taking courses at TC, held several student pastorates, and graduated in 1947. He was appointed chair of the Publication Committee in 1948. DP, "Evangelism and Discipleship: Elmo Warkentin's Legacy," *Christian Leader* (6 October 1992), 19. See Index for references to E. Stanley Jones.

46. Elmo Warkentin, "The Federal Council of Churches and the Association of Evangelicals Compared," *Christian Leader*, 1 and 15 January 1947, 1-2, 5-6, resp.; Arthur Willems, "How to Detect the First Signs of Modernism," *CL*, 15 February and 1 March 1947, 1-3, 5-6, respectively. For earlier warnings about liberal tendencies, see R. C. Seibel, student, "Bedarf unsere Gemeinschaft einer hoeheren Lehranstalt?," *Zionsbote*, 26 October 1927, 5; and J. H. Voth, "Eine Reise im Nordwesten [Kanadas]," 10 August 1927, 4-6.

47. G. W. Peters, "The Christian Teacher," *Christian Leader*, 15 July 1949, 12-13; J. W. Vogt Editorial, "The Curse of Modernism" followed by a guest article by Baptist W.A. Criswell, *CL*, 1 and 15 February 1950, 3 ff.; Jack Adrian, "Trends to Modernism," *CL*, 1 July 1950, 3-4; cf. Frank C. Peters, "Religious Authority," *CL*, 15 October 1953, 3, and many more.

48. Education Committee, Minutes, 17-18 January 1946, A 280, CMBS/F; B. B. Janz to P. E. Schellenberg, 20 January 1945; Peter R. Lange to Henry S. Voth, wondering whether "we are at the point of disintegration," 12 February 1945, H. S. Voth File, CMBS/W. This was the very time when Henry W. Lohrenz was near collapse; he died in March 1945.

49. In essence, Harder did not agree with the sharp lines drawn between "eternal verities" and "cultural variables," Roy Just, interview by author, Fresno, 6 December 1988; cf. Education Committee, Minutes, 17-18 January 1946 and 24-25 January 1947, CMBS/F.

50. Education Committee, Minutes, 23 October 1947, CMBS/F.

51. This brought together B. J. Braun, J. B. Toews, H. R. Wiens, B. B. Janz, A. H. Unruh, J. W. Vogt, H. H. Flaming of the Board of Reference and Counsel; with J. W. Warkentin, J. K. Warkentin, Orlando Harms, J. J. Toews, William Neufeld, and J. H. Quiring of the Education Committee, *GC Yearbook* (1948), 155-156. By 1951 Schellenberg had fewer defenders, especially in the EC. His friend J. W. Warkentin was gone; added to the most conservative members, J. J. Toews and William Neufeld, were Dan E. Friesen, Leo Wiens, and Waldo Wiebe, *GC Yearbook* (1951), 220.

52. Education Committee, Minutes, and Statement of "policies and procedures" attached, 29 November 1948, and 21-25 January 1949; P. E. Schellenberg to J. W. Warkentin, November 1948, CMBS/F.

53. Education Committee, Minutes, 22-3 March 1949, CMBS/F.

54. Cf. J. J. Toews, "Report of the Board of Education of Tabor College," *GC Yearbook* (Winkler, 1951), 24-29; and Das Erziehungskomittee, "An die Konferenz der Mennoniten Bruedergemeinde von Nordamerika," *Zionsbote*, 6 April 1949, 10-11; Roy Just and many others, interviews by author, 1988 to 1992, Peter Penner Collection.

55. P. E. Schellenberg to Education Committee, 1 June 1951, Maryon Schellenberg Troyer Collection.

56. A. A. Unruh, J. H. Lohrenz, and P. V. Balzer, "General Statement to the Board of Foreign Missions of the Mennonite Brethren Church [on the call and **recall** of missionaries, November 1951]," 3 foolscap pages, Missionary Conference, India, Minutes; A. E. Janzen, "An Analysis of the Memorandum of the [India Missionary Conference] re the Recall of Missionaries," 19-20 November 1951; and "A word from the Board of Foreign Missions relative to releasing Missionary John Hiebert to serve Tabor College," Board of Foreign Missions, Minutes, CMBS/F. Cf. Harry Neufeld, "Reaction of a Missionary to the Spirit in the Home Churches," *Christian Leader*, 1 June 1952, 2-4; and Orlando Harms to Peter Penner, 9 September 1991, Penner Collection.

57. Editorials, "Rev. Hiebert Will Be Inaugurated to Tabor Presidency February 3," *Christian Leader*, 15 January 1952, 1; "WELCOME TO AND PRAYER FOR OUR NEW COLLEGE PRESIDENT," 1 February 1952, 2.

58. There was no prior indication of emotional breakdown in India. In 1939 he wrote that the terrible heat wore at the physical and nervous strength of missionaries, in "Mitteilungen von der Arbeit in Nagarkurnool," *Zionsbote*, 14 June 1939, 2-3. During his last term (1947-51), Hiebert found work draining on his health. He wrote Janzen: "Sleep often does not come at nights when one weighs the problems and tries to solve them," cf. 22 July 1948 and 17 September 1949; Janzen to Hiebert, 28 September 1950; 17 January 1951. Hiebert worked at an accelerated pace on such projects as getting Ernest Schmidt to replace him, and the Krauses established at Bruton. In the hot season of 1951 he had to get away from the heat and "fatigue" of year end activities, Hiebert to Janzen, 11 April 1951, Hiebert File, CMBS/F.

59. Hiebert Family Correspondence, Peter Penner Collection.

60. Roy Just, interview by author, Fresno, 6 December 1988, Penner Collection. For the conservative view of movies at the time, when the Canadian Conference had pronounced against the use of TV, see Frank C. Peters, "The Christian and the Commercial Movie," *Christian Leader*, 15 April 1955, 4-5.

61. Education Committee, Minutes, "The Charge to John Hiebert," January 1952, 2 pp., CMBS/F.

62. Before his recall, John Hiebert had learned he was to be replaced at the Central High School (by Ernest Schmidt) so that he could be relieved of his multi-faceted "station work" and spend time in evangelization; A. E. Janzen, *Survey of Five of the Mission Fields...India* (Hillsboro: BFM, 1950), 25-27.

Education Committee, Minutes, "Word from the Incoming President," 31 January - 2 February 1952, 2; 2 April 1952; "The Presidency of the School," 14 September 1953, A 280, CMBS/F. Missionaries who said goodbye to him at Secunderabad railway station remember one of his last words: "I wish this train were going in the other direction (instead of to Bombay and America)"; Frieda Neufeld, interview by author, Vancouver, September 1988; Margaret Willems Balzer, Saskatoon, February 1989; also Hiebert Family Correspondence, Penner Collection.

63. Hiebert Family Correspondence, Penner Collection. For the Conference delegation vote, see *GC Yearbook* (Winkler 1951), 30-31.

John Hiebert's *Weltanschauung* was probably far more cosmopolitan than most Mennonite Brethren in North America. He had rubbed shoulders in India with world mission leaders, including the internationalist John R. Mott. In 1948 he had articulated in a matchless way "The Unchanging Gospel in a Changing World," *Christian Leader*, 15 May 1948, 5-8; and in 1952 he made a ringing statement on the Mennonite Brethren mission as in truth a "faith mission," see "Glaubens=Mission," in *Konferenz=Jugendblatt*, September 1953 - February 1954, 3-7.

64. John Hiebert served in this capacity briefly. See Frank C. Peters' statement to the Pastors of the Central District Conference, 17 May 1954, Tabor College, C-11, Folder 119/116, CMBS/Hillsboro. Margaret Willems saw Hiebert in her Mountain Lake audience about this time. He seemed interested when she told him the people of India would like him to come back; interview by author, Saskatoon, February 1989, Penner Collection.

65. J. B. Toews to A. E. Janzen, Orlando Harms, and Marvin Jost, 16 July 1954, Board Members File, CMBS/F.

66. In a September 1953 interview F. C. Peters seemed to satisfy the board on all counts, though one board member recommended strongly that this brilliant and popular preacher from Canada should not be made president without first teaching at Tabor under interim arrangements which were in place; Education Committee, Minutes, September 1953, 13; Orlando Harms to Peter Penner, 9 September 1991; others feared that Peters would turn Tabor into a Bible school; Cornelius J. Rempel, interview by author, Kitchener, June, 1990, Penner Collection.

67. The Board resolved that "because of disagreement in policy and idealism and in order to give the administration the fullest possible freedom ... it appears inadvisable to renew the teaching contract of Dr. Schellenberg for the com-

ing year," Education Committee, Minutes, 28 January - 1 February 1954, 3, 10-12, 15; J. J. Toews, secretary, to F. C. Peters, 7 April 1954, CMBS/F; Orlando Harms to Peter Penner, 9 September 1991, Penner Collection.

68. Obituary: "Dr. P. E. Schellenberg Dies [with a brief eulogy from Clarence Hiebert]," *Christian Leader*, 1 May 1973, 15; Richard Schellenberg (son), *CL*, 29 May 1973, 15. Schellenberg was overlooked by the editors of *Mennonite Encyclopedia* in 1990.

69. Loyal Funk to F. C. Peters, 18 April 1955, CMBS/F; Education Committee: "Die Erziehungsbehoerde macht weitgreifende Plaene [the Education Committee makes far-reaching plans]," *Zionsbote*, 5 January 1955, 13.

70. Henry R. Wiens to A. H. Unruh, 16 August 1956, A 280, CMBS/F; Herbert and Rose Krause, interview by author, Fresno, 12 November 1992, Penner Collection.

71. J. B. Toews to J. A. Harder, 21 July 1956, Board Members, Box 12; A. E. Janzen referred to the "tragedies in the missionary families Hiebert and [J. J. and Anna] Dick," which "have shocked both the home constituency as well as the whole staff of the missionaries on foreign fields," Board of Foreign Mission, Minutes, 29 October 1956, CMBS/F.

72. In the 1940s some brethren equated suicide as "eine geistliche Umnachtung [death in spiritual darkness]," Theodore Regehr, interview by author, Fresno, 1 February 1993, Penner Daybook.

73. For these brief obituaries, see *The Christian Leader*, 15 September 1956, 21; Board of Foreign Missions, "Eine Trauerbotschaft," *Zionsbote*, 25 July 1956, 2; Obituary of John N. C. Hiebert, *Zionsbote*, 8 August 1956, 14-15.

74. John Hiebert Family Correspondence, October 1991, Penner Collection. Cf. Patty Duke and Gloria Hochman, *A Brilliant Madness: Living with Manic-Depressive Illness* (New York, 1992). This book covers the whole range of mental illnesses, the stigma attached, as well as former and current treatments, case studies, psychotherapy, and modern resources. Lithium, the most widely-used drug, was not approved until 1970. Even if lithium had been available in 1953, there is no claim here that it would have been the answer to Hiebert's illness.

75. H. R. Wiens to P. C. Hiebert, Hillsboro, 1 August 1956; Hiebert to Wiens, 6 August 1956; Wiens to A. H. Unruh, 16 August 1956, Board of Reference and Counsel (BORAC), CMBS/F.

76. The J. N. C. Hiebert Story, "Reminiscences by Anna J. Hiebert," to Peter Penner, 31 August 1991, Penner Collection.

77. A. E. Janzen to H. R. Wiens, 21 July 1956, Secretariat Correspondence; J. B. Toews to J. A. Harder, 21 July 1956, Board Members, Box 12, CMBS/F.

78. H. R. Wiens to P. C. Hiebert, 1 August 1956; A. H. Unruh to H. R. Wiens, 5 August 1956, BORAC, CMBS/F.

79. A. H. Unruh to H. R. Wiens, 5 August; and P. C. Hiebert to H. R. Wiens, 6 August 1956; Wiens to Unruh and Hiebert, 16 August 1956, BORAC, CMBS/F.

80. H. R. Wiens to P. C. Hiebert, 16 August, and Hiebert to Wiens, 20 August 1956, BORAC, CMBS/F.

81. H. R. Wiens to A. H. Unruh, 16 August 1956, BORAC, CMBS/F.

## CHAPTER 13

1. I have coined the word **meditorial** (a combination of meditation on some passage of Scripture and a didactic editorial). Janzen's memoir, which is particularly interesting for his early life, must be compared with these thousands of letters: Abram E. Janzen, "Each Step of the Way," unpublished Memoir, in five parts, 96 chapters, 851 pages, 1985, CMBS/Hillsboro.

2. Many letters are missing, having been discarded before the Secretariat files were carried from Hillsboro to Fresno in 1975; John Wall, interview by author, Kitchener, 25 June 1991, Penner Collection.
J. B. Toews, as Executive Secretary of the Historical Commission of the General Conference of MB Churches, expressed his appreciation for Abram Ewell Janzen's many contributions between 1945 and 1975. "Your sense of history . . . has drawn the framework in which the works of God . . . will be interpreted in the future." J. B. Toews to A. E. Janzen, 5 September 1975, an uncategorized Janzen File, # 4, CMBS/F.

3. Janzen easily switched from total devotion to Tabor College (1939-1942) to that of the Board of Foreign Mission; see his first article on foreign mission: "Aeusere Mission," *Christian Leader*, 22 August 1945, 2.

4. Cornelius J. Rempel, interview by author, Kitchener, 25 June 1991, Penner Collection.

5. Various chapters (see index for details) provide illustrations of those like Henry S. Voth who wanted to staff the India mission with **Amerikaner** and **Kanadier** missionaries rather than **Russländer**. Henry Voth's fear of a **Russländer** takeover was expressed in 1933: "it is unique how these Russians know how to force issues in their favor!" H. S. Voth to H. W. Lohrenz, 18 March 1933, Lohrenz Papers, CMBS/F; cf. A. E. Janzen, "Der Missionsgeist in den Gemeinden," *Zionsbote*, 15 March 1950, 3-4.

6. (A. E. Janzen), *Foreign Missions: Guiding Principles and Field Policies* (Hillsboro: BFM, 1947), 15; cf. G. W. Peters, *Foundations of Mennonite Brethren Missions* (Hillsboro: Kindred Press, 1984), 93-94.

7. A. E. Janzen, *Survey of Five of the Mission Fields ... India*, typescript bound, pictorial (Hillsboro: BFM, 1950), 1-39.

8. A. E. Janzen, *Survey . . . India,* 6; by 1961 he had changed his mind about the compounds. He saw them as "rather pretentious," following the colonial pattern; cf. Janzen, "The Development of Missionary Dynamic Among American Mennonite Brethren," in *The Church in Mission: A Sixtieth Anniversary Tribute to J. B. Toews*, ed. A. J. Klassen (Fresno: Board of Christian Literature, 1967), 160.

9. A. E. Janzen, *Survey,* 6-10.

10. A. E. Janzen, *Survey*, 34; cf. Paul D. Wiebe, *Christians in Andhra Pradesh: The Mennonites of Mahbubnagar* (Bangalore: Christian Literature Society, 1988), 61.

11. A. E. Janzen, *Survey*, 26.

12. Janzen, *Survey*, 12-14, 25-27.

13. Janzen, *Survey*, 14-16.

14. A year after receiving this report, the Board of Foreign Missions recommended consolidation rather than proliferation of medical work and urged concentration on evangelization along lines suggested by Janzen; Board of Foreign Missions, Minutes, 18-20 October 1949, and 6-8 November 1950, 4-7, CMBS/F. Still later they tended to concentrate evangelism **through** medical work.

15. A. E. Janzen, "Aeussere Mission," *CC Yearbook* (1950), 15; *GC Yearbook* (1951), 34.

16. J. H. Lohrenz, "Our Telugu MB Church in India," *GC Yearbook* (Mountain Lake, 1948), 31 (**emphasis added**).

17. A. E. Janzen, "Foreign Mission," *CC Yearbook* (1956), 31.

18. A. E. Janzen to P. V. Balzer, J. J. Kasper, and J. N. C. Hiebert, 21 September 1950, Balzer File, CMBS/F.

19. Much later, G. W. Peters admitted that the relationship between the Missionary Council and the Board "[was] nowhere clearly defined." For a survey of "the period of [Board] centralization," see Peters, *Foundations*, 91 ff.

20. For the history and details of the agreement with Billington (30 January 1954), see J. A. Wiebe to the Administrative Committee of the Missionary Council, and to Hillsboro, 22 July 1953, CMBS/F.

21. P. V. Balzer, "The Newly-Acquired Field in India," *Christian Leader*, 15 July 1955, 6-7; "Berean Bible Institute in India," *CL*, 1 February 1956, 6; "Narayanpet Church Dedicated," *CL*, 15 August 1957, 6; Balzer to the Board of Foreign Missions, 24 December 1954, Balzer File, CMBS/F.

22. P. V. Balzer, "Bethany Bible Institute Trains Christian Workers," *Christian Leader*, 18 April 1961, 8-9.

23. Henry G. Krahn to A. E. Janzen, 6 January and 23 February 1958; Krahn to J. B. Toews, 10 March 1958; Janzen to Krahn, 8 April, and Krahn to Janzen, 14 July 1958, H. G. Krahn File; Caleb had already gone to hospital once before from stress. See John J. Krahn, "Life Story of Henry G. Krahn (1923-1985)," 1993, 9 ff, Peter Penner Collection.

24. R. S. Aseervadam, "The Mennonite Brethren Church in Andhra Pradesh: A Historical Treatise" (Ph. D. diss., Osmania University, Hyderabad, 1980), 186-187.

25. John J. Krahn, "Life Story of Henry J. Krahn," 12 ff.

26. Jake Friesen, "Wiens [Howard Roy] Memorial Building," *Konferenz - Jugendblatt*, June to October 1954, 18; "The Medical Center at Jadcherla," in *Andhra Mennonite Brethren Church of India: Fifty Years in Retrospect, 1904-1954* (Hillsboro: BFM, 1954), 28-29; cf. Catharine A. Reimer's desire to see a Maternity Hospital and Women's Industrial Home built at Jadcherla; Reimer to J. H. Lohrenz, 31 May 1939, Reimer File, CMBS/F.

27. The medical staff in alphabetical order:

Peter J. Block, MD, Deverakonda, 1961-66, 1968-71
Helen Dueck, RN, Gadwal, 1956-62, 1963-67
Jake Friesen, MD, Jadcherla, 1951-58, 1960-66, 1967-72
Ruth Friesen, RN, Jadcherla, 1951-58, 1960-66, 1967-72
George J. Froese, MD, Jadcherla, Wanaparty, 1954-60, 1961-67, 1972-3
Helen Harder, RN, Shamshabad, Hyderabad, 1946-53, 1954-60, 1962-66, 1966-71
Frieda Neufeld, RN, Jadcherla, Bangladesh, 1951-57, 1959-65, 1966-69, 1969-72
Marie Riediger, RN, Jadcherla, 1957-63, 1964-66
Margaret Suderman, RN, Wanaparty, 1929-38, 1938-46, 1947-55, 1956-62
Regina Suderman, RN, Jadcherla, 1951-58, 1959-65, 1966-69, 1969-72
Rosella Toews, RN, Nagarkurnool, Jadcherla, Bangladesh, 1946-53, 1954-60, 1961-66, 1967-71
Maria C. Wall, RN, Deverakonda, 1915-23, 1924-32, 1933-45, 1947-57
Ronald Wall, MD, Jadcherla, dental short-term, 1962-64
David Wiebe, MD, Jadcherla, short-term, 1966-68
Margaret Willems, RN, Gadwal, Wanaparty, 1946-53, 1955-61

28. Helen Harder to J. B. Toews, 10 December 1962, Harder File, CMBS/F.

29. J. A. Wiebe to A. E. Janzen, 13 March 1952, 18 September 1952, and 23 December 1957, Wiebe File, CMBS/F.

30. J. A. Wiebe's letter regarding "power of attorney," to H. G. Krahn, 2 May 1959; Krahn to A. E. Janzen, 6 June 1959, H. G. Krahn File, CMBS/F.

31. J. A. Wiebe to A. E. Janzen, 13 March, 18 September, 6 October 1952; 1 July, 17 October 1953; and 4 December 1955, CMBS/F.

The author has omitted discussion of many aspects of these years, including the "defamation" case lodged against Wiebe repeatedly by a Rubin between September 1955 and January 1957.

32. J. A. Wiebe to A. E. Janzen, 1 July 1953, and Janzen to Wiebe, 11 December 1954, CMBS/F.

33. J. Friesen, "History of Jadcherla Medical Center [1955]"; J. A. Wiebe to A. E. Janzen, 13 March 1952 and 12 September 1958, CMBS/F; J. A. Wiebe, "Dedicate Indian Medical Center Buildings," 21/16 (15 August 1957), 6; MBM/S staff, "Twenty-Five Years of Healing," *MBH*, 17/10 (12 May 1978), 25.

34. R.S. Aseervadam, *"The MB Church in Andhra Pradesh"*, 233 ff., 285; R.S. Lemuel, "R. S. Aseervadam," *Christian Leader*, 25 January 1983, 14; for a summary of all the medical personnel, both North American and Indian, see Dr. N. S. Isaiah, "A Brief Sketch: Medical Ministry," in *Diamond Jubilee: Seventy-Five Years of Grace* (Hyderabad: MB Church India, 1974), 50-54.

35. A. E. Janzen, "Foreign Missions," *GC Yearbook* (1948), 13-14, 24, 40, 43; this meant one missionary to 152 members, a very competitive ratio; cf. J. B. Toews, "Conference Missionaries - 1945-1963," *GC Yearbook*, (1963), 62.

36. Missionary Council, Minutes, 29 December 1948 - 2 January 1949, 212, CMBS/F.

37. Administrative Committee, Missionary Council, Minutes, 29 June 1951; and AC, Minutes, 19-20 November 1951; see "Special Session," Missionary Council, 25 January 1952, CMBS/F. A. A. Unruh, whose story follows later in this Chapter, like D. F. Bergthold before him, understood his call as coming from God and the sending church, not from the Board or Secretariat, hence the objection to such tampering with that call; Margaret (Unruh) Regehr, interview by author, Winnipeg, 9 July 1993, Peter Penner Collection.

38. See Niyogi Committee, "The Madya Pradesh Report on Missionary Activity: Conclusions," in Blaise Levai, ed., *Revolution in Missions: The Role of Missions in Present Day India* (Vellore: Popular Press, 1957), 274-278.

The (Old) Mennonites at Dhamtari, MP, were actually investigated in 1954. The charge was that one of their converts had been induced by money to become a Christian, and that others in their Christian village had been disrespectful of Hindu gods. The Dhamtari mission and church passed the test without curtailment of its activity, see John Lapp, *The Mennonite Church in India, 1897-1962* (Scottdale: Herald Press, 1972), 196-199. In fact, this commission's work had little impact in the short run.

39. Blaise Levai, ed., *Revolution in Missions*, 5-6.

40. William Hocking, Chair, *Rethinking Missions* (New York: Harper and Sons, 1932), 33 ff.; cf. Grant Wacker, "Second Thoughts on the Great Commission: Liberal Protestants and Foreign Missions, 1890-1940," in *Earthen Vessels: American Evangelicals and Foreign Missions, 1880-1980,* ed. J. A. Carpenter and W. R. Shenk (Grand Rapids: Eerdmans, 1990), 281 ff.

41. David Chellappa, The Bishop of Madras, "The Need for Revaluation of Missions," in Blaise Levai, 1 ff; cf, Michael Hollis, *Paternalism and the Church: A Study of South Indian Church History* (London: Oxford University Press, 1962).

42. See Peter Penner, *No Longer At Arm's Length: Mennonite Brethren Church Planting in Canada* (Winnipeg: Kindred Press, 1987), 25-26, 63-64.

43. For the launching of the Western Children's Mission in Saskatchewan, see Penner, *No Longer At Arm's Length*, 21-24; Henry W. Lohrenz' view was that if G. W. Peters could not have his way "to the dot, he knocks things 'kurz und klein' [into small pieces]," Lohrenz to J. A. Wiebe, 17 February 1945, Lohrenz Papers, CMBS/F.

44. A. H. Unruh to G. W. Peters in Columbia, 8 April 1944; Peters in Bogota to H. W. Lohrenz, 24 May 1944; Peters to P. R. Lange, 1 or 11 January 1946, G. W. Peters Papers, CMBS/F.

45. G. W. Peters, *The Growth of Foreign Missions in the Mennonite Brethren Church* (Hillsboro: MB Publishing House, 1952); cf. A. E. Janzen, *Foreign Missions: The India American MB Mission in India, 1898-1948* (Hillsboro; BFM, 1948).

46. J. B. Toews, "G. W. Peters: God's chosen instrument," *Christian Leader*, 14 February 1989, 20.

47. J. B. Toews, *JB: A Twentieth-Century Mennonite Pilgrim* (Fresno: Center for Mennonite Brethren Studies, 1995), 64 ff.

48. These incidents indicate how some brethren "played God"; J. B. Toews, interview by author, Fresno, 11 December 1988, 7 January and 2 February 1989; cf. Toews, *JB*, 123 ff.

49. J. B. Toews, *JB*, 151 ff.

50. J. B. Toews, interview by author, Fresno, 14 December 1992, Penner Collection.

51. J. B. Toews to A. E. Janzen, 16 June 1954, Board Members' Files, CMBS/F.

52. This financial motive was stated more clearly in 1961: we must "find ways and means of a considerable reduction in operational cost," J. B. Toews to Ted Fast, chair of Mission Administrative Committee, 2 September 1961, Fast File, CMBS/F.

53. G. W. Peters, "Statement of the General Conference of the M. B. Church on the Effects of the Changes of Our Age on the World-Wide Missionary Assignment," *GC Yearbook* (Yarrow, 1957), 41-43; cf. Peters, *Foundations of Mennonite Brethren Missions* (Hillsboro: Kindred Press, 1984), 91 ff.; J. B. Toews, interview by author, Fresno, 14 December 1992, Penner Collection.

54. For example, M. W. Kliewer (who was appointed media secretary in 1955) "Nachrichten vom Missionsbureau," *Zionsbote*, 19 January 1955, 4-5; George J. Froese to M. W. Kliewer, 7 March 1957, Froese File.

Strangely, Marion Kliewer had instructions to limit the coverage to bona fide conference papers. Because the Christian Press, Winnipeg, was not then owned by the Canadian Conference, he wanted to exclude such publications as the *Mennonitische Rundschau* and the *Mennonite Observer*. Kliewer wrote: "To mail essentially the same material to **non-conference** periodicals tends to **undermine and displace our brotherhood's publication efforts** (emphasis added)," Kliewer to Margaret Willems, 7 February 1957, Willems File, CMBS/F.

55. A. E. Janzen, "Deputation," *CC Yearbook* (1955), 54; J. B. Toews, "Der Kampf fuer den Glauben in der Vorbereitung des Missionsarbeiters," *CC Yearbook* (1956), 178-179.

56. Jake Friesen, interview by author, Reedley, CA, 30 October 1988; Vernon R. Wiebe, interview by author, Hillsboro, April 1989, Penner Collection; Wally Kroeker, "Looking ahead to the second century," *Mennonite Brethren Herald*, 21 September 1984, 7.

57. Missionary Council, Minutes, # 75, June 1952; Board of Foreign Missions, Minutes, October 1952, and a supplement to "Guiding Principles and Policies," 22 January 1953, CMBS/F.

58. Board of Foreign Missions, "Pessimism," Minutes, 19-21 October 1954 and 10-12 October 1955; Secretariat, the resolution regarding a Governing Council for India, Minutes, 20-24 April 1956, A 250-0-2, CMBS/F.

59. J. A. Wiebe to A. E. Janzen, 22 February 1957, Wiebe File, CMBS/F.

60. J. A. Wiebe to A. E. Janzen, 22 February 1957, Wiebe File, CMBS/F

61. Cf. J. B. Toews on the "modified Presbyterian church polity" followed by Mennonite Brethren, in "How then shall we be led?" *The Pilgrimage of Faith: The Mennonite Brethren Church* (Winnipeg: Kindred Press, 1993), 218-219.

62. Board of Foreign Missions, Minutes, 26-29 March 1957; A. E. Janzen to J. A. Wiebe, 17 April 1957, Wiebe File, CMBS/F.

63. A. A. Unruh to A. E. Janzen, 2 September 1957, Unruh File, CMBS/F.

64. A. A. Unruh to A. E. Janzen, 2 September 1957, Unruh File; J. A. Wiebe to A. E. Janzen, 23 May, 2 and 5 September 1957, Wiebe File, CMBS/F.

65. As shown, each missionary had found it gratifying to build his own empire; when J. B. Toews deplaned in Bombay in 1957, he was greeted gruffly, in Low German: "What do you want here?"; cf. J. B. Toews, interview by author, Fresno, 2 February 1989, Penner Collection; and Toews, *JB*, 160.

66. Anna Suderman, "Memoirs of Anna Suderman, 1902-1980," ed. Laurene Peters, (1983), 64, Suderman File, CMBS/F; Emma Lepp Baerg, interview by author, Saskatoon, 19 February 1989, Penner Collection.

67. G. W. Peters, *Foundations*, 96-9; Hans Kasdorf wrote much later that the reasons for this radical shift were "not entirely clear" to him. He saw it as a "unilateral action," in "A Century of Mennonite Mission Thinking," D. of Theology diss., University of South Africa, 1986, 375-379.

68. Donald J. Unruh to Peter Penner, 12 April 1990, Peter Penner Collection.

69. The India missionaries present at Yarrow were J. J. Dick, J. H. Lohrenz, and Frieda Neufeld. E. E. Schmidt, also there, and just returned from his one term in India, was seated beside Frank C. Peters. The latter did not think anything remarkable was taking shape, whereas Schmidt did; Ernest and Evelyn Schmidt, interview by author, Sanger, CA, January and May 1989, Penner Collection.

70. See C. Peter Williams, *The Ideal of the Self-Governing Church: A Study in Victorian Missionary Strategy* (indigenization defined by Henry Venn, expanded, threatened, undermined, replaced, compromised) (Leyden: E. J. Brill, 1990).

71. J. B. Toews, "Foreign Missions Report," *GC Yearbook* (1960), 49.

72. The chart is most misleading, though not intentionally so; in 1957 it **could not** yet show the powerful body that was set up to control matters (1960-1968): the Mission Administrative Committee. The MAC displaced the "Missionary Fellowship," and related directly to the Governing Council; and the MF in terms of authority slipped below MAC. The black "legislative" line leading to the committees of the Administrative Committee of the Governing Council is totally wrong.

73. *GC Yearbook* (1960), 47; see Board of Foreign Missions, *Guiding Principles and Policies* (1961), 11.

74. Missionary Council, "Report of the Constitution Committee on the 'New Plan' for India, presented to the Missionary Council in Jadcherla," 6 September 1958; J. A. Wiebe to A. E. Janzen, 29 July and 12 September 1958, CMBS/F.

75. Board of Foreign Missions, Minutes, 17 January 1959; Administrative Committee, India, Minutes, 27-28 January 1959, CMBS/F.

76. Board of Foreign Missions, Minutes, March 1959, 6-7, 40, 42; 17-23 February 1960, CMBS/F.

77. A. A. Unruh to A. E. Janzen, 28 November 1957, Unruh File, CMBS/F.

78. A. E. Janzen to A. A. Unruh, 21 June 1958, Unruh File, CMBS/F.

79. A. A. Unruh to A. E. Janzen, 10 May 1958; Janzen to Unruh, 21 May 1958, Unruh File, CMBS/F; Unruh to J. B. Toews, 14 May 1958, Unruh Papers, CMBS/W. Having come to Canada at age 21, in 1925, Unruh never overcame his weakness in English spelling and syntax. At Unruh's request, his private papers were never sent to Fresno. The two sets of papers, those in Winnipeg and those in Fresno, are dovetailed in this study.

80. A. A. Unruh to "Werte Brueder im Herrn," 30 May 1958, Unruh File, CMBS/F.

81. A. E. Janzen to A. A. Unruh, 27 October 1958; Unruh to Janzen, 8 November 1958, Unruh File, CMBS/F.

82. A. A. Unruh, "Aufruf aus Wanaparty," *Mennonitische Rundschau,* 5 November 1958, 2-3; cf. Unruh to J. B. Toews, 30 May 1958, Unruh Papers, CMBS/W.

83. Administrative Committee, Minutes, India, 1 June 1959, CMBS/F.

84. Board of Foreign Missions, Minutes, March 1959, 6-7, 41, CMBS/F.

85. Margaret Suderman, "Medical Missionary Service," *Christian Leader*, 15 February 1956, Suderman File, CMBS/F; cf. J. B. Toews, "A New Direction," *JB*, 161-163.

86. Anna Suderman, "Memoirs," 57; Dorothy Siebert, "From Southern Manitoba to India: Margaret Suderman at Wanaparty," *Mennonite Brethren Herald*, 30 December 1983, 8-10.

87. J. B. Toews, interview by author, Fresno, 2 February 1989); Paul G. Hiebert, interview by author, Fresno, 6 November 1988, Penner Collection.
When Elizabeth died in 1966, the Missionary Fellowship remembered her faithful ministry: A. A. Unruh, Tribute to Elizabeth Kornelson Balzer, 17-18 December, Mahbubnagar, in Peter M. Hamm to P. V. Balzer, 28 December 1966, Shamshabad Letters, P. M. Hamm Collection, Abbotsford, BC.

88. See Anne L. Ediger, "India Church Sets Stage for New Chapter," *Mennonite Brethren Herald,* 26 April 1968, 9; "Personalia," *MBH*, 21 September 1973, 25; Margaret Willems Balzer, interview by author, Saskatoon, February 1989; Benjamin (Balzer whom Peter Balzer adopted, and whose two sons married Lois and Eunice, two adoptees of Margaret Willems Balzer), interview by author, Hyderabad, 6 October 1990, Penner Collection; Mary Willems, "Margaret (Willems) Balzer: A Story of Resilient Faith," *MBH*, 19 February 1988, 31-32; obituaries: "Peter V. Balzer," *Christian Leader*, 20 August 1985; "Margaret Willems Balzer," *MBH*, 26 August 1994, 32.

89. John H. Lohrenz, *A Life for Christ in India: Mrs. Maria Lohrenz, 1892-1962* (Hillsboro: BFM, 1963); obituary, "Maria Klaassen Lohrenz," *Mennonite Brethren Herald,* 10 August 1962, 9.

90. J. H. Lohrenz to J. J. Kasper, 30 July 1962, Kasper File; Lohrenz to Mission Administrative Committee, 23 March 1963, John Lohrenz Papers, CMBS/F.

91. Maria C. Wall to A. E. Janzen, 3 and 24 October 1956 and 19 February 1957, March 1958; Janzen to Wall 5 October 1957, Wall File, CMBS/F.

92. Ted Fast to the Administrative Committee, 13 August 1957; to "The Board Members, AMBM," 18 August 1957; to A. E. Janzen, 12 December 1957, Fast File, CMBS/F.

93. Anna Suderman, "Students Meet for Reunion," *Christian Leader*, 15 January 1957, 6, 13; "Farewell Addresses to Missionaries Maria C. Wall and Helene L. Warkentin," *CL*, 28 January 1958, 6-7.

94. J. J. Kasper to the Board in Hillsboro, 9 January 1959, Kasper File, CMBS/F.

95. J. J. Kasper to A. E. Janzen, 22 August 1959, 12 January and 13 September 1960; Janzen to Kasper, 21 January 1960, Kasper File; many worried about the side-effects in financial terms of MB John's visit to America in 1960.

96. A. E. Janzen to J. J. Kasper, 3 December 1960 and 18 July 1961, Kasper File, CMBS/F.

## CHAPTER 14

1. Abram E. Janzen to Unruh, Kasper, Friesen, Fast, and Poetker, 3 September 1960, see Unruh File; Missionary Council, Minutes, # 91, Secunderabad, 22-23 June 1960; Missionary Administrative Committee, Minutes, # 1, 6 October 1960, A 250-6-1, CMBS/F.

2. J. B. Toews, *The Mennonite Brethren Church in Zaire* (Fresno: Board of Christian Literature, 1978), 135-142.

3. Ted Fast to A. E. Janzen, 26 September 1960; Anne L. Ediger to Janzen, 25 October 1960, Fast and Ediger Files, CMBS/F.

4. A. E. Janzen to Ted Fast, 30 August 1960, 4 February and 5 May 1961; Fast to Janzen 26 September and 15 November 1960, Fast File, CMBS/F; Abram A. Unruh, "Some questions regarding the Policies governing the relation of the National Church and the M.B. Conference in America," 1961, Unruh Papers, CMBS/W.

5. Margaret Willems, "The Present Status of the India Program," (August 1961), 9 pp., Willems File; Helen Dueck to J. B. Toews, 13 January 1962, Dueck File; Ted Fast to A. E. Janzen, 26 September and 15 November 1960, Fast File; Henry P. Poetker to Janzen, 6 April 1961; Toews to Poetker 6 June 1962, Poetker File, CMBS/F.

6. Ted Fast to A. E. Janzen, 26 September and 15 November 1960; though Fast was co-signer with D. J. Arthur for the budget, he was held responsible for a shortage of rupees 2,500, Fast to Peter Penner, 22 September 1991, Penner Collection; Henry G. Krahn to Janzen, 22 August 1961, Krahn File, CMBS/F.
E. E. Schmidt, "Moving Toward Self-Propagation [at Gadwal]," *India: The Mennonite Brethren Church* [May 1956], 3 pp.

7. John A. Wiebe to A. E. Janzen, 15 and 17 April 1958, Wiebe File, CMBS/F.

8. Ernest E. Schmidt, "Mennonite Brethren Central High School, Mahbubnagar, Hyderabad, India," 1991, 37, 39; "Replies [to author's questions]," 1991, 4, Penner Collection.
The Gadwal people asked for the Schmidts' return. They had heard that "there had been ambiguous and irrelevant reports concerning the work of our Missionary Rev. Ernest E Schmidt," B. Aaron, Chair of Gadwal Field, and fifty signatures to Hillsboro, 6 February 1959; cf. J. A. Wiebe File, 10 June 1959, CMBS/F; a corroborating Gadwal letter, stating that an "Indian pastor and a missionary" had "reported adversely about you to the [BFM]," to E. E. Schmidt, 18 August 1958, in Schmdit, *Ibid.*, 37, Penner Collection.

9. H. P. Poetker to J. B. Toews, 16 April 1962, Poetker File; A. Suderman to A. E. Janzen, 23 January 1959, and Janzen to Suderman, 3 February 1959, Suderman File, CMBS/F.

10. The former mission cottages at Ootacumund were sold in 1957, J. A. Wiebe to A. E. Janzen, 21 October 1957, Wiebe File, CMBS/F.

11. George J. Froese to A. E. Janzen, 3 August 1957, Froese File; M. Willems to J. B. Toews, 13 November 1957 and 3 June 1958; Toews and Janzen to Willems, 7 and 8 April 1958, Willems File; H. P. Poetker to Janzen, 14 August 1957, Poetker File; it was ironic that John Hiebert, who was recalled from the field in 1951 to help eradicate 'modernism' from TC, preferred the more liberal Kodaikanal over Ootacumund, see Hiebert to Janzen, 12 January 1948, and 24 August 1950, Hiebert File, CMBS/F.

12. A. E. Janzen to Ted Fast, 26 October 1960, Fast File, CMBS/F; Fast to Peter Penner, 22 September 1991, Penner Collection.

13. A. E. Janzen to H. P. Poetker, 25 January 1961, Poetker File; J. A. Wiebe to J. B. Toews, 7 October 1961 and 17 February 1962, Wiebe File, CMBS/F; cf. J. D. Mosteller, "Ramapatnam, Jewel in the South India Mission," *Foundations: A Baptist Journal of History and Theology* (October-December 1968), 315.

14. Missionary Fellowship, Minutes, Kodaikanal, 7 June 1963, in J. A. Wiebe File, CMBS/F.

15. H. P. Poetker to J. B. Toews, 19 August 1962, Poetker File, CMBS/F; cf. J. D. Mosteller, "Ramapatnam," 308-325.

16. Ted Fast to J. B. Toews, 30 June and 19 August 1962; Toews to Fast, 22 May 1963, Fast File; H. P. Poetker to Toews, 3 July 1963, Poetker File, CMBS/F; cf. David Ewert, "Indian Seminary [Yeotmal] Attempts an Exacting Task," *Mennonite Brethren Herald*, 16 October 1970, 17.

17. Ted Fast to J. B. Toews, 19 August 1962; Toews to Fast, 22 May 1963, Fast File, CMBS/F.

18. Ted Fast to Henry R. Wiens, 7 October 1963; 29 July and 22 November 1964, and other similar references in 1965, Fast File, CMBS/F.

19. Ted Fast to Board of Missions, 9 October 1964; Peter J. Funk to Ted Fast, 19 November 1964, Fast File, CMBS/F.

20. For example, the Governing Council approved a scooter for Shamshabad teachers; instead one **not** approved was purchased for the personal use of a missionary; Frank C. Peters, "read this letter and then throw it away!" to H. R. Wiens, 22 August 1964, Board Members' File, CMBS/F.

21. Paul G. Hiebert to P. J. Funk, 23 August 1965, Hiebert File, CMBS/F.

22. P. J. Funk, quoting Frank Peters, in a letter from Jadcherla, to H. R. Wiens, 1 August 1964, CMBS/F; cf. Frank Peters' series of articles about his India trip in the *Mennonite Brethren Herald*, beginning 31 July 1964, and running through to 23 October 1964.

23. Katie Siemens Esau, interview by author, Abbotsford, 24 November 1988; Rosella Toews to Peter Penner, 4 January 1994, Penner Collection.

24. These caveats notwithstanding, much was made easier once the seniors had retired, as in 1957. Frieda Neufeld, interview by author, Vancouver, November 1988; Margaret Willems Balzer, interview by author, Saskatoon, February 1989; Katie Siemens Esau, interview by author, Abbotsford, 24 November 1988, Penner Collection.

25. Cf. J. B. Toews *JB: The Autobiography of a Twentieth-Century Mennonite Pilgrim* (Fresno: Center for Mennonite Brethren Studies, 1995), 160.

26. Margaret Willems, "The Cry for Mercy," *Christian Leader*, 15 April 1954, 6.

27. M. Willems to J. B. Toews, 22 August 1958; A. L. Ediger to Toews, 5 November 1958, Willems and Ediger Files, CMBS/F.

28. Cf. A. L. Ediger to J. B. Toews, **emphasis added,** 5 and 28 November 1958, Ediger File; G. J. Froese to A. E. Janzen, 8 November 1958, Froese File, CMBS/F; M. W. Balzer, interview by author, Saskatoon, February 1989; Helen Dueck, interview by author, Coaldale, September 1992, Penner Collection.

29. M. Willems, "Your Prayers Answered," *Christian Leader*, 10 March 1959, 8-9.

30. M. Willems to A. E. Janzen, 7 January and 23 September 1961; Willems, "The Present Status of the India Program," [August 1961], Willems File, CMBS/F.

31. M. Willems, "The Present Status of the India Program," [August 1961], Willems File.

32. Helen Harder thought that Margaret Willems could come back if only she would reduce some of her personal demands, Harder to J. B. Toews, 10 December 1962, Harder File, CMBS/F. The story of Willems' attempt to return, under certain conditions, is omitted.

33. Jake Friesen to A. E. Janzen, 12 May 1961, Friesen File, CMBS/F.

34. Helen Dueck, from Wanaparty, to J. B. Toews, 7 February 1962, Dueck File; Toews to the MAC, 8 March 1962; Toews to J. Friesen, 5 October 1962, Friesen File, CMBS/F.

35. G. J. Froese accepted the diagnosis of Dr. J. R. Donaldson, made at Miraj Center, and reported on this and Marie Riediger's search for healing and victory, to Jake H. Epp, Hillsboro, 22 January 1966, 15 November 1966; A. A. Dick, Medical Commissioner, advised that Riediger should go home, but he wanted the Jadcherla medical staff to **agree** on the MS diagnosis, H. R. Wiens to Froese, 27 January 1966; J. Friesen to Wiens, 2 February 1966; Wiens to Friesen, 7 February 1966, Friesen File, CMBS/F.

36. Board of Missions, "Marie Riediger," Minutes, May 1967, CMBS/F; Riediger to Peter Penner, 14 August 1990; Marie Riediger, interview by author, Abbotsford, September 1992, Penner Collection; Elsie Neufeld, "[Marie Riediger] A Human Bridge to Healing," *Mennonite Brethren Herald*, 20 April 1990, 31-32.

37. The doctor who diagnosed her problem and did the corrective surgery was David Harder, Vancouver, son of John A. Harder, Yarrow; Marie Riediger, interview by author, Abbotsford, September 1992, Penner Collection.

38. Marie Riediger to Peter Penner, 14 August 1990, Penner Collection; Elsie Neufeld, "A Human Bridge to Healing," 31-32.

39. Helen Harder Loewen, "Mennonite Brethren Medical Missions," Report to Medical Commission, n.d., 5, 9-10; Harder, "Medical Work at Shadnagar, India," *Christian Leader*, 15 April 1957, 8-9.

40. H. Harder to J. B. Toews, 10 December 1962; "Autobiography of Helen Harder (Loewen)" (n.d.), 7 pp.; Harder to J. H. Epp, 26 October 1966, Harder File, CMBS/F; Harder, "India Women Meet God," *Mennonite Brethren Herald*, 21 June 1963, 9.

In retirement, Helen Harder Loewen wrote a booklet: *Sky-Lace* (India stories and poems, dedicated to Anne L. Ediger) (Waterloo: Sky Lace Books, 1995).

41. Helen Dueck was not alone. Paul Hiebert wrote about the new attitudes required in India: "[She] must see [herself] as a [sister] to the national [sisters], a student of their culture, and ... a sinner with them on the path to Divine Grace," in "A Position Paper," 1967, in A. A. Unruh Papers, CMBS/W; Ted Fast to Peter Penner, 22 September 1991, Penner Collection.

42. G. F. Froese and Peter M. Hamm letters to J. H. Epp; and Epp to the MAC, March-April 1967, in Board of Missions, Agenda, May 1967, Board Files, Box 11; H. Harder to Epp, 5 January 1969, Harder File, CMBS/F.

43. Helen Dueck, interview by author, Coaldale, 17 September 1992, Penner Collection.

44. Mildred Enns to A. E. Janzen, 31 July 1953, Enns File, CMBS/F; Rosella Toews to Peter Penner, 4 January 1993, Penner Collection.

Enns attended Winkler Bible School for one year and Mennonite Brethren Bible College, 1948-9. See *Missionary Album* (Hillsboro: BFM, 1951), 38, and *Rainbow* (Winnipeg: MBBC Yearbook, 1949).

Mildred Enns (of **Kanadier** background) was accepted as a missionary candidate by Henry S. Voth and A. E. Janzen over the objection of J. B. Toews and his faculty at Mennonite Brethren Bible College. Voth, pastor at Winkler, is alleged to have retorted: "Since when will **Russlaender** tell us [**Amerikaner**] whom we can or cannot send out?", see J. B. Toews, interview by author, Fresno, 1988-89; cf. Toews, *JB*, 121-122.

45. I am grateful to Helen Harder Loewen for copy of an obituary of Mildred Enns. She was twice-married, to Robert G. Deacon in 1972, and to Helmut H. Toews in 1979, and died 24 June 1986, Penner Collection.

46. Katie Siemens to J. B. Toews, 4 September 1957 and 21 February 1958, Siemens File, CMBS/F.

47. Katie Siemens to A. E. Janzen, 27 July 1958; P. V. Balzer to MAC, 1 July 1961; P. M. Hamm to Janzen, 30 March 1961; Janzen, letter of reference for Siemens, to Hamm, 20 April 1961, Hamm File, CMBS/F; Katie Siemens Esau, interview by author, Abbotsford, 24 November 1988, Penner Collection.

48. K. Siemens, "India Girls' Camp Held in October," *The Christian Leader*, 15 December 1959, 6; some of the things she was asked to do seemed "irrelevant" to the task of church planting for which she had come to India: see Siemens, "Summarized Report [to BFM]," 26 January 1966, Siemens File, CMBS/F.

49. Emma Lepp to A. E. Janzen, 22 April 1958; Janzen to Lepp, 21 July 1959, Lepp File, CMBS/F; E. Lepp, "Can Christian Schools Survive?," *The Christian Leader*, 23 August 1960, 8-9.

50. A. E. Janzen to Edna Gerdes, 5 December 1957, Gerdes File, CMBS/F.

51. E. Gerdes to A. E. Janzen, 26 July 1957, 25 February, 2 April, 5 May, 30 June 1958; Janzen to Gerdes, 5 December 1957, 10 April, 14 May 1958, Gerdes File; Margaret Willems to Janzen, 3 January 1960, Willems File, CMBS/F.

52. A. A. Unruh and P. V. Balzer to Hillsboro, 15 March 1960, Unruh File, CMBS/F.

53. Jake Friesen to A. E. Janzen, 11 and 25 March 1960, Friesen File, CMBS/F.

54. A. E. Janzen to Margaret Willems, 16 September 1960, Willems File.

55. J. B. Toews, P. J. Funk, John Ratzlaff, Memo regarding E. Gerdes, 18 May 1961, in Secretariat Minutes; cf. H. P. Poetker to A. E. Janzen, 6 December 1961, Poetker File, CMBS/F; Edna Gerdes to Peter Penner, September 1990, Penner Collection.

56. A. A. Unruh, "Authority in Mission Fields," 1960, Unruh Papers, CMBS/W.

57. [J. B. Toews], "Our Fundamental Concept and Purpose of Missions." *The Christian Leader*, 20 October 1959, 8; "1959 Foreign Missions Report," *CL*, 29 December 1959, and 12 January 1960, 8, 7 respectively; A. A. Unruh, "Threatening by the Board in its Minutes," 3 June 1960; "Relationship of Churches, Missionaries and Board of Missions," 1963, Unruh Papers, CMBS/W.

58. Unruh wrote Dick in Clearbrook he was not looking forward to the "brainwashing" in Hillsboro, A. A. Unruh to J. J. Dick, 14 February 1960, Unruh File; Board of Foreign Missions, Minutes, involving Toews, Janzen, Lando Hiebert, and I. H. Tiessen, in Hillsboro and Abbotsford, 28 February and 2 March 1962; 1 July 1962; 24-29 August 1962, resp., CMBS/F.

59. [J. B. Toews], "Statement of Evaluation of our MB Program in India (November 1961)," 4 pp.; "Principles and Practices to Govern Future Relationships," [1962], 11 pp.; A. A. Unruh, "Some Concern about the Mission Organization of the MB Churches," 5 February 1962; "Co-laborers in the Lord's Vineyard [re identification in the *Mennonitische Rundschau*, 20 March 1963]," Shamshabad, 1963, CMBS/W; Unruh, "Words of Farewell to our Churches," *Mennonite Brethren Herald,* 7 December 1962, 9-10.

60. Donald J. Unruh, interview by author, Winnipeg, July 1990; and D. J. Unruh to Peter Penner, 12 April 1990; Margaret Unruh Regehr, interview by author, Winnipeg, September 1992, Penner Collection.

61. Unruh called the advisory role of the Missionary Fellowship "a wrong procedure," in "To whom is the MAC responsible?" 2 March 1965, Unruh Papers, CMBS/W; A. A. Unruh to H. R. Wiens, 1 April 1964; cf. G. J. Froese to J. H. Epp, 11 April 1965; Epp simply replied that MAC speaks for the MF, Epp to Froese, 1 April 1965, Unruh and Froese Files, CMBS/F.

62. A. A. Unruh, "An Evaluation of the Evangelistic Program of the National Church," Shamshabad, 1965, 13-21, Unruh Papers, CMBS/W; "Men Committed to Evangelism," *Mennonite Brethren Herald*, 6 August 1965, 9; D. J. Arthur, "Report from the India Mennonite Brethren Church, AP, India," *GC Yearbook* (Corn, 1966), 83-86.

63. A. A. Unruh, "Report on the Ministers Course", Exhibit 4, Board of Missions, Minutes, February 1964, 127-128, CMBS/F.

64. F. C. Peters to H. R. Wiens, 22 August 1964, Wiens Papers, CMBS/F.

65. A. A. Unruh to J. H. Epp, 3 May 1965, Unruh File, CMBS/F.

66. A. A. Unruh to Vernon R. Wiebe, 5 August 1970, Unruh Files, CMBS/F; Unruh, "The Election of the Board of Mission Members," 11 December 1970, Unruh Papers, CMBS/W; there may be an oblique reference here to G. W. Peters and his many theoretically-based suggestions to the Board; cf. C. J. Rempel, interview by author, Kitchener, June 1991, Penner Collection.

67. When Annie (Elias) Unruh died in 1972, Unruh married Agatha Klassen Friesen of Waldheim, Saskatchewan. Abram died at age eighty-four in September 1988. Donald J. Unruh, "Tribute to Abraham A. Unruh," Winnipeg, September 1990, 5 pp., Penner Collection.

68. Peter V. Balzer handed over accounts, but not until his departure at the end of March 1961, Paul G. Hiebert (the son of John Hiebert and grandson of Nicolai Hiebert), to A. E. Janzen, 26 March 1961, Paul Hiebert File, CMBS/F.

69. A. E. Janzen to P. G. Hiebert, 16 July 1960; Hiebert to Janzen, 29 December 1960, 21 January and 14 August 1961, Hiebert File, CMBS/F.

70. P. G. Hiebert, "Report of the Bethany Bible School," in Board of Missions, Minutes, February 1964, 129; Hiebert to H. R. Wiens, 31 August 1964, Hiebert File, CMBS/F.

71. Frances Hiebert, "The Eleventh Hour of Christian Missions," *Mennonite Brethren Herald*, 18 January 1963, 7-8; P. G. Hiebert, "Some Personal Observations Regarding the Missionary Task," 4 October 1962, Hiebert File, CMBS/F.

72. The overriding factor was Frances' illness at the time, requiring quick access to medical attention, P. G. Hiebert to Peter Penner, 28 May 1994, Penner Collection; Paul G. Hiebert, *Anthropological Insights for Missionaries* (Grand Rapids: Eerdmans, 1985).

73. Emma Lepp to J. H. Epp, 9 February 1962, Lepp File, CMBS/F.

74. P. G. Hiebert to J. H. Epp, 31 August 1964, Hiebert File, CMBS/F.

75. P. M. Hamm, "Bethany Bible Institute and College Report for 1966," Board of Missions Agenda, February 1967, 22-27; cf. [Vernon R. Wiebe], "Yeotmal's Growth is Fantastic [article with picture of key graduates]," *Mennonite Brethren Herald*, 16 May 1969, 19.

76. S. Joseph and Hannah said changes at Bethany induced them to begin an independent ministry called The Christian Concern Mission, interview by author, Shamshabad, October 1990, Penner Collection; P. M. Hamm to P. G. Hiebert, 5 August 1968; to G. J. Froese, 22 September 1968, Shamshabad Letters, Peter Hamm Collection.

77. P. M. Hamm, *Reflections on My Journey* (Abbotsford, BC: Private, 1993), 139 ff.

## CHAPTER 15

1. Whitby was one in a series of conferences sponsored by the International Missionary Council since 1910; see Herbert Kane, *Understanding Christian Missions* (Grand Rapids: Baker, 2nd. ed., 1978), 180; cf. Blaise Lavai, ed., *Revolution in Missions: The Role of Missions in Present Day India* (Vellore: Popular Press, 1957), 72 ff.

2. *GC Yearbook* (Winnipeg, 1963), 52, 54.

3. J. B. Toews, "Obedience in Partnership," *GC Yearbook* (1963), 95-96; cf. handbook *Obedience in Partnership: Mennonite Brethren Church Missions* (Hillsboro: BFM, 1963); for an appraisal, cf. Blaise Levai, *Revolution in Missions*, 72-86; Hans Kasdorf, "A Century of MB Mission Thinking," D. Theology diss., University of South Africa, 556 ff; J. B. Toews, thirty years later, *A Pilgrimage of Faith: The MB Church, 1860-1990* (Winnipeg: Kindred Press, 1993), 272 ff.

4. *GC Yearbook* (Reedley, 1960), 49, 54, 64; (Winnipeg, 1963), 57.

5. *GC Yearbook* (1963), 60, **emphasis added.**

6. A. E. Janzen, "Joy in MB Foreign Missions Administrative Service," Board of Foreign Missions, Minutes, August-November 1960; A. E. Janzen, "A Charted Life in an Uncharted World," *The Christian Leader*, 28 June and 12 July 1960, 4-5.

7. This accident seemed as inexplicable as the death of his brother John in 1956. Editor, "Lando Hiebert Dies in Car Crash," *The Christian Leader*, 24 July 1962, 24; J. A. Harder, Yarrow, died 22 March 1964; Hugo Jantz, "John A. Harder, Valiant for the Truth," *Mennonite Brethren Herald*, 24 January 1969, 6-8.

8. Hans Kasdorf, "MB Mission Thinking," 384.

9. *GC Yearbook* (1963), 60.

10. Peter R. Lange to G. W. Peters, 16 April 1962, Peters Papers, CMBS/F.

11. Board of Missions Report, *GC Yearbook* (Reedley, 1960), 48 ff.; (Winnipeg, 1963), 56. ff. Many in India complained about these staff changes; V. K. Rufus to V. R. Wiebe, n.d., received 3 January 1979, Wiebe File, CMBS/F.

12. Board of Missions Report, *GC Yearbook* (1963), 56 ff.; (1966), 106; "Major Policy Matters to Come Before General Conference," *Mennonite Brethren Herald*, 21 October 1966, 10; and Board Agenda, September 1967; A. A. Unruh to J. H. Epp, 10 January 1967, Unruh File, CMBS/F.

13. A. L. Ediger to A. E. Janzen, 25 October 1960; J. B. Toews to Ediger, 25 October 1960, Ediger File, CMBS/F.

14. A. L. Ediger to J. B. Toews, 19 January and 21 March 1961, Ediger File; A. A. Unruh agreed: "It is not the acceptance of another peoples' culture ... which is appreciated, but the ability to let culture not become a barrier [to] communication and love," [1964], Unruh Papers, CMBS/W.
Henry Poetker interpreted this directive as the Board's way of saying they had been too "itinerant." He was not about to do without his own vehicle; H. P. Poetker to A. A. Unruh, 26 May 1962, Poetker File, CMBS/F.

15. V. R. Wiebe, "A church with promise and struggles," *Mennonite Brethren Herald*, 8 June 1979, 23-24.

16. Martha Pullman Bergthold, interview by author, Fresno, 22 January 1993; regarding pensions, Peter Penner to S. V. Epp, Winnipeg, 18 February 1994; Epp to Penner, 4 March and 28 May 1994, Penner Collection.

17. G. W. Peters, *Foundations of Mennonite Brethren Missions* (Winnipeg: Kindred Press, 1984), 74.

18. Valerie Rempel, "She Hath Done What She Could: The Development of the Women's Missionary Service in the Mennonite Brethren Churches of the United States" and Gloria Redekop, "Canadian Mennonite Women's Societies: More Than Meets the Eye," in *Bridging Troubled Waters: The Mennonite Brethren at Mid-Twentieth Century*, ed. Paul Toews, Perspectives on Mennonite Life and Thought, no. 9 (Winnipeg: Kindred Productions, 1995), 149-174.

19. A. L. Ediger, "Increased Indian Personnel in Hospitals," *Mennonite Brethren Herald*, 10 May 1963, 9; several Indian doctors were assisted by technicians and compounders, several were completing medical training.

20. G. J. Froese to P. J. Funk, 6 January 1963; Funk to Froese, 28 December 1963, Froese File, CMBS/F.

21. Ted Fast to J. H. Epp, 16 March 1965, Fast File, CMBS/F.

22. J. H. Epp to Peter J. Block, 8 April 1965, Block File; G. J. Froese to Epp, 11 April 1966; Epp to Froese, 21 and 22 April 1966, Froese File, CMBS/F.

23. P. J. Block to P. J. Funk, 16 March 1965, and Funk to Block, 29 March 1965, and 29 April 1966, Block File; G. J. Froese to J. H. Epp, 7 April 1966, Froese File, CMBS/F.

24. P. M. Hamm to P. J. Block, 16 March 1967, Block File, CMBS/F.

25. P. J. Block to P. J. Funk, 5 January 1970, Block File, CMBS/F; Peter and Arlene Block have since worked medically in Ethiopia and in Nepal: see news item in *Mennonite Brethren Herald*, 28 June 1974, 19; and 25 August 1989, 30; Peter Block, "Saskatoon Couple work with Ethiopian Mennonites," *MBH*, 3 September 1976, 21.

26. J. Friesen to P. J. Funk, 13 August 1969; Friesen to V. R. Wiebe, 31 August 1969; Wiebe to Friesen, 11 September 1969, Friesen File, CMBS/F.

27. V. R. Wiebe to P. J. Block, 20 February; Block to Wiebe, 15 March 1971, Block File, CMBS/F.

28. David Wiebe, MD, "Some Medical Memories," for the Medical Commission (n.d., probably 1970s), 7 pp., Peter Penner Collection.

29 Dan A. Nickel to P. J. Funk, 7 July and 16 October 1967; 3 April 1968, Nickel File, CMBS/F.

30. Ted Fast to J. H. Epp, 30 December 1968; Fast to V. R. Wiebe, 5 April 1969, Fast File, CMBS/F; Fast thought of these monies as disappearing into "the bottomless pit" of the general treasury. He wrote: "They never sanctioned [the car] and I never got to designate one penny. This is still a very sore point in my heart." Ted Fast to Peter Penner, 22 September 1991, Penner Collection.
Dan Nickel to J. H. Epp, 10 August and 21 October 1970; cf. Missionary Fellowship, Minutes, India, #37, with V. R. Wiebe and J. H. Epp present, 21 March 1972; CMBS/F; Dan Nickel, "Shifting into New Role: India," *Mennonite Brethren Herald*, 10 January 1969, 19.

31. Ted Fast to V. R. Wiebe, 17 May 1969, Fast File, CMBS/F.

32. H. P. Poetker to J. H. Epp, 23 June 1972; and Dan Nickel to Poetker, 16 August 1972, Poetker File, CMBS/F.

33. Secretariat, "Major Policy Matters to Come Before GC," *Mennonite Brethren Herald*, 21 October 1966, 10; G. W. Peters, Board Report, *GC Yearbook* (Winnipeg, 1963), 56 ff.; Ted Fast to Marion Kliewer, Hillsboro, 9 February 1969, Fast File, CMBS/F.

34. Ted Fast to V. R. Wiebe, 17 May 1969, Fast File, CMBS/F.

35. Ted Fast to V. R. Wiebe, 13 May and 2 July 1969; Ted Fast, "Answers to a [Debriefing] Questionnaire," August 1969, Fast File, CMBS/F.

36. Ted Fast to Peter Penner, 22 September 1991, Penner Collection; LaVernae J. Dick, "To Begin Again," *Mennonite Brethren Herald*, 28 November 1975, 8-9.

37. J. Friesen to P. J. Funk, 17 July 1963, Friesen File, CMBS/F.

38. Board of Missions, Minutes, November 1950, 108, February 1965, 13; Secretariat, Minutes, 5 May 1963; Ted Fast to P. J. Funk, 6 October 1961, Fast File, CMBS/F.

39. S. V. Epp to Peter Penner, 4 March and 14 June 1994, Penner Collection.

40. The house parents for the Bruton years were as follows: Rose and Herb Krause, 1950-53; Linda and Jacob Ewert, 1953-58; Betty and Peter Hamm, 1958-63; Nancy and Jerry Neufeld, 1963-67; Martha and David Friesen, 1967-72.

41. Peter M. Hamm, *Reflections On My Journey* (Abbotsford: Private, 1993), 143.

42. Nancy Neufeld, interview by author, Fresno, 17 November 1992; P. G. Hiebert to Peter Penner, 28 May 1994, Penner Collection.

43. Maryann Peters Wall, interview by author, Reedley, 3 November 1992, Penner Collection.

44. Jerry Neufeld to H. R. Wiens, 4 December 1964, Neufeld File, CMBS/F.

45. G. J. Froese to J. H. Epp, 24 August 1965, and 30 January 1966, Froese File, CMBS/F.

46. P. M. Hamm, *Reflections*, 143.

47. G. J. Froese to J. H. Epp, 7 June 1966, Froese File, CMBS/F; Herbert and Rose Krause, interview by author, Fresno, November 1992, Penner Collection.

48. Jerry Neufeld to J. H. Epp, 24 February 1966; and Epp to Neufeld, 17 March 1966, Neufeld File, CMBS/S; Nancy Neufeld, interview by author, Fresno, November 1992, Penner Collection.

49. G. J. Froese to J. H. Epp, 7 June 1966, Froese File, CMBS/F.

50. J. Neufeld to J. H. Epp, 20 September 1966, Neufeld File, CMBS/F.

51. Evan Adams, "Why Christian Students Resist Missions Recruitment," *The Christian Leader*, 30 January 1968, 6-7.

52. Gordon Nickel, from Thandiani, Pakistan (for some years associate editor of the *Mennonite Brethren Herald*), 11 July 1990; Alden Poetker, from Brazil,

July 1990; Tim Froese, Winnipeg, 12 September 1990, to Peter Penner, Penner Collection.

53. Alden Poetker, Response to author's questionnaire, November 1990, Penner Collection; "Inspired by Parents [Henry and Amanda Poetker]," *Mennonite Brethren Herald*, 7 March 1986, 17.

54. Cathy Froese Baerg, who discussed the author's questions with her siblings, May 1991; Tim Froese to Peter Penner, 12 September 1990, Penner Collection.

55. Missionary Fellowship Paper, India, "Hill Seasons: Pros and Cons," 9-10 July 1966, CMBS/F.

56. For example, between May 1968 and March 1976 he contributed thirty-seven articles to the *Mennonite Brethren Herald*.

57. V. R. Wiebe, "Memo to the Brotherhood," 3 March 1969, 6 pp.; the real deficit on 30 September was $539,632.; see Special Meeting in Chicago, MBM/S Files, 29 March 1969, CMBS/F.

58. V. R. Wiebe, "A Vision for the Seventies," *Mennonite Brethren Herald*, 20 March 1970, 12; the younger board members in the 1960s chafed under the continuing influence of "strong personalities" like G. W. Peters, Wiebe to Peter Penner, 9 February 1994, Penner Collection.

59. V. R. Wiebe, "Performance Reviews for Missionaries?" *Mennonite Brethren Herald*, 1 May 1970, 15; cf. A. A. Unruh's call for an evaluation of all **board** members; Unruh to Wiebe, 5 August 1970, Unruh Files, CMBS/F.

60. V. R. Wiebe for MBM/S, "An Open Letter to the Brotherhood," *Mennonite Brethren Herald*, 26 June 1970, 10-11.

61. Harold Jantz, Editorial, "The 'Open Letter'," *Mennonite Brethren Herald*, 26 June 1970, 9.

62. V. R. Wiebe, "Three Months Have Passed," *Mennonite Brethren Herald*, 18 September 1970, 18.

63. V. R. Wiebe, "Free to Win Many to Christ," *GC Yearbook* (Reedley, 1972), 27-30; cf. Wiebe to J. Friesen, 11 September 1969, Friesen File, CMBS/F.

64. Emma Lepp to J. H. Epp, 16 August 1970, Lepp File, CMBS/F.

65. E. Lepp to J. H. Epp, 13 February 1973; H. P. Poetker to Epp, 29 September 1971; Lepp, "The Development of the India Mennonite Brethren Sunday School from 1946 to 1972," 13 February 1973, 2 pp.; Lepp File, CMBS/F; cf. P. Menno Joel, "Dedicated to Serve Through Teaching," *Christian Leader*, 25 January 1983, 13.

66. H. P. Poetker to J. H. Epp, 29 September 1971, Poetker File; E. Lepp to Epp, 16 September 1972, Lepp File, CMBS/F.

67. H. P. Poetker to J. H. Epp, 3 June 1972; Epp to Poetker, 16 January 1973, Poetker File, CMBS/F.

68. Emma Lepp explained that Yalla John of the American Baptists had desired to join the MB church at Mahbubnagar, but "no move was made to allow him to join." Lepp to Epp, 21 October 1972; cf. Poetker to Epp, 2 October 1973, Lepp File, CMBS/F.

69. This bungalow is still reserved for such visitors; E. Lepp to J. H. Epp, 1 February 1973, Lepp File; Epp to H. P. Poetker, 16 January 1973, Poetker File; Missionary Fellowship, Minutes, # 45, 23 January 1973, CMBS/F.

70. Secretariat, "Twenty-five years of healing," *Mennonite Brethren Herald*, 12 May 1978, 25; "Medical Report from India," Board of Mission, Agenda, 1-5 October 1971; Frieda Neufeld, "MB Medical Missions," (n.d.), Medical Commission, 14 pp., CMBS/F; cf. Dr. N. S. Isaiah, "A Brief Sketch: Medical Ministry," in *Diamond Jubilee: Seventy-Five Years of Grace* (Hyderabad: MB Church of India, 1974), 50-54.

71. P. B. Arnold, the son of P. B. Benjamin, Wanaparty, completed his MA in surgery at Ludhiana, Punjab. MBM/S, Minutes, 1-5 October 1971, CMBS/F; P. B. Arnold, "A new vision for the church emerging," *Mennonite Brethren Herald*, 29 September 1978, 19-20.

72. G. J. Froese to J. H. Epp, 12 December 1972, Froese File, CMBS/F.

73. A. E. Janzen, *Survey of Five of the Mission Fields ... India* (Hillsboro: BFM, 1950), 15.

74. This revolt led to the evacuation of all MB personnel; J. B. Toews, *The Mennonite Brethren Church in Zaire* (Hillsboro: Board of Christian Literature, 1978), 135 ff.

75. A. E. Janzen to Unruh, Kasper, Friesen, Fast, and Poetker, 3 September 1960, Unruh File; this policy change was one John Lohrenz could not fathom, J. H. Lohrenz to H. P. Poetker, 1 September 1961, Lohrenz Papers, CMBS/F.

76. A. E. Janzen, regarding $25,000. for a house in Hyderabad, to H. P. Poetker, 7 March 1961; Missionary Fellowship, Minutes, Mahbubnagar, 14 October 1972, CMBS/F.

77. J. B. Toews to Board of Missions, Hillsboro, "Policy of the Board of Missions in Regard to Places of Worship in Mission Compounds," Mahbubnagar, 22 November 1961, CMBS/F.

78. It proved almost impossible to do evangelism in the midst of property matters; Dan Nickel to J. H. Epp, 26 January 1971, Nickel File; Missionary Fellowship, Minutes, # 37, 3, CMBS/F.

79. Dan Nickel, "The Story of the Transfer of Mission Properties," 9 February 1993, 2 page summary, Penner Collection.

80. Dan Nickel to J. H. Epp, 26 January 1971, Nickel File, CMBS/F.

81. Dan Nickel to M. B. John, Property Committee, 22 September 1972, Nickel File, CMBS/F; cf. P. B. Arnold, "Origin, Growth and Activities of M. B. Property Association," in *A Festival of 100 Years* (1990), 61-62.

82. Dan Nickel to J. H. Epp, 26 January 1971, Nickel File, CMBS/F; Nickel, "The Story of the Transfer of Mission Properties," 9 February 1993, Penner Collection.

83. The executive of the MB Property Association elected on 8 February 1975 were M. B. John, N. P. James, and P. B. Arnold. Other directors were T. G. Gipson, B. A. George, P. B. Richard, and M. P. Devadass. Louis F. Knoll of the American Baptist Society, then located in Madras, was given power of attorney. Advocates for the Company were Messrs. Devadason and Sagar; Dan Nickel, "The Story of the Transfer of Mission Properties," 1993, Penner Collection; cf. James D. Mosteller, "Ramapatnam, Jewel of the South India Mission," *Foundations* 11 (October-December, 1968), 320 ff.

84. L. P. Knoll to William Wiebe, Hillsboro, 6 June 1978, Secretariat Files, CMBS/F. **Note:** Indian currency may be understood as follows:
100 pisa = 1 rupee
1,00,000 rupees = 1 lakh
10 million rupees = one crore or 100 lakhs.
At that time one Canadian dollar bought about 7 rupees. Hence the investment Knoll was reporting on was 1/10 of a crore or 10 lakhs = about $142,857.

85. Bill Wiebe to Advocate Devadason, 4 September 1979, Secretariat File, CMBS/F.

86. Editor, "Last Missionary Pulled Out," *Mennonite Brethren Herald*, 3 August 1973, 6.

87. V. R. Wiebe, "Does [MBM/S] Have Too Much Money?" *Mennonite Brethren Herald*, 25 January 1974, 21; "Moratorium on Western Missionaries," 1 November 1974, 21.

88. V. R. Wiebe, "Should Missionaries be allowed to Moonlight?" *Mennonite Brethren Herald*, 24 August 1973, 12. Interestingly, Wiebe's own family developed a travel agency in Hillsboro in which the general secretary was somewhat active.

89. Hans Kasdorf, "A Century of Mennonite Brethren Mission Thinking," D. Theology diss., University of South Africa, 1986, vol. 1, 332-336.

90. Cf. V. R. Wiebe, "The Family of God," *GC Yearbook* (Winnipeg, 1975), 60 ff.; and Secretariat, "State of the Mission is Stable," *Mennonite Brethren Herald,* 8 March 1974, 26-27.

91. J. B. Toews, former general secretary, was most critical of the home side in the partnership, in "Missions in the Context of Change," *A Pilgrimage of Faith*, 261-280.

## CHAPTER 16

1. MBM/S, "Many open doors and some adversaries," *Mennonite Brethren Herald*, 27 April 1979, 14-15.

2. The author and his wife Justina visited the Nalgonda site and were able to spend a day with Suryapet Christians in October 1990. See Chapter Seven for comparative figures of 1930.

3. This chart shows the British regime prevailing in the rest of India until 1947; the Hyderabad regime until its incorporation by Nehru in 1948; the prevailing Hindu caste system; and the Republic of India.
Horizontally, there is the leadership level at the top, the military at the second (the British army, the Resident's cantonment in Secunderabad), the corresponding warrior caste in the Hindu system, and in Nehru's India his military establishment; the civil services and professions at the third; and the farming element in fourth rank.
Below the double line are the "outcastes," so to speak, in each formation. The Constitution of 1950 offcially took that line away.
The **arrow** shows the two major outcaste groups which **moved up** into a new Christian caste grouping. The majority Madigas were calling themselves **Telengana** by 1969.

4. Statistical Sources: for 1939, Henry W. Lohrenz, ed. *Our Mission Among the Telugus*, 34-35; for 1950, A. E. Janzen, *Survey*, 31 ff.; for 1970, P. M. Hamm, *India MB Church Statistical Report*, 65; for 1978, V. K. Rufus, in Paul D. Wiebe, *Christians in Andhra Pradesh*, 18-20, 60-61, 93-94; for India, J. E. Schwartzberg, ed., *A Historical Atlas of South Asia* (New York: Oxford University Press, 1992).

5. Cf. "Growth of Patterns in MB Conference," *GC Yearbook* (Vancouver, 1969), 71, 111.

6. Peter M. Hamm, *Reflections On My Journey* (Abbotsford: Private, 1993), 62-63; cf. Hamm, *India MB Church Statistical Report*, 66 ff.
Regrettably, Peter Martin Hamm died in August 1993; Gary Hardaway, "Former MBM/S administrator/missionary dies," *Mennonite Brethren Herald*, 24 September 1993, 24.

7. R. S. Lemuel, "M. B. Board of Evangelism and Church Ministries (GC)," in *A Festival of 100 Years, 1889-1989: Souvenir* (Mahbubnagar: Centenary Editorial Committee, 1990), 11-14.

8. Afraid of "wrong impressions" being given, Henry Poetker personally asked Peter Hamm and his assistants: "How many of those registered ... are born again?" H. P. Poetker to J. H. Epp, 7 June 1971, Poetker File, CMBS/F.

9. G. A. Oddie, ed., *Religion in South Asia: Religious Conversion and Revival Movements in Medieval and Modern Times* (New Delhi: Manohar, 1977), 4-6.

10. The military and national rebellion against British India (1857) was comparable to the Taiping Rebellion in China or the Pugachev Revolt in Russia. D. B. Forrester, "The Depressed Classes and Conversions to Christianity, 1860-1960," in G. A. Oddie, *Religion in South Asia*, 35-66.

11. A. E. Janzen, ed., *The Andhra Mennonite Brethren Church of India: Fifty Years in Retrospect* (Hillsboro: BFM, 1954). This helped to create confusion later about anniversary dates.

12. J. Paranjyothy, "The Spiritual Significance of the Telugu Faith Convention of the Mennonite Brethren Church in India," in *A New Vision for the Church Today*, ed. J. H. Epp (Hillsboro: MBM/S, 1968), 38-39.

13. G. W. Peters, "Report of the Board," *GC Yearbook* (Corn, 1966), 56 ff.

14. Secretariat, "Churches in India Ordain 10," *Mennonite Brethren Herald*, 21 April 1967, 11.

15. Ted Fast, "The Missionary Situation in India Today," *A New Vision for the Church Today* (1968), 31-36; see A. E. Janzen, ed., *Guiding Principles and Policies* (Hillsboro: BFM, 1961), 8 ff.

16. Board of Foreign Missions, Minutes, "The New India Plan" (1958), 18-22 August 1958, 66-72; H. P. Poetker to A. E. Janzen, 4 April 1961, Poetker File, CMBS/F.

17. Margaret Willems to J. B. Toews, 5 July 1959, and 28 February 1960, Willems File; Toews to Ted Fast, 20 January 1962, Fast File, CMBS/F.

18. G. W. Peters, "Observations and Impressions on the Work in India and Japan," (1964-5), in Board Agenda, February 1965, 2; on this occasion Henry R. Wiens made it plain that Peters had been in India voluntarily and had no assignment from the Board, Wiens to Ted Fast, 17 July 1964, Fast File, CMBS/F.

19. Mission Administrative Committee, Minutes, 31 December 1965; G. J. Froese to J. H. Epp, 16 March 1966, Froese File, CMBS/F.

20. A. A. Unruh to M. B. John, May 1966, M. B. John File, CMBS/F.

21. P. G. Hiebert to P. J. Funk, 23 August 1965, Hiebert File, CMBS/F.

22. Cf. A. L. Ediger to J. B. Toews, 8 August 1960, Ediger File; and H. G. Krahn, on the near fisticuffs in Mahbubnagar church, to A. E. Janzen, 28 March 1961, Krahn File, CMBS/F.

23. Ted Fast, re the "physical struggle" which went on until 0300 hours at Hughestown church on Christmas Eve, to J. B. Toews, 1 January 1963, Fast File; cf. Mission Administrative Committee, Minutes, 13 April 1963; cf. Bethel M. B. Church, Hughestown, Hyderabad, to "Rev. Sir and Madam [A Welcome Address to the Lohrenzes]," 17 October 1963, Lohrenz Papers, CMBS/F.

24. D. J. Arthur, "Report from the India M. B. Church," *GC Yearbook* (Corn, 1966), 83-86; cf. Arthur, "The India Church and its Self-Support," *A New Vision for the Church Today* (1968), 85-88.

25. M. B. John, "The Growth and Responsibility of Our Church in India," *Christian Leader*, 15 December 1957, 9; Ted Fast to J. B. Toews, 6 October 1953, Fast File, CMBS/F; cf. Chapter Ten.

26. A. A. Unruh recalled how M. B. John treated the Andhras as "foreigners," in the "Y[alla] John Case," 15 March 1973, CMBS/W.

27. Stanley Wolpert, *A New History of India* (New York: Oxford University Press, 1990), 368; A. Suderman, "Memoir of Anna Suderman, 1902-1981," ed. Laurene Peters, 60-61, CMBS/F.

28. P. M. Hamm, *Reflections On My Journey*, 141.

29. P. M. Hamm to David Ewert, 4 June 1969, Shamshabad Letters, Peter Hamm Collection. Something comparable happened in Nigeria in 1966 in the "Biafran War," when Ibos appeared to want to take over the country.

30. Anna Suderman to J. H. Epp, 10 January 1968, CMBS/F; Suderman, "First Writers' Workshop," *Mennonite Brethren Herald*, 5 April 1968, 8.

31. A. Suderman to J. H. Epp, 30 September 1966, 23 August 1967, and 14 November 1968; to P. J. Funk, 24 January 1968, Suderman File, CMBS/F.
   In September 1966 Anna Suderman requested the services of Margaret Enns because she saw a great shortage of workers. Margaret had been teaching at Hebron School, Coonoor, since 1959. After fourteen years there she moved with the school to Ootacumund and stayed until 1979. She was not appointed for service until she joined Katie Siemens at Shamshabad and taught there from 1981 to 1987.

32. R. R. K. Murthy to M. W. Kliewer, 27 October 1964; to P. J. Funk, 26 December 1964, Murthy File, CMBS/F.

33. A. Suderman, "The M. B. Church Makes Advance in Andhra Pradesh," [1970]; "Memoir," 94-5, Suderman File; A. L. Ediger to J. H. Epp, 29 December 1967; to P. J. Funk, 13 September 1968, Ediger File, CMBS/F.

34. A. L. Ediger to J. H. Epp, 2 February 1965; Ediger to P. J. Funk, 20 February and 2 August 1965, Ediger File, CMBS/F; P. M. Hamm to Epp, 28 March and 25 May 1967, Shamshabad Letters, Peter Hamm Collection.

35. A. L. Ediger to J. H. Epp, 14 February 1969, Ediger File; cf. Epp to R. R. K. Murthy, 25 September 1968; G. Bhagvandos had been warmly endorsed by John A. Wiebe and was prepared to join the MB church, see Murthy to Epp, 8 October 1968, Murthy File, CMBS/F.

36. Even the Nickels were once "mobbed" while riding a rickshaw; Dan Nickel, interview by author, Abbotsford, 24 September 1992, Penner Collection.

37. A. Suderman, "Memoir," 94-5, Suderman File; A. L. Ediger to J. H. Epp, 15 April 1969, Ediger File, CMBS/F; Ediger, "India Church Ordains to the Ministry," *Mennonite Brethren Herald*, 15 March 1968, 8.

38. The reference was to J. Paranjyothy, a Yeotmal graduate and Bible school teacher, who took over the radio work, see his "Radio and Correspondence School Ministry," in *Diamond Jubilee: Seventy-Five Years of Grace: Mennonite Brethren Church of India* (Hyderabad: MB Church of India, 1974), 6-8.
The GC now insisted that all evangelism programs must be "'church based' and actively involve the national churches"; A. Suderman, "Memoir," 94-95; cf. the partnership principle in Board of Missions, "Major Policy Matters to Come Before General Conference," *Mennonite Brethren Herald*, 21 October 1966, 10.

39. A. L. Ediger to J. H. Epp, 15 April 1969, Ediger File; R. R. K. Murthy to Epp, 16 April 1969, Murthy File, CMBS/F.

40. Dan Nickel, interview by author, Abbotsford, 24 September 1992, Penner Collection.

41. P. G. Hiebert, "A Position Paper: The Mennonite Brethren Mission in India," (1967), Hiebert File, CMBS/F.

42. P. M. Hamm to R. R. K. Murthy, 21 September 1969; Hamm to J. H. Epp, 25 October 1969, Shamshabad Letters, Peter Hamm Collection.

43. A. Suderman to J. H. Epp [received from Michigan 12 January 1970]; Suderman, "M. B. Church Makes Advance," [1970]; Epp, **emphasis added** to Suderman, 14 January 1970, Suderman File, CMBS/F.

44. A. Suderman, "M. B. Church Makes Advance in Andhra Pradesh," Suderman File, CMBS/F.

45. Leoda Buckwalter, Far Eastern Broadcasting Association, "Why God Scattered the Team [in Mahbubnagar]," n. d., 7 pp.; Buckwalter, interview by author, Elizabethtown, PA, May 1989, Penner Collection.

46. A. L. Ediger to J. H. Epp, 22 June 1969, Ediger File, CMBS/F.

47. Allen Buckwalter to J. H. Epp, 18 July 1969; Ediger to Epp, 9 August 1969, Ediger File, CMBS/F.

48. A. L. Ediger, also telling how the GC were now targeting D. J. Arthur, to J. H. Epp, 22 October 1969, Ediger File, CMBS/F.

49. Leoda Buckwalter: "Mahbubnagar's loss of Ediger was FEBA's gain," interview by author, Elizabethtown, PA, May 1989, Penner Collection.

50. Byron Burkholder, "Anne Ediger: the celebration of a life," *Mennonite Brethren Herald*, 23 October 1981, 25; Dan Nickel gave the tribute to Ediger in St. Catharines, ON; the author met Anne in New Delhi in the midst of her work and friends, Peter Penner, New Delhi, to Justina Penner, London, 18 February 1973, Penner Collection.

51. Paul Wiebe, "Conclusion," *Christians in Andhra Pradesh*, 198 ff.

52. Peter Hamm, *Statistical Report* (1970), 65.

53. R. R. K. Murthy, "Evangelism in the Brahmin Community," 14 October 1968, 2 pp.; Murthy to J. H. Epp, 16 April 1969, Murthy File, CMBS/F.

54. Murthy, "From Hindu to Christian," *Mennonite Brethren Herald*, 11 April 1963, 6; Murthy to Bill Wiebe [received in Hillsboro, 7 February 1975], CMBS/F.

55. H. P. Poetker to J. H. Epp, 25 September 1972, Poetker File, CMBS/F.

56. A. L. Ediger, "India Church Ordains [Murthy] to the Ministry," *Mennonite Brethren Herald*, 15 March 1968, 8; cf. Murthy, "Indian Church - MB of the Heart; 'there are no born Mennonites,'" *MBH*, 7 March 1969, 21; Ted Fast to Board of Foreign Missions, 12 August 1957, Fast File, CMBS/F.

57. Paul Wiebe, *Christians in Andhra Pradesh*, 125, 180 ff.; cf. Bill Wiebe, "New freedom spurred problems in India," *Christian Leader*, 5 June 1979, 14-5; many Christians called themselves "Harijans" in order not to be cut off from government welfare programs; they hardly dared vote against the party of their landlords; see M. A. Solomon, "Where are the peacemakers?" *Mennonite Brethren Herald*, 31 January 1989, 16-17.

58. Though no name is mentioned, the person Paul Wiebe identifies as from a "low-caste Dakkali" family, "historically associated with begging from the Madigas in making a living," is the same person mentioned in the letter by H. P. Poetker to J. H. Epp, 8 February 1973, Poetker File; somehow Arthur had attained a higher sta-

tus, thus making it easy for him to get support for his studies abroad and a position with the GC; cf. *Christians in Andhra Pradesh*, 127-128, and the church certificate with biographical details issued for Arthur by M. B. John, pastor of Calvary MB Church, Mahbubnagar, 7 February 1974, Secretariat Files, CMBS/F.

59. Marie K. Wiens, "Visit with Indian Leader D. J. Arthur," *Mennonite Brethren Herald*, 31 October 1969; Wiens, "Persecution coming, says church leader," *MBH*, 10 August 1979, 25.

60. Paul Wiebe, *Christians in Andhra Pradesh*, 123-125; cf. J. H. Voth, "Probleme im Missionsleben," *Zionsbote*, 9 June 1926, 4-5.

61. D. J. Arthur, "The Church in India Today and its Response to the Present Challenge," *A New Vision for the Church Today*, 2.

62. H. P. Poetker to J. H. Epp, 8 February 1973, Poetker File, CMBS/F.

63. H. P. Poetker to G. W. Peters, 20 March 1972, Peters' Papers, CMBS/F.

64. Cf. Harold Jantz, "Radio opens wide new doors in India," *Mennonite Brethren Herald*, 16 January 1981, 6-8; and other views of this radio ministry: N. P. James to V. R. Wiebe, 21 March 1979; and Wiebe to James, 5 April 1979; and a critical evaluation by J. D. Manoranjan [advocate for P. B. Arnold] to Wiebe, [received in Hillsboro, 28 August 1979), Wiebe File, CMBS/F.

65. H. P. Poetker to G. W. Peters, 20 March 1972, Peters' Papers, CMBS/F.

66. H. P. Poetker to J. H. Epp, 25 September 1972, 8 February 1973, Poetker File, CMBS/F; note that the criticism in the September letter about the way GC business was done came very close to the criticism which Frank C. Peters made in 1964 of the MAC's way of doing business, in which Poetker was implicated. Too often in both cases, one or two were acting alone. In retrospect, this seemed a portent of the future, before P. B. Arnold became a power broker.

67. H. P. Poetker to J. H. Epp, 29 August and 2 October 1973, Poetker File, CMBS/F.

68. M. A. Solomon, and others, Letter to "Dear Brethren in Christ [in the international MB community]," Mennonite Brethren Laymen Evangelical Fellowship, Mahbubnagar, including an appendix of [23] "Questions the India MB Church Leadership Should Answer on the Matters of Stewardship," 14 September 1991, 12 pp. (hereafter MBLEF Letter) in Penner Collection.; cf. Paul Wiebe, *Christians in Andhra Pradesh*, 159, 170-171.

69. J. D. Manoranjan, advocate for the Governing Council, "Open Letter" [received in Hillsboro 9 July 1979]; to H. P. Poetker, drawing a comparison between the two antagonists, George and Arnold [18 December 1979]; cf. P. B. Arnold to Bill Wiebe, 6 June 1978; and B. P. Abel to V. R. Wiebe, 15 July 1978, Secretariat Files, CMBS.

70. P. M. Hamm and H. P. Poetker to Bill Wiebe, 24 July and 27 August 1979, respectively; R. R. K. Murthy and Poetker to Bill Wiebe, 9 December 1979, Secretariat File, CMBS/F.

71. V. K. Rufus listed all the visitors (11) representing MBM/S between 1972 and 1978, yet "our relations have not been strengthened." Not knowing what was reported by Hillsboro, he wrote: "So you went on your own way, and we have continued in our own weaknesses"; Rufus to V. R. Wiebe [received 3 January 1979]; cf. J. D. Manoranjan to Bill Wiebe [received 28 August 1979], Secretariat, CMBS/F.

72. V. R. Wiebe, "A church with promise and struggles,"; Bill Wiebe, "Understanding the India MB," *Mennonite Brethren Herald*, 8 June 1979, 22-25.

73. MBLEF Letter, 14 September 1991.

74. Werner Kroeker, interview by author, Fresno, 21 October 1994, Penner Daybook.

75. Ernest Friesen and Edmund Janzen, on behalf of the Executive Committees of MBM/S and the General Conference of Mennonite Brethren Churches, "Update on India Mennonite Brethren Conference," *Mennonite Brethren Herald*, 18 March 1994, 22.

# CHAPTER 17

1. John A. Wiebe, "The Madiga and Christianity: a Study in Acculturation," unpublished M. A. thesis, University of Minnesota, 1949, 2 vols., 226 pp., CMBS/F; Peter M. Hamm, *India Mennonite Brethren Church Statistical Report 1970* (Shamshabad: Mennonite Brethren Mission, 1970), 65, 70; Paul D. Wiebe, *Christians in Andhra Pradesh: The Mennonites of Mahbubnagar* (Bangalore: Christian Literature Society, 1988), 99 ff.; Peter Penner, "The India Mennonite Brethren Church," *Mennonite Reporter*, 11 June 1973, 2.

2. M. C. Emmanuel, "Prophet feeds ravens!" *Mennonite Brethren Herald*, 19 April 1996, 12.

3. Amanda Poetker, "A Village Church in India," *Mennonite Brethren Herald*, 29 October 1976, 21-22.

4. Henry P. Poetker to G. W. Peters, 20 March 1972, Poetker File, CMBS/F.

5. See the many references to Murthy and Yalla John in Chapter Sixteen; also H. P. Poetker to Peter Penner, 16 April 1996, Penner Collection.

6. Harold Jantz, "Radio opens wide new doors in India," *Mennonite Brethren Herald,* 16 January 1981; cf. H. P. Poetker to Peter Penner, 16 April 1996, Penner Collection.

7. R. S. Lemuel, "M. B. Board of Evangelism and Church Ministries (G. C.)," in *A Festival of 100 Years, 1889-1989* (Mahbubnagar, 1990), 11-14, 32, 35; cf. Vernon R. Wiebe, "A church with promise and struggles," *Mennonite Brethren Herald,* 8 June 1979, 23-24.

8. J. B. Toews to A. E. Janzen, 5 September 1975, Janzen File, # 4, CMBS/F.

9. My wife Justina and I attended the Centennial in October 1990 as private persons, not representing any conference; see PP, "Who are the people of God?" in *Suvarthamani* (February 1991), 26-28; I was pleased that the Governing Council considered 1889 the founding date of Mennonite Brethren work in India rather than 1899: see *A Festival of 100 Years of MB Church, India, 1889-1989* (Mahbubnagar: India MB Church, 1990).

10. The 1980 doctoral thesis of R.S. Aseervadam, "The Mennonite Brethren in Andhra Pradesh, India: A Historical Treatise," unpublished Ph.D. thesis, Osmania University, Hyderabad, 1980, CMBS/F, does not tell the story "through Telugu eyes." It is a fairly typical dissertation, thematic, largely based on secondary sources, many of them American. Paul D. Wiebe's 1988 book brings together much more understanding of the social and cultural context in which the Church was born, based on his sociological approach, *The Christians in Andhra Pradesh: the Mennonites of Mahbubnagar* (Bangalore, Christian Literature Society, 1988).

11. Gary Hardaway, "Tragic accident kills India women's leader," *MBH,* 30 August 1996, 15.

12. A. E. Janzen, ed., *The Andhra MB Church of India: Fifty Years in Retrospect, 1904-1954* (Hillsboro: BFM, 1954); [Jake H. Epp, ed.], *A New Vision of the Church Today,* being a compilation of papers written upon the occasion of the 50th Golden Jubilee [Faith] Convention of the India MB Church, Wanaparty, India, 1968 (Hillsboro: MBM/S, 1968); Bhoompag Aaron George, ed., *Diamond Jubilee Souvenir: Seventy Five Years of Grace [1899-1974],* dedicated to Pioneer Missionaries and the Nationals (Hyderabad: MB Church of India, 1975); Centenary Editorial Board [E. D. Solomon], *A Festival of 100 Years of MB Church, India: 1889-1989* (Mahbubnagar: Governing Council, 1990).

13. See Preface of *Joy Turned to Mourning: Life and Ministry of D. F. Bergthold, Missionary to India,* by M. A. Solomon (Mahbubnagar: Aseervadam, 1979).

14. A. E. Janzen, *Survey of Five of the Mission Fields ... India,* typescript bound, gloss sheets of photographs (Hillsboro: BFM, 1950), 1-39.

15. The author and his wife were privileged, like many others, to have the wonderful hospitality of this bungalow in October 1990, graced by the person of Chendraleela, who was trained for her duties by Emma Lepp and Esther Fast.

16. John H. Lohrenz to P. A. Klaassen Family, 20 March 1966; cf. Lohrenz to E. J. Peters, Wasco, CA, 31 July 1967, Lohrenz Papers.

17. P. B. and Sharada Arnold, "Medical Ministry in India," in *A Festival of 100 Years*. 49, 51; Dr. N. S. Isaiah, "A Brief sketch: Medical Ministry," in *Diamond Jubilee*, 50-54.

18. M. A. Solomon to Peter Penner, 18 April 1991, Solomon File, Peter Penner Collection.

19. Peter Penner, "James Thomason and the Company's Imperium in North India," in *The Patronage Bureaucracy in North India: The Robert M. Bird and James Thomason School, 1820-1870* (Delhi: Chanakya Publications, 1987), Chapter 4, 82 ff.

20. G. J. Froese to J. H. Epp, 12 December 1972, Froese File; cf. R. R. K. Murthy to Bill Wiebe, received 7 February 1975, Murthy File, CMBS/F.

21. Though the author did not have simultaneous translation, one person from each camp explained the gist of his rendition.

22. M. A. Solomon to Peter Penner, 18 December 1990, Solomon File, Penner Collection

23. MBM/S Report: "Our Fields: India," *GC Yearbook* (Reedley, 1984), 51.

24. P. B. Arnold, "Witnessing Discipleship in Asia," *Mission Focus* 14, (December 1986), 49-52.

25. Paul Wiebe, *Christians in Andhra Pradesh*, 201 ff.

26. *Ibid.*

27. Murthy to Bill Wiebe, 7 February 1975, Murthy File, CMBS/F; cf. J. A. Loewen, Letter to Editor regarding the "whole person ministry" issue, *MBH*, 23 January 1987, 11.

28. V. R. Wiebe, "A church with promise and struggles," *MBH*, 8 June 1979, 23-24; Bill Wiebe, "New freedom spurred problems in India," *Christian Leader*, 5 June 1979, 14-15.

29. Cf. J. B. Toews, *The Pilgrimage of Faith: The MB Church, 1860-1990* (Winnipeg: Kindred Press, 1993), 280; and *JB: the Autobiography of a Twentieth Century Pilgrim* (Fresno: Center for MB Studies, 1995), 163, 165. In retrospect, his disappointments were very great.

## APPENDIX

1. Four years of study at the Baptist "seminaries" at Hamburg-Horn, Germany, and German-language division at the Baptist Seminary at Rochester, NY, are here considered the equivalent of a Bachelor of Theology (ThB). This rational is based on the assumption of high school equivalency, two years of preparatory work, and two years of theology. While this does not add up to a BD degree, those Russians and American pioneers who acquired this education seemed secure enough in their preparation. None of them felt the need to advance their education during furloughs as was the pattern later.

2. High school or secondary education usually equals Grade Twelve (senior matriculation).

3. The teaching certificates here may have varied all the way from war-time "teaching permits" to certification at the Bachelor of Education (BEd) level, which means at least one year of post-secondary work in education.

4. The personal records of the missionaries are not available to researchers. Though they vary somewhat between America and Canada, the matriculation standards for this study are assumed to be as follows:

> **Registered Nursing Certificate (RN)**: three years training beyond senior matriculation;
> **Bachelor of Nursing (BN)**: a post-secondary degree;
> **Doctor of Medicine (MD)**: four to five years of medical training beyond a BSc;
> **Bachelor of Arts (BA)**: successful graduation from a three-year university or college course;
> **Master of Arts (MA)**: usually one full year of work beyond the BA;
> **PhD**: three to six years beyond the BA;
> **Note**: Only the RN and the MD were consistently acquired **before** leaving for India the first time.

Theology diplomas and degrees, BRE, BTh, or GTh, from Bible institutes and Bible departments varied a great deal. Only a few certfcates and diplomas received from the Bible colleges and Institutes of the day can be recorded with certainty. At best one can indicate where they studied and how many years of such study preceded going out.

See **Endnote #2** for an assessment of the Hamburg-Horn and Rochester (German) Baptists degrees.

# INDEX: Names and Selected Subjects

# About the Author

Peter Penner was born in Siberia in 1925 and came to Canada with his parents the next year. He grew up in the Vineland (Ont.) Mennonite Brethren Church, where he was converted and baptized at the age of sixteen.

Penner attended the Mennonite Brethren Bible College in Winnipeg and earned two degrees from that institution: the B.R.E. in 1953 and the Th.B. in 1957. His B.A. came from the University of Western Ontario (Waterloo College) in 1955. Penner earned his M.A. and Ph.D. degrees in History at McMaster University in 1962 and 1970, respectively.

In 1965 Penner took a lecturer's position in History at Mount Allison University in Sackville, New Brunswick. He was made Professor of History there in 1983. Over a period of twenty-seven years he taught British and European history with a specialty in British India. After retirement in 1992 he was named Emeritus Professor of History.

Penner has served in two MB home mission fields: Lindal, Manitoba (1955-57), and Toronto (1962-64), having been ordained to the Gospel ministry by the Kitchener (Ont.) MB Church in 1954. He also taught in two Fraser Valley schools: East Chilliwack Bible School (1957-59) and Mennonite Educational Institute, Clearbrook (1959-60).

Penner has been a frequent contributor since 1956 to various Mennonite papers and journals, and since the 1970s has published reviews, articles, and four books in the area of his speciality. He has published two books on the Mennonite Brethren: *Reaching the Otherwise Unreached* (1959), a history of MB outreach in British Columbia, and *No Longer at Arm's Length: MB Church Planting in Canada* (1987). Penner also has written *The Chignecto 'Connexion': The History of Sackville Methodist/United Church, 1772 to 1990* (1990).

Penner is married to Justina Janzen. They have two children: Ruth and Robert, and two grandsons, Justin David and Jonathan William Penner.

In New Brunswick the Penners became members of the Sackville United Church and worked in that church and conference from 1967 to 1991. They joined the Petitcodiac Mennonite Church, Petitcodiac, New Brunswick in 1991, and after relocating to Calgary, Alberta, in July 1994, joined First Mennonite Church.

413